GOAL

Best wishes Dear
from
Steve Perryman

In a very short time
this teenage Tottenham
dynamo has
established himself
among the talented stars
at White Hart Lane. Usually
a real cool
character, young Steve
may be forgiven for
getting a few nerves before
Saturday's League Cup
final at Wembley, his
first big occasion. But
you can be certain of
one thing from the midfield
terrier. Once the game
has started he won't be
worrying about Wembley, All
the hundred thousand fans
or the atmosphere. And
he'll be thinking about is beating
Aston Villa and getting
the first of what promises to be
a big haul of honours

match
action

OFFICIAL PROGRAMME
price 5p

U.E.F.A. CUP, Semi-final,
1st Leg

TOTTENHAM HOTSPUR

v

A.C. MILAN

Wed., 5th April, 1972
Kick-off 7.45 p.m.

1971-72
No. 49

Steve Perryman
Tottenham

players

pins

TOTTENHAM HOTSPUR
F.A. CUP FINALISTS 1981

THE 100th F.A. C

spurs art no.23 Steve PERRYMAN

To STEVE
LOVE
Paul

TO
STEVE
THE
GREATEST
CLUB MAN
TOTTENHAM
HAVE EVER
HAD
TREVILLION

ON (BBC Local Radio London, Medway, Oxford: page 66)

22-28 May 1982 Price 25p

RadioTimes

Can Spurs win again?

Will Steve Perryman
celebrate another FA Cup
Final triumph — or can QPR
topple holders Tottenham?
Saturday's spectacular
is live on BBC1 and Radio 2.
Inside: preview by John Mo

's a man's 'oh

STEVE PERRYMAN

A Spur Forever!

My Lilywhite and Blue Life

With Adam Powley

VSP

To Kim, for following me to Japan, the adventure
that changed our lives; being brave enough to
have children while we were out there; and nursing
me back to health when I needed it most.

Also to all of the Perryman family, especially Mum and
Dad, who are no longer with us but who set me on my
way and always supported me through thick or thin.

STEVE PERRYMAN

A SPUR FOREVER!

My Lilywhite and Blue Life

"This is the story of the game seen through my eyes and told in my words. But central to the tale is Tottenham Hotspur – how could the club not be? It moulded my life and still does. I am a Spur forever"

Published by Vision Sports Publishing Ltd in 2019

Vision Sports Publishing
19–23 High Street
Kingston upon Thames
Surrey
KT1 1LL
www.visionsp.co.uk

Copyright © Steve Perryman

ISBN: 978-1909534-92-6

Written by: Steve Perryman with Adam Powley
Editor: Jim Drewett
Design: Doug Cheeseman
Imaging: Jörn Kröger
Editorial production: Ed Davis and Toby Trotman
Proofreader: Ian Turner
Portrait photography: Nick Maroudias

Photography: Getty Images, Colorsport, PA Images, Shutterstock, Offside, Mirrorpix, Alamy
Additional images: Steve Perryman, Exeter City FC, Bob Goodwin, Vivienne Goldstein, Kevin Hill

A CIP Catalogue record for this book is available from the British Library

Printed in Slovakia by Neografia

MIX
Paper from
responsible sources
FSC® C020353
FSC
www.fsc.org

CONTENTS

FOREWORD
by GLENN HODDLE

first saw Steve Perryman nearly 50 years ago, almost right back to when he first wore a lilywhite shirt. As a kid on associated schoolboy forms at Tottenham Hotspur, the club I supported, I watched him play in the FA Youth Cup-winning side of 1970; I also saw him score twice in the memorable UEFA Cup tie of 1972 against mighty AC Milan. That didn't happen often! They were probably two of the best goals he scored, though he scored an even better one at Derby once.

But what a night that Milan game was. I was one among tens of thousands delighted to see Steve perform so well, because he meant so much to the supporters. Spurs then was a team of hugely talented players, most of them bought. Steve was different. He'd come through the ranks, and it was evident he was popular and endeared himself to the crowd. He really did seem to be 'one of us' – a young home-grown player who gave his all to the Spurs cause.

I wanted to learn from Steve and watched him intently. When he got into the first team he was a model pro. He was someone the young players really admired and aspired to follow. He certainly inspired me. I wanted to wear that white shirt too. He was a midfielder then. Us youth players would watch him in action from the touchline, sitting on low benches around the perimeter of the pitch. We could smell the linament on the players' legs and could almost have tripped the linesman up we were that close. As a young kid watching Steve play, with the physical commitment he had, was a great experience.

This was seeing Steve in action. I first properly met him when I was an apprentice, when I watched players to observe how they were off the pitch as well as on it. I got the opportunity to train with Steve on occasion, and saw him in the dressing room that I had to clean. He was a class act – smart, intelligent, funny and quick-witted with a dry sense of humour. The way he held himself was impressive. He was always very professional, providing a great example.

When I broke into the first team and was doing well, Steve gave me a great bit of advice, probably the best single piece of guidance I've ever had. By all accounts Steve was very much a forward-minded, creative player in his younger days, but to get into the first team he had to adapt his game to a more defensive midfield role that the side required. I think he saw something in me that he recognised from when he broke through. He pulled me aside one day and said, 'Glenn, make sure you listen to your coaches and

"Steve was a class act – smart, intelligent, funny and quick-witted with a dry sense of humour"

Glenn and Steve lead the traditional Wembley lap of honour following Tottenham Hotspur's famous 1981 FA Cup Final victory

the players, and heed the advice you get. But what you don't want to take on, leave. You decide. You don't want to lose your natural ability. Don't lose what you are gifted at.'

It was wonderful advice. It made me feel strong. I was aware I was a bit different as a player. At that time being creative was difficult, and Steve just settled me down and gave me the confidence to play to my strengths. He probably won't remember saying it, but it stayed with me all my career.

Steve and I soon complemented each other in the Spurs team to great effect. We had a routine which Steve explains here, in this terrific book. It was the 'moving set piece' that evolved from when he moved to full-back. Steve was such a great captain, and he was so selfless. He showed leadership by the way he played – how he tackled, how he would drive through a brick wall for us – which always demonstrated immense bravery. But he was also a great communicator. When he passed the ball to me it was always with information, telling me whether I had time to turn, if there was a man on, or if I could play a long ball out to Tony Galvin haring up the wing. My dad said to me once, 'How did you see that pass to Tony was on?' I said, 'Skip helped me out there, telling me I could play it.' Steve gave a message with every pass.

He was also honest. If you made a mistake, on or off the pitch, he let you know, but was always fair. Some people often described me as a luxury player just waiting for the ball. Believe me, if you played on the right side of a diamond in front of Steve Perryman as I did, he made sure you did your fair share of hard work. He knew it wasn't the strongest aspect of my

Glenn (second from left) and Steve (far right), amongst a group of Spurs players pictured in the summer of 1976 following Keith Burkinshaw's appointment as manager

game but he would always encourage me to get back and defend. He gave praise when it was merited too, which was lovely because Steve has always appreciated good football. And he could play himself. He moved to sweeper for the season we were in Division Two with considerable success because of his qualities as a footballer, and his ability to adjust so well. He didn't get the England caps he deserved, but I joined him on the trip for the single senior appearance he did make, and I was so pleased for him.

Steve was a very good player indeed, efficient and able to simplify the game. I learned so much from him. You can't always hit a 40-yard wonder pass, there has to be a balance, and Steve was great at explaining that. He was the best captain I played under, and I've played with some good ones. The biggest compliment I can pay is that a good captain is the extension of the manager on the field. Steve was the prime example of that. He was very close to Keith Burkinshaw and then Peter Shreeve, and was the perfect foil for them, providing such a positive influence to the benefit of the team. He would make adjustments on the pitch, not tactical so much as making us aware and communicating effectively. He had a very astute understanding of what was required for a teammate in any given game, be it praise or a rollicking. And furthermore, if Steve himself wasn't playing particularly well, he still had the character to guide his teammates. That's real strength of mind, and another kind of bravery, which I always admired in him.

You wanted to do well by Steve. I was scared I was going to do something he wouldn't like one day, after I had opened up a couple of sports shops, again inspired by what Steve had done with his own stores. Steve used to ask the players to autograph footballs to display in his shops and donate to charities. I did the same thing, bringing footballs in to get signed, thinking, 'I'll have a bit of that', but then also thinking, 'Hang on, what's Steve going to say?' I was like a little kid going to the headmaster telling him what I was planning, but he laughed and said it was no problem. He was good as gold.

After his playing career, Steve went into coaching and management and was particularly successful in Japan, and then in his role at Exeter City. It's not through any fault of his own, but I feel his managerial talents haven't been as utilised by the game as well as they could have been, especially in England. The players at Spurs all thought he was the obvious candidate to go into management. With the right tools and environment I think he would have done a fantastic job somewhere.

Steve and I have been through a lot together – glorious success with Spurs, great games and occasions, and some difficult times as well, sharing similar experiences with our health in recent years. I've played with and against some truly world-class footballers, but if I was asked who I respect the most in football I would say 'Skip' above anyone else, without any shadow of a doubt. A great player, leader and man, on and off the pitch. He is very unselfish, be it with players or the fans or anyone. He has been a fantastic example and it was a pleasure to play with him for so many years.

As Spurs players we all called him 'Skip', and still do to this day. When we speak on the phone or meet up it's always, 'Alright Skip!' It's a measure of our liking for a lovely bloke, and enduring respect for our leader – one of Tottenham's greatest players and a true legend of the club.

Glenn Hoddle
September 2019

"If I was asked who I respect the most in football I would say 'Skip' above anyone else, without any shadow of a doubt"

INTRODUCTION

"For good and ill, Spurs made me. Not just as a footballer, but to a large extent as an individual"

When I left Spurs as a player in 1986, I went on to play for, then coach and manage, a number of other clubs. I would often meet with their supporters to talk about their teams and what I was striving to do for them. But that was partly my point. I would say to the supporters, 'I want to do the best for *your* team. But this isn't my club. I've got a club.'

That club was and is Tottenham Hotspur. For good and ill, Spurs made me. Not just as a footballer, but to a large extent as an individual. I joined Spurs as a teenager and became a man, made in the image of Tottenham, White Hart Lane and the people who believed in the Spurs cause – my teammates, the coaches and managers, the fans and, above all, Bill Nicholson. His ways of working, his ethics and values and his belief in how the game should be played have stayed with me all my professional life, and I have tried to live up to them in my own work and principles. I learned lessons in football and life from Bill Nick, and have never forgotten them.

One of the things that Bill and one of his successors, Keith Burkinshaw, drilled into us players was that the fans are the most important people at a football club. Without them it is simply not a club. It's why I've always taken my responsibility seriously in speaking to fans, meeting them and answering their letters. I know a chap called Scott Russell, who wrote a letter to me when he was a kid. I've still got that letter and he's still got my reply. He's a Tottenham fan to this day, and has twin boys who are also Spurs supporters. Scott wrote to me when I left Tottenham and he has always written to me whenever I've got a job elsewhere. The letters sent between us have carried on for decades, and Scott says he's a fan because I answered that first letter he wrote to me.

I have never been able to understand when modern players at clubs I have worked at get letters or emails but leave them unread and unanswered. I'm a naturally tidy person and will put those letters into a pile when I see them. If they stay unchecked by who they are addressed to I'll take a look. Often it's just someone wanting a photo or something signed. So next day I put the photo in front of the player and say, 'Sign that for us.' And then I'll put it in the envelope and send it to the fan. I think that's what a supporter deserves. That's not just a Steve Perryman thing – it's a Bill Nicholson, Tottenham thing.

I draw on those values, and my long experience, when passing on advice to youngsters right at the start of their careers. A few years ago when I was

The hard graft. We had some very tough games against Bolton during the 1977–78 campaign in the Second Division, and in the FA Cup that season as well, going out after a replay at a muddy Burnden Park

director of football at Exeter City, I had a chat with Ethan Ampadu – son of Kwame, who was a key player for us at Exeter. Ethan, who moved on to Chelsea, was very talented as a 12-year-old, so advanced that he was playing with 15-year-olds, but I didn't speak to him about how good he was – I ribbed him, asking how he could play football with his long hair getting in his eyes. It was good-natured, but the reason I was saying it was to keep him in check – to not let him get above himself. At Spurs that was drummed into us all the time. 'Don't get above yourself; don't think you've made it.' Ethan wasn't like that but what I said to him had a purposeful message that he should stay humble and focused.

I recently passed on a good-luck message to a young Norwegian player, Eirik Lereng, advising him to work hard, to seek improvement every day, and to use any praise received to fuel his desire and to take full advantage of the gifts he's been given. I stressed the importance of integrity, about earning his wages with total dedication to his profession and never taking these rewards for granted. I asked him to be honest in his performances, be humble and treat people as he wishes to be treated, but also to make every opponent know that he's as tough as he is fair. I laid out the importance of 'listening to your body' to guard against injuries. To try and add imagination in coaching sessions to bring more life and realism to the practice.

I advised Eirik about the importance of not just being in the right place and time, say, for a set piece, but also thinking the right thoughts when he gets there: being aware of the situation and prepared. I talked of looking at his own performance before blaming others, helping teammates with a positive voice and encouraging their improvement – it's a team game after all. That's my philosophy in a nutshell, and to a large extent it has been formed by those 19 years as a Spurs player.

Now, I love seeing young players on the path to what I hope will be long and successful careers. Their fresh stories make me reflect on my own journey. I can hardly believe it, but it is half a century since I became a top-flight professional footballer. Had I been told way back then, as a nervous 17-year-old eager to ply his trade on the big stage, that I'd spend the next 50 years in the sport, I'd have been shocked. If I'd been told that I'd become the record appearance holder for Tottenham Hotspur, I would have laughed at the idea. Yet here I am, half a century on, reflecting on an incredible career and life, and with that record firmly in the books: 866 games with a proud cockerel on my chest. I am immensely honoured to be the man with that distinction.

It's been 50 years of a remarkable, eventful career, first as a young player trying to make his way in the game, then as an emerging, industrious midfielder, before becoming a cup-winning captain, then a coach, a trophy-winning manager and a director of football. I've been there and basically done it at all levels of the game at home and abroad. I've played and worked with and against some of the greatest footballers and managers ever to grace this wonderful, at times maddening, but always fascinating sport. It is the beautiful game – well, most of the time – but it has provided me with an enviable job.

There have been some incredible highs and lows, successes and reverses. I've appreciated and enjoyed the good times, because you can never be sure what is coming next. That has been one of the key aspects of my character: keeping an eye out for what lies around the corner. I have learned so much and continue to do so, about the game and more besides. After all, it's no good getting older if you don't get wiser.

I've seen great changes in how football is played and run, and not all of them positive. But some things never change. There is very little I hear today, concerning tactics for example, that I didn't hear from Bill Nick, his assistant Eddie Baily and their coaching team way back in the 1960s. The words and phrases might have changed, and the technology to analyse and communicate a message about playing the game is different, but the meaning and essential truths haven't altered.

This is because at its heart, football is still basically about one group of players against another, still about winning and maintaining control of the ball, still a thrilling game of skill, endeavour and imagination. It's the game I played at the highest level for one of the biggest and most famous clubs in the world, winning glittering trophies, and it's the game I played as kid more than 50 years ago, just for the sheer joy of running around with my brothers and mates.

This is the story of that game seen through my eyes and told in my words. It includes a cast of the most colourful characters, takes you behind the scenes into the world of ruthlessly competitive football and ranges across Europe and even as far afield as Japan, which was an amazing adventure for me and my family. But central to the tale is Tottenham Hotspur – how could the club not be? It moulded my life and still does. I am a Spur forever.

"There have been some incredible highs and lows, successes and reverses. I've appreciated and enjoyed the good times, because you can never be sure what is coming next"

I am a Spur forever!

THE GIFTED ONE

For a footballer, my upbringing was about as normal as you can get. The vast majority of us who played in my era came from very similar backgrounds: growing up in hardworking working-class families, living modestly but happily, and with football at the centre of our young lives.

My upbringing began on 21st December 1951, arriving into the world as the youngest of three boys. I was born at home in a prefab, a hangover from the Second World War which had ended just six years before and which loomed over our generation.

We moved when I was two into a cul-de-sac on a new council estate in Northolt, which became part of my football development. There were not a lot of cars around anyway then, but the layout of the road made it a pretty safe place to kick a ball around with your mates. Having two older brothers also pulled me along the football path. Ted was the oldest and Bill the second, with two years between each of us. I suppose I was meant to be the girl, but it didn't happen.

My abiding memories of that time usually revolve around being outside and playing football of some kind. At a very young age there was something that is not in my character at all now, but I liked playing with dirt. I'd be rolling in it in the middle of a game. My brother would ask, 'What are you doing?!' but I just liked it. And then the ball would come my way and I'd play. I don't know if it was going back to nature or whatever, but that was one of my first ever football memories. Strangely enough in Japan, where I spent some of the best times in my career, they have a way of playing with mud that is actually an art form. They turn mud into little spheres and they are judged on how perfectly round they are. There are songs about it – 'dorodango' balls, they are called. Kids practise making them at playtime.

Things like that in a culture like Japan were unimaginable to me and my family in the 1950s. Back then we were just a normal family. My dad Ron was a coal-delivery man. He had gone down the mines in Yorkshire during the war, picked out by National Insurance number for what was essential work during the conflict. It was hard work and a tough experience – on his first day down the mine someone got crushed to death.

My mum Joyce Barwick was, well, a mum, the classic homemaker. She looked after the shopping, cooking and ran the household. Barwick is quite a famous name in Ealing. Mum was one of nine, and had seven brothers, two of whom died in the war. The oldest brother, Victor, emigrated to Australia

> "The vast majority of us who played in my era came from hardworking working-class families, living modestly but happily, and with football at the centre of our young lives"

My brothers Ted (left) and Bill (right) – two wonderful and inspirational siblings who put me (centre) on the path to a life in football

and had a big family there. Another, John, was called the black sheep of the family because he ended up becoming a senior police officer. It was said in jest that he had to move out of London to take up a post on the Isle of Wight so that he wouldn't have to pinch his brothers.

My dad Ron's side were from Hounslow and Ealing. He had a sister and a brother, also John, who was football mad. Their father Jack – my grandfather – played for Hounslow Ivydene in a 1921 final. He played, but not to a professional level; you would have thought if any of Jack's sons would have produced a pro it would have been John but it turned out to be my dad.

My paternal grandmother was Bridget. She was Irish and had black hair in a bun that when undone came a very long way down her back. I think that's where I get my strong hair from.

My mum's parents were Christian and Mabel, who had an ulcerated leg due to varicose veins that led to it being amputated. Christian signed up to be in the First World War but was too young so made out he was his brother to get in uniform. They lived close to Gunnersbury Park Tavern, which is where my granddad drank. His surviving kids would all congregate around that pub. My nan and granddad are both buried in the cemetery between the pub and the park. We spent family afternoons outside the pub and they'd send us a packet of crisps and a bottle of lemonade and we were more than happy.

My mum used to be very critical of her dad, saying that he'd buy everyone in the pub a drink but keep her mum short of money. Christian had beautiful grey hair and was called the Grey Ghost. He would have his chair right by the fire and now and again he would push a log in a bit further with his foot. He'd spit in the fire. Sometimes it would hit the top and drip down. We'd all look at each other in disgust.

I have all sorts of memories from that time, some hazy, some still very clear. One was of a family next door to Christian and Mabel. The family had a daughter who had some kind of medical condition. She was huge and had what would now be described as learning difficulties, or special needs. My uncles would muck about and sort of cuddle her and have a mock fight with her. Her name was Lillian. There was no harm in her, but as a little

My paternal grandad Jack (bottom row, far right) with his team Hounslow Ivydene. Jack was left-footed like my dad and older brother Ted, but my right foot was my strongest

Hounslow Ivydene's F.C. Season 1924-1925.

Taking centre stage in the lap of my paternal grandmother, Bridget. Back row (left to right): my cousin John Stone, grandad Jack, my brother Ted, and my cousin David Stone. Front row (left to right): Janet Perryman, another cousin, Bridget and me, and finally my brother Bill

kid I was scared witless by her. When she came in my nan's house the door would crash open. I knew it would be Lillian coming in. You could hear her stomping down the hall. I'd be so frightened I would jump out of the window and run off. I was very young then. I walked into Mabel's house one day to find her lying on the floor. I ran quickly to the pub to tell everyone. She eventually died; it was not good for me to see and experience that at such a young age.

This large extended family naturally made a big impression on our lives. Who am I to judge, but visiting each set of grandparents' households provided different levels of comfort. The house of mum's parents was all floorboards and lino and you could hear your feet when you walked through it. At Jack and Bridget's house there was more comfort. We got sweets and fizzy pop. We'd always go there for Christmas. Bridget saved for the next Christmas the moment one was over – it was all about festive season for her in that house, and we knew we were going to get a present.

Part of our visits there was to go and watch a game. We'd watch Southall v Hounslow or Hayes on Christmas morning. Jack watched Brentford play in the 1940s, and we would follow suit a decade later.

Like most people looking back on their childhood, I tend to remember the good times. But we were genuinely so happy. The summers were always hot, though the winters were always freezing cold in a council house. I would run downstairs to get dressed in front of the electric fire to keep warm.

Being the youngest had its pros and cons. My mum said Ted had all the inoculations and she did it all by the book with him; with Bill she held back a bit more and he had half the jabs, while I had none. I asked her why one day and she said, 'Those two are colour blind.' As if that was a justifiable reason! In those days you couldn't do certain jobs – drive a train for example – if you were colour blind.

My mum was a character. Every few years or so at Christmas she'd pull this one story out, in front of the whole family. We knew what was coming. She'd say that one day there had been a knock on the door. It was a gypsy lady selling pegs or lace. In those days it was thought to be bad luck to not

At home in the Perryman prefab (left to right): Ted, me, our mum Joyce and Bill

buy anything from a traveller. The lady said, 'Thank you, madam. So, I see you have three sons. The oldest is the most intelligent, the middle one is the luckiest, and the youngest is the gifted one.' Bill used to always respond, 'Tell me how I'm supposed to be lucky!' And Mum would say, 'Because you've got an intelligent brother, and a gifted one.'

It wasn't non-stop laughs all day, every day. My dad had to really graft in his job delivering coal. There must have been some hard times – not that I was really aware of them, other than knowing that the pennies were closely watched. If my mum came home with the shopping at two o'clock on a Saturday having ridden her bike to Greenford five miles away, balancing the shopping bags on the handlebars, only to find she was a few pence short on the change, she'd cycle all the way back to get it. My dad would offer her double not to go, but she wouldn't have it.

Having brought the shopping home, by four o'clock there would be nothing left. Three hungry young boys would devour the lot. The last resort was to eat blocks of jelly – the base ingredient that would be diluted in hot water to make an actual jelly. We were annoyed if that was all that was left. Cornflakes were a staple. In our house treats, like Libby's Milk for example, disappeared almost before they were out of the shopping basket.

I remember going over to my cousin's house on my dad's side and seeing a fruit bowl with fruit in it. Even a bit of chocolate on the side. Why hadn't it all been snapped up? That didn't happen in our house – if it was there, it was gone. We were happy with whatever we got. Mum made our food go further – toad in the hole with just a couple of sausages but cut into 20 pieces to try and share them around. I would say, 'I've only got half a sausage here!' She would look and say, 'That's too much for you' and put it on someone else's plate. She did not miss a trick.

My mum worked but when I got home from school she was always there – ironing, cooking, cleaning. As I grew up she had the odd part-time job with Lyon's Maid working evening shifts. My dad would pick her up and sometimes she'd bring home 'seconds' – choc ices. She'd come home, wake us up and give us a choc ice to eat, knowing we'd be so happy.

I would share bedrooms with my brothers in turn because neither would do it permanently as they got fed up with me. Mums would do things for their kids in those days in ways that they wouldn't do now. One day Mum woke me up and said, 'You don't want to go to school, do you?' And I went back to sleep.

She was a one-off, with a sense of humour that could be cutting. She'd put my dad down pretty easily in a row. He'd look at us and say, 'See? See what I have to put up with?' It was cockney wit really, even if we weren't strictly speaking cockneys.

With my big brother Ted, who is holding our cousin Bill

Tobacco was a big thing. We were always going down the shop to get tobacco for my dad – Old Holborn, Golden Virginia, papers and matches – he was always missing something. There might be a bit of chocolate as a reward but if ever there was a way to put kids off smoking, that was it: seeing him run out of tobacco if the shop was shut and how it affected him. He died aged 75 in the end from emphysema, a legacy of smoking from a young age, mine work, work in foundries and coal delivery, before ending up airside at Heathrow Airport. The fumes he must have been exposed to over that time did for him, so it was not a surprise. But it was a really sad sight to see him deteriorate so badly, and it gave our whole family a firm insight into the damage smoking can do.

Dad was out at work at lot and Mum was at home, so she had more of an influence. She made the decisions about whether I could go to watch football or not. QPR one week, Brentford the next. If I got money at Christmas, she'd say, 'I'll look after that.' I'd ask where. 'My secret compartment.' It would be for the nice things – fares and entrance money to the football.

My dad was supportive of my interest in football but it was Ted who took responsibility for me. Bill was more his own man with his job. Ted was educated. He went to university, the only one in the family who did. He studied at Brunel and went on to work for Air Traffic Control. He wasn't a teacher but had the skill of a teacher in his thinking. If I couldn't do homework, Ted would be the one to help me. My dad was pretty good with numbers – adding up the cost for coal sacks must have helped – but it was Ted who had the education.

Having three boys in a family, separated by only four years, could have made things feisty, but we got along fine. If there was competition it was probably between Bill and Ted. I never saw myself as the favourite but I was the youngest and they would do things with me, taking me places. My mum would give them permission to go somewhere but only if they took me along.

What I think was an important part of our childhood was the cinema, and in particular cowboy films. Saturday mornings, we'd go to Woolworths and buy some sweets – that was a real treat – and then run to the pics. They provided moral lessons: the good guy always won; fair play always ruled; if you worked hard you'd be successful. There was a moral guideline there to what we were watching. It's not there today. I sometimes watch *EastEnders* and wonder why I am I watching it. Everyone has a drink the moment there's a problem. And the gambling. I can't stand it.

On holiday
in Gosport in
our relatives'
driveway. I'm
in between Ted
(left) and Bill,
and they clearly
had the height
that I lacked,
although maybe
not the eyesight
as they were both
colour blind...

There were plenty of other formative experiences. My brothers both used to go with my dad on his coal round in the summer holidays to collect the beer money, the theory being that customers would be inclined to give a bit more of a tip to a kid then a coal-faced man. I pestered them to tag along. I was a little kid hanging on to the back of a coal lorry with no regard for health and safety. I was trying to be helpful but got in the way. A bit of coal dust got in my eye and I had to be taken to a chemist to get it out. I created such a fuss that the word from my dad was, 'Never again!'

It was Ted and Bill and their mates who I followed into what became my life in football. There was very little else to do. A bit of fishing perhaps, a spot of cricket in the summer, maybe even some tennis if we had rackets. There was another family across the cul-de-sac, the Whittakers. The dad was a plumber and they always had what we needed to play with – a cricket bat, football, whatever. The mum – also called Joyce – would come out and shout, 'Get in here, you!' They would have to go but also have to take their balls and stuff with them.

All the neighbours and families got on. We were all in the same boat – living on a council estate, with no real airs and graces, and pretty much the same standard of living. My dad did always have a car, though, and it was a big moment when he traded up from a little van to a Ford Cortina. Saloon cars in those days still had running boards, and our footballs would get stuck under these, or in a rosebush hedge where they would burst so you'd end up kicking a burst ball about.

I just had to play football, all the time. I spent hours and hours indoors kicking a balloon, or a boxing glove, aiming to kick them against the bit of glass on top of the door in the hall. Rainy days were the end of the world. A wet Saturday meant watching speedway or, worse, wrestling. Or rugby. I can't understand that game now, let alone then.

The joy in our parents' life was seeing three boys grow up and do all right – even the gifted one. When my dad got a foreman-type job at Heathrow Airport it coincided with me breaking into the Spurs team. He and his mates would come and watch us in Europe for 10 per cent of the normal flight fee thanks to his work for Air France. It came at the right time, when the coal business was declining but Heathrow was building up. So they could travel around Europe, and I could get them tickets. Not many people travelled then – it was a rare experience. It's one of my happy memories, thinking about what my career did for his quality of life.

Decades later, when I got my first managerial job at Brentford, Dad gave me a talk about how people are liberty-takers and will try and do as little as they can, and how you need to give them a kick up the you-know-what. It was a very down-to-earth way of explaining leadership and management to me, but served me well in lots of contexts.

Our holidays as kids were going to visit my mum's cousin Audrey and her husband Derek. That side of the clan was a lovely naval family who lived in Portsmouth, Southsea and Lee-on-Solent. Audrey and Derek lived in Gosport and when they went on holiday we could use their bungalow; otherwise we wouldn't get a holiday. All our joy was make-do-and-mend, nothing on a plate,

all earned and due to people being a bit clever with their thinking. We were resourceful, growing up around families with similar values and interests.

One of the consequences was that all the kids played football. It was an obsession. When there were too many of us playing football in the street, we'd head over to a nearby field. It wasn't good enough, really – it had horses in it and the grass was unkempt. We thought if there was a park there, that would be handy. So we got a petition up, and we went round the estate getting signatures. We were always getting grief where we played, so plenty of people signed, and it was successful. The council turned it into a park – Lime Trees Park, which is still there today. It's a legacy from all those kids who wanted somewhere decent to play the game they loved.

My first organised team was at Gifford Junior School. I would have seen Ted and Bill playing for it, so the expectation was, 'You're next.' By the time I went there they had their own playing field. Our school was great for saying, 'It's too hot to sit inside in class. Steve, go and speak to Mrs So-and-so's class and ask if they want a game of rounders.' Getting outside and doing sport was encouraged. Six-a-sides were a regular thing.

As a second-year, I was picked for my house team that usually had fourth-formers playing for it. They pulled me out of class to play. I was above my station, really, looked upon as a good player without me being conscious of it. I didn't really know if I was good or not – partly because at that age I didn't know what good meant in terms of being a footballer; we were just playing for fun.

We played football every single playtime. Not with a proper football, but it dominated your life, even with it not being on telly. We played every day on the street or in the park. We made our own decisions. I'd be out the front, doing keep-ups, and would be joined by a boy called Steven Groves. He was the same age as me and went to a different school, but lived close by and we played as young kids together. I still know him now, a very nice and loyal chap.

Two more kids would turn up and we'd have a little game passing to each other. Then a bit of head tennis. No one told us how to play – we just made up our own rules. It was the start of coaching, really. Even without a ball, if it was raining and I was indoors I'd be knocking that balloon around. What I could gain from that I don't know but all the time it was playing, gaining a ball sense. I am a product of street football. That's hard to do today – there are too many cars, and it's too dangerous.

I was quite good academically, and passed the 11-plus. I never had great confidence for reading out loud in class but maths was about finding the key to something. As soon as I found the key I could do it. That applies to a lot of things, be it a crossword or problem-solving. As a manager, Paul Tisdale gives players the key to their career. At Exeter we could lose in a transfer auction but he could convince a player to come because he could improve them. As a kid I couldn't find the key to unlock learning and understanding English, or geography. But maths was easy.

With two brothers going to Eliots Green Grammar School it was assumed I'd go, and sure enough I did. There was the practical consideration of being able to recycle uniform, and the fact my brothers could provide me with valuable family protection.

On my first day at senior school I turned up in my purple blazer. Sixth-formers wore black blazers and one of them pointed to something on the ground and said to me, 'Oi, you, pick that up.' I said meekly, 'I didn't put it there.' 'I know you didn't. Pick it up.' I said to him, 'My name's Perryman, and I've got two older brothers.' He stormed off. It was survival instinct in a way, standing up to a bully. I think I've always done that. I've given that talk at half-time. The manager has said his bit and he's asked me to speak.

The first photo of me in action in a proper kit. Here I am playing on Ealing Common for Gifford School. Ted had seen the school's geography teacher – by chance taking photos on the common – and asked him to take a picture of me

GIFFORD STEAL HONOURS

Gifford School, Northolt, stole the limelight at Ealing School Football Association's annual presentation at Walford Schoo Northolt, on Monday. They are pictured with the four trophi they have won this season.
The presentation was carried out by Queens Park Range manager Alec Stock.

'Do not forget what you've just been told,' I say, 'but you are being bullied. You know why they are called bullies? Because when someone answers or fights back, they back off. So do yourself a favour – go and front the bully and see what happens.' And it always happens: they back down.

I played football with my older brothers and their mates, so when I played with my own age group, it didn't make it easy but it meant I could handle it a little easier. It's why I got in the junior-school team early, and the district team. I just enjoyed playing. Looking back I remember the things I was taught as a schoolboy: don't pass across your own area, for example. Pep Guardiola must have missed that lesson...

But from very early on I had an instinct. I knew when a goalkeeper was taking his kick where that ball would land – I could anticipate it. I would have seen where the first one dropped, so I knew where it would go the next time. I had an awareness. I could read what would happen. It seemed like I was the only one who could see it. That was my first thought, not that I could play better than anyone else but that I could read the game better.

That was the start of me as a footballer, really. At that age I think it was just an intelligence. I've barely read a book, even when I was doing an exam. When I read anything my legs ached. It was as if my body was saying, 'Move!' Whether that's me lacking concentration or something else, I could never sit down and read a book. But I read people. And I was reading where this goal kick was going. It's a down-to-earth, applied intelligence.

If I had to explain what coaching is, I'd say it's trying to help your players have a better than 50/50 chance of knowing what is going to happen. It's thinking three or four moves ahead. Thinking where a pass is going to go, or even before it happens. Bill Nicholson used to say playing football is like driving a car. You're not just driving *your* car, you're not just playing *your* game – you have to know what that driver in front of you is doing, even the one behind you, to help you make a better decision. To which John Pratt said, 'So that's why I have so many car accidents!'

Properly competitive football didn't happen for me until I was 15. I was playing football for my school house teams, but that could be nine

The Gifford School fourth-year team in 1960–61 (above left) – the year of the great Spurs Double – with me seated on the far right. I was aged 10 and in the third year but good enough to play with boys a year older than me. Bobby Drumm, holding the ball, went for a trial with me at QPR and later played for Reading

Making the local paper (above) for our exploits that season, with a medal to show for it (left)

Another medal, this time for the Ealing Schools district team. I was making progress through the representative sides

Lifting silverware – something I hoped might be repeated. This was with the Ealing district side, with Mr Butcher acting as our manager. Second from the right on the back row is Dave Coxhill, who later turned pro at Millwall

against eight, not even 11 versus 11. Eliots was very serious about basketball but we were not allowed to play competitive football with other schools; when Eliots had played in a league, even in those days there had been trouble. Being a grammar school was also a factor. We had St Vincent's next to us, the best boxing school in the county! In our purple blazers we stood out like sore thumbs. We regularly had to run the gauntlet of a chasing pack, which probably helped my fitness but it meant no more competitive football, just occasional friendlies against other schools at weekends.

As a child back then it was hard to be unfit. To the junior school was about three miles; I used to run there, walk fast, walk backwards, run on walls, all the things kids do, and it made me fit. It made my legs strong. And whatever I was doing I wanted to do it right. It could be kicking a tennis ball against a wall, I'd want to do it well and not just for the sake of it. I wanted to hit the ball without it bouncing on the ground and make my kick more difficult. There was a wish for me to do things right and an intelligence to know what was going to happen next.

The vital ingredient in my development then was Ted. Even before I was rated by any club, Ted wrote to them suggesting they take a look at me or asking for a trial. I did have trials at Brentford and Reading, where a friend of mine from junior school had gone. The Reading manager, Roy Bentley, said I was OK but no better than what they already had.

I played on the main pitch at Brentford when I was 13, with the apprentices and triallists, who at 16 seemed like giants. I never even sniffed the ball let alone touched it. Jimmy Sirrel, who became manager at Brentford, was the trainer and in charge of the trial. It must have been the end of season or pre-season because he was up a ladder painting the stand – that was what managers and coaches had to do back then. It seemed every time I did something good Sirrel was painting something difficult up in the corner. When he turned round to look at the game again my good bit was over. Well, that was my excuse for not getting taken on by Brentford anyway.

I'd been highly rated as an 11-year-old at junior school but when organised schools football had stopped for me after I left Gifford, I dropped off the radar. Ted was still thinking I was good enough and said to me one day after one of the Eliots weekend friendlies, 'You'll be a better player when you tell the man on the ball what you think he can do. Not because he's a bad player; not because you're better than him. But because, like us all, he hasn't got eyes in the back of his head. So if you can tell him what you think he can do – be it turn, pass, get rid, whatever – it makes you a better player because even without touching the ball you've helped your team. And it will also give you an opinion on the game.'

This is not a coach. This is my 17-year-old brother. I tried it and it didn't work. Ted said, 'Ask yourself why. Were you too quiet? Or too late? Because the man on the ball might be hearing two or three things said to him. You have to break into his thought processes. If it still doesn't work at least you've tried your hardest. It's not because you're a better player – it might just be he's not the type of player to listen to it.'

That talk and my response to it did help me become a better player and a captain. It gave me an opinion. From my position of old-fashioned inside-forward it helped as the game was going on around me. That advice had a profound and lasting effect on me. It taught me not to be afraid to use my voice; it taught me not to be disheartened if that voice was not listened to, and to keep using it. I'm not demanding players listen and do what I say – I'm suggesting it because I'm trying to help them.

Ted provided the intervention I needed then. The letters clubs sent to me offering trials and whatnot were addressed to my dad – but it was Ted behind him, pulling the strings about how to word the reply. Solicitors were not an option. I was relying on Ted's intelligence to drive it all.

It was going to become invaluable because soon enough I would be leaving the world of kids' football and playing with the bigger boys.

"Soon enough I would be leaving the world of kids' football and playing with the bigger boys"

The original photo used in the local paper article on page 25, featuring the under-11s and under-10s – I played for both teams. We might have had knobbly knees but were very smart in our blazers, reflecting the good values we were taught by our teachers, including how to shake hands properly: 'Take the medal with the left and shake with the right, and look people in the eye when they present it to you'

The 1961–62 Gifford School team sport a new kit – in Arsenal colours! Cedric Smith, on the far left, managed the team, assisted by Mr Lewis (far right)

Box of delights: a collection of my early schoolboy medals

I missed out on competitive football for a number of years after moving to Eliots Grammar School, where basketball was the main sport, but a change of teacher put football back on the agenda and eventually saw me selected for Ealing district under-15s, which proved to be the launchpad for my football career. Here I'm shaking hands with dignitaries before a match (top). On the far right is Mr Jamieson, who ran the team. Dave Coxhill is on my left, with Brian Hicks to his left. To my right is Gary Fowles, while to his right is Doug Dimmock, who played basketball for England. Two internationals in a year was pretty good going

After winning the match we hoisted our captain Peter Keary, who was later signed by West Ham, on our shoulders while he held the impressive-looking trophy (bottom)

CHAPTER TWO

IN DEMAND

Football is like a small village. Although there are hundreds of clubs ranged all over the country, and in the modern global game the sport's reach is of course far wider, it is still a pretty tight-knit community in which plenty of people know each other and some know the game inside out.

That held true in the mid-1960s, when there were few secrets about young players who could potentially make it as a professional. I was one of them. At 15, soon after I started to play competitive schools football again, there were a bevy of clubs following me. London clubs were showing a particular interest, but so were others from much further afield.

The key was a sudden change for what turned out to be my final year at school. At Eliots most of my football was in the playground with a tennis ball as the school wasn't keen on football. Our existing sports master Jack Barrett did like the sport because he was a Man United fan – and he let us all know it – but the school had made the decision not to play competitively, and focused on basketball.

What changed was that Jack went on a refresher course and his replacement was a young teacher who had different ideas and started some trials for a school football team. I had doubts I would get in as I genuinely didn't particularly rate myself, but it kickstarted my career in youth football and ultimately the professional game.

The background was that this new teacher had some involvement with the borough's district-team manager Jack Jamieson, and he put us in for the team's trials. There were only about six schools that entered players so there was a need for fresh blood. I went to the trial and got selected for a competitive match against Harrow Schools at Salvatorian College. It was a lovely welcoming venue but we murdered them 9–1. I played inside-forward. Ted took me home; we discussed the game, how I played and spoke again about me needing to have an opinion and express it.

I got home very pleased with things and at some point in the afternoon the doorbell rang. My brother answered it. Standing on the doorstep was a dapper man who was the next to have a profound influence on my life.

Charlie Faulkner was Tottenham's chief scout and had formerly been at QPR. He lived in Hillingdon, so was obviously keeping tabs on players in West London. Ted said, 'Oh, hello Mr Faulkner, how are you?' Charlie was a bit taken aback by the fact Ted had recognised him.

'I've seen your brother play today,' said Charlie.

> "At 15 there were a bevy of clubs following me. London clubs were showing a particular interest, but so were others from much further afield"

A very talented Middlesex Schools team line-up, along with my metal and embroidered badges. I'm second from the right of the front row, with Phil Holder, who became a great and lifelong friend of mine, on the far left of the same row. Back row, third from right is Ray Bowles, who joined Spurs at same time as Phil and I. Peter Keary, who joined West Ham, is third from left on the back row, while standing on the far left is Dave Shipperley, who played more than 100 games for Charlton and was the father of Neil Shipperley, who played for a number of clubs, including Crystal Palace

Ted said, 'I wrote to you about him when you were at QPR.'

'Ah, OK, well, that didn't quite get through to me for whatever reason.'

Charlie was invited in. We made him a cup of tea before we all sat around the table. He said, 'I really liked your play and I'd like to invite you to Tottenham for schoolboy training. If you sign this form you can come training…'

Ted stopped him short. 'No, sorry, he's not signing.' I was thinking, 'What?!' This was the chief scout of Spurs, Ted! This was Tottenham: Bill Nicholson, the Double, glory glory football, Blanchflower, Mackay, Greaves and so many others. A few weeks before I was barely kicking a ball in anger and now one of the biggest clubs in the country is interested in me and my brother is saying no.

Ted was about 18 then. That took some mental strength for him to say no, and was tribute to his knowledge, to know that if I signed that form my options would immediately be limited and I'd be tied to one club. Charlie was persistent. 'But to come training you have to sign this form.' Ted said, 'No, you don't. He's not signing that form.'

It didn't put Charlie off, and despite me not signing, arrangements were made for me to train at Tottenham one or two nights a week. Now we had to work out how I was going to get there. Ted and my dad talked it through and between them they got me to North London. From that moment on, my schoolwork fell away. It don't stop me having a brain, but my focus changed.

So did the opportunities before me. When we got picked for the district team, one of my mates at school said, 'You could end up playing for England Schoolboys, Steve.' I didn't pay much attention but I was soon picked for Middlesex. Playing trials and district football was a test, but more in terms of putting me out of my comfort zone and making me deal with new people. I coped with the standard of football fine.

The trials for Middlesex were at Kingsbury FC. I have a distinct memory of looking across the changing room and seeing two lads who were taking the piss out of everything and everyone. I found out they were from Kilburn,

KEARY, PERRYMAN PLAY FOR LONDON

EALING SCHOOLS' F.A. have two 15-year-olds selected for London Schools in their annual match with Liverpool at Anfield next Monday (November 7).

The two schoolboys who have won through a series of trial matches all over London are wing half Peter Keary (Twyford School, Acton) and inside-forward Stephen Perryman of Eliot's Green School, Northolt.

Another local boy, Barry Drake (Brentside), won through to the final side but has not been selected.

This is the first time two Ealing boys have been chosen for the same London representative match.

Keary, Perryman, Drake and centre - half Gary Fowles (Eliots Green) were playing in Middlesex trials this week as well.

Professional scouts have been following the careers of Keary and Perryman with considerable interest in the past year.

STEVE PERRYMAN . . . comes from Ealing.

and were definitely more streetwise than I was. 'Stay clear of them two,' I said to myself.

One of those Kilburn lads was Phil Holder, who would become a lifelong pal and an individual who has had such a big impact on my life. He had the confidence as a 15-year-old to stand up for himself and take on everyone else if he needed to. We formed a real bond that was invaluable as we made our way through the game, but back then he was such a forceful character it did make me wonder how I was going to handle this new world of more serious football.

That takes a bit of dealing with. No one ever thinks about how to survive the dressing room at a trial, which can be a real test. You didn't know if you're going to be starting a trial game or not. The selection process was ruthless. Players were divided into colours – yellows against reds, only we might be told to play in green because we weren't good enough to get in either the yellow or red teams. We might be thrown on at some point with no real clue about what we were supposed to do, playing with a lot of kids we didn't know.

I wasn't comfortable with that. To this day I am never really comfortable going into situations with new people. I'm wary. In 1966, that year of representative games, trials and training, and being coveted by clubs, I met new people all the time. Because I had not signed forms for Tottenham – very unusual for a kid in the under-15 age group – I could be invited to other clubs who by then were seeing me at the various trials. I had been absent from the schools football picture, and therefore I was ripe for chasing.

After playing for Middlesex, I was put forward to play for London Schools. The trial was successful and I played for London at Anfield. That was my first trip to a ground I always loved to visit. You'd be hard pressed if you were a scout not to get to that game, because the vibes were that London had got a good player who was not 'on a form', and therefore available. In a way all the scouts were going only to look at one player – me, not because I was a superstar but because I was not signed up.

There were better players than me in the Middlesex team, but a local newspaper article (above left) highlighted my progress in being selected for London Schools and reported that scouts were showing a keen interest

The team line-up from the game against Liverpool (above right). It was my first visit to Anfield which became a favourite ground of mine – playing there was the biggest test of a player's ability in football

More representative mementoes from my London Schools days

After I'd been initially scouted, the letters came from the different clubs asking if they could visit our house. In the school holidays particularly, clubs would make their approaches. QPR, West Ham, Orient, Fulham, Chelsea and Arsenal all showed interest. Manchester City and Malcolm Allison were keen and wrote a letter, and I have a vague memory of Joe Mercer visiting.

The fact that all these scouts and managers were interested and coming to the house was a good reason for me to think, 'I must be a good player.' But it still all seemed strange. We lived in a corner of the cul-de-sac on the end of the terrace and these big clubs were visiting to try and sign me.

The visits started about 7pm. They wouldn't want to interrupt us if we were having tea, so they'd phone up ahead and arrange to come. Until 9:30pm there would be a constant flow of people arriving.

At first they would be shown into the 'normal' living room with my brother, or if he wasn't there my mum would be talking to them from the kitchen. She was making cups of tea all night. Everyone seemed to bring a box of biscuits. My mum would say, 'Oh, how nice, thank you', and then add it to a pile of about a dozen boxes. The scouts would have seen from that alone that they were definitely not the only ones interested in me.

It was like an assembly line. They were then shown into what all families like us had in those days, the room only used on a Sunday or for special visitors. Ours was called the front room. It was in a better state of decoration. There would be tea, biscuits and chat, with all the clubs making their pitch for me to sign for them.

The conversations were very interesting. Ron Greenwood at West Ham saw that Ted was keeping scrapbooks of my progress, with cuttings from local papers saying how good I was in the various schoolboy representative games. 'Well that's OK,' said Ron. 'But if there's a bad one make sure you put that in as well.' He was quietly telling me to keep my feet on the ground. Very wise.

The phrase 'mind games' is used all the time now but they were going on then as well. As an illustration my mum, who wouldn't have known who any of these visitors were, would have chats. Once, when Ron stood in the kitchen waiting for his cuppa, she said to him, 'Love, I wouldn't sign him. He's never gonna be strong enough.'

'What?'

'Well, he was born with a heart murmur. He don't eat proper food, all he eats is cornflakes, and I just don't think he's going be strong enough.' My mum was right: I had been diagnosed with a slight heart murmur in infancy, though the prognosis was it would correct itself as I grew, which turned out to be the case. That was Mum just speaking her mind but it could have been interpreted by Greenwood as a message that my family and I didn't want me to sign for West Ham.

Clubs would do all kinds of things to try and get me to sign. QPR got their players Jim Langley and Frank Sibley to pick me up and take me to training. They were good players and good people, and made an impression. If I supported any club, it was QPR. I watched Brentford as well, but if ever my brothers went to an away game, they'd go for little adventures to watch Rangers at places like Southend or Bournemouth, and I'd go with them.

Rodney Marsh was QPR's main player, which was another lure. After one particular training session he presented me with his shirt. It strengthened the attachment I had with Rangers. They trained within walking distance from my house at the London Transport Ground, which made it practical. They had players like Mark Lazarus, Mike Keen the captain, Peter Springett, Tony Ingham and Peter Angell. QPR might have been Third Division but they were a producing club who reared players like the Morgan twins, Roger and Ian, Frank Sibley and Tony Hazel.

The chief scout Derek Healey and coach – and later manager – Bill Dodgin would come around and take me to play golf. I didn't play and never really have since, but it showed that clubs would try anything to win us over. It wasn't the size of the club, necessarily, but how we felt they were treating us that made a good impression.

Nonetheless I knew that as soon as I signed apprenticeship forms all that would end. No one was going to pick me up to play golf. Rod Marsh wouldn't be presenting me with a shirt. The glad-handing, the smiles and the boxes of biscuits would soon stop.

The efforts to sign me became less subtle. I went to the marble halls of Arsenal. Straight away I didn't feel warmth. Arsenal were all over me, but the feeling wasn't right. I played a game for Ealing against Islington Schools at Highbury. Arsenal's manager Bertie Mee invited my brother Ted and my dad, who had gone to the game, into his office afterwards, and they told me later what had happened. Mee said something like, 'We've had eight different people watching Steve', presumably to show how serious they were. One of them was George Male, the former England international and Arsenal captain in the 1930s and later chief scout.

I was told years later that Male said I should never have played for Tottenham and that I was a 'born Arsenal player'. What they apparently looked for was balance. I'm not sure that literally meant physical balance so much as a balanced mental attitude and a strength of character. George Male was proper and correct. Arsenal were correct. I think they do things right, on the whole. But at that meeting with Mee, something was said which just confirmed how I felt about the club.

'We're still not sure about him,' he said. 'But actually we think that you're after a backhander.'

My dad and Ted were taken aback. Ted said, 'Where did you get that from?'

'Well,' said Mee, as if it was just a casual turn of phrase, 'it's just that… well, you know, there's a lot of clubs after him.'

It could have been Arsenal's indirect way of saying, 'Do you want a backhander? Is that what it's going to take?' Whatever it was, it backfired. We took it completely the other way.

'Steve's going to make the decision on where he feels comfortable, and therefore the money aspect you're talking about will not affect anything,' said Ted. 'If you don't want to sign him that's OK, that's very honest, but don't worry about that decision, because there are enough clubs that do want to sign him.'

Tottenham by contrast did do it right. I had a good feeling about the place the moment I first walked through the door. They didn't just look after me, they were welcoming and friendly to my family. One incident stood out when I was selected to join up with England Schoolboys on a tour to Germany. It was a very proud moment, naturally, for all of us Perrymans. Tottenham recognised this and

Berlin bound! Charlie Faulkner, my dad and brother Bill in Germany after my call-up to the England Schoolboys squad. This was my first ever flight (below) and while I didn't play in the first game of the tour I was selected for the second in Saarbrücken, with Ted capturing the moment I was substituted (bottom)

took my dad and two brothers to Germany. I didn't actually play in the first game, but the English Schools officials were so affronted by my family being flown out by Spurs that they completely ignored them.

The match was in Berlin at the Olympic Stadium that had hosted the Games in 1936. Ted said they got to the stadium and every door they went to, there was no check of tickets or direction about where to go. He and Bill and my dad just kept saying, 'England' and a door would be opened. Eventually they got into a room. It was where Hitler would have been during the Olympics. There were people in there in official blazers, so they must have been on some committee to do with English Schools. My dad and two brothers were obviously somewhere where they shouldn't be, and they were looked at as though they were peasants and asked, 'What are you doing here?'

Why do that to the parent of one of your players, just because a club has brought him over? The contrast with how Spurs treated my family was so different. I think they took my dad and mum to see me play in Belfast for England Schoolboys – though she never saw me play at White Hart Lane. 'Stephen,' she'd say, 'Wembley's not far. If you get to Wembley I'll come and watch you.'

In Berlin, England lost 6–0 to a really powerful German team and so had to make changes. I then played in Saarbrücken and we drew 0–0, putting myself in contention to be picked for the next game, which was at Wembley against Scotland and which my mum did go to. I ended up playing four games, including another game against Scotland at Old Trafford, and it raised my profile. Reports compared me to Johnny Haynes, which was nice but surely over the top. Strong criticism from Ted saying I played poorly kept my feet firmly on the ground. But that raised profile added to the pressure. Where was I going to go to? Everyone else in those England teams seemed settled. Tony Towers was going to Man City, Len Cantello to West Brom; Tommy Taylor, Richie Pitt and others were signed.

It was Spurs who were making the running. Charlie Faulkner was almost living in our house, turning up in his camel coat with his cigarette holder. He wasn't a former player. No disrespect to Charlie but it was a wonder how he was working with such a total football man in Bill Nicholson. That's not to say that Charlie didn't know his stuff. He must have had an eye for a player as he found Graeme Souness as well.

None of us had ever met someone like Charlie before. He was a nice guy but beyond our comprehension in some ways with his style, manner and the world he came from. He was a man of his word, though. Everything he promised in turning up, taking us somewhere or doing something, he did it.

Meanwhile I was still training at Spurs. We were put through our paces by two young pros, Roger Hoy and John Sainty. That might seem odd, given the specialist coaching much younger players now receive at clubs, but the sessions were good. Overall Spurs did things right. It could be I had forgotten my socks and someone would get me a pair without looking like they were doing me a favour. The place just felt right. But not enough to make it nailed on that I would sign, partly because of the distance I was having to travel. It was nearly 20 miles and it took two hours getting there after school and an hour home when the roads were not so busy.

Those journeys were useful, however. Ted had passed his driving test so would share the lifts with my dad and take me to various games. We'd talk about my game or particular points, such as a referee's decision, or a passage of play. Not necessarily something about me, but an aspect of

Facing page: The England Schoolboys squad gathered for a group photo at a training camp in Stoke. David Mills, who went on to play for Middlesbrough, is second from left on the bottom row, while I'm second from right on the same row. The squad also included Len Cantello, later of West Bromwich Albion (back row, sixth from left); Richie Pitt, who played for Sunderland (back row, fifth from left); Steve Whitworth, who went to Leicester (middle row, first from left), and Tony Towers of Manchester City (middle row, third from left). On the far right on the middle row is David Rogers, who played for Bristol City, while on his right is goalkeeper Mervyn Cawston, later of Norwich City and Southend. Above are the embroidered badge for my blazer and a pin badge

Leyton Orient Football Club Ltd.

TELEPHONE
OFFICE—LEYTONSTONE 1369

TELEGRAMS
"ORIENT," BRISBANE ROAD, LEYTON, E.10

PRESIDENT—F. JOHN YOUNG

CHAIRMAN . . . . H. S. ZUSSMAN
VICE-CHAIRMAN - H. E. LEA, F. F. HARRIS
DIRECTORS . . . . . . C. BENT-MARSHALL.
R. DELFONT, A. E. PAGE, L. GRADE
SECRETARY . . . . G. A. HICKS
MANAGER . . . . D. R. GRAHAM

LEYTON STADIUM
BRISBANE ROAD
LEYTON :: E.10

12TH Oct 66.

Dear Mr Perryman

I've been asked by Mr Graham to contact you regarding your son. I believe he spoke to you asking if you would like the boy to join our Club. I can assure you we will look after him, and further his football Education. I realise you live the other side of Town, but if you give us permission to play the boy in one of our Schoolboy friendly games we can make arrangements to get him here. Hoping to hear from

---

PHONE: GRANGEWOOD 0704

West Ham United Football Co., Limited

SECRETARY
E. CHAPMAN
MANAGER-COACH
R. GREENWOOD

REGISTERED OFFICE
BOLEYN GROUND
GREEN STREET
UPTON PARK, E.13

10th October 1966

Your Ref........

Our Ref........

Mr E. Perryman,
39, Bancroft Court,
Greenford,
Northolt,
Middlesex.

Dear Ted,

    I sincerely hope that you enjoyed your visit to West Ham on Saturday and also the match.

    The reason for this letter Ted is to forward on to you your train fare for Saturday's journey. I have enclosed the sum of 30/- and I trust that this will cover the cost.

    I trust that we shall have the pleasure of meeting you again in the not too distant future.

        Best wishes.

        Yours sincerely.
        W. St Pier.
        Chief representative.

HAROLD BUNCE

Stephen Perryman

70, Springwell Road,
Heston,
Middlesex.

HOUnslow 1241

17. 4. 67

As a representative of Crystal Palace F.C. may I offer to you an invitation to visit Selhurst Park. at one of the remaining games in company with myself.

Like others they are interested in your future and would like you at least to see the set-up etc of their club.

You will not be pestered to sign. That would be left to you and your parents discretion.

I would point out that this is a very friendly club. and at least you could enjoy an evening out.

Would you kindly write me your views. Sorry but could not attend game this evening.

H. Bunce.

'Dear Mr Perryman...' West Ham, Leyton Orient, Crystal Palace, Fulham and Manchester City were just some of the clubs, along with Spurs, to pitch for my signature

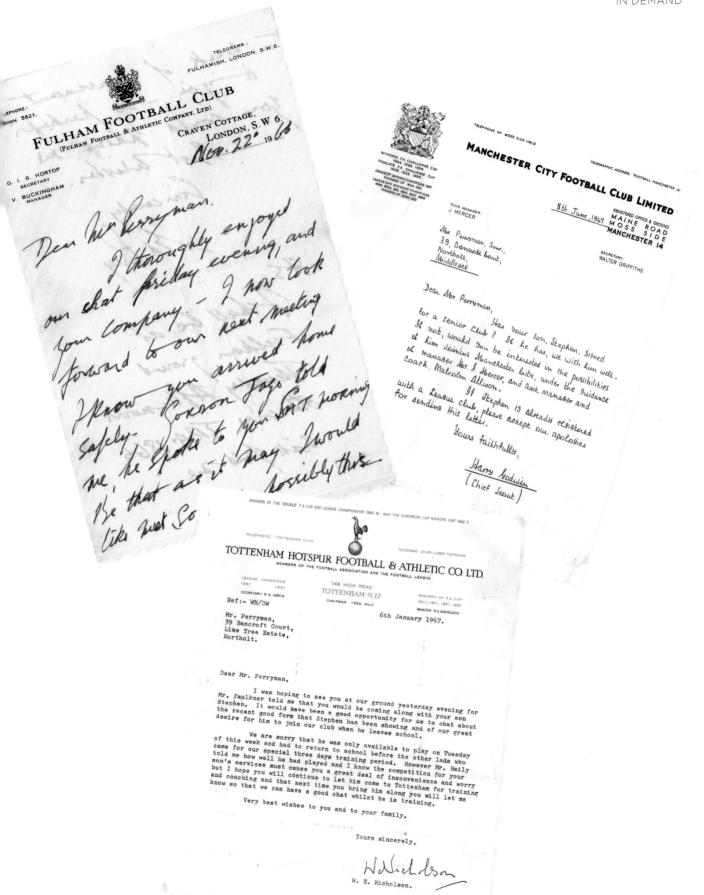

FULHAM FOOTBALL CLUB
(Fulham Football & Athletic Company, Ltd)

TELEPHONE:
~~OWN~~ 5621.

TELEGRAMS:
FULHAMISH, LONDON, S.W.6.

CRAVEN COTTAGE,
LONDON, S.W.6.

Nov. 22nd 1966

G. I. S. HORTOP
SECRETARY

V. BUCKINGHAM
MANAGER

Dear Mr Perryman,

I thoroughly enjoyed our chat friday evening, and your company – I now look forward to our next meeting

I know you arrived home safely. Gordon Jago told me, he spoke to you last morning

Be that as it may I would like next So . . . . . possibly this . . .

MANCHESTER CITY FOOTBALL CLUB LIMITED

TELEPHONE Nº MOSS SIDE 1181/2

TELEGRAPHIC ADDRESS: "FOOTBALL MANCHESTER 14"

TEAM MANAGER:
J. MERCER

REGISTERED OFFICE & GROUND
MAINE ROAD
MOSS SIDE
MANCHESTER 14

SECRETARY:
WALTER GRIFFITHS

8th. June, 1967

Mr. Perryman, Senr.,
39, Bancroft Court,
Northolt,
Middlesex

Dear Mr. Perryman,

Has your son, Stephen, signed for a senior club? If he has, we wish him well. If not, would you be interested in the possibilities of him joining Manchester City, under the guidance of manager Mr. J. Mercer, and Asst. manager and coach, Malcolm Allison. If Stephen is already registered with a League club, please accept our apologies for sending this letter.

Yours faithfully,

Harry Godwin
(Chief Scout)

TOTTENHAM HOTSPUR FOOTBALL & ATHLETIC CO. LTD.
MEMBERS OF THE FOOTBALL ASSOCIATION AND THE FOOTBALL LEAGUE

WINNERS OF THE 'DOUBLE' F.A. CUP AND LEAGUE CHAMPIONSHIP 1960 61. AND 'THE EUROPEAN CUP WINNERS CUP' 1962 3

TELEPHONE: TOTTENHAM 1020

TELEGRAMS: SPURS-LOWER-TOTTENHAM

LEAGUE CHAMPIONS
1951   1961
SECRETARY: R. S. JARVIS

748 HIGH ROAD
TOTTENHAM · N.17
CHAIRMAN · FRED. WALE

WINNERS OF F.A. CUP
1901, 1921, 1961, 1962
MANAGER · W. E. NICHOLSON

Ref:- WN/DW

6th January 1967.

Mr. Perryman,
39 Bancroft Court,
Lime Tree Estate,
Northolt.

Dear Mr. Perryman,

I was hoping to see you at our ground yesterday evening for Mr. Faulkner told me that you would be coming along with your son Stephen. It would have been a good opportunity for us to chat about the recent good form that Stephen has been showing and of our great desire for him to join our club when he leaves school.

We are sorry that he was only available to play on Tuesday of this week and had to return to school before the other lads who came for our special three days training period. However Mr. Baily told me how well he had played and I know the competition for your son's services must cause you a great deal of inconvenience and worry but I hope you will continue to let him come to Tottenham for training and coaching and that next time you bring him along you will let me know so that we can have a good chat whilst he is training.

Very best wishes to you and to your family.

Yours sincerely,

W. E. Nicholson.

If the cap fits! We received an England cap for a series of fixtures in a Schoolboys international season, rather than for individual matches

The England Schoolboys team line-up for 1966–67

ABOVE: England Schoolboys 1966-7, back row left to right: Mr. T. Saunders (trainer), G. Jones, D. Dangerfield, L. Cantello, M. Simmonds, G. Crudgington, R. Pitt, S. Howie, S. Whitworth, D. Rogers, Mr. E. T. King (manager). Front row left to right: L. Millerchip, A. Towers, D. Spencer, T. Taylor (Capt.), S. Perryman, W. Kenny, P. Cuff. (Prov. 1.)

football that helped my understanding and development. It was like having my own personal teacher. As a young kid I might say, 'The ref was crap.' 'Yeah but,' Ted would say, 'you didn't lose the game because of him.' Ted provided context, insight. It was good sense that helped me develop my own opinion and what I became known for – my leadership, using my brain, on and off the field. It was all driven by Ted. I don't even think he knew what he was doing or where it was going to lead for me, but it worked.

Ted might have been living his football through me a bit, but it was never apparent. I used to watch him play Sunday football. He wasn't captain but I'd have to walk away at half-time sometimes. He didn't swear as much as I do – my dad swore and that's where I got it from – but with Ted when it came to football, ooh, could he give it out. That was a passion for him. He did things right and expected that of those around him.

It rubbed off onto me. If I did 40 kicks against the wall keeping the ball off the ground, the next day I wanted to do 41. My mentality was, 'I can do better than that.' But it can't be football 24 hours a day. I say to kids now, 'As much as you want to be a player, don't ignore cricket, or cross country, or table tennis. Break it up a bit. You can't have football all the time. As much as you might need to do it, break it up to keep things fresh.'

Back in 1967 my dad was leaning towards Tottenham. They treated him well. He would be taken out by the scout Dickie Walker and Mrs Bick from the office. They would sometimes pick him up in a club car and take Dad out for lunch or for a drink. Spurs actually made it as enticing and welcoming as they could do without showering our family with gifts or anything more than that.

Dickie was smart, an ex-army man with a moustache and always dressed in a tie and a blazer, with a handkerchief in his top pocket. There was some debate about who actually signed me for Spurs; both Dickie and Charlie thought they did but it was Charlie who was the one on the doorstep with the first knock. Dickie was the man who handled administration in the office because Charlie was off around the country doing his job for Bill Nick.

It wasn't all positive vibes from Spurs, mind. I can't remember it word for word, but I got a distinctly dismissive impression from Eddie Baily, Bill Nick's assistant, and a brilliant player in the 'Push and Run' team that won the title in 1950–51. Charlie said that Eddie said to him, 'There is no way he's joining us. Switch off, stop worrying, he's not joining.' I would come to discover that was typical Eddie. If he had an opinion, he had to voice it.

So, of course, did Bill Nick. The first time I met him I thought he had a rock-like face. The Tottenham players, if they called him anything other than Bill, actually called him 'Granite'. It wasn't taking the mick, it was out of respect. He was immaculate; the creases in his trousers were razor sharp, the shoes were polished. I don't think it hurt that he spoke in a different manner to people as well, with a Yorkshire accent softened by being in North London for so long. He wasn't a cockney, cheeky-chappy, Terry Venables type, but he had a simple, clear, directness of voice.

I would see him at night-time training. He would poke his head around the corner, to show interest in the session but also because he heard that this young player that Charlie really rated was now in for his third session.

Bill followed it up, and also came to our house. There would be me, my dad and my brother talking to Bill Nick. Imagine that. Bill Nicholson, one of the greatest managers Britain has ever produced. The Double winner,

"If I did 40 kicks against the wall keeping the ball off the ground, the next day I wanted to do 41. My mentality was, 'I can do better than that'"

STEVE IS SIGNED UP BY SPURS!

MOST youngsters are football crazy, and Steve Perryman was no exception. Steve attended Eliots Green School, Northolt and he played at inside-forward for his school team. Even at this time it was obvious that he had great potential as a footballer. And he made the Middlesex, London and England Boys teams.

In July 1967 Steve decided that football was to be his career and joined Tottenham Hotspurs as an apprentice. He has now appeared five times for Spurs Combination side, and seventeen times for the Metropolitan League side. And just last week, Steve, who lives in Ealing, signed as a full-time professional for world-famous Spurs.

the man who won the first ever European trophy for a British team, Mr Tottenham. And he's sitting in our front room asking me to come and play for him. He was a busy man, on the lookout for new players and talent, but he wasn't doing this for every 15-year-old.

Tottenham at that time felt they needed to produce home-grown players. They had been reliant on Bill Nick being clever in the transfer market, but wanted to show they could develop their own. This was to bear fruit in a few years to come and have a major impact on my career, but for now the immediate aim was to get me to sign on as an apprentice.

The complimentary tickets that Tottenham sent us were certainly no hindrance. The visits from Charlie and Bill, and the follow-up letters that backed up the talk kept them in the forefront of our minds. There was a constant communication with the club due to the regular training sessions, whereas the other clubs would dip in and out.

I had enough knowledge of how important loyalty was to recognise that Tottenham were delivering on their promises, and their honesty was impressive. Bill Nick's down-to-earth approach won me over. 'This is how it is' was his no-nonsense style. But I always felt welcome at White Hart Lane. It just felt warm.

I couldn't hang around thinking about how pleasant things might be, however. A decision had to be made. It's happened in my life that if I've got a decision to make I leave it as late as I can to give the answer every chance to pop up. I was putting eggs in the Tottenham basket but without actually telling them that I was veering their way. But it still came down to a toss-up. QPR had a lot going for them, while Ted was keen on West Ham.

It wasn't just because of Moore, Hurst and Peters, the World Cup and all that. I was invited by West Ham to go to their Youth Cup nights, which were always a bit special. Ted tuned in to Ron Greenwood's philosophy. He had a soft voice, and was a teacher type. Bill Nick's voice was direct – 'I say it, you do it.' Greenwood was more, 'Let's try this.' That appealed to Ted.

The problem was that at 15 when I left school it was two hours to travel to Tottenham, but West Ham would have been another 20 minutes. If it had been up to me completely, I'd have joined QPR for local reasons. I'm a home bird and didn't fancy digs one iota. But while it would be a bit of a grind in getting to Tottenham, it had its benefits. I discussed this years later with Don Howe about the journey, but also having to be up early and home late, working hard just to get to the club. Don said, 'Steve, that's what gave you a long career.' It was the discipline and application needed to do that day after day at a young age.

EMPHASIS ON YOUTH—HERE'S A STAR OF THE FUTURE

SPURS manager Bill Nicholson rates 17-year-old STEVE PERRYMAN as a star of the future. A Northolt boy, Steve joined Spurs straight from school, and has made such remarkable progress

TOTTENHAM SIGN UP PERRYMAN

STEPHEN PERRYMAN, the 15-year-old, and much sought-after inside-forward, has finally signed for Tottenham Hotspur.

Stephen, an England Schoolboy international who comes from Northolt and went to Eliots Green Grammar School, has signed on as an apprentice professional, having trained at White Hart Lane last winter.

This brings an end to a chase for his signature which has involved Manchester United and several London clubs, including Queen's Park Rangers who were just beaten by Spurs.

It came to the spring of 1967. Spurs had reached the FA Cup Final against Chelsea and both clubs were the talk of London. But for one 15-year-old there was a very different kind of expectation. Who was I going to join? One evening at Spurs training at White Hart Lane I went into the car park and Bill Nick was walking towards me.

He said, quite abruptly, 'Hello. Are you going to join us or not? Because if you don't, you're not getting a cup final ticket.' Chelsea were making all sorts of offers for the final, promising to take my family, giving me an invite to the post-match banquet, for me to sit on the team bus and even go in their dressing room at Wembley. They knew the crunch was coming, and their manager, Tommy Docherty, came round to our house as well to try and sway me.

I don't know exactly at what point I decided to join Spurs but I did indeed go to the final – and it was with a ticket provided by Spurs. I had officially joined Tottenham Hotspur. What edged it was Bill Nick. Training at the club was obviously important and it gave them more of a chance to treat me right and make me feel good about them. But Bill's straightforwardness was something that I responded to.

Now the hard work really began.

A precious artefact – a letter from Bill Nick, Mr Tottenham, to the father of the player who ended up playing the most games for the club

WINNERS OF THE "DOUBLE" F A CUP AND LEAGUE CHAMPIONSHIP 1960 61, AND "THE EUROPEAN CUP WINNERS CUP" 1962-3

TELEPHONE: TOTTENHAM 1020   TELEGRAMS: SPURS-LOWER-TOTTENHAM

TOTTENHAM HOTSPUR FOOTBALL & ATHLETIC CO. LTD.

MEMBERS OF THE FOOTBALL ASSOCIATION AND THE FOOTBALL LEAGUE

LEAGUE CHAMPIONS	748 HIGH ROAD	WINNERS OF F.A. CUP
1951 1961	TOTTENHAM · N. 17	1901, 1921, 1961, 1962

SECRETARY: R S. JARVIS   CHAIRMAN: FRED. WALE   MANAGER: W. E. NICHOLSON

26. 6. 67.

R. Perryman Esq.,
39 Bancroft Court,
Lime Trees Estate,
Northolt.

Dear Mr. Perryman,

Mr. Faulkener has just 'phoned me to say that you have heard from the Football League that they do not intend to take any action in regards to your decision to ask permission for Steve to leave school this summer. I was informed, by one of our local headmasters last saturday, that the school can take no action against you either, so it seems that everything is in order for your son to be registered by a Professional Football Club.

Naturally we are hoping that it is going to be ours and I can tell you that if it is we shall never have been more pleased to welcome any boy to our Club. Charlie mentioned about bringing Steve along on wednesday - if you can manage to come with him I shall be more than pleased, and any other members of the family too.

I am very pleased to hear of the decision of the F/L which seems to have been a complete reversal of the attitude they were taking in the first place. You must also be happy and relieved in feeling that it was worth all the worry.

Closing in haste with best wishes to all.

Yours sincerely,

W Nicholson,

Manager.

My England Schoolboys shirt, presented at the end of the international season

ELIOTS GREEN GRAMMAR SCHOOL

PUPIL'S REPORT BOOK

NAME S. PERRYMAN

COUNTY COUNCIL OF MIDDLESEX
BOROUGH OF EALING EDUCATION COMMITTEE

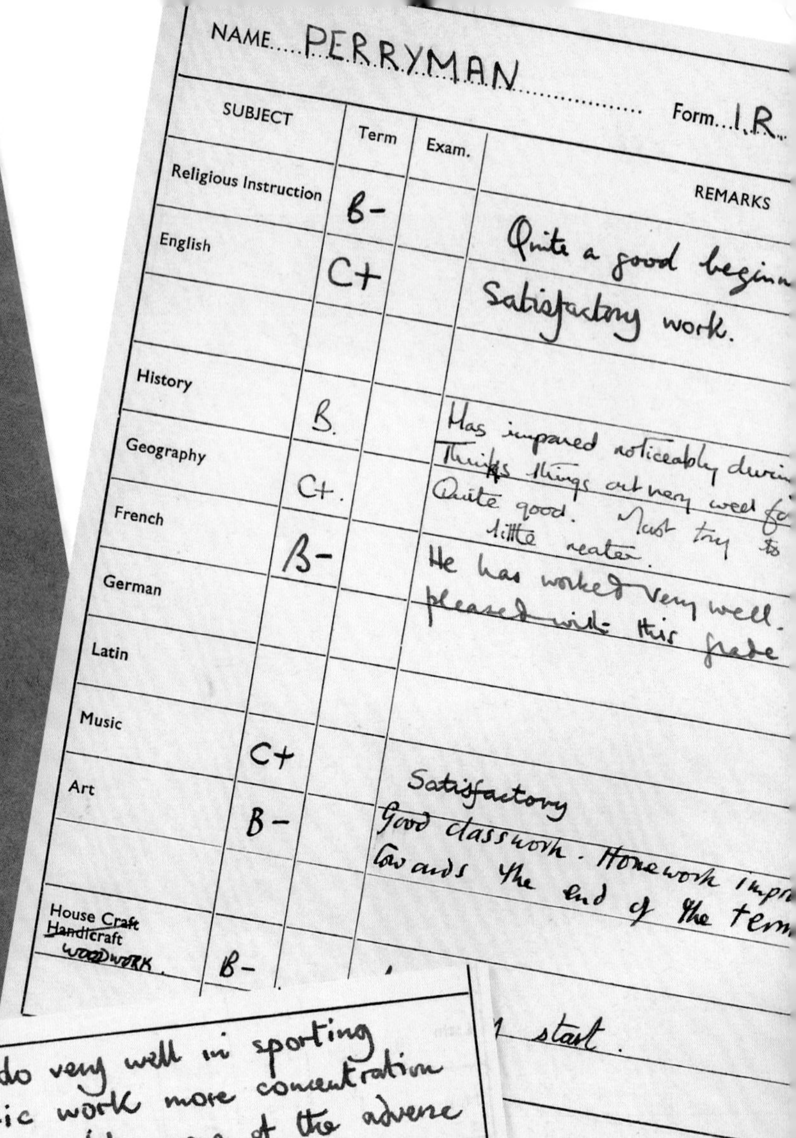

NAME..... PERRYMAN .... Form... I.R.

SUBJECT	Term	Exam.	REMARKS
Religious Instruction	B-		
English	C+		Quite a good begin... Satisfactory work.
History	B.		Has improved noticeably durin... Thinks things out very well fo...
Geography	C+.		Quite good. Must try to... little neater.
French	B-		He has worked very well. ... pleased with his prate...
German			
Latin			
Music	C+		Satisfactory
Art	B-		Good classwork. Homework imp... towards the end of the term...
House Craft Handicraft WOODWORK	B-		

... start.

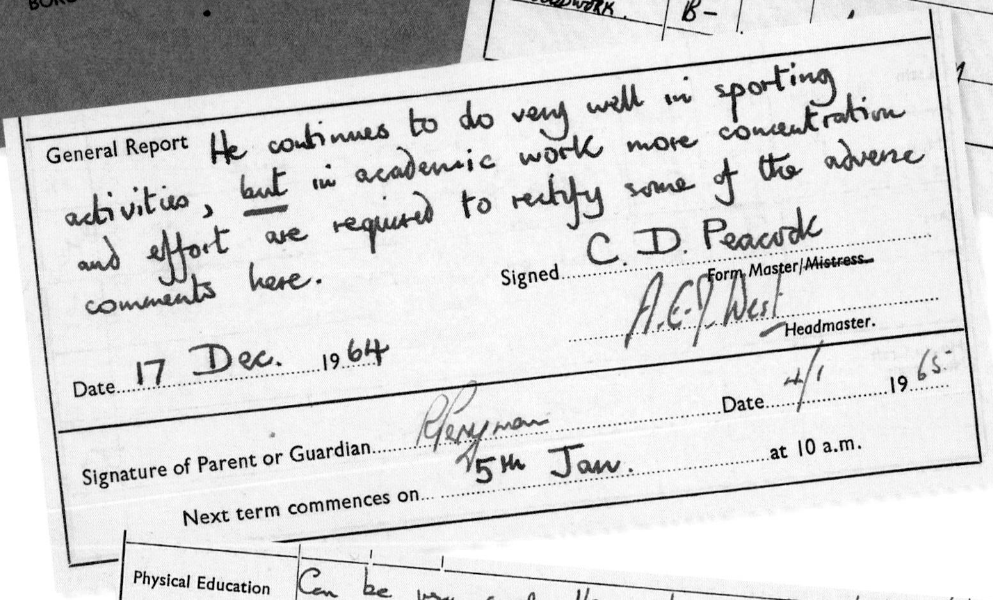

General Report	He continues to do very well in sporting activities, but in academic work more concentration and effort are required to rectify some of the adverse comments here.

Signed C. D. Peacock — Form Master/Mistress

A.E.J.West — Headmaster.

Date 17 Dec. 1964   Date 4/1 1965

Signature of Parent or Guardian...... RPerryman

Next term commences on...... 5th Jan. ...... at 10 a.m.

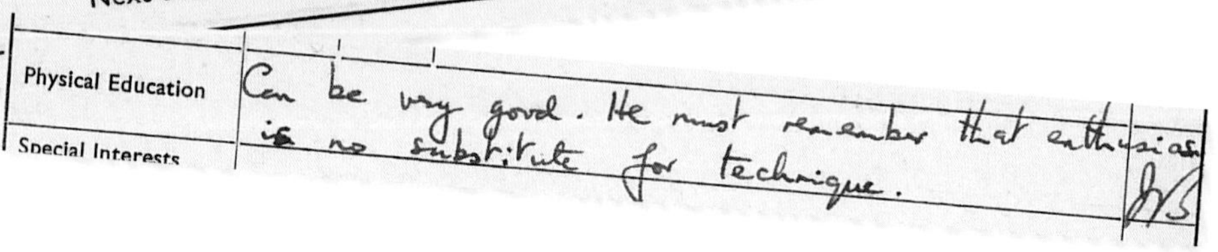

Physical Education			Can be very good. He must remember that enthusias... is no substitute for technique.	
Special Interests				

Year 2

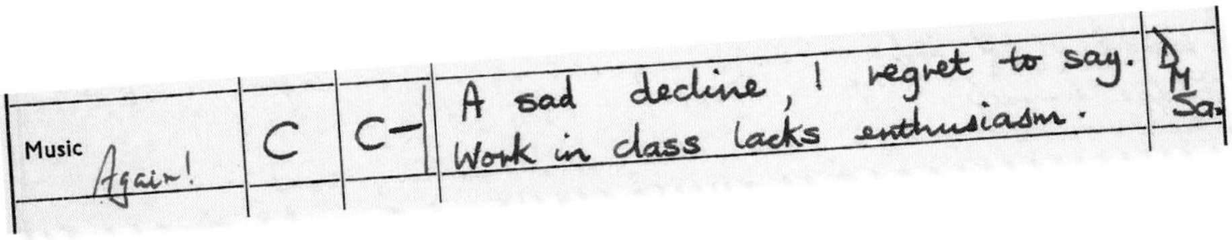

Music	Again!	C	C-	A sad decline, I regret to say. Work in class lacks enthusiasm.	Sa...

Year 3

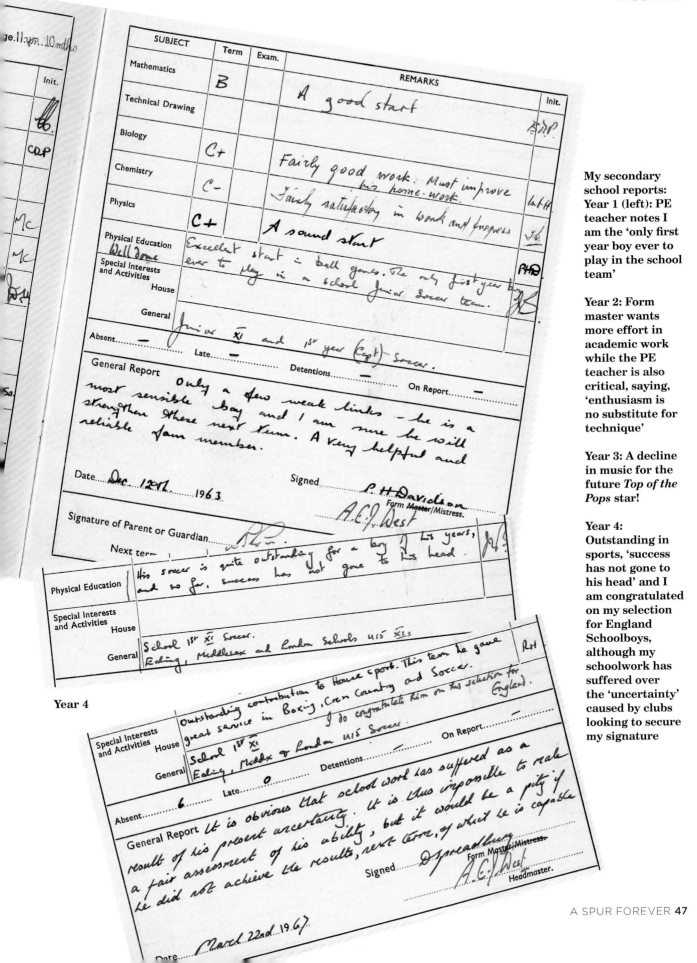

SUBJECT	Term	Exam.	REMARKS	Init.
Mathematics	B		A good start	
Technical Drawing				BDP
Biology	C+		Fairly good work. Must improve his home-work.	
Chemistry	C-		Fairly satisfactory in work and progress	
Physics	C+		A sound start	
Physical Education	Well done		Excellent start in ball games. The only first year boy ever to play in a school Junior Soccer team.	
Special Interests and Activities				
House				
General			Junior XI and 1st year (capt) Soccer.	

Absent ___   Late ___   Detentions ___   On Report ___

General Report Only a few weak links – he is a most sensible boy and I am sure he will strengthen these next term. A very helpful and reliable form member.

Date Dec. 12th 1963   Signed P H Davidson Form Master/Mistress.

A.E.J. West

Signature of Parent or Guardian ___

Next term His soccer is quite outstanding for a boy of his years, and so far, success has not gone to his head.

Physical Education		
Special Interests and Activities		
House		School 1st XI Soccer.
General		Ealing, Middlesex and London Schools U15 XIs

Year 4

Special Interests and Activities		Outstanding contribution to House sport. This term he gave great service in Boxing, Cross Country and Soccer.
House		I do congratulate him on this selection for England.
General		School 1st XI
		Ealing, Middx & London U15 Soccer

Absent 6   Late 0   Detentions ___   On Report ___

General Report It is obvious that school work has suffered as a result of his present uncertainty. It is thus impossible to make a fair assessment of his ability, but it would be a pity if he did not achieve the results, next term, of which he is capable.

Signed D Spreadbury Form Master/Mistress.

A.E.J. West Headmaster.

Date March 22nd 1967

My secondary school reports: Year 1 (left): PE teacher notes I am the 'only first year boy ever to play in the school team'

Year 2: Form master wants more effort in academic work while the PE teacher is also critical, saying, 'enthusiasm is no substitute for technique'

Year 3: A decline in music for the future *Top of the Pops* star!

Year 4: Outstanding in sports, 'success has not gone to his head' and I am congratulated on my selection for England Schoolboys, although my schoolwork has suffered over the 'uncertainty' caused by clubs looking to secure my signature

MEN IN WHITE COATS

The name Paul Shoemark probably doesn't mean much to people outside of his family, friends and colleagues. There are probably a few journalists who remember the name, and maybe some fans with very good memories of youth-team football in the late 1960s. That is no slur against Paul, who was a nice lad and a very talented young player. But those of us who were young footballers at Tottenham will certainly remember him.

Paul Shoemark's experience at Spurs is a salutary lesson in how tough it was and still is to make it in the game. He had signed for the club, arriving as a top-rated England schoolboy four years before me. I heard stories about how the youth players hammered him every day. He was from Northamptonshire, so they didn't like the way he spoke or dressed, or any other supposed negative characteristic.

He was a winger and everyone thought wingers were 'milky' – that they were bottlers, scared of a tackle. That is not true. Bravery comes in many forms and wanting the ball when you know you are going to get clattered can be brave. Having a bad game in front of 50,000 but still wanting the ball, that's brave.

But Shoemark didn't get the chance to prove it, because he didn't last. John Pratt and Tony Want, two of my new young clubmates warned me not to think I'd made it just because I'd played for England Schoolboys. They'd seen what happened to Paul, who had joined us with all the pomp and fanfare and other players didn't take kindly to it. He was living away from home in digs, with no real support, no back-up. None of it made sense why he was singled out, other than he was seen as a 'special' talent and thus became a target. By the time I arrived at Spurs, Paul was a shadow of his former self. They kicked him in training and killed his confidence. He never recovered from it, eventually left the club and drifted out of the game.

As soon as I arrived at Tottenham as a signed-on apprentice, I felt the 'Paul Shoemark vibes' aimed at me. Factors conspired to mark me out as someone who the rest thought was 'special'. I wasn't and never thought that about myself. But it made those first few months at White Hart Lane very tough.

There had been problems around me signing what were called Associated Schoolboy forms at 15 and leaving school. Eliots had objected, pointing to the fact that as a grammar-school pupil, I was committed to staying until I

> "Factors conspired to mark me out as someone who the rest thought was 'special'. I wasn't and never thought that about myself. But it made those first few months at White Hart Lane very tough"

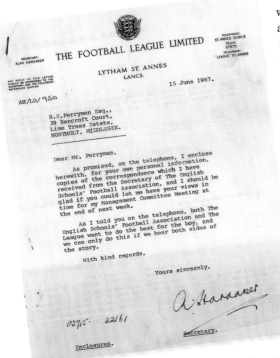

THE FOOTBALL LEAGUE LIMITED

LYTHAM ST. ANNES
LANCS.

15 June 1967.

AH/LD/950

R.E.Perryman Esq.,
39 Bancroft Court,
Lime Trees Estate,
NORTHOLT. MIDDLESEX.

Dear Mr. Perryman,

As promised, on the telephone, I enclose
herewith, for your own personal information,
copies of the correspondence which I have
received from the Secretary of The English
Schools' Football Association, and I should be
glad if you could let me have your views in
time for my Management Committee Meeting at
the end of next week.

As I told you on the telephone, both The
English Schools' Football Association and The
League want to do the best for the boy, and
we can only do this if we hear both sides of
the story.

With kind regards,

Yours sincerely,

A.Hardaker

Secretary.

Enclosures.

There was a dispute between my school and Tottenham over me signing and leaving school. Alan Hardaker, secretary of the Football League, wrote to intervene

was 16. The row was eventually settled in my favour, but it meant I arrived at Spurs at just 15. In those days, the apprenticeships lasted three years; that meant I was having to deal with 18-year-olds who were older, wiser and much more sure of themselves.

That is quite an age gap. In addition there were rumours flying around about me. One was that me and my family had been offered money to sign for Tottenham. It wasn't true – what was, as I later found out, was that QPR had offered £5,000 to sign me. It wasn't allowed, so it would have been offered on a nod and a wink. Ted and my dad kept it from me, so as not to put any more pressure on my decision. Five grand in those days was life-changing money.

The gossip I picked up on was that there had been a payment made. At 15 you don't say to your new teammates, 'I didn't get money for signing.' To bring it up would have sounded like admitting to it and others would have thought, 'Why is he saying it if it didn't happen?' But that didn't stop people thinking I'd been paid to join Spurs.

Not only that, but I arrived with big hype to live up to. The comparisons to Johnny Haynes were the kind of thing to cause jealousy, envy and instant resentment in the dressing room. It marked me out, and there were other things that only added to that unwanted label of being 'special'. Spurs made a big deal in the press about signing me as there was pressure on them to produce their own players, rather than just get the chequebook out.

I saw that newspaper coverage when I walked into Doll's Caff, which was a Tottenham institution. Turning right out of the main gate onto the High Road, the café was about two shops along. The name above the door was actually 'George's Café' but everybody knew it as Doll's Caff because she was his wife and ran it when he passed away. The first time I walked in there, I saw it pinned on the wall: a cutting from a paper. There was nothing else on the wall, just this article about me signing for Spurs. 'Spurs sign superstar schoolboy' or something like that. It made me cringe with embarrassment. It was exactly the kind of thing that would put the focus on me; a daily reminder and every player that went into Doll's would see it. It almost made me start to think I'd be better off being an average player, so I wouldn't be marked out as special. It took me three weeks to ask Doll to remove it from the wall. I went early one day when no one was around. 'Please Doll,' I said. 'Please take it down.'

Getting in early was the exception for me, however. Part of Charlie's sales pitch to get me to join Spurs was that I wouldn't have to go by public transport every day, because, as he was local, he would give me a lift now and then. The traffic was not as bad in those days as it is now and it was a very kind offer but Charlie was not quite so desperate to be in on time as me, knowing I was going to get my head taken off if I was late. The agony I felt when the traffic on the North Circular was bad was so stressful.

For whatever reason, Charlie did not get on with Johnny Wallis. Johnny was another legendary Tottenham character who I would get to know, work with and really like for decades. He was the man in charge of the day-to-day work with the apprentices, and someone we dared not cross. Johnny was the man I had to answer to if I was late, and there were times when I was

SOCCER NEWS—by JAMES CONNOLLY

Spurs scoop London rivals for schools star

SPURS, the confirmed spenders, have just beaten all the big clubs for a player who didn't cost a penny. Yesterday, England Schoolboys inside forward **STEPHEN PERRYMAN** joined them as an apprentice professional.

Spurs chief scout Charlie Faulkner should be very happy with his coup. Manchester United and all the top London clubs were in on the greatest schoolboy chase since Terry Venables signed for Chelsea some years ago.

Q.P.R., in at the death with Spurs, made a dramatic late night effort to sign Perryman on Friday.

'BETTER FUTURE'

"Stephen trained at White Hart Lane last winter and liked the set-up," his father, Ronald Perryman told me last night, "I let him make up his own mind. He felt that he had a better future with Spurs and I am quite happy about him going there as an apprentice. Now it is entirely up to him."

Stephen, whose home is at Northolt (Middlesex), will be 16 in December.
* * *

● Young Stephen, now on Spurs books, gets in some heading practice—in his garden !

This was the actual cutting that was pinned to the wall of Doll's Caff and caused me so much embarrassment

delayed, either on public transport or in the car when Charlie gave me a lift. I had to be at White Hart Lane by 9am to meet Johnny and the other ~~young players to drive up~~ on the coach to the training ground at Cheshunt. Given Charlie and Johnny didn't see eye-to-eye, if I was late when I'd had a lift that would wind Johnny up even more. I'd be running up to the gates on the High Road seconds before 9am. Johnny would be in the coach, sat in the front passenger seat and looking along the High Road. He'd see me but still have the bus drive off.

Then I would have to work out how I was going to get to Cheshunt myself. I'd be thumbing a lift along the A10. The worry was intense. I'd be imagining the players on the coach mocking me. 'Thinks he's special… family must have got paid.'

Being a minute late was bad enough. But I was later to find out that I'd been a *week* late when I first joined. The very first morning I was due at White Hart Lane I made sure I was on time. I was there at 8:30am, but discovered that the rest of the players had already been training for a week. Because Spurs were so pleased that I had signed for them and had literally just left school, they had given me a week off, presumably for a rest, but without actually telling me. I certainly didn't get the message that the other apprentices had started a week before. Not to do skills and play football, either, but to graft, lumping equipment around to get the club ready for pre-season training in earnest. You can imagine how my absence went down with the rest.

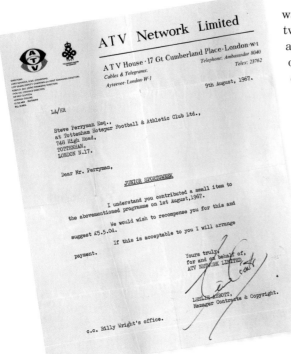

Another letter, and further cause for my embarrassment, on this occasion relating to the time I appeared on television in a segment of a TV programme, describing the life of an apprentice footballer. I'd barely been one for five minutes!

Within days it got worse. The dressing room layout at Cheshunt was different to the one at White Hart Lane, where there were just two dressing rooms, one home one and one away. There were three at Cheshunt: one for the young players aged between 15 and 18, one for the reserves and then another for the first team. A call came down the corridor from that first-team end to ours: 'Bill Nick wants to speak to Steve Perryman.'

'What the hell does he want to talk to you for?' someone said.

'I... I dunno.'

'Well, you better go and find out what he fucking wants then come back and tell us.'

So I went and knocked on Bill's door. 'Come in' he said.

I'm standing in front of the great man. 'In a couple of days' time a camera crew is coming in because the first team are playing Celtic and it's a big game.' Tottenham playing Celtic, even in a pre-season friendly, was a big deal.

'They want to talk to the players,' Bill continued. 'We're the FA Cup winners, they're European champions, there's going to be a lot of press and TV people here to do the build-up and at the same time they want to talk to a young player about the life of an apprentice professional and I've said you're going to do it.'

I was stunned into silence.

'Well, what's up?' said Bill.

'I've only been here a few days, Bill, I don't know the life.' I said, hesitantly.

'No? Well I've told them you're doing it' said Bill, curtly. 'Off you go.' What was I going to do? The players back in the changing room demanded to know what Bill wanted. I couldn't tell them – they would have slaughtered me, and it would have made some very resentful. I'd only been at the club five minutes and suddenly I was getting attention from TV. That would have made things very difficult for me.

I muttered, 'My dad needs to sign something.'

'What? What's he got to sign?' someone said, all suspicious.

'I don't know, something. I didn't understand it, really.'

Now I was telling lies. I had to get myself out of this. If I told them what Bill Nick had just told me they'd have verbally killed me.

I didn't sleep for two nights. In this new role and life, this new chance and opportunity, I should have been excited. Instead I was worried sick about how I came across to my peers. I couldn't be seen to be going up to that other end of the corridor because a youth-team player just didn't do that. But I had to because I had to speak to Bill Nick.

Two days after he first summoned me I managed to get back to Bill Nick's office. I knocked on his door. 'Come in!'

'What do you want?' he said, looking stern.

'Bill,' I said, 'I can't do that TV thing.' He said, quietly, 'Now listen to me. I've said you're doing it. And you're doing it.'

And so I did it, squirming with embarrassment, self-conscious and dreading what the reaction would be. There was plenty of mickey-taking. I got more than my fair share of the usual rituals a new face would have to go through, like getting chucked in the bath with all the cold dirty water they'd been ringing out mops in, for example. But there was a more direct and sinister threat.

As was common practice then, Johnny would appoint an older apprentice to effectively act as a foreman to the rest of us. It gave that young player a bit of clout and power. When I joined it was a chap called John Gilroy. His nickname was 'Wishbone' for some reason, I've never found out why. One day he caught me alone in the changing room. 'You think you're something special, don't you?' Nothing I said to deny it would make a difference. 'Well, you ain't. And I'm going to make your life a misery.'

I was 15 years old, in a completely new, very challenging environment. I'd been for training at Tottenham before, and that was hard, physically demanding with testing drills. But this was in another league. This wasn't just hard work for your body – it was a test of mental strength. Shoemark and others before and after him couldn't survive it. I had to make my mind up quickly and toughen up. Did I have the mental strength required to get through this?

What helped hugely was having Phil Holder alongside me, who had also joined the Spurs youth system. He became another of the people who had major impacts on my life at various stages. He was a month younger than me and I knew him from Middlesex Schoolboys days. He wasn't at Spurs at first as he was in hospital getting treated for an injury or something, but he soon became my 'go-to' man. We developed a strong friendship through our young days from apprenticeship to emerging professionals. Between us we weren't taking bullshit off anyone. Even older players, the young pros when we were apprentices, soon came to know that if they wanted to take me and Phil on they had it all to do.

Phil was later to become youth-team captain, and with good reason. Phil was streetwise and could look after himself. I came from the suburban edge of London but Phil was from Kilburn, born right in the middle of 12 kids. He was mentally more grown-up because in that domestic situation he had

Phil and I with the FA Youth Cup which Spurs won in 1970 – interestingly wearing all-white. We have been big mates for so long, and it was lovely to share some success early on in our Spurs careers

Bill Nick in his office, where he practiced tackling with me!

to fight to cope – getting his share of food, getting his shirt ironed. It made him competitive, and in a competitive environment like a football club a good ally to have on your side. So I leaned on him a bit.

If anyone gave us bother, he'd either say, 'Steve, sod them' or take them on. He helped me become aggressively competitive on and off the field, not to take crap off anyone. It proved invaluable in years to come playing against the likes of Leeds or Liverpool away. You cannot be a shrinking violet or they are going to walk all over you, then piss on you as they walk past. What I gleaned from Phil was something that I paraphrase when I speak to young players today. 'What do you think about your next opponent?' I'll ask them.

They usually answer that they are going to be good.

'Yep, you're better off thinking he's going to be good than bad. But you need to be thinking, "He wants to piss all over me, beat me in the tackle and rub my nose in the dirt. He wants a win bonus, he wants to brag about it to his mates after the game." So what I'm saying is you have got to think your opponent is a bastard. And then if he's only half a bastard, you're in front.'

Phil had an attitude of 'Get ready for battle', but as a friend you couldn't have better. He was generous. If six of us apprentices got on the bus, he'd say, 'I've got these', meaning to pay for the fares. We knew he didn't have a lot of money. But that encouraged us next time to say, 'I'll get this', because that's fair. Phil lived by a code, a set of rules with his own strong sense of right and wrong. He turned up to training one day with blood dripping off his face. 'It was the bus conductor, he wanted paying,' was his explanation. Phil riled against authority. But he's probably one of the most respectful people I know.

He loved Bill Nick. When I sent Phil a photo of Bill recently, he wrote back, 'The man – don't make them like him any more.' Bill used to return that respect by calling him 'Chief'. The rest of us were 'Perryman, Clark, Daines'. On a day when he was feeling a bit soft, Bill might say 'Steve'. But Phil was always 'Chief'.

In January 1968 we were clearing snow off the pitch as apprentices for the first team's FA Cup replay against Man United, a huge game. It was a hive of activity, with planks of wood everywhere for the wheelbarrows to run over, and shovels and all sorts of stuff. We youngsters joined in with the ground staff and Bill Nick came out in his suit.

'Chief!' he said to Phil. 'How's the boys?'

'Er, good Bill, yeah, but it's hard graft. Be a little bit better if you treated us all to fish and chips.'

Bill had to think about it. The club were going to get a 50,000-plus crowd for the replay and it wasn't going to be on unless we got the pitch sorted. There was big gate money at stake if a club had a replay against a team like that, and Bill was in charge of the purse strings.

'Yeah, all right Chief, you organise it.'

Phil was talking back to the manager, respectfully but with a purpose; it was right and it was fair. It was the same when I played alongside him. Well, sometimes. I'd hear him say to an opponent, 'Why don't you fuck off? Who do you think you are?' and the effect that had was predictable. But it rubbed off on me. It gave me purposeful aggressiveness – nastiness, even – that would stand me in good stead.

Phil had that attitude in spades. He relished the battle. Whether it was training or a game, the whistle blew, a tackle came in and he'd turn to me and say, 'Game on.' It was one of Phil's sayings.

From those early days he protected me. Phil was short but would take on all sizes. He got sent off one day against the Metropolitan Police team. I knew he was going to get sent off the moment someone said to us, 'See that fella there, just by the centre spot? He's the youngest ever sergeant in the Met Police.' I knew then that poor sarge was going to get it. The ball went out of play, there was a throw-in down the line and as it bounced up and the sergeant headed it forward, Phil scissor-kicked his head. Forget the ball. Phil didn't even look at the referee, he just walked.

Bill Nick adored Phil but he never really made it at Spurs – at least not in a football sense. Everyone he played with or against knew his name and about Phil personally as he was such a character. There is an irony in me, his close friend, being the one who largely blocked his opportunity to get into the team – there simply weren't enough spaces in midfield. Additionally Phil had a problem with his body shape. When he picked up an injury, usually because he was too brave, his body took too long to get back to where it should be because he put on weight easily.

There was little chance of me putting on too much weight in those early days at Tottenham. The intensity of the training, the work we did as apprentices and the travelling, coupled with the mental pressure I was under left me totally exhausted. I'd get up early and, if I wasn't getting a lift from Charlie, leave at 7am, get the bus to Northolt station, get on the Tube, change at Oxford Circus then on the Tube again, change for Manor House and another bus to get to White Hart Lane by 9am. I'd have plenty of jobs – sweeping up, hanging up kit and cleaning boots, to name just a few, and have training and playing. I'd leave at 5pm and then have another two hours of travel home. Four hours a day of travel at that age is a lot.

I had moved worlds. I was not a full professional but an apprentice and that demanded professional commitment and effort. I was being paid to be a footballer now and had to earn my money. It was going from the edge of West London to North London, which felt much more like being in the

"A bit of Phil Holder rubbed off on me. It gave me purposeful aggressiveness – nastiness, even – that would stand me in good stead"

The five wise men (left to right): Eddie Baily, Pat Welton, Johnny Wallis, Cecil Poynton and Bill Nick

inner city. I was working with lads broadly in my age group, but now also with much older, serious, professional men. Bill Nick and Eddie Baily were Tottenham legends and giants of the game, but there were lots of coaches, trainers and other people I had to look up to and respect.

There was an interesting little detail in how they dressed. Bill was often in his suit but day-to-day wore a tracksuit, as did Eddie. Those involved with the apprentices, like Cecil Poynton and Johnny Wallis, wore white coats, as did Andy Thompson, who was a pre-war veteran player and part of the 1921 FA Cup-winning squad. Jack Coxford was another, and former player Sid Tickridge. They were all part of my early education.

I would sit there, cleaning boots or doing some other chore, listening to them jaw away and it was all washing over me. Andy never really talked about 1921 and all that. Johnny might make the odd mention of a player from the past, but the farthest they would usually go back was to the 1950–51 team. They talked about Ron Burgess being in a different class to Dave Mackay. Ron must have been some player.

The change in my life was amazing. I had gone from non-competitive schools football to working flat out at a major club in barely a year. From a 20-minute walk to school and back, to four hours on my own traipsing across London. The physical and mental tests of that first pre-season were punishing. I was so glad that I made that early decision never to go into digs, because if I did I would have been left on my own to go back to a bedroom in a strange house, brooding on what I was going through, and it could have been damaging.

Being at home I did have the support of my family. Not that they always understood the situation I was in, because when I came home absolutely shattered they wanted to know who I'd spoken to, which star player I'd seen, all those things a parent interested in their son making his way in professional sport would want to know. But I simply didn't have the energy to talk to them. I came home, had dinner and just wanted to sleep. My head was spinning and I didn't want to talk about it.

Looking back at those first few months I don't quite know how I got through it. For a 15-year-old there was a hell of a lot to carry. It was a test of character and coming through that helped give me a long career. But other problems soon arose. In the summer weeks before I started at Spurs I carried on playing football over the park with my brothers and mates. It was fun, unstructured with no one telling me what to do, and had been a big part of my development, especially in the absence of competitive football for a time at school. In one of those park games in the summer of 1967 I fell over and put my hand down to stop the fall, breaking a bone in it. There was no treatment for it as such – it was going to heal itself. But after the first couple of weeks at Tottenham when the balls started coming out for actual skills training and matches between the various teams – the A team against the B team, for example – I was told by Eddie not to touch the ball, just to chase it. Literally to run around after the ball without tackling or kicking. The idea was to protect my injured hand, or so I thought.

I was an inside-forward, but in an odd way that instruction from Eddie was a sign of things to come for me. After the 1966 World Cup, the game had changed. An inside-forward was now a midfield player, either attack-minded or defensive. Everyone wanted an Alan Ball or a Nobby Styles. People followed the winners, and formations changed from 4–2–4 to 4–4–2. No one was going to allow as many people up the park, especially as wingers were viewed as a bit lazy. They were becoming obsolete, though we still had wide players at the club. The focus shifted more to fitness. Eddie and Bill always believed in fitness: 'If you can't run, you can't play' was the message from them.

That pre-season, particularly in the first four-week spell, I was doing more running than I could imagine. I was not unfit as a schoolboy but not as fit as the club wanted me to be. The players who had had a two- or three-month break had it worse. Players today who are in summer tournaments maintain their fitness, but if we stopped playing in April like some did

Showing my competitive side in a youth-team match at Cheshunt. My natural game was more passing oriented but I was evolving my style to make me more 'selectable'. This match took place on the top pitch at Cheshunt, which meant it was an important game

"At Tottenham there was an aura hanging over us. We were Spurs players and expected to do things right – with style, panache"

then we lost a lot of fitness and had to start again. Christ, did they put us through it.

But that instruction for me to chase the ball was a precursor to how I developed as a player, and I started to focus more on my work-rate and expending energy, though my young body couldn't really cope and I got a bad back. This meant treatment, another new experience for me.

Yet for all the newness of this world, there wasn't that much in the way of instruction about how to play. It is difficult to describe but at Tottenham there was an aura hanging over us. We were Spurs players and expected to do things right – with style, panache. One of the earliest quotes to me was, 'If you play it easy, quick and accurate you'll be all right.' And I still say to this day, 'Why not?'

I wasn't a dribbler, or someone who could pick the ball up on the touchline and run past the full-back with pace. I needed to get it, give it, and move around the field, and that suited Tottenham's way of playing.

Pundits can say all they want about touch, reactions, playing through the lines and transitions. If you cannot cope with that first challenge that's coming your way – getting possession of the ball – anything else is redundant. I could get the ball, give it and get into position to receive it back. And that was the key to me making it through that testing first spell. Football comes to the rescue. Can you play or not? Because if you can play, you get selected, whatever the level, and you make your way up.

That might mean getting picked over 16-year-olds, or even older, and that was another reason for me to be concerned about any resentment and perception of being special. I didn't really care what the coaches thought. I was focusing on dealing with the players. We spent most of our time at Cheshunt in pre-season but when the season started we would be in the away dressing room at White Hart Lane. The home dressing room was for first-team players who we barely interacted with; all the others were in the away one which meant I – as a 15-year-old – would be mixing with players in their mid-20s who weren't in the first-team frame. That was another test. There were a lot of verbals and piss-taking to cope with.

My strategy was to keep quiet and keep my head down. I virtually didn't open my mouth in the first few months. I did what I was told and got on with my work. We would do our menial jobs before lots of ball work in the mornings and a lot of running in the afternoons around the roads of Cheshunt, into the woods at Cuffley and back. Hard yards to get us fit.

We were like a military unit on those runs. A lot of the fitness aspect of football then stemmed from physical training in the army. Both Bill and Eddie would have been influenced by their time during the war. Bill Nick was a PT instructor while Eddie saw active service and was listed as missing in action at one point.

So we had to be fit. By God, we had to be fit. We had Bill Watson, the ex-Olympic weightlifter, come in. We did small weights and lots of stepping on and off benches. Allied to what I went through as a schoolboy running to school and home, this led to me having strong legs and strong joints so that people had to go some way to injure me. And it enabled me to challenge with purpose.

We were pushed hard, but when the football started there was the encouragement to play. The men in white coats would trot out the lines that Bill used, that were part of the language of White Hart Lane. If the ball went out of play, the call would go up: 'When the ball goes dead, come alive.'

That was one of the Bill Nick's favourites. 'One ball back, the next one should go forward' was another. It was drummed into you.

There was something old school about it all. It was general coaching and guidance. We weren't given explicit instruction on how to play a particular pass, for example. But they might focus on aspects at half-time, in uncompromising language. 'We're playing a right-winger and a left-winger and none of you are giving them the ball. Start giving them the fucking ball. And by the way, wingers: start fucking demanding the ball. Let's get it right; let's start getting a bit of something about us.' It was all common sense stuff – 'play what you see', 'the first thing you see is probably the best', 'play the way you're facing' – which suited me fine. We were given a base of play, 'shop-floor football'. It was about learning by doing, about recognising the things that keep happening in a game so that they were not a surprise when they did occur. For example, if the keeper kicked the ball long to the strikers it was either going to come back from them into our midfield, and I better be there to meet it, or it was going to get flicked on and someone else better be there to meet it. None of it was backed up by video or detailed software analysis. It was about experienced trainers and coaches knowing the game, reading it and passing on their knowledge.

If we didn't do certain things they let us know in no uncertain terms. You were pulled up for not putting your foot in. If they decided someone was a coward, he never had a prayer. They always had it in for Jimmy Neighbour. I heard two white-coated trainers talking about Jimmy after a Youth Cup game, and they were very critical about him. I thought to myself: 'They're never gonna talk about me like that.'

One of my favourite photographs, a famous insight into the White Hart Lane dressing room – look at the intensity in how Bill Nick is talking

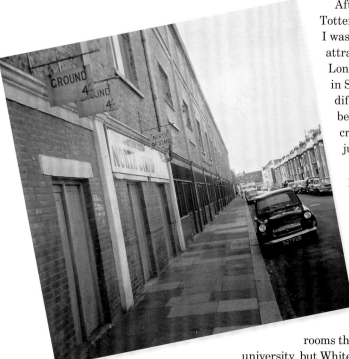

White Hart Lane as it was in the late 1960s – my old stomping ground

After those first few months, I felt more settled. Cheshunt, Tottenham and White Hart Lane became familiar places I was comfortable in. I'm a West London boy, but I was attracted to Tottenham – the club and the place – and North London straight away. I've never really felt comfortable in South London. Not that I dislike it but it just feels different. If, for instance, Crystal Palace or Charlton had been an option for me to sign I think I would have gone crazy: not only would the journey have been hellish but it just did not feel right.

But at Tottenham I felt a link with the people and the place. It obviously played a part in why I stayed there so long. I feel when I go back now that while I know it's all changed, something about the area persists. It had, like the club, a culture of common sense.

I'd seen White Hart Lane when I had gone for evening schoolboys training. Being someone paid to work in it gave me a different perspective. I always thought it was not plush or certainly posh but a place of industry. It was workmanlike, serving a purpose, be it the terraces and the stands or the offices and rooms the public didn't see. My school had wanted me to go to university, but White Hart Lane was my university, my next place of learning.

It all looked like it was well-thought-out and maintained. There is a famous photo of Bill Nick in the dressing room with the Double team and Cecil Poynton, this time wearing a tracksuit instead of his white coat and pouring tea from a jug with an H on it *(see page 59)*. The wood panelling in that photo went at some point. You can also see wooden boards, a bit like duck boards, on the floor to save the players from having to put their feet on the actual floor, which might have been wet or cold. I was responsible for scrubbing those boards. They were well-made, solid and functional. They didn't crack or splinter and it seemed there was no chance of that happening at Tottenham – it was all well-planned. Money was spent correctly.

The surfaces in the gym and the ball courts were not spotless, because they were being used constantly by people walking in and out. But they were clean and well-kept. Everything was proper and correct. That's how Bill Nick was – he ran the whole show.

It was a down-to-earth but purposeful place. I remember thinking, 'I wonder who chose the colours light blue and white' for the balustrade on the East Stand where the Shelf was. Who designed the way that we could get from the running track in the corner through to the tunnel, then out through another corner to get through to the gym? It felt like it was a considered place.

People often described White Hart Lane as its own little kingdom and that was accurate. The immediate area felt like part of the club. I picked up very quickly what the club meant to the community. Even as a kid I felt a responsibility to that area if the first team lost a game, because I knew the place and the people.

We had two cafés right on our doorstep. Tony's was left out of the main gate, Doll's on the right. Although the bank was further along it felt like an annexe of White Hart Lane. The staff were pleased to see you, even as an apprentice. When we went out into the street people would talk to us.

Tottenham Hotspur was so much a part of Tottenham. The bank, the pubs, the railway station, the shops and the cafés were all getting their living out of Spurs really, but their support was genuine and heartfelt. The schools were all pro-Spurs, the church over the road let the club use their car park. The club's influence spread everywhere: I was part of a big organisation, a proper force in the area.

Not that I could take liberties with it because I could go out and meet some of the ground staff in the cafés who would just take the piss. They might have seen your last FA Youth Cup game and say, 'You were nowhere near it, Steve; any chance of you ever having another shot?'

I could even have easily seen Bill Nick's wife, Darkie, riding her bike along the road while waving to me. That's quite special.

I began to learn about the history of the area and the club, from overhearing conversations or people telling me things here and there. Like the history of Bruce Grove and the Duke of Northumberland and the Harry Hotspur connections that gave the club its name. It enveloped everything. It was a place that stood on its own two feet, saying, 'This is how we are and this is what we do.'

Of course there were supporters everywhere up and down the country – Spurs were one of the biggest clubs in Britain and had been for a long time. But being there it still felt local. It was unmistakably a North London club. And I guess I became a North Londoner.

Before I joined Tottenham I wasn't that aware of all the grief with Arsenal. I soon knew Bill's feelings about it. Driving a red car or wearing a red tie were strict no-nos. But I gained more awareness watching the North London derby from the touchline in January 1968. Us apprentices sat on low benches around the touchlines on the running track, rather than seats in the stands. That probably earned the club a few bob from being able to sell tickets that would otherwise be given for free to us!

We sat low so we didn't obscure anyone's view, the fans breathing down the back of our necks while we watched the game unfold, and I was stunned. I thought, 'How the hell am I going to compete in this?' All I could see were a blur of legs as the players battled it out. It was so fast and frantic – there was no time on the ball. The tackles were flying in. Alan Gilzean, who scored the winner, was at the heart of it, getting all kinds of treatment but giving as good as he got. And the noise from the crowd was deafening. I couldn't believe it. If I wanted to be one of them, a first-team pro, how was I going to be able to cope with this pressure of such full-on physical commitment? No one gave an inch. I was seeing how serious this game is and how much supporters live off the back of that result.

I don't think I could have been in a better place to see it. Not to judge it tactically but in terms of the energy, commitment and purposeful attitude needed. If anything taught me what was coming, it was that.

We were hearing what the punters were saying and I remember thinking, 'Blimey, they really don't like Venables!' Many years later I said to him, 'Terry, you were the best player I ever saw in a warm-up' and he laughed, but he didn't quite do it from a supporters' point of view and was given a hard time. They liked the Alan Mullery style more than the Venables style.

That Arsenal game was such a lesson in what I needed to do to survive. I'd come through my first steps to becoming a footballer, only to see there was much harder work still ahead of me.

"My school had wanted me to go to university, but White Hart Lane was my university, my next place of learning"

CHAPTER FOUR

BABY NEEDS NEW SHOES

The bell rang and it was time. Just before 3pm, Saturday. I was standing in the corridor outside the home dressing room at White Hart Lane. I'd played my youth match in the morning, returned with the rest to do our matchday jobs and was now waiting for the show to start, ready with my broom to sweep the corridor. Around 60,000 people were waiting outside. I could hear the hum of expectation.

The door opened, and there stood this colossus of a footballer, Dave Mackay. Not a giant in height, but definitely in stature and hard-won reputation. The hardest of hard men. Not dirty, not snide – just tough. He'd won the Double, broken his leg twice yet somehow still come back and won the FA Cup again the season just gone.

He was in his gleaming lilywhite shirt, the navy cockerel on the left of his barrel chest. Behind him were football superstars. Jimmy Greaves, Alan Mullery, Alan Gilzean and Pat Jennings. Mackay glanced at me, but barely noticed I was there. He bounced a ball and the sound smacked around the corridor. He shouted back to his teammates, 'Any of yous feels like panicking today, just give me the ball.' The shouts went up and the players walked out, their studs clattering down the corridor, up the steps and out of the tunnel into the light, the roar that greeted them a signal for the battle to come. Game on.

Having come through those testing first months as an apprentice, I was experiencing what it was like to be at the heart of a big club. I wasn't playing with the first-teamers, but would see them in training and around the club. I felt involved, part of the wider club, the Tottenham cause. I wanted to get on and get better.

I was making good progress and started playing for the under-17s and under-18s in the South-East Counties League under Sid Tickridge. For some reason, Johnny trained and managed us during the day, but not for games. That didn't seem to make sense, particularly for a manager like Bill Nicholson who was so organised and thorough. But that's the way they did it and it seemed to work.

The club had five teams: the first team, the reserves, the A team (which played in the Met League), the youth team (broadly under-18s and including the Youth Cup team), and the junior team (under-17s). I played only a handful of games for the juniors and youth team. Getting in the A team was the next step for aspiring apprentices and young pros. We didn't work on a Friday if picked for the A team because that was the side Johnny

> "I felt involved, part of the wider club, the Tottenham cause. I wanted to get on and get better"

The A team.
Back row (left
to right): Mike
Dillon, Les
Charker, John
Cutbush, Terry
Lee, Barry
Daines, Ray
Bunkell, Billy
Edwards and
Ray Evans. Front
row: Phil Holder,
me, Jimmy
Neighbour, Paul
Shoemark, John
Gilroy (aka
'Wishbone') and
Graeme Souness

actually managed. We got in if we were good enough or they had injuries and needed cover.

I felt the step up each time in terms of quality. The ball moved quicker and sharper. I was playing against more experienced, older players who knew a few tricks and it was more physical. Matches against Millwall, West Ham, and Orient were tasty. If you played, for example, at Crystal Palace for the youth team, matches would be played on a common, and it almost felt like a park game. The higher the level, the more likely it was to be played in a stadium.

Pulling on a Spurs shirt for the first time was such an honour. We're all intrigued by shirts, but I liked it for its simplicity, and what it meant. Putting on the white shirt with the proud cockerel, feeling the significance of it – the Double team had worn it, albeit a slightly different style – it's historic. There were no replicas in those days, so it was a very rare opportunity to wear the shirt and I felt proud that I was considered worthy of pulling it on.

Despite progressing on the field I was still an apprentice, scrubbing baths, cleaning brasses and toilets, and usually armed with a broom. Sweeping the gym out was a bastard job. Our lungs filled with dust. We were taught to sprinkle water beforehand and brush at an angle, so as not to kick up the dust. But it was boring and more often than not we'd stop and have a game of five-a-side. If Johnny caught us, the punishment was to not be allowed in the gym for a small-sided training game for a week.

On the days when we were training at White Hart Lane, we changed in the away dressing room and as the nights drew in it would be getting dark by the time we were due to finish. We'd report to Johnny and tell him we were finished – cleaning the tiles in the treatment room, for example. He'd come and inspect and do the typical old-soldier trick, running his finger over the tile and then rubbing any dirt onto your shirt. 'You ain't finished. Do it again.'

It was old-fashioned but in the right way. It taught us respect and that we had to look after the place, taking pride in who we were working for. Now and again though, Johnny would upset Phil and Phil would bite, saying, 'You fat bastard.' As far as Johnny was concerned, Phil was dead to him for a month.

Another time Phil went to Johnny and said, 'My boots have worn out.'

'Nah. Four more games in them.'

'You know they're wearing out, John.'

'Four more games.'

'Ok, I'm gonna see the manager.'

'Good. I'll phone him and tell him you're coming.'

Phil didn't get his new boots. If you made life hard for Johnny he made it double hard for you. He had this technique of saying, 'Volunteer!' Another time when Phil had just called him fat, whoever put their hand up when he asked for a volunteer, Johnny ignored them. 'Phil!'

'Yes boss, that's me,' said Phil.

'Follow me, the rest of you bugger off home.'

Johnny got Phil to take the dustbin over to the incinerator in the East Stand, a horrible job. It was a late afternoon in winter and no one wanted to head over that far side where it was dark and said to be haunted.

So I used to treat John right. Not crawl, just do what I was told. I didn't know any other way. You'd learn when he was in a good mood, so that when he said, 'Volunteer!' you'd say, 'Yes John, that's me' and he'd say, 'Good, get yourself home, you've a long way to go.'

Another thing he'd do at the end of the day was say, 'Follow me!' We'd all follow and he'd unlock the away dressing room, where we changed. All our clothes had been thrown in a pile on the table. Johnny shouted, 'Last one out of here takes that dustbin to the incinerator.' Cue a mad fight to get your stuff. You'd go home without socks because someone would nick yours just to avoid being the last one changed.

Mayhem, but with a purpose. It was a classic school of hard knocks, learning how to stand up for ourselves and then proving we were willing to learn and develop. I often say that Tottenham made me and it's true: not just as a player but as a man. The years of 15–17 are crucial in how you turn out as a person and naturally this great sporting institution was having a massive influence on me. I learned about the rules of life and how to accept the consequences of my actions.

It was army-style discipline. We wore old training kit that had holes in it and knackered plimsolls. Some alleyways in the ground probably had rats running around, and they'd send us down them on our own. It was about testing your mettle and absolutely no one was allowed to get above themselves.

Compounding all this was that as teenagers we were still growing. It wasn't really taken into account like it is today. Even years after I was an apprentice, there was not enough consideration for individual physical development. One time in the 1980s we were, unusually, training on a Sunday at Cheshunt. There was an under-15s game and I stood in the stand watching. Keith Burkinshaw was with some coaches and they were talking about some of the players. I listened in.

They discussed Des Walker, then a schoolboy on Tottenham's books. The conversation went round with each coach or trainer saying, 'No', meaning 'Not good enough'. Lack of pace was cited. Finally, Robbie Stepney said, 'Listen to you lot talking bollocks. He *is* quick. He will get his quickness back – it's just that he's growing and his body is having to adjust. Yes, he looks ordinary-paced now, but if you let this kid go you must be mad.'

"This great sporting institution was having a massive influence on me. I learned about rules of life and how to take the consequences of my actions"

They let him go. Next time I saw Des was at Nottingham Forest for a First Division game. He was leaning on a broom in the tunnel. 'Hello Des,' I said, 'What are you doing here?' He said he'd got a phone call to come to Forest and try out there. 'Well done, you' I said. Next time we went he was playing superbly against us, their fans singing, 'You'll never beat Des Walker'. And he got turned down at Tottenham for lacking pace.

Such stories are common in football. It is far easier and understandable for a manager or a coach to err on the side of caution and not sign a young player up. As Harry Redknapp has said, 'If you say "No" every time, you're constantly being proved right.' Making decisions on players is a percentage game, fraught with risk. It's a calculated guess. Walker's situation was that he was not quite physically ready. Things are going on in a young player's body but back in the late 1960s there was little in the way of acknowledging them.

I was quite small but I had good strength, and needed it. Like in any organisation there would be a little bit of bullying. Wishbone had promised to make my life a misery but even though Phil and I were younger we wouldn't take that. We didn't have an actual fight with him – it was more he saw we were no pushovers.

There would be punch-ups in the gym. Training was quick and razor-sharp, all one- and two-touch in small-sides games. The maximum was probably seven-a-side. If it got to nine-a-side it was a different type of game because there was no space and it became a war. Opponents would go *bang* – smack you against the wall like no tomorrow.

Johnny liked it and almost encouraged it. One day Phil and his mate Terry Shanahan fell out during a game. Everyone in the ball court had to back their own man and as I was on Terry's side I had to back him even though he was taking on my mate Phil. There was no fight as such, more an added intensity of tackles and challenges. We emerged with ripped shirts and some of us limping – we tore into each other, anything went and Johnny had just watched it happen. At the end he said, 'You bastards. You want to kick your own fucking players and yet you don't kick your opponents. You'll have to learn something from this.' We weren't allowed back in the gym for about two weeks, but we sensed he also admired us for it. He couldn't say, 'Well done', but I think inside that's what he was thinking.

There were about 15 to 18 apprentices for Johnny to look after. Eddie Baily dropped by and contributed with a drill or a session here and there. There was no goalkeeper coach. Pat Jennings trained with the first team. Stuart Skeet and Barry Daines, the youth-team keepers, trained with us as apprentices but were just part of the overall sessions.

Having so many youngsters inevitably resulted in capers. Phil and Terry Shanahan got hold of a new machine the club had brought into the treatment room. It was a glorified sunlamp, I think to clear up skin problems. Users were supposed to wear thick dark glasses and you couldn't do more than 10 minutes in its glare. But if you were young and carefree, you didn't know that and thought it was for tanning. So Phil and Terry had a go with it for half an hour with no glasses on. They came out with literally red faces and at one stage there was genuine concern they might even lose their sight.

More common injuries were part and parcel of life at the club. With multiple teams, the knocks piled up in the treatment room on Mondays. The regular schedule would be to train at Cheshunt on a Tuesday, have a day off on Wednesday and be in the gym and ball courts on Thursdays, before

Before the days of image rights! The Spurs Shop began to sell photos of players when I was starting out, and this is one of the first examples

Friday's track work. We wouldn't really go on grass after a Tuesday. In the old days – the very old days – there was the perceived wisdom of trainers not allowing players to have the ball in the week so that they wanted more of it on a Saturday. In our case, not going on the grass was old-school thinking but more enlightened because we did have a lot of the ball, doing extensive skills work indoors.

The White Hart Lane ball courts are part of Tottenham legend. It's said the 'Push and Run' title and the Double were won in the gym and I can see some truth in that. Those places were hothouses for footballing excellence. A premium was placed on skill. It was where we could prove that we were players, aside from actual games. There would be exercises involving chipping the ball onto a line painted on the wall, or hitting it into a circle. That was part of afternoon training for the apprentices but we'd see first-team players in there doing it as well and it was marvellous.

Johnny had this routine where he would get us in a row hitting alternate left- and right-foot volleys against the wall. You'd practise and do it right 20 times but when he came along the row to where you were, you'd make a mistake and only do two. He'd lick his pencil and write on his notepad, saying, 'Two', with a withering look. There would be a forfeit for the worst score, often having to take the dustbin to the incinerator.

This was how we were judged, encouraging competitiveness. There was a smaller ball court where I remember Mackay training. He had the record for the number of volleys – not Johnny's left-and-right drill but one where you couldn't step over a middle line so had to hit the ball hard enough every time so that it would come back over this line to you. Dave rattled off 36.

The 1969–70 FA Youth Cup-winning squad, a group of young men poised for success

It was all rooted in what was needed on the field. We see it today, with modern defenders when a ball comes in and they volley it but it goes miles or drops short. They haven't mastered the skill we were practising. It was useful: watch the ball, keep your head still, make good contact. Now do it again. And again. And again…

The Spurs coaches and trainers didn't get many things wrong. Eddie was instrumental in pushing the interests of young players, promoting the home-grown policy that the club wanted. We had a good array of talent. Brian Parkinson was a very good footballer but went under the radar a bit. Richie Pitt was a bit better known. Ray Bunkell, Ray Evans, Pratty and Tony Want were all Londoners, solid but ambitious: they thought they should be higher up the reckoning than they were. But to make progress we had to be good enough, given the quality above. In retrospect, some were wasting the early part of their career because while they did turn pro they didn't make it to regular reserve or first-team football at Spurs. They could perhaps have spent that time at another club, playing at a more senior level albeit a club without Tottenham's status.

Of course a player can leave and have a career elsewhere. Of my predecessors in the Spurs youth system, Derek Possee went on to Millwall and Keith Weller played for the Tottenham first team but became a bigger name at Leicester, but not many home-grown players made it through at Spurs and lasted. Phil Beal and Joe Kinnear were the exceptions, not the rule.

The reason was because Spurs was a club of the highest standing. It was a proper club from top to bottom and all of it was led by Bill Nick. Your future would be decided by the opinion that the leaders of the club had of you. Bill Nick was the ultimate judge. As an apprentice, I would watch the first team play and realise this was a special club, and it was going to be mighty hard to break into that team.

The way that Tottenham asked us to play at that time was basic. We were there because we could play, of course, so the general feeling was why would they need to teach us too much about how to play? There would be instances when the instruction and coaching would be more specific. Bill Nick showed us specific moves or actions on a board with counters, particularly if he'd watched us playing in the FA Youth Cup. But, as ever, it would not be complicated. It was all rooted in common sense.

This great manager would be telling us the same things he said to his first-team players. 'When the ball goes out of play, don't die – you've got to be alive!' The key was to think how you would take that further in your own head. What did he actually mean by it? It could mean getting into position. If the ball went out for a throw-in, you had to get back to protect your centre-backs. There was no science as such. It was common-sense thinking for yourself.

Graeme Souness arrived at Tottenham as an apprentice in 1969. I saw him on television recently and he made a comment that made my ears prick up. 'The ball moves quicker than any player,' he said, meaning that it's better to pass the ball rather than run with it. That came from Bill Nick. It was true then and is true today, because it is fundamental common sense.

It went back further than Bill Nick. He got a lot of his wisdom and sayings from Arthur Rowe, and he probably got them from Peter McWilliam. People talk about the culture of a club and there's lots said about the 'Spurs Way'. But it was real: there was an expectation about how to play and conduct yourself.

"The White Hart Lane ball courts are part of Tottenham legend. Those places were hothouses for footballing excellence"

Essentially it was just a framework. If you had ability and a brain to link into that framework then you'd benefit, establishing structure and purpose to your game. Eddie drilled something into me early on, and it was to have a profound influence on the player I became.

Talking about the opponent I was about to face, Eddie would say, 'Make sure every time he gets the ball, particularly in the first 20 minutes, you get his head down on it. You don't let him pass forward – you make him play square or back. Make sure he can hear your feet coming, your breathing, that you are hunting him. You are not going to give him a free kick of the ball, to get his head up and pick out a lovely pass that causes damage. You get close.'

He'd continue by saying, 'This is for 20 minutes. If you come up against a bloody good opponent you've got to do that for 93, 94 minutes. You don't ever get a blow [meaning a breather] and that's why you've got to train hard – because you'll need it for that day when you have to hunt an opponent down the whole game.'

The ethos was work first, play second, win third. Glenn Hoddle and I were different players because he didn't come through my era: his mentality was probably 'play first'. My mentality was about responsibility to the team and what I had to do as an individual. Football is a team game but it is you against him as well: individual battles. Win your battle. Who's having the bonus?

There was a great saying that trainers and coaches at the time used to gee players up: 'Baby needs new shoes. Whose baby's getting them?' The meaning was you were being challenged to want to win enough, to get the win bonus and ensure it would be your kid getting a new pair of shoes. I wasn't a father at the time but that didn't matter – the meaning was obvious.

That was an old pro saying if ever there was one. I've used it over the years myself because it's what I believe in. It's virtually saying, 'Who's having a bonus today, you or them?' The wording might change – nowadays at the top level it might be, 'Who's having a new Lamborghini?' But the meaning doesn't alter: do you want to win more than them?

That kind of talk suited me. I relished the battle. I lacked half a yard of pace and I needed something to give me half a yard to compensate, so it was my work-rate and energy that were becoming my strengths. I assumed that was being noticed in my performances in the South-East Counties matches, but nothing explicit was said. It was implied. There were signs that I was making encouraging progress, that the guvnors were pleased with me. Or at least that I could be trusted, which is so important in terms of being selected for teams.

One indication, perhaps, was being invited to join the first team on an away trip to Newcastle at the end of the 1967–68 season. This was quite something for an apprentice. Older lads in the A team who had become pros didn't get to travel with the first team. I had turned 16 by then; I still didn't want to be marked out as special, but that Friday before the Newcastle game I got a surprise.

We changed into our training gear at White Hart Lane. The routine would be to go on to the running track and do a two-lap warm-up, then a dozen sprints running to the old alphabet hoarding on the sideline that they used to put up the scores of the other First Division games when the first team were playing at home on a Saturday. Each fixture had a corresponding letter, so Arsenal v Liverpool would be letter A for example.

On the puffer, with Jimmy Greaves (left) on his puffer! This is an evocative shot of how we used to travel by train in the late 1960s. I made a similar trip to Newcastle, helping out with shifting the kit and rubbing shoulders with the stars of the first team

I was getting ready to start this session when Bill Nick came over and said, 'You got a suit?' I struggled to answer, while all the other youth players were looking and no doubt thinking, 'Why is he asking Steve that?'

'Yes,' I said. He said, 'I suggest you go home, put it on and meet us on the platform at King's Cross for the 4:30pm train. You're going to go with the first team, not because you're a good player but because Cecil Poynton is not well and you're going to help him move the skips [which were used to transport all the kit].'

I was thinking, 'What are they – my teammates – thinking?' Bill Nick was thinking, 'Just get a move on!'

Joyful as I was that I was going to be travelling with the first team, I was conscious that I was going to get it on Monday from the apprentices. But you do what you are told.

I rushed home, put on my suit and dashed back to King's Cross. Suddenly I was on this train being served food. This was another world. The players didn't know me – why would they? – but now I was sitting among them. They were playing cards for money. Mackay was captain and the man in charge. There was Jennings, Knowles, England, Kinnear, Mullery, Greaves, Gilzean. I'd had no real contact with them at all before. I assume someone must have explained why I was there. I was in dreamland. The players were being kind to me. They weren't dismissive at all.

I had to graft that weekend. Every time we got off somewhere – the station, hotel or stadium – the skips with all the kit had to be moved. On the Friday night we stayed at the hotel at Gosforth Park racecourse, which had recently opened. The hotel had a cast-iron gas fireplace as a centrepiece – I'd never seen anything like that in my life – and I could see the racetrack outside the hotel windows and lounges. There was a big race on the telly on Saturday lunchtime before we left, and yet I was seeing it live outside the window. It all felt so strange.

> "Pat was sitting next to me and when he'd signed his name I took the book and passed it on. Pat said to the waitress, 'Love, get his autograph – he's going to be some player'"

The night before, we sat at the dinner table in a private room. When the plates were cleared away the waitress passed an autograph book around the players. Pat was sitting next to me and when he'd signed his name I took the book and passed it on. Pat said to the waitress, 'Love, get his autograph – he's going to be some player.' I'd just come out of school and Pat Jennings, *the* Pat Jennings, was saying that. Just to be around them was pure class. I roomed with Pat that night. He rang down to room service for sandwiches despite having just had dinner. What luxury this all was.

I was getting a privileged insight into the world that top professional footballers lived in. For whatever reason, the players hadn't yet signed an agreement on bonuses and were discussing it the next day with the management. I think Bill Nick forgot I was there. He told them, 'This is the bonus' – I vaguely recollect it was £20 per point away from home. As they trooped out I came out last and Bill pulled me aside and said I wasn't to breathe a word. He needn't have worried. Virtually the whole trip I just sat there. If you had to write a manual for young players going on their first trip with the first team, the first rule would be: 'Do not open your mouth. Just smile. If someone talks to you, smile. If someone gives you something, say thank you.'

The game itself was amazing. The atmosphere at St James' Park was incredible. I sat in the dugout and could barely see anything of the game, but could see and hear the huge crowd on the Gallowgate terrace. The tension and elation and disappointment, wow, it was just the extremes of everything. It said to me, 'This is really serious.'

I'd been to Wembley for the 1967 FA Cup Final. Why it was so different at Newcastle to Wembley I don't fully know but it was more compact and felt more intense and serious. Why wouldn't the FA Cup Final seem serious? I guess it was a fun, showcase event and that we were all glad to be there, but this was business: points to be played for.

I recall a Newcastle player rolling the ball into the net with Pat stranded but Cyril Knowles was on the goal line and stopped it. Two attackers ran at him and he just ran through the middle of them and everyone went, 'Fucking hell!' Typical Knowlesy – that was his character.

I watched the game alongside Bill Nick and Eddie. Bill was controlled, Eddie shouting and swearing the odds. We saw the victory out, winning 3–1 after going 3–0 up. Mackay ran the show, in one of his last games for the club; he was just magnificent. Overall it was a very impressive performance.

Then it was back to the train station. It was Newcastle's first defeat for a while and their supporters were not happy, so 2,000 of them were there waiting for us. Police stood on both sides as we came off the coach and their fans were booing us for their lives. I just put my head down and pushed the skip. Apparently one of these fans threw a cup of hot chocolate at Mullery, who saw it coming and swerved out of the way, only for the contents to hit Mike England.

That was not a wise thing for that fan to do. Mike took a step forward and – boom! – punched whoever threw the hot drink. We sat on the train afterwards and the police came on asking questions about the incident. They were not saying Mike had done anything wrong: they just needed to know what he did and hear it from him. That was that, and we were sent on our way. It was all a bit different to today: now there would be running news updates, phone-ins, footage on Twitter and all sorts of commotion.

What an experience that was. I got the last Tube home. Monday morning I had to tell everyone what I'd been up to and heard. I hadn't 'arrived' by any means, but I was treated to something very special even if I was still at such pains not to be thought of as such.

But I was becoming a professional footballer, regardless. The actual monetary rewards at the time for apprentices were good but modest. From under-16 to under-17 to under-18 levels, the pay was £6, £7 and £8 a week respectively. Fortunately, my hard work paid off.

It got to 21st December 1968 and my 17th birthday. About a week before, Bill Nick had said those magic words: 'Steve, we're going to sign you as a pro. Well done. But we won't do it next week. Phil's 17 in the middle of January, so we'll do you both together.' No fuss, no wasted words – just a simple statement.

I was thrilled for myself and my family but I couldn't wait to tell Phil he was going to be turn pro as well. We'd looked after each other and were reaping the dividend.

The appointed day came. Phil and I sat outside Bill's office. I went in first, signed swiftly and came out. Phil then went in and did the same. It took five minutes, max. We didn't say a word to each other until we were out on the High Road waiting for the 279 bus, all pleased with ourselves without saying anything. Eventually, Phil said, 'Go on then: how much?'

'Same as you I guess, £18 a week,' I said.

'Bastard. I'm on £17.'

Bill Nick lets us know what team we would be playing for in early season matches at Cheshunt. This was probably taken on the day of the pre-season photocall when the photographers would get images to use through the season, including head shots and action pictures

THE CONTENDER

I n the 1968–69 season, when I turned pro, the team and the club were going through a period of transition. Dave Mackay had gone to Derby in the summer. Jimmy Greaves was in his last full season, though he played all 42 league games and was still banging goals in for fun. But a number of players – including a trio of home-growns in Jimmy Pearce, Ray Evans and John Pratt, as well as Peter Collins who was signed as a youngster from Chelmsford – made their debuts. Bill Nick was rebuilding, assembling what was to become his third trophy-winning side, and looking to promote from within.

For all my swift progress and experiences like the trip to Newcastle, I was still a fresh-faced kid and very much a youth-team player. I might have bought my first car, a Wolseley, but it cost £90 and for a kid on 18 quid a week that was a major commitment and I had to save up for it. I was still living at home, but paying my mum something for my keep. I was kept grounded at home and at work.

For all the visible changes in first-team personnel, behind the scenes the club still exuded stability and routine. Bill Nick ruled. Everyone called him 'Bill', there was no 'Sir' or 'Mr Nicholson' or 'Gaffer'. He was at pains to let us know that plain 'Bill' was fine. He didn't need any titles or ways to denote that he was in charge. He and Eddie dealt with the professionals while keeping an eye on anyone coming through. Johnny, Sid and the men in white coats put us through our paces. Work and training were now familiar to us youngsters. Bill Watson, for instance, would come in the mornings to do what would now be called strength and conditioning.

I struggled with doing weights. We did a series of exercises using equipment along the wall in the gym and going from one to the next. The one where it required you to sit on a bench and lift a weight by 'kicking' through a lever to strengthen the top of the thigh, I just couldn't do, it was as if something in my brain was telling me, 'Don't do it'. I've heard since that it's not a good exercise for the knees. But when I look at pictures of me in my young days my muscles were well-formed, and that was due to Bill Watson's routines and all the running that we used to do.

We did sit-ups, hundreds and hundreds of them. Bill Nick loved sit-ups. Without really knowing the science behind it, it was working the core muscles. He believed fitness and strength came from the stomach muscles. While Bill's methods were rooted in experience and know-how honed over decades, he was ahead of his time in many ways.

"For all my swift progress and experiences like the trip to Newcastle, I was still a fresh-faced kid and very much a youth-team player"

Aged 17, proudly showing my first car at Cheshunt, a Wolseley 1500, that cost me £90 when I was earning £18 per week. Note the Fred Perry shirt – all the trappings of an aspiring first-team player!

The same could not be said for nutrition. We were pretty much left to our own devices, which meant either eating at home or in the local cafés. The club only really intervened with pre-match meals; they thought I needed to have steak, but something told me again, like the knees, not to have it. Tough. 'You're eating steak – we've ordered it for you.' We were given meat and carbs in the form of potatoes, which is just about the worst thing you can eat before a match as the sport nutritionists later worked out.

Dealing with injuries and medical matters also seemed fairly rudimentary by today's standards. The treatment room would be busy on a Monday after all the weekend games. There might be four swollen or 'fat' ankles, two eye injuries, a hamstring, all sorts. If you were one of the injured, you would be called in to see the doctor, who was another of those long-serving Tottenham institutions, Dr Brian Curtin. We never saw him the rest of the week until Saturday, or occasionally on a Friday if a decision needed to be made on a player's fitness.

Dr Curtin would look at you, along with Cecil Poynton; they'd discuss something between them and give you tablets. 'Take two yellow ones in the morning, three blue ones after lunch and four red ones before bed.' They never gave them in a packet, it was always in your hand. I would see the other players with fat ankles walk out and throw the pills away. 'Blimey,' I thought, 'they know more than the doctor.' But then I'd think again. If I threw them away and my ankle didn't get better maybe it would be because I hadn't taken the pills, and I couldn't admit that when they were assessing my ankle a week later thinking I'd taken the tablets. So then I thought I *should* take the tablets. Dr Curtin was the man who went to university, after all. The pills were anti-inflammatories most likely, but for a club that was so organised it didn't feel right that they didn't explain things in more detail.

On a day when Dr Curtin was not in, Bill Nick would walk into the treatment room. There were four beds, one player on each, with a couple waiting their turn. Bill would be as immaculate as ever, the picture of smartness. But he would look around with an expression of almost disgust on his face. He wouldn't say a word and then he'd just walk out. No 'Hello', no 'How you feeling?' Just disdain. What he was saying with that look was, 'You are no good to me because you're injured.' His message was, 'You're soft.'

Still, we could cope with a hit. We were hard-nosed and hard-wearing. My legs were building up strength and would be further developed playing on the sandy pitches of those days. I am convinced the strong muscles in my legs protected my knees through all the hard running I was doing and continued to do so. And no one ever mentioned being tired ever. It was a word that was never used.

While the steak and the pills of various colours might not have been to my taste, the physical training suited me fine. As a young pro I became part of Tottenham's culture, exposed to a history and tradition that I had to adhere to. I was a ball player as a young footballer, but when I got the chance to impress at Spurs it wasn't pure football that was going to push me up the ladder: it was going to be energy, allied to football skill, which would make me selectable. Energy was what they didn't really have, particularly in the first team.

I would have to impress Eddie. As I made the transition from youth player to contending for a first-team place, he would take more notice and be involved. One day I played an A-team game, making a mistake in not tracking an opponent. I'd hoped had he missed it but nothing got past Eddie. He pulled me to one side after the match. 'You little bastard,' he said. 'Your player got in our box and you let him run. If you ever do that again I'm making sure you're taken off. Even if we have to go down to 10 men. You lazy little bastard.'

You had nowhere to hide with Eddie, nor Bill. One of them would get you. The more they watched, the more they were on you. They weren't intimidating or bullying at all. I just felt that I did not want to let them down. They were very exacting, as they had to be. If they thought you were a coward, you stood no chance. The big word of the era was 'bottle'. They loved anyone who put a foot in. Although I was still an inside-forward, when I put my foot in in those seven-a-sides it really *went* in, so I don't think there was ever any concern with me on that score.

I did used to worry about playing, though. I wasn't an extreme worrier but in the build-up to a game I would be yawning, which is apparently not a sign of tiredness in that context but more of stress. My thinking was, 'I'm going to play badly – I'm tired,' but apparently it would have been nerves. I wish I'd known that at the time.

It was all part of my development. Helping that progress was that I could learn from what I was doing, good or bad. If it was the latter we would be told in stark terms: 'Don't fucking do that again.' But as much as I learned through the youth team, and limited reserve games, allied

"When I put my foot in in those seven-a-sides it really went in, so I don't think there was ever any concern with me on that score"

Johnny Wallis, a man I learned so much from, not just about football but about how to conduct myself and be respectful. He treated you like you treated him. It was all part of my learning curve

to all the coaching sessions, I had not yet made my appearance on the big stage. That still seemed distant, something I could only really dream of rather than expect. And even if I had confidence in my am bitions, everyone in any position of authority or seniority was all too ready to take me down a peg or two.

You'd get it from all the characters around White Hart Lane. Jimmy 'Dodger' Joyce was unlike any person I had met in my life. I first met him at schoolboy training when he would pay our travel expenses, and any time we needed reimbursing for something we had to see Dodger. He was an ageing, short fella carrying a bit of weight, who shuffled along on two big feet and wore a pocket watch in his waistcoat. We would go to him and put in our request for payment.

'Son?'

'Two and six, Jim.'

'Two and six? You brothel-bred bastard,' he would say, but with a smile. 'If you think you're getting away with two and six from me you must be a… who brought you up?' Dodger would then do that thing of licking the pencil tip before he wrote something and gave us our money.

It was the same thing every time. Cutting but oh so funny. Dodger would go away on the youth-team trips every year and one time we went to Holland. At Feyenoord they treated him like a king. Bill Nick was Mr Tottenham? No, as far as the Dutch were concerned Dodger was the top man. He loved cheese and he was in his element eating all the Edam.

It was distinctive, working-class, old-London wit and humour mixed in with no-nonsense discipline to keep us in check. We couldn't take any liberties, but they liked it if we bit back a little bit. It was like an extension of training, but this time teaching us how to handle ourselves and build our confidence. Don't talk out of turn. Don't be lairy. But don't shrink into your shell either. We learned quick. 'If I'm a brothel-bred bastard, Jim,' I said to Dodger one day, 'what does that make him?' and I'd point at Phil.

These people became part of our life. Johnny Wallis was at the fore in this regard, very old-school and the embodiment of the character of the club. Lenny Warren was clerk of works, and what a bastard he was for keeping us in check. We had to go and see Len to get the carbolic soap for cleaning the dressing rooms. 'Shit roll, soap and soda' was what we had to collect. The soda was for cleaning the big bath.

Bill Beeby, who was in charge of the ticket office, was an ex-copper and quite stern, and we had to address him correctly, 'Yes, Mr Beeby'. Henry Naylor was the groundsman at White Hart Lane, Don Coulsdon was in charge at Cheshunt, and together they all had an influence. We got to know the workings of the club, the people involved and how to talk to them. We were being taught North London values and ways – an 'etiquette' in how to conduct yourself.

Ron Henry was another great character. As a key man in the Double team, Ron was Spurs royalty in any case, but he did coaching and would still turn out for the A team, in between running his market garden. He would be hard, merciless even, on the young players but was popular – Chris Hughton loved him when he came to Spurs in the mid-1970s.

Phil could get a rise out of Ron. We'd be meeting up for the A team to go and travel by bus somewhere and Ron would walk in wearing a belt with a big buckle on it. Phil would say, 'Ron? Steve reckons you look like a cowboy with that belt.' Cheers, Phil. Ron would catch up with anyone who took him on in the end, calling them all sorts of names. But then he'd be playing alongside us in the A team and be the staunchest of teammates, looking out for us, encouraging us and if need be right up for it if it got a bit physical.

White Hart Lane was just full of these characters. Micky 'Dripping', or Micky Stockwell to give him his actual name, was the general maintenance man. He always walked with a 2x1 length of wood under his arm. He would walk past us and say, 'Bounce!' We never did find out what he meant but it was his catchphrase. As we got older and a bit bolder, we'd see him in Tony's café and say, 'Mick, we got to ask you: what is the 2x1 bit of wood for? You've carried it for the last 10 years. What is it?'

'Listen,' he said, warming to his task of educating us. 'You carry it around with you, then no one can say, "What are you doing?" because you can just point at the bit of wood as if they are an idiot for asking.'

It was gold dust to impressionable lads like us. What characters. Probably earning thruppence, but proper fans who loved the club, even if the last thing they would do was show us any affection. They'd never praise us. It was always: 'You lazy bastard. I didn't want to watch the game but there was nothing on the telly so I came and watched you lot. Blimey, you were shit.'

That was all we got out of them. And we loved getting it. The character building of that group was phenomenal. Me and Phil laugh ourselves silly when we start talking about those times; they were brilliant.

Another A team, a mix of old hands, ages, and abilities, each of us on a different path in our careers. Andy McCulloch (top left) came from non-league and went to QPR. Andy Bish is second from right on the back row, with the great Double winner Ron Henry to his right. Others in the frame include John Gilroy, Terry Naylor, Barry Daines and John Collins

"We were growing in confidence and were now not overawed by the stars of the club. Daily interaction with the first team increased and training with them began to step up"

Bill Nick appointed all those people if they hadn't been there already when he arrived as manager in 1958. It was his extended way of managing, and he wanted those kinds of people in those roles so that we were treated the same way throughout the club, whether it was playing in a match or having the piss taken out of us by the ground staff. All of them would encourage us to do the right things and act the right way – and they'd let Bill Nick know if we didn't. That's not being a grass – it is upholding the standards needed, particularly at a football club with such tradition. We had to carry it off. It wasn't just about kicking a ball. It was about how we acted and worked, and who we were as people. Johnny always said, 'My belief is you play as you work. Cheat them jobs,' – cleaning boots, for example – 'and you'll cheat me on a Saturday, and you'll cheat this club.'

We learned fast. Phil said something to me one day after the first team played a practice match and we were in the team against them. We were driving home when he said 'Mullers' – meaning Alan Mullery – 'took the piss out of you today. When you slid under him and you knocked the ball away, didn't you see how he looked at you? He looked at you like you was a piece of shit.'

I said, 'Phil, I never saw that. So what are you saying?'

Phil said, 'Nail him tomorrow.'

I'm pretty certain I didn't but we were growing in confidence and were now not overawed by the stars of the club. Daily interaction with the first team increased and training with them began to step up. I hadn't really learned to kick a ball properly until I was about 15, but even then I never kicked it more than about 30 yards, or at least not accurately. I'd see Bobby Charlton hit a long left-to-right ball to precision and think, 'Christ, how did he do that?' I never really trusted my 'laces': I had a strong side-foot, but couldn't kick through the ball with both distance and accuracy.

But when I was in the ball court training with the first team and I had to drive the ball accurately for Gilly, Chivers, Greaves and Co, I needed to find a way to do it and fast. The ball needed to be served up to the forwards. I couldn't get away with hitting it too hard so it went over their heads or too soft so that it dribbled along the floor: I'd get shouted at.

There was a pressure to be consistent and reliable. My left foot was poor and that weakness was exposed in a drill where we'd have to change from right-foot crossing to left-foot crossing. I would get criticised by Bill Nick. 'Any chance, Steve?!', as in 'Any chance of you doing that better?' I was finding out how demanding Bill Nick could be. Looking back, I do wonder if there should have been more constructive criticism – someone taking me to one side and saying, 'Come here, your weight is wrong' or 'I'll get you back for a couple of afternoon sessions.' I never felt that *care*, as if it was perceived as being too caring to give it to a young player – too soft, even. Andy Thompson, veteran of the 1920s, might make the odd kind comment. If he watched an FA Youth Cup game he would say something to us like 'Loved your shot'. But he was the last line of opinion, someone who filled in with the coaching and training hierarchy. There was very little in the way of football training from him. He limped about and obviously had a dodgy hip, and we sort of felt sorry for him.

That very old, established way of coaching and training the youth players was about to be altered, however, when Pat Welton arrived to take charge of the youth system in August 1969. A former Orient goalkeeper, his brief was to bring the successful methods he had used as head coach with the England under-18s team that he had twice won the UEFA Under-18

Championship with. Hitherto our training consisted of drills and small-sided games; Pat brought in things like training grids – the squares and triangles that have developed into the drills of today. It was a more modern way of thinking.

This was Bill being forward-looking yet again. There was always method and purpose to what he and Eddie did, even if sometimes it seemed off the cuff. I found out later from Eddie that he and Bill devised their own sessions to a fine detail in their offices. They were very highly regarded, and foreign coaches would turn up and sit on the bank at Cheshunt taking notes, Sven-Göran Eriksson among them.

It was their way of seeing top coaches work at the coalface rather than just going on a course. But when Pat came Bill tried to make the youth area of the club a bit more about teaching in its style and structure, as Spurs decided they needed to produce more players. Johnny moved to be more of a kit man while still training us when needed, so it was a case of evolution rather than the end of an era.

Getting surprised by a snapper on a press day. Peter Collins and Alan Gilzean are in the background

Working with Pat in 1969–70 was to be my last season playing in the youth team, and even then it was intermittent because a grander stage awaited. The management had bigger things in mind for me and an early indication of what these might be had come at the end of 1968–69 season.

The first team were due to go on tour to North America in May and the first week of June in 1969, playing against British and European teams. A week or so beforehand, I finished an evening A-team game at Cheshunt. I hadn't got into the reserves yet, but was playing against sides like Braintree who had good solid old pros to test you. I walked off at the end of the match into the corner where the changing rooms were. Eddie always used to stand there.

I was vaguely aware he was there and I was wary of him saying anything because it wasn't likely to be, 'Well done.' Sure enough – 'Perryman!' he shouted.

'Someone tells me,' he continued, with a heavy sarcastic tone, 'that you're on some list in there. I don't quite believe it, or how it's happened but apparently you're on the list – probably last on the list – to go to America with the first team. How the hell's that happened?'

'I don't know, Eddie,' I said, a bit bewildered.

'Well, I suggest you do have a look at the list just in case there's some instruction on there about passports or something that you need to know. I doubt that you'll be going, but anyway, just make sure you make yourself aware.'

As a captain, coach or manager I would have been saying to a young player in that situation: 'Well done, son, you've had a very good season and made it to America – well done.' But not Eddie. This was evident whatever we were doing. If I drove into the car park, he'd say, 'Two weeks of pushing that clutch down and you'll end up with a calf injury.' There always had to be a piss-take to anything he said.

But sure enough, I was on the list to go on the tour. Blimey. I'd been on an away trip with the first team before, but this was another step up. I'd had a good season, and was obviously making headway. Because of international commitments, Mullers wasn't going to the USA, and Gilly wasn't due to join the trip until later, so there was an element of me making up the numbers. But there was more to it than just that. I played games and supposed that Bill Nick was having more of a look at me.

I played in the first game, a 4–3 win against West Ham in Baltimore. The Hammers were based there, while Aston Villa were resident in Atlanta. That meant that those two teams stayed there for the duration of the tour and various teams, including us, visited them to play.

That first game was an experience on and off the pitch. It was played in a baseball stadium, with the pitch running across the baseball diamond, so that felt odd. Afterwards we went back to the hotel that both teams stayed in. On the Sunday, I was told by one of our players to go up to one of the rooms. This is a bit strange, I thought. I went up, knocked on the door and inside there was a group of Spurs

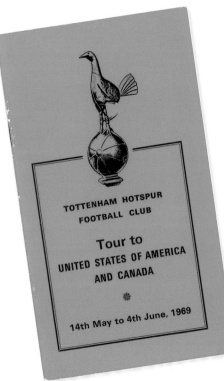

TOTTENHAM HOTSPUR
FOOTBALL CLUB

Tour to
UNITED STATES OF AMERICA
AND CANADA

14th May to 4th June, 1969

A handbook for the US tour of 1969 that provided me with a doorway into the first team

Perryman the patient

Steve Perryman guessed wrong when Spurs manager Bill Nicholson made a last-minute decision to include him in the first team's summer tour of America.

The 17-year-old reserve forward admits: "I couldn't believe it at first and more or less accepted that I was going along for the ride."

It did not turn out that way. Perryman played in four games

STEVE PERRYMAN

and though the youngest and most inexperienced member of the Spurs party was an outstanding success.

and West Ham players having a drink. The bath was full of bottles and cans of beer. It might have been Bobby Moore's room, and he was certainly there.

In America at that time you couldn't get a beer on a Sunday in some places – dry Sunday I think it was called. So instead the players, World Cup winners and superstars among them, were having a drink in one of the hotel rooms, having stocked up on beer.

This was an initiation like none I had had before. It wasn't a mad piss-up, more of a relaxed drink, but the significance was the company I was being invited into. I only spoke when I was spoken to and didn't stay long but I was one of the lads now. Here I was, 17, barely two years out of school and yet to play first-team football, having a social with Bobby Moore. Bill Nick had always wanted to sign Bobby, and we found out later that Bobby had wanted to come to Tottenham. It's a real 'what if'.

America as a whole was some experience. When we went to Atlanta to play Villa we stayed at the Hyatt Regency. In the atrium four lifts came down like something out of a space station – it was amazing. All the rooms were facing in towards the centre, so you could see all the people walking along to go to their rooms.

America was all so new, bright and sparkling. My brothers had asked me to buy them short-sleeved collared shirts while I was out there, as they were the in thing to wear at the time. So I went out shopping, got the shirts, came back into the hotel reception and asked for the key. The lady on reception said, 'When you turned out of here did you go left or right?' I said left. She replied, 'My God. Don't ever do that again.' I'd walked down into the most dangerous area in the city, apparently. Nothing happened. My naivety got me through it, perhaps.

Having bought these shirts, I was now walking through the hotel. Tony Want appeared. He said, 'Steve, the chaps are a bit disappointed with you. You're not drinking.'

I told him I didn't drink. He said, 'You'll have to start.'

He showed me where to meet them, in a lounge at the back. This was a new experience, mixing with the big boys. I popped upstairs to drop the shirts off, came back down and walked into the room where the others were.

'Ah, Steve is here, where you been? Get him a beer!'

They didn't ask if I wanted one. This huge beer was plonked down in front of me. I was thinking that if Bill Nick walked through that door, he was going to take my head off. So I took a sip and put it on the floor. Just out of sight, thinking I've got to be part of it but I don't want to be doing it. I didn't drink at all then. I stayed for a bit, then made an excuse to go. Bill Nick wouldn't have minded about the rest of them, it was the end of the season and it wasn't a club rule not to have a modest drink. But for a 17-year-old on his first trip, that would be different.

Later I found the private room where we were having our evening meal. It was seven o'clock, I was on time. Eddie and Bill Nick were there but none

STEPHEN, 17, PLAYS AGAINST WORLD'S TOP CLUB TEAMS

By Gazette Soccer reporter

Seventeen-year-old Stephen Perryman of 39 Bancroft Court, South Ruislip, arrived home from Canada at the weekend a fully fledged professional footballer having played for Tottenham Hotspur against four of the greatest club teams in the world — after being taken to Canada for "experience."

Stephen, who turned full time pro' for Spurs early this year, is a former local schoolboy player who represented Ealing, Middlesex and London boys and played for England boys against Scotland at Wembley last year.

He was spotted by Mr. C. Faulkner, Spurs, chief representative, who lives in Westbourne Road, Hillingdon, taken to White Hart Lane for trials and signed by Mr. Faulkner for Tottenham in the face of fierce competition.

Now former England and leading First Division scorer Jimmy Greaves says of him: "He is a great natural player who could be wearing England's colours in a couple of seasons.

Spurs' manager Bill Nicholson took Stephen to Canada for the recent Toronto Cup tournament to give him experience and intending to send him back to England after a week or so so that the youngster could accompany Spurs Youth Team to the Hague for a youth tournament.

But the youngster played so well against West Ham in the opening game that he was retained and another player was sent home. Subsequently Stephen played in every match of the competition, against Glasgow Rangers, Aston Villa and Italian champions Fiorentina, who finally won the tournament on Sunday beating Glasgow Rangers 2-0 in the final match.

Stephen Perryman and, of course, a football.

The local paper catches up on my progress

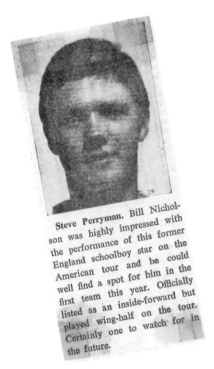

Steve Perryman. Bill Nicholson was highly impressed with the performance of this former England schoolboy star on the American tour and he could well find a spot for him in the first team this year. Officially listed as an inside-forward but played wing-half on the tour. Certainly one to watch for in the future.

More clippings from the American tour, including a report of my appearance against Rangers on 1st June 1969

Perryman is Spurs star on U.S. tour

The greatest satisfaction Tottenham manager Bill Nicholson gained from taking his side to America was in the excellent showing of his younger players, writes Harold Palmer.

He was particularly pleased with Steve Perryman, who, wearing the number four shirt, in effect took over the mantle of Alan Mullery, lost to the England party in South America. Just back from a trip which he said 'Went better than we expected.' Nicholson told me that the only snag had been a spell of 11 days between games during which the players had "kicked their heels."

Mostly his comment, however, was in praise of the play of the 17-year-old Perryman. "He is on the small side," said Nicholson, "but he did extremely well."

OOOOOH, THAT SMARTS! Ronnie MacKinnon of Glasgow Rangers winces as he gets in way of a hard shot by John Pratt of Tottenham during action near Scots' goal. Spurs' Steve Perryman (4)

of the other players. 'All right?' they said. 'What you been doing?' I told them I'd bought some clothes.

It got to 7:10pm and no one had turned up. Eddie said, 'Steve, do you know where they are?' I pleaded ignorance. 'I expect they're fucking drinking somewhere,' said Eddie and I tried not to show any sign that I knew that was indeed what they were doing.

Finally at 7:20pm they came in, in straggles. They weren't blind drunk but giggly, which was a cue for Eddie to proceed to verbally annihilate them one by one, so much so I was thinking, 'I've gotta write this down. I gotta tell my brothers all this.'

'Do you know what the time is?' Bill let Eddie rip into them. Eventually Ray Evans came in with Jimmy Greaves. They were sharing a little joke. 'Oh! Oh, Evans is here! Oh, you've decided to turn up have you? I suppose you're going to write a book when you get home – *Me and Jimmy Greaves*.'

Eddie found something on everyone. The funniest bit was reserved for Roger Morgan, who had been bought for a lot of money but hadn't done particularly well.

'Blimey it's our birthday. Roger Morgan's turned up. Bill, Roger has graced us with his presence.' It carried on and Roger had a bit of a bite back. Eddie said, 'Do you know what you remind me of, Morgan? You always look dirty. In fact you look like a car mechanic who hasn't had a wash.' And so from that moment on for his whole time at the club, Roger was called 'Spanner'.

Things settled down. We were enjoying the meal. At least they were all there – apart from Venables and Phil Beal, who never showed up. We didn't know what had happened but Eddie was passing comments, saying, 'We're two short? I suppose they've fucking gone out somewhere!'

As players we were not entitled to do that, especially when meals had been booked, but Bill was more lenient on end-of-season tours, so they got away with it. The rule was not to take liberties or cause trouble, but we were on a longer leash.

Back at the dinner table, it came up that we were moving on to Canada to play in Toronto. Eddie asked who wanted to go to Niagara Falls. I didn't put my hand up as I was not expecting to be going any further on the tour. Alan Gilzean was joining us and I assumed I'd be sent home. Only about three of the rest put their hands up.

'So, Morgan,' Eddie started up again, 'you're not going to Niagara Falls? Have you been to Niagara Falls before then?'

'No, Ed,' said Roger, 'and I haven't been to the Moon but I don't fucking want to go there either.' This was comedy gold and the back and forth was just flying, all led by Eddie. He was the ringmaster and no one was brave enough to really take him on. Roger, however, was a happy-go-lucky type and probably thought it was the right thing to join in. I felt I was better off staying quiet.

It was dawning on me that I was now with a special group. It was fantastic but I needed to work out how to cope with it all. I needed to look good in front of the class, so to speak, but I mustn't look bad in front of Bill and Eddie. It required mental boxing all the time.

Then I got the shout. 'Steve, by the way, you're staying.' They told me David Jenkins was going home instead. I asked why. 'Because he's got fucking sunburn on top of his feet, laying round the pool yesterday, that's why,' said Eddie with absolute contempt. That had been reported back to Eddie and Bill, and they weren't happy and ordered Jenkins home.

I suppose I must have done enough for them to think I was worth another look. Gilly did come out and David went back. He never really cracked it at Tottenham. He'd been swapped from Arsenal for Jimmy Robertson, who had been a bit of a favourite. No one could understand why that was done. I thought, sat on the touchline as a schoolboy, that Jimmy was so fast, like shit off a shovel. He was quick and could cross it. David Jenkins looked like he lacked confidence and purpose.

So I stayed and played against Aston Villa in Atlanta and then we went to Toronto, where I played the games against Glasgow Rangers and Fiorentina. There were a lot of people at the Rangers game, as there were so many Scottish fans in Toronto. We played against Eusebio on AstroTurf – he was a guest player for Toronto.

I must have done all right to stay in. Although it might have been about giving the others a rest at the end of the season, everyone thought I was doing well. I was on cloud nine playing with the first team. There I was next to them, socialising with them. It was a validation of progress and travel represented another level of development.

Alan Mullery tells the story that when he got home from international duty that summer, Bill Nick phoned him to ask how he had got on with England in the home internationals and a tour of Central and South America. Mullers said he'd done well, and that people had said he was the best player. Bill said to Mullers, 'Well, that's good because I've found your replacement.' Bill told him it was me.

'He ain't taking my place,' Mullers replied.

I didn't know it at the time, but I would be battling with the likes of England international Alan Mullery to play in the Tottenham first team. I had become a contender.

"Mullers said he'd done well, and that people had said he was the best player. Bill said to Mullers, 'Well, that's good because I've found your replacement.' Bill told him it was me"

THE BIG STAGE

The American tour was a turning point for me. As a young player I was just pleased to be closer to the first team; this was Spurs, after all, and my opportunity had been a shot out the blue. But I'd done well. The fact I'd played in all the games enabled me to gain the trust of the management and the players, though tour games are of course less pressurised. I had learned from being around the chaps and witnessing all the piss-taking that the best way of dealing with it was to say nothing and do what I was asked. I ended up going to Niagara Falls and the fact that I didn't want to drink must also have gone down well with Bill and Eddie.

I had been playing well in the A team, and Bill and Eddie had been getting good reports about me. They came to see the odd game; Bill Nick would sometimes turn up on the Saturday morning. I would just see his head over the top of the mound at Cheshunt and think, 'Blimey, Bill Nick's here.'

I always had an appetite to play, I trained as well as anyone else and I had imagination. 'When the game dies you come alive' was now a natural part of my thinking. Yet I started pre-season not really knowing where I stood. Was I going to be sticking with the youth and A team or playing more for the reserves? As luck would have it, for the first time since I'd had a bad back I picked up a muscle injury. At the club's media day about a week before the first game of the 1969–70 season, the players lined up to have their individual photos taken. I wasn't included, and didn't expect to be. But Bill Nick came up and said, 'If it weren't for that injury, you'd have been photographed.' I think I just blurted out, 'I don't want to be injured, Bill.'

Things changed fast. The team had a reasonable start but then produced some poor performances, including defeats to Leeds and Liverpool, and a 3–0 loss at Man City. Arsenal were then beaten but a trip to Derby was next and I was taken as 13th man. There was only one sub then, so the matchday squad was 12, with an extra player taken along in case anyone got taken ill or injured in the warm-up. The fixture had added intrigue because it was Derby's manager, Brian Clough, pitting his wits against Bill, with Dave Mackay playing for the home side.

The Baseball Ground was an old-fashioned stadium full of character and the match was a big occasion. I'd played there in an England Schoolboys trial but with no one there. Packed stadiums are completely different places. But the game was a horror show. Mackay bossed it, strutting around the pitch like he was a god and we were thrashed. Willie Carlin, five foot one tall, scored with a header.

"I started pre-season not really knowing where I stood. Was I going to be sticking with the youth and A team or playing more for the reserves?"

BRIAN SCOVELL brings you all the Soccerday news

Spurs set to gamble

SPURS manager Bill Nicholson is ready to introduce 17-year-old Steve Perryman to First Division football against Sunderland at White Hart-lane today. Last night Perryman was in Spurs' squad of 13. Today he could find himself slotted into the midfield spot.

Nicholson told me: "I shall not decide until the morning but it won't be a bad time to push him in, especially as Sunderland have a lot of young players. I won't be afraid to play him. We have been having problems in midfield and this might be a good time to try to do something about it.

"He's a small lad but very industrious and he tackles well.

"Perryman came to us straight from school as a 15-year-old. Age doesn't concern me, only how good a player is."

Young Steve and Dennis Bond, another midfield player, have been added to the team who lost 5—0 at Derby.

MYSTERY INJURY STOPS CHIVERS

Nicholson: This proves we can find our own players

Boy Perryman joins Spurs stars

By JEFF POWELL

STEVE Perryman, 17, stands this morning on the threshold of the First Division in defiance of those who doubt Tottenham's capacity to produce players of their own.

Whether or not he plays against Sunderland, he is destined to become one of the youngest ever to appear in Spurs' first team.

Skipper Mullery with Perryman yesterday
Picture PATRICK LARKIN

Newspaper reports announcing my elevation to the first team

Spurs had problems in midfield. Venables had gone and when we played Liverpool, Bill was reported as 'unashamedly' picking a 4–4–2, as if it *was* something to be ashamed of. Mullery was even partnered with Jimmy Greaves at some point and Roger Morgan played, but midfield energy was lacking.

In the aftermath a distraught Bill was under pressure and made changes. Thus my opportunity to get on the big stage came about because of a game that finished Derby 5 Spurs 0. It's fine being a good player or having a good pre-season, but the opportunities have still got to arise. You can't allow yourself to dwell on the thought that you have a chance to get in the team, you have to be ready and willing to take that chance.

There were all sorts of rumours that week after the Derby defeat. There was a reserve game at Reading the following Tuesday night and I travelled expecting to play but wasn't selected. I was so disappointed but it transpired that the plan was I might be involved on Saturday for the first team against Sunderland, though typically none of that was communicated to me.

It wasn't until Friday that the manager's intentions became at least slightly clearer. Dennis Bond, who had made his debut two years before, and I were called into Bill Nick's office at White Hart Lane in the West Stand. It was wood-panelled and appropriately for Bill very organised and neat. His back was to the window that looked out onto the High Road. The secretary wasn't present – I only ever saw Bill in there. It was his domain.

Bill simply said, 'One of you is definitely playing; possibly both.'

There was a team meeting later. The talk was quite negative after the Derby result. Bill said he'd been thinking about making changes but hadn't quite decided yet. Given that I was there, the other players must have had an inkling, and Mullers ruffled my hair. It was left at that. We didn't work on anything specific in training.

The odds-on favourite to play would have been Dennis with me as sub. Bill always said he had more trouble with the decision of who was going to be sub than picking the team. I was too surprised to process it all. My mind had been building up to this for so long and suddenly the prospect of playing was there. Driving home on Friday, Phil said, 'You're playing – trust me. Bill wouldn't say that unless you were playing.' Phil was Mr Positive about everything but I wasn't nearly as sure.

Saturday arrived. I woke up thinking, as I always did, 'How do I feel?' That feeling would have been heightened because I knew I was possibly playing, but I've always had this thing whereby I think the worst of, say, carrying a knock before thinking it through and ending up feeling positive. That morning, 27th September 1969, my legs ached a little bit. There were so many thoughts swirling around in my head. Naturally I was nervous. I think being anxious is something positive – nerves help to put your mind on the right track. I had scrambled eggs for lunch at home. A newspaper article claimed I might be playing as Roger had a stomach bug. I didn't pay much attention. I was 17 and naive, but naivety can be a good thing. I was driven to Tottenham with my head in a muddle. A decade later, when I was driving myself to a game, my head would be full of specific thoughts, thinking in minute detail about the game to come. But at 17, not knowing if I was playing or not, it was a blur.

In that era, the deadline to be in the dressing room was 2pm. We got to the ground by 1:50pm, through the famous Bill Nick gates and parked up. I went to the ticket office to sort my complimentary tickets as the crowd built up.

I went into the dressing room with the rest of the players and Bill Nick just announced the team to the group. Dennis was in – and so was I. I was given the No.11 shirt and took Roger's place. The fact that me, Dennis and Mullery played meant Bill changed to a 4–3–3. John Pratt didn't play and neither did Tony Want, who had both appeared several times already that season.

So I was in. This club that I'd played for, practised for, cleaned up for, I was now going to be playing for in the first team at White Hart Lane. This was a whole new ball game. I'd been watching matches for two years and now *I* was on the big stage. Some other little kid was going to be on that touchline watching my legs, like I had been watching Gilly and Venables's legs in that frenzied game against Arsenal. This wasn't the derby, it was Sunderland, a team who got relegated that season. But I was playing.

The team were obviously lacking confidence. I was certainly nervous but not in a negative way; I wanted to prove to those people who didn't yet know me that I could play. There was no real reaction from my new teammates. They were pleased for me but they couldn't say so in the room then because Bill Nick was talking. Getting closer to kick off it was different. I got a couple of 'Well done's and a 'You can do it'. No words were exchanged with Roger, but they didn't need to be. This was professional football and we acted professionally.

Pat Jennings says when he was struggling in his early days, Jimmy Greaves walked off the pitch with him after one game and said, 'Son, let me tell you, you're going to be one of the greatest goalkeepers this world has ever seen.' Reassurance like that can be very important. A word here and there can be a real boost but it's best not to say too much to the person making his debut because it's like you're saying they are not really ready. Sometimes things are best left unsaid.

The programme from my first-team debut, against Sunderland on 27th September 1969

"I wasn't worried about making mistakes. I just wanted the game to start and to play well. If I'd known then it would lead to 17 years in the team, most of them as captain..."

Over the course of the years I've seen a lot of people make their debuts and they tend to do well. I went into that Sunderland game reverting to that simple instruction: play quick, play easy, play accurate. Try not to speed yourself up; try and play the first pass you see.

In the dressing room beforehand it was business. Some were louder than others – Mullery was skipper and was shouting, 'This is the day, come on! Let's put it right from last week!' Mike England was a powerful man and had a strong voice. Pat made some comments but more quietly. Jimmy Greaves just got on with it. Gilly was quietly confident; if you watched him strut around the dressing room you picked up a bit of confidence off him.

They were all disciples of Dave Mackay. Gilly liked to tell the story years later about how, in the tunnel before the 1967 FA Cup Final, Mackay looked at the young Chelsea players and seeing how nervous they were said, 'You don't fancy this, do you?' They were beaten before a ball was kicked.

Everyone went through their own routines. On cold winter days, the trainer would give a little brandy – just to make your throat 'warm'. There was no brandy on this day in September, but there were nerves and anxiety. Some players went their whole careers like that. I was told that Arsenal's Charlie George would be physically sick before games. We all had different ways of coping with it. I blocked out the thought of having to perform in front of 50,000 people. I have a vague recollection of someone saying something to me along the lines of: 'First pass, first tackle, first thing you do – just get it right.' Wise words: make it easy. Don't pick the ball up and try to dribble through the opponents. Simple is best: work your way into the game.

The dressing room is a sealed-off, sacred place before kick-off. There was no warm-up: I did a few steps onto the bench to get my legs going. But I didn't want to look too serious as that might have suggested I was too nervous. There wasn't much in the way of talk, and none on tactics. There might have been one or two warnings from Bill and Eddie about Sunderland, a team near the bottom of the table, along the lines of: 'You think this is going to be easy – trust me, this ain't easy.'

The last moments ticked away. It was then that everyone wished me well, remembering how they felt in this situation. There was a knock on the door from the ref. There wasn't any checking of the boots back then. We just wore what we wore – no undershirts, gloves and all that nonsense. We stood waiting to go out, moving our legs, looking around. A buzzer went off. Game on, as Phil would say.

The good thing about being home-grown is you know every step you're taking because you've worked every inch of the place. I stepped out of the dressing room door, went on a 10-metre walk to the steps that led down, and then up a few more steps onto the pitch. The away team went out first; there wasn't enough room in the tunnel for both teams then in any case.

I came out to what was the fans' special day. They looked forward to it all week, and for some people who might only be able to come occasionally it was even more special. There was a burst of noise. Every player and fan of Tottenham in that era has that image of Mackay striding out, booting the ball miles into the air and then controlling it on his instep. That was an entrance. I was just wondering where my family was. In later years when I became established, they had season tickets so I knew exactly where they were. It was a moment then to reflect back on my family, the effort they had gone to bring me up and the help they had all given me.

Now I had to focus on the game. I wasn't worried about making mistakes. I just wanted the game to start and to play well. From Friday, having been told I might be playing, it had been a long time but this was it: it was happening. I assumed it would be all right; I'd never had a bad run, no one ever said I was in bad form. But if I'd known then it would lead to 17 years in the team, most of them as captain…

Any reflective thoughts I did have ended when the whistle blew. In those first moments it was difficult to get the ball. Sunderland were lively. I was wondering about getting my first touch and when it came it was a relief, a simple pass. But my next contribution wasn't so good. After seven minutes I controlled the ball and was looking for the easy pass that wasn't quite on. I began to veer around, having too many touches and getting pressed. Maybe they sensed a bit of weakness in a 17-year-old debutant. Eventually I laid a ball back to Pat but it was too obvious. Gordon Harris, who was in the England team in the build-up to the 1966 World Cup, nipped in and shot but Pat saved it and it went for a corner.

What had I done? But there was no panic from my teammates. 'Stevie, no problem. Come on, get on with it, defend this corner.' There was so much happening in the match that I couldn't afford to dwell on messing up. After that I played myself into the game. If it had been live on telly and 40,000 people had seen it and another four million people at

Positive reviews for my debut, despite the defeat

NIC SALUTES YOUNG STEVE

Spurs ... 0   Sunderland ... 1

OUT of this mess came a star of the future ... 17-year-old Steve Perryman.

When the last jeer had died away, Tottenham's costly stars went to him in turn and congratulated him on his successful debut.

Manager Bill Nicholson told him: "Well played, son." Said Nic: "I asked him how he felt and he said it wasn't as bad as he thought it would be.

TEMPERAMENT

"He's got a great temperament, this kid. The first time he touched the ball he could have given away a goal.

"But he didn't worry about it. He got on with

his job and worked very hard.

"He showed he was brave and he had a lot of good touches, things you can't teach a youngster.

"I'd like to keep him in, but I don't want to rush him."

Nicholson absolved one other player from blame— Perryman's midfield partner Dennis Bond. Sunderland's teenagers— especially 20-year-old Bobby Kerr—ran and ran, but on this day Spurs could have lost to anyone.

The fact that Mik England should score th goal (42 minutes) with beautiful header summ it all up. Everything w wrong for Spurs. T started badly and away.

Brian Sc

Tottenham 0, Sunderland 1
By DICK MILFORD

SPURS CHOSE an "easy" match against bottom-of-the-table Sunderland to give 17-year-old Steve Perryman his League baptism. He didn't disgrace himself. But this was far from an easy match.

A Sunderland team with plenty of their own youngsters to boast about won their Second First Division victory of the season. They did it with industry and method, and they could have won more convincingly.

But they could hardly believe their luck in meeting one of the worst Spurs sides for years. At times it looked really easy for Sunderland. The hangover of last week's thrashing at Derby lingered painfully for Spurs. They got the slow handclap even before the interval, and manager Bill Nicholson was told by barrackers in the best seats to "buy some wingers."

Sunderland won the match by an own goal headed by centre-half Mike England just before the interval.

They could have been 3—1 ahead by then. And so desperate were Spurs that they switched England to centre-forward for the whole of the second-half.

Faded

This was a bid by Nicholson to take an aerial route past the Sunderland defence that boxed in strikers Greaves and Gilze It made no differenc England got in three header but Alan Brown's defence wer still the bosses.

And behind the crowd of red shirts was that competent goalkeeper Montgomery, who saved England's third header spectacularly.

Spurs lacked midfield skill to open up Sunderland. Young Perryman hit the right passes before the interval, then faded. Bond, back after 11 months in the reserves, was their most consistent performer. Pearce has never been so disappointing. Mullery wasn't inventive enough, and Greaves and Gilzean were disarmed by the Sunderland defence.

In their programme Spurs expressed disgust at last week's hooliganism in Bedfordshire and told the rowdies: "Stay away, we don't want you."

Unfortunately, some of their sane supporters may stay away, too, if Spurs don't improve soon.
● Manager Bill Nicholson said later: "I can't remember when Spurs played successive matches without scoring."

SPURS: Jennings 6; Beal 6, England 6, Collins 5, Knowles 5; Mullery 5, Perryman 6, *BOND 8; Pearce 5, Gilzean 5, Greaves 5.
SUNDERLAND: Montgomery 7; *IRWIN 8, Heslop 6, Todd 6, Ashurst 7; McG-ven 6, Harris 6, Kerr (inj) 7; Hughes 7, Baker 7, Tueart 7. Sub.: Park.
Referee: G. Kew (Yorkshire) 6.

DEBUT for Spurs boy

'Let's play' – my
attitude was to
get on with it and
go to work

home, more of it might have stayed with me, but we didn't have that sort of coverage then, thankfully.

I had barely touched the ball, made an error that nearly led to a goal, and was gasping for air. I looked at the clock, thinking, 'How am I going to last?' But a second wind kicked in. It's why teams warm-up properly today, so that the players have got rid of their first wind and are onto their second. We never warmed up and it showed.

The rest of the game passed by in what seemed an instant, and a forgettable one at that. I remember Mike England's own goal and that we ended up with a 1–0 defeat. A home defeat for Spurs was catastrophic, especially to a team that went down that year. There was disbelief, with the players very down in the dressing room, and Mullers even had a confrontation with a trouble-making fan in the car park afterwards, which I was unaware of at the time. But no one seemed to be down on me.

I was proud. I was thinking of my nans and granddads and their pride. At that point I didn't even really consider that I was representing the supporters. I was too young to take on that responsibility just yet. I was representing my family; the crowd came later.

Sometimes in my career I've seen managers use debut players to take the stress out of the team because the team cares so much for the person making his debut that they rally around him and as a team more generally. It wasn't for lack of trying but it didn't work out that day, and the inquests were severe in the press.

Bill Nick had to think I was good enough and could cope; otherwise he wouldn't have put me in. Trusting a kid of 17 said a lot. The opinion was that despite my first mistake in the game I had recovered straight away – which is how it should be. One mistake shouldn't be two. I've always believed in never letting the crowd know that you know you've made an error. I hate seeing players who make a mistake show their anguish. That makes it a double mistake. I can't remember Bill Nick saying well done to me but as a manager you're proud that your club produces players. All of a sudden you've got an extra man to select so there were positives out of that day for Bill.

I had been blooded. Despite the defeat, I was too naive to think any negatives about myself. I was just happy that I had played and knew a bit more about what to do next time. And there *would* be a next time. I was now going to be allowed to train with the first team more and change in the home dressing room. A threshold had been crossed. I hadn't made it by any means, but I was now in the frame.

There was no chance of me cutting off contact with the youth players. Phil became their leader as he progressed into the reserves and it remained his patch. Wishbone was gone by the end of the season. They were my group too and I was not going to be thought of as a big-time Charlie. They were genuinely pleased for me and if you'd told me at 15 that two years later they were going to be delighted that I'd got into the first team, at least to my face, I'd have found that hard to believe. But I was one of them still. It would take about 50 games to be moving in first-team circles. If a first-teamer had a party there would probably be an invite but I would politely decline. I knew my place.

My place in the team persisted, however. In my third game I played at Liverpool. Someone told me that Bill Shankly said to Bill Nick after the game, 'Where did you get your tiger from?' I might not have done my job against Sunderland but by Christ I did my job perfectly at Liverpool.

It was the start of me doing 'extra' away from home because of the 'game on' atmosphere. Liverpool hadn't quite the hit the heights then but Shankly and a team of Ian St John, Ron Yeats and Tommy Smith, with Tommy Lawrence in goal and 26,000 on the Kop, provided an unforgettable test and experience.

I had played at Anfield for London Schoolboys but this was something else. Liverpool and Anfield had such an effect on me. Over the course of the years we had some incredible games but I was struck then by just how serious a football club it was, from the oldest supporter to the youngest.

There was an intensity of noise, feeling, desire and unity. I couldn't imagine any Liverpool player turning down an autograph. Before the game we stayed in the Adelphi Hotel and went to the cinema on Friday night out of habit. When we were around Liverpool it smelt of football. This was a serious game and we had to be so right in our attitude and performance. That game, a 0–0 draw, I got it right. Jimmy Greaves missed a one-on-one against Lawrence and could have put all those years of Spurs never winning at Anfield to bed years before we eventually did. But it was a decent result.

Eddie Baily's lesson to me about getting close to my opponent for 20 minutes but doing it for the whole game if need be was writ large at Liverpool. It was game on *all* game. That's what they expected from their players and that's what they got.

Over the course of a run of 18 league games I did good things in wins against Newcastle and Sheffield Wednesday. Against Newcastle I tackled Bobby Moncur and the ball popped out to the halfway line, where Jimmy Greaves got it, turned and beat about four players, rounded the keeper and walked it into the net. It was one of his greatest goals and in the papers the next day it said I made the goal. These days I'd get an assist but it was really only a tackle.

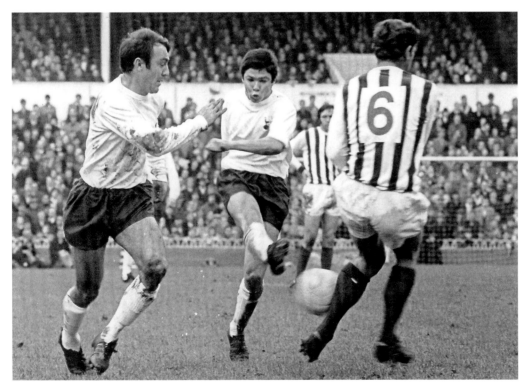

Taking a shot at goal with Jimmy Greaves and West Brom's Jeff Astle ahead of me. I'm quite pleased to see I've got my head over the ball

STICK-OUT STEVE
Gave Ron Yeats the surprise of his life

SO often does a player's car represent his status in the game. George Best and his Iso Rivolta, for instance. Or the "Jags" of Francis Lee, Colin Bell and other Manchester City players.

You'll come across the occasional Aston Martin. Even a Mercedes.

But one of Saturday's key Cup fighters, attached to one of our biggest clubs, climbs into a second-hand Wolseley after training.

Of course, Steve Perryman is only a 17-year-old beginner. But at present rate of progress, I'd say the Spurs youngster will have graduated to executive-style motoring by this time next year.

Works hard

Spurs' Cup date before an all-ticket crowd at Bradford City's Valley Parade will be Perryman's first taste of Cup warfare. He'll also be one of the youngest players taking part in the 32 ties.

But not one of the 768 men stripped for action will graft harder than this all-purpose teenager in the No. 11 shirt.

Perryman came into the Spurs side after that crushing 5-0 defeat at Derby—"And has done really well," says skipper Alan Mullery. "He gets through a tremen-

dous amount of work."

Manager Bill Nicholson is on record as saying of Perryman, "Th's boy has shown some of our established players a thing or two about work-rate."

This from two football characters who are so demanding in their approach to the game—Nicholson, a manager who never gives praise lightly; Mullery, a mid-field man who never fails to cover every blade of grass.

Perryman, born at Ealing, joined Spurs as an apprentice professional in July 1967. Was a surprise addition to the first-team squad that toured the United States and Canada last close season. Made a tremendous impression.

Only thing old-fashioned about him is his crew-cut. Still, in spite of Georgie Best, it seems a haircut more in keeping with an up-and-comer.

A growing 5 ft. 7½ ins., Steve himself is unaffected

STEVE PERRYMAN — a dream come true.

by suddenly being thrust into the First Division limelight.

"I always dreamed of playing with people like Jimmy Greaves and Alan

Gilzean," he says. "I'm enjoying every minute of it. Get plenty of encouragement from players like Alan Mullery."

The Spurs fans can be very critical of a side that is not doing well — perhaps because they have been spoiled in the past. But no one gets on to young Perryman. Probably it's because of his will-to-win attitude.

Anticipation

Bill Nicholson cites a case in point—against two of the Liverpool giants at Anfield. "I've never seen anyone so surprised as Ron Yeats was when he was tackled by Steve. This was directly after he had dived in to tackle Tommy Smith."

Young players often "show" for two or three games, then drift out for a spell. Not Perryman.

To really assess what he is putting into a game, you must watch Perryman closely. He shields the ball like a natural player. Is not obvious with his passes. He anticipates moves by the opposition.

Of course, he still has a lot to learn. But playing against Bradford City in the Cup on Saturday will help put an old head on young shoulders.

Further praise, this time for my performance against Liverpool

We beat West Brom but then lost against Man United. This was the big English game of the season. It was Best, Law and Charlton against Greaves, Gilzean and Jennings, Busby versus Bill Nick, the two 5–1 games in 1965 and all that. They were a major team with huge support, with 53,000 roaring them on at Old Trafford. Waves of attack came at you. There was a distinct glamour about both clubs – that was the game everyone wanted to see, and I was now part of it, and having to face George Best.

I'd seen him first-hand in the FA Cup replay of 1968. There was a moment then when Best got in from the halfway line and was one-on-one with Pat, and Pat stopped him scoring. It was pure theatre. The whole ground stood up.

Best was reaching the heights at this time as the first football superstar. Bobby Charlton was always a big name but, because of his youth, looks and the aura surrounding him, Best represented a coming-together of the pop and football worlds. If you were working-class and successful then it was usually either in showbiz or football. He was in both camps.

Playing against him was astonishing. You couldn't sell yourself against Best because he could just take you. He was so lithe and could twist his body like no other player. He'd wait for you and then woosh – gone. I never won a tackle against him. I might have won a loose ball that wasn't meant for either of us, but I remember thinking, 'Put your foot in there and he's gone.'

He gave the impression he resisted discipline, like he was a player out on his own. There was always the narrative of the more acceptable brilliance of Charlton jarring against the flamboyant brilliance of Best. When we played against them we were always looking for signs of uneasiness or needle between them, though there never was.

After United, we lost at Coventry away which was one of the first English matches beamed live to Scandinavia. I ended up meeting the man responsible for it, Lars-Gunnar Björklund. He was a Spurs fan who worked for a company called Tips Extra, a pools company in Sweden, and his idea was to take one live game every Saturday. It must have been a deal with Midlands TV because it was always a game from that region, and usually seemed to involve us so it helped make my name in Scandinavia, which would be important for the future.

Back in 1969–70 I was getting a rapid introduction to the top flight. We lost 2–0 at home to West Ham, and I was made aware of the London derby edge. We faced Crystal Palace on Boxing Day and I recorded the next marker in my progress when I scored my first goal. I played a one-two on the edge of the box and ran on to finish. It was a Tottenham-taught goal – pass and move.

Challenging – fairly – the great Bobby Charlton. I was so respectful of him. I was now playing with and against true legends of the game, the real icons

We got Palace in the FA Cup a month later, but it ended much more unhappily, as we lost a replay at Selhurst Park. That defeat was pivotal and prompted big changes. Gilly, Knowlesy, Kinnear and Greaves were dropped, as was I. Without me and the others, we got a 1–1 against reigning champions Leeds, with a young, virtually reserve team that included the returning Want and Pratty, Bond and Ray Evans. Leeds finished second that season and were a proper team so that was a good result.

Still, I'd had a very good run. Bill Nick explained my absence by saying he was resting me. He didn't hold me in any way responsible for that Palace defeat, whereas he was critical of the others, and publicly, which was rare for him to be. The supporters always knew when Bill wasn't happy with a performance.

I went back to playing for the reserves and in the important youth games. I trusted absolutely that Bill was telling the truth that he was resting me and I didn't feel embarrassed that I was out of the team. In the meantime, pretty momentous moves were taking place. Jimmy Greaves never got back in the side and was transferred to West Ham, with Martin Peters coming the other way.

Jimmy was always great with me and was adored by the fans, for whom he couldn't do anything wrong, but I thought Eddie had something against him. That came through in meetings. Jimmy had only just turned 30. I don't know what was happening behind the scenes and if his drinking problems played a part, but it felt like he was being singled out for criticism.

It came to a head earlier in January in the third round of the FA Cup at Bradford City, which had banana skin written all over it. We drew there 2–2 and I gave the ball away for their first goal. At half-time, Bill Nick kept making a play of it, saying, 'Jim, make an angle!' I'd tried to nutmeg

A report of my first ever goal, scored against Crystal Palace on Boxing Day 1969

THE SUN, Saturday, December 27, 1969

SUN Sport

LONDON'S TWO WHIZZ KIDS TURN ON A GOALDEN SHOW

NO wonder they call them the whizz kids, Steve Perryman (left) gives Crystal Palace no Christmas cheer as he shoots the second goal in Spurs' 2-0 win. And Southampton's Eric Martin (right) doesn't seem to know if it's Boxing Day or Good Friday as Ian Hutchinson scores his second to help Chelsea to a 3-1 victory. Yes, Perryman and Hutchinson should silence those Northern knockers.

a player to get the ball to Jim so Bill Nick wasn't going to criticise me for it because at that point I think the sun was shining out of my arse. In Bill's opinion it must have been Jim's fault. He mentioned it about four times until Jim stood up and said, 'Steve, don't try any more clever gear, because it gets me a bollocking!'

That was Jim's humour, which didn't always go down well. Friday team meetings were getting longer as the inquests into our poor form continued. After 90 minutes, maybe two hours, it seemed Bill always looked at Jim and said, 'Anything to say?'

Jim would reply, 'Bill, it's all right you talking to us, but really, you can either play or you can't play. All this talking isn't doing us any good.'

Bill would get agitated and tell him on the spur of the moment, 'Ah, off you go then!' But Jimmy really did go. Thirty years later, Jimmy and I were at a fans' Q&A event and I was asked why I chose Spurs. I mentioned that West Ham wanted me, and Jimmy said, 'I played for West Ham and for Spurs. You made the right decision, Steve, trust me – because West Ham was a fucking holiday camp.'

My first game back was against Everton away in the new year, where we lost 3–2. They were champions that season with the Holy Trinity of Ball, Kendall and Harvey. Goodison, with its triple-decker main stand, was another jaw-dropping sight. It was also the first time I crossed midfield swords with Alan Ball, who said to me during that game, 'If your team ever wins anything son, I'll eat my hat.'

I stayed in the team for most of the rest of that season. I'd been lucky with my fitness. I played in the rearranged home game against Everton that was abandoned at 0–0 due to floodlight failure. Initially that game was supposed to be played in November. The day of that game, I woke up feeling ill and my mum rang Bill to say I wasn't fit. Bill Nick said to put me back to bed, and see how I felt in an hour. By then it started snowing. By the time that hour was up Bill rang to say, 'Don't worry Mrs Perryman, the game won't be played.' That fixture seemed cursed – Peter Collins got injured in the rearranged game, was stretchered off and never really recovered.

We got revenge over Manchester United in the penultimate game of the season. They fielded Carlo Sartori that day, an Italian raised in Manchester, and they were going through some troubles themselves. John Fitzpatrick and Denis Law had a fallout while Gilly and Chivers scored, a foretaste of the brilliant strike partnership they were going to forge now that Jimmy had gone.

As for me, I was pleased with my season's work. The crowd had responded to my energy and industry. The fact that I played with my sleeves rolled up – because the sleeves were too long for me – and had a short haircut probably helped. I've read that I came across as 'pugnacious'. All of a sudden an image started to appear. Skinheads and suedeheads started around that time so I was seen as one of the new breed.

It all left me shattered physically. I'd crash out on the settee at home for at least an hour after training and games. No one told me to do it; I just needed it. Your body is your best messenger. Food, drink, sleep, your body tells you what it needs. I listened to my body and it helped me to play so many games.

I sometimes watch matches now and think, 'Why is that player walking?' I never walked, unless there was an extended break in play. I was on the move the whole time because the ball changes position the whole time, therefore you have to adjust your position. You have to be thinking, 'What do I think will happen next?' and that affects how and where you move to in preparation.

I would come off the pitch absolutely spent, taking up to half an hour before I even got in the shower. I wasn't the type to go out or have a drink. My absolute focus was staying in the team and doing as well as I could and I needed a fit and rested body to do that.

That was brought into even sharper relief by me playing in the FA Youth Cup campaign that season when first-team duties allowed, as I was still eligible to play youth football. Pat Welton's influence started to be felt and the side made very good progress. I think it won every tournament that year other than a Southern Junior Floodlit Cup defeat to Colchester – the kind of shock that can happen at any level.

There was one particular day when I was in the first team but was withdrawn to be sub for the youth team, only no one told me. After a few

> "Alan Ball said to me during the game, 'If your team ever wins anything son, I'll eat my hat'"

In the muck and bullets challenging Alan Whittle of Everton, with Tony Want beside me and Alan Ball on the right

Competing for the youth team against Coventry (left) and lining up with the FA Youth Cup-winning side (right) – Bill Nick said he didn't like the length of our hair!

rushed phone calls and a frantic drive to get to the game, when I arrived the youths were losing 2–0. I came on and we won 3–2. I wasn't really the type of player that could turn a game, but it looked as if I had. It added to my reputation.

It was a good team with fine players: Barry Daines, Mike 'Matt' Dillon (nicknamed after the TV character in *Gunsmoke*), Ray Clarke who went on to play for Ajax, Phil Holder, Bobby Wiles and Brian Turner from Australia, called 'Bluey'. Billy Edwards ended up playing for Wimbledon and Bobby Almond played for New Zealand in the 1982 World Cup. John Oliver was a fast right-winger; Mike Flanagan was an amateur that Spurs decided not to take on as a pro but who did very good things at Charlton and Palace. Eddie Jones, Ron Gilson, and Joe Peck were all local boys. And of course there was Graeme Souness. He had played for Scotland Schoolboys against England at Tottenham, which would have confirmed his promise and led to Spurs signing him. We all knew he was a good player, and he had a sort of superior character about him. It was based on technical ability not raw competitiveness, but he was a player then who was kicked rather than one who did the kicking. I think he learned to become a hard man at Middlesbrough from Bobby Murdoch, the former Celtic midfielder who once sorted out Leeds in the European Cup. Jack Charlton was in charge up there as well. With him you had to pull your weight. It's unfair to say Souness was just a hard man because he was very skilful and talented. Toughening up added that vital ingredient that would turn him into a European Cup winner.

There is some regret for Spurs that Graeme didn't come through because of the player he became. He had a style about him as a player and a person. He would have outskilled me whereas I was probably playing a more aggressive game that suggested I was ready for senior football earlier. I was a year older so I was more developed, but I broke in first because the gap was there to break into. Graeme didn't have that gap and the more he couldn't break in the more frustrated he got. He probably thought the coaches didn't respect his ability by not taking the ultimate step of putting him in the team.

Bill Nick used to explain to him, 'Perryman works too hard compared to you, and Mullery and now Peters – two England internationals – are ahead of you. How are you going to break into the team?'

Bill in effect was encouraging Souness to be patient, but Graeme may never have felt that was made clear to him. In the end he wanted to get away. By the time we were leading players for Spurs and Liverpool we lined up against each other but never really in an individual battle, out of respect.

Our youth team played good football at this time. I played against Ipswich one day and Brian Talbot was man-marking me. I wasn't the type of player to warrant being man-marked. I said to him, 'Are you a mug or what? Why are you following me around?'

'Because it's my job. It's what I've been told to do.'

'You must be stupid. While you're standing with me here, we're killing you over there.'

The quality we had got us to the FA Youth Cup Final. This was a big deal, as we had never won it before and it was a chance to prove that the club's focus on home-grown players had credibility. It actually took us three games, including two replays, to beat a Coventry side in which David Icke was goalkeeper. I wonder what happened to him?

Those games were hard. Everyone expected the world from me. I gave it my full effort, but I couldn't always quite produce what I'd just produced in the first team. Youth-team football should be easy, right? Wrong. Sometimes it's easier to play against better players. I was being judged in a different way. If I put my foot into a challenge with the youth team, people would think: 'So what? Of course he does, he's a first-team player.'

Crowds had built up as we progressed. Fans were reading about it in the match programme every week. Spurs supporters were clever enough to know that if they watched a youth-team game they would be watching the possibles of the future. We eventually won the second replay 1–0, a great achievement and a fantastic honour for a really good bunch of lads. But by then I was seen by some not just as a possible future first-team player, but a probable one.

One of my favourite articles, in which I am compared to Danny Blanchflower, no less (right). The intro at the top is a bit misleading – Bill Nick meant I was reliable and that I had the anticipation of Danny, not that I was the new version of him, even if some fans might have been saying it – but it was high praise indeed. Bill also made reference to a 'more colourful player'. This was Graeme Souness, though he didn't mention him by name

A full-page image from *Goal* magazine (opposite), showing me doing what I did: challenging for the ball, which I was brought into the side to do and which the crowd seemed to respond to

SOCCER IN ACTION

SO far this series has told you about the £100,000 players of today. Today Spurs' manager Bill Nicholson, in an interview with Steve Richards, talks about a star of tomorrow —Steve Perryman (pictured right), the 17-year-old White Hart Lane star fans are already calling the new Danny Blanchflower.

Spurs' Mr Reliable is just 17

By BILL NICHOLSON

STEVE PERRYMAN is still 17. I decided to make him a First Division player when Spurs were hardly threatening to be the best team in the country.

They're still not — but Perryman remains in the side. The reason for this is simple enough.

He is establishing himself as a first-team player. He has yet to dig out a path of personal glory for himself. He hasn't captured the public imagination with any special brilliance.

Early

You couldn't say he was going to be another George Best, or anyone nearly as spectacular in style. He is —at this early stage of his development — a reliable player.

I stress the word RELIABLE because this is so vital in a youngster's make-up.

I have got a far more colourful player still waiting to get into the First Division. With a sway of either shoulder he can send two defenders the wrong way and take the ball between them.

But, as yet, he isn't ready. Perryman is.

Perryman, who comes from Ealing, is completely unspoiled and we are hoping he will stay that way. He is a steadying influence for us. He has got a certain efficiency, enough skill, in my opinion, and is basically accurate in what he does.

He has control and the intelligence not to try ridiculously risky passes. He prefers the simple way. He paces his passes. He times them.

This is so important in the art of distribution. He anticipates the game. As some would put it, he reads it. As a link man, he moves up in anticipation. He moves back after perceiving a situation.

In this respect, he helps to make up for a certain lack of speed in his running. He is like Danny Blanchflower in this way. He is always ready.

He starts to move before the other man (the opponent) and usually reaches his destination first because of this anticipation. I am not saying that Perryman is another Blanchflower.

He hasn't got the imagination of Danny, who was a master of the unexpected. Blanchflower used to conceal his intended passes. But Perryman is doing this to a certain extent.

Unfair

After all, he is only 17 and a serious comparison is unfair to him. It is all the more to his credit that he can be likened to Danny in some aspects of the game.

Perryman is a good trainer who enjoys work. In fact, his appetite for football is difficult to satisfy.

Some have already predicted that he will be in the full England side in five years. I am not inclined to make such forecasts about beginners.

I am sure that he will become a consistently good club man if he hasn't already. You see, as I said, he is so **RELIABLE.**

GOAL

STEVE PERRYMAN
Spurs

GERRY YOUNG
Sheffield Wednesday

The Spurs boy who does a man's job

KEN MONTGOMERY says he's a bright star at seventeen

SO STEVE HAS WON HIS SPURS

JIMMY GREAVES, deservedly, got all the praise, mine included, for his majestic two-goal blitz on Newcastle United last Saturday.

Yet as the Geordies left White Hart Lane, their talk was not of goal genius Greaves. "Who's the little perisher in the number 11 shirt?" they asked. "He can play a bit."

For the benefit of almost all but the Tottenham faithful, let me introduce the "little perisher."

He looks more like a choirboy than a professional footballer. And he has an appetite for overtime work in midfield.

Steve Perryman is the name. Five feet eight inches and 10 ½ st. of football promise. He could become the best thing to hit the London Soccer scene this season.

Talk about it Tottenham and the mind automatically registers big-money buys like Greaves, Alan Gilzean, Martin Chivers, Roger Morgan, Mike England, Alan Mullery, etc. etc. etc.

Home-grown winners have been few and far between at White Hart Lane in recent years.

Yet, while these are early days in the Football League career of youngster Stephen Perryman, more people than manager Bill Nicholson will be disappointed if the little lad from Ealing doesn't become a very big footballing name.

The one-time England schoolboy international, chased by every top club in London, and by Manchester United is relatively unknown to the Soccer masses.

After all, he has played in only a handful of First Division matches.

Many miles from home

Steve's Tottenham debut was made against West Ham, complete with World Cup trio Bobby Moore, Geoff Hurst and Martin Peters.

Nothing unusual in that? Not at face value. But the match was played 3,148 miles from White Hart Lane, in Baltimore, Maryland, USA.

Tell me of another player who has made his debut in a London derby so many miles from home.

The game was back in mid-May, on Tottenham's close-season tour of America and Canada.

Spurs manager Bill Nicholson surprised many people by naming the former Ealing schoolboy in their tour party.

Awful lot of modesty

"I was amazed when the boss put a list of twenty players on the board, with my name among them," Steve recalls.

"I had only played twelve reserve-team matches. I knew that the party was to be set to sixteen, and assumed that I would be one of the unlucky four.

"Then, two days before we flew out, Mr. Nicholson told me to get my bags packed. I was in."

Even then, this youth.

Florentina of Italy in Toronto, and although we lost 3—0, I was kept in for the final game against Glasgow Rangers, which we won 4—3.

That four-match tour was the launching of a League career which has been equally short but successful.

Bill Nicholson is not a man to lavish extravagant praise on any of his players, whether £100,000 star or a £7 staff boy.

Yet he obvious tremendous respect the Perryman p

Tremendous tackler

Last Wednesday, after a gruelling training spell at Cheshunt, Nicholson told me: "For a little 'un, he has got tremendous guts, and a natural aptitude for the game. He is a

_____ tackler and

_____ just as quietly as he in-troduced him to the big-time in the first place.

And I doubt very much if this level-headed lad will complain.

Nicholson's _____ Yorkshire summing up of his most promising find for seasons simple. 'He has his head _____ the right wa

Level

te

Exam _____ been _____ played _____ every _____ and _____ all _____ read

he ___

to ___

_____ of ever-

SOCCER STAR, April 3, 1970

---

18   MANCHESTER EVENING NEWS, Friday, Nov. 21, 1969

in town tomorrow

ANOTHER DANNY ON THE WAY UP

SPURS ARE the big spenders of the past few seasons: the pace-setters in the ever-spiralling transfer market. But things could be different in the future.

For Spurs are quietly launching a crop of home-bred youngsters and some of these new starlets can be seen in action against Manchester United at Old Trafford tomorrow.

He is slim, 17-year-old, London-born Steve Perryman, who brightened the club's long-awaited revival.

Bill Nicholson predicts is going to play a major part in the club's long-awaited revival.

Perryman was thrown into the First team nine games ago. Since then he has proved he is there to stay.

11 jersey he is marked down as a great midfield prospect. The form of Perryman but when to keep playing him only played him in the No

Steve Perryman, one of a crop of home-bred youngsters who is being groomed to play a major part in a partnership Spurs hope will be as successful as the Dave Mackay-Danny Blanchflower one

By David Meek

_____ Division _____ out of _____ in the _____ keeps coming back _____ fact he has played 25 _____ the last _____ junior _____ trials _____ reported to _____

"He is remarkably strong for his age and doesn't know what it means to be beaten. His play just moves so mature it is hard to accept that in three years' time he will still be only twenty.

Spurs are grooming Perryman to team up with another young Spurs Hart Lane discovery, 16-year-old Graeme Souness.

Not long ago, but Nicholson is already comparing him even now to Dave Mackay-Danny Blanchflower one. Perryman, international and got his firs

Confident

"When Souness is ready for the first team I'm sure many people will note the uncanny likeness to Mackay," says Nicholson.

"Everybody at Spurs is confident the emergence of _____ years could see _____ the next couple of _____ partnership _____ as successful _____ every bit as _____

when he travelled with Spurs to America last close season. He played in four games and was an outstanding success. But he had to wait until the end of September to make his League debut against Sunderland."

No one, not even his manager, forecast a long run for him, but his strong, decisive play and flourish lacking has kept him in the side.

It is no exaggeration to say this teenager has been the only unquali-

fied success of this astonishing season, and it is coincidence that side, and it is that since his arrival in the team Spurs have lost only twice. They will be the harder for Manchester United to beat tomorrow.

Come on Steve is Spurs' hope for a winner

Spurs star in embryo

RIGHT up until Tottenham signed West Ham's Martin Peters in exchange for Jimmy Greaves, plus a cash adjustment, the Spurs were reported to being interested in Peter Marinello (£100,000-plus class and a terrific asset to Tottenham, or come to that, any club, yet a player who cost nothing when he joined looks set to become a Tottenham star in a year or two.

He is Steve Perryman, a Spur since he left school in 1967. Ealing-born Perryman won almost every honour in boys' soccer playing for Eal-

ing, London, Middlesex and England. Among the players with whom he played the England Boys are Dick Pitt (Sunderland), Len Cantello (West Bromwich), Tommy Taylor (Orient) and Tony Towers (Manchester City).

Tottenham must thank Charles Faulkner, their chief scout, for signing Perryman for it was he who spotted the boy's promise and Faulkner lost no time in recommending the player to Tottenham — he knew he had to move quickly or other clubs would have been after him. It did not take Tottenham long to realise Perryman was the type who would make the grade, and that is how Tottenham came to sign him.

With such an array as Tottenham have, youngsters are apt to get overlooked as far as the Press is concerned and there was little news of Perryman until this season, and although a season is a proving for him. He won his first Youth cap, playing away against the Republic of Ire-land and is now a key-man

in the national Youth side. Later came his first Division 1 match, one which all Spurs' supporters will recall for it proved one of the upsets of the season — Sunderland visiting White Hart Lane on September 27 and winning through the only goal of the match, only their second victory of the season.

However, Perryman, playing outside-left, did well, so well in fact, that he held the position for several matches and besides playing on the wing also played inside-left, and when he did return to the reserves it was not because of any loss of form or poor performances, but because manager Bill Nicholson decided to rest the youngster who has beginning to come in for some "stick".

His ball-play is fast developing and his tenacity, never accepting defeat, always fighting for the ball and the way he sticks to his task has made him a big favourite with Tottenham fans, as well as being recognised in soccer circles as a youngster who will develop into a really classy player.

Although Perry is just starting his career he has already played in eight other countries — Eire, Northern Ireland, Wales, Scotland, United States, Canada, Hol-

land and West Germany and enjoys watching football, especially if his younger brothers are playing and he watches them whenever he can.

Perryman has played in over half Tottenham's first team games this season, and looks set to make a first team place his own in a year or two.

TWENTY-TWO

STEVE PERRYMAN

STARMAN STEVE

Young Steve Perryman turned in star-man performances against both West Ham and Coventry.

STEVE PERRYMAN

Spurs new ace finds that even the big-name stars also make mistakes

STEVE PERRYMAN for Munich '74 is a suggestion with which few would argue. But while the Soccer world raves about the prospects of Spurs' finest find, the kid everyone wants to see remains oblivious to all the shouting around him.

Mention Munich to Perryman and you draw an immediate blank. He even talks of it as though he had never heard of the World Cup.

"Munich? I've never thought about it," he told me. "I have to play for this season. I want to establish myself at Tottenham this year. Right now I'm

by ERIC NICHOLLS

not looking any further than that."

It is this genuine modesty, this realisation that he is still learning his trade, that will help him to become the star his fellow professionals and his believe he will be.

His work-rate is beyond question, his skills superb and his attitude to the game beyond reproach.

GRATITUDE

But all the time he was striding towards an obvious bright future through his early days with Middlesex and London Boys, he demanded nothing and expected less.

Says Steve: "I didn't know what I wanted to do. I enjoyed my football, but I didn't give it a thought that I might become a professional until I played for England.

"Then I noticed scouts at matches and it all happened from there. It was a good way out really, because I still don't know what other job I would have gone into."

Stardom hasn't changed him. He still talks with gratitude of those who have helped him and shows a perception beyond his 18 years when he speaks of the big-name players.

Steve spent his last year as an apprentice being guided by former England youth manager Pat Welton and the young Spur says: "All our training under Pat has specialised. This way everybody got help.

ORDINARY

"I really learned a lot from Pat and I think everybody here realises what a good job he is doing for the club."

And Steve's feet were just as firmly on the ground when he stepped out to join his more famous colleagues as a first-team player.

"Names didn't worry me," he says. "They're big names to people outside, but when you are training with them you know them as ordinary fellows. They can make mistakes, too."

The progress Steve has made sends Bill Nicholson, his normally reticent manager, into raptures.

The Spurs boss who almost had second thoughts about signing the young Perryman because he felt he might be too small to make the grade, says now: "I'm delighted with Steve's progress. He hasn't grown much taller, but he has certainly grown up in the football sense."

And Alan Mullery, the skipper who, Perryman says, "coaxes us along," is just as generous in his praise: "Steve's work-rate is phenomenal. He never stops running and finds some great positions."

Martin Peters, who should know what it takes to earn a place in Sir Alf Ramsey's note-book says: "Steve's going to be one of England's great players. He is always buzzing."

ELUSIVE

The unflappable Perryman has shown all the qualities of stardom as Spurs struggled through their early season games, reaching desperately for the mantle of greatness that still eludes them.

But the signs were already there when he made his first-team debut on the summer tour of Canada and the United States last year. They were still there when he scored his first League goal for the club last Boxing Day.

He may stand little more than 5 ft. 7 in. He may have yet to top 10 st. on the scales. But if character is second only to ability in the making of great players, I hope he never changes.

STEVE PERRYMAN . . . unspoiled by star treatment

Coverage of my first season

STARS OF THE FUTURE

by JASON TOMAS

STEVE PERRYMAN

SOCCER STARS OF THE '70s

On the threshold of 1970 stand the up-and-coming stars of England . . . the boys with golden feet who will take over from the Mexico World Cup squad for Munich in 1974.

Who are they? The Sketch team of soccer writers tell you in a powerful series that will mark your card for the Seventies.

Today we introduce London's Pride, 18 - year - old Charlie George, of Arsenal, and Steve Perryman, Spurs' brilliant 17-old.

Both are on the fringe of Under-23 honours and both should head for full England places.

✻ STARBOUND ✻

STEVE PERRYMAN
SPURS

★ STEVE PERRYMAN . . . shook Ron Yeats

Steve in action with Wolves' Mike O'Grady

PERRYMAN—KID WHO JUST LOVES WORK

STEVE PERRYMAN looks just like the kids who stand on the North Bank at White Hart-lane — hair cut short, face white, eyes eagerly looking around.

This alertness shows on the field. He's always looking for the ball. Always running. Always fighting.

As Spurs manager Bill Nicholson says: "This boy has shown some of the established players a thing or two about work rate.

"He's never worried if he makes a mistake — and at his age he's entitled to make a few mistakes.

"He's as game as they come. I shall always remember the look on Ron Yeats's face

when Steve slid him at Anfield. That was right after he had dived in to tackle Tommy Smith.

"I ask you—a kid of 17, only ten stone, throwing himself in against those two!

In low

"Steve gets in low on the tackle and he uses all his weight. This is what I want from a mid-field player — someone who can win the ball as well as use it.

"He's got this skill of taking a pass and shield-

ing it in the same movement. You can see he's got a great future by the way he gets out of trouble sometimes.

"I brought him into the side sooner than I intended. His form has been so good I can't rest him. He plays in all our youth games and England Youth games and trials—four matches a week sometimes, but he never asks to miss anything."

Perryman himself is just about waking up to what has happened to him—a rise from the apprentice ranks to the

First Division in two years.

"I always dreamed of playing with Greavsie, Gilly and the rest," he says. "I'm enjoying every minute of it and I gets lots of encouragement from people like Alan Mullery. The fans are very fair to me, too."

Says skipper Mullery: "His work rate is tremendous. He never stops running and finds some great positions."

Has graft

Little Steve—he's 5ft. 7in. tall—has the graft that Sir Alf Ramsey demands.

I wouldn't be surprised to see him taking over from Alan Mullery in the 1974 World Cup!

fields behind the Perryman house.

Skipper Alan Mullery says: 'He is always on the go and this will make up for the fact that he is not very quick. If he lacks anything it is pace — but he has played well and is perpetual motion. He will get to places other people can't. He's not a Jimmy Robertson for pace — who is? but Bill Nicholson has faith in him and it is easy to see why.

Standards

Spurs set their standards higher than most. The aim is Europe and a place at the top — which is a compliment to a 17 year-old who can hold down a place.

'It is easier for teams lower down to take more chances and play youngsters early,' says Eddie Bailey.

'We have to test youngsters because we have always set the highest standards. We think Steve Perryman will be OK.'

Spurs lost 1-0 at home to bottom-of-the-table Sunderland on Perryman's First Division debut, but he held his place alongside Jimmy Greaves and Alan Gilzean.

Bill Nicholson, a man who chooses his words carefully, spoke up for Perryman's promise at the after-match Press conference.

Spurs boast internationals and players who cost six-figure fees. Young Perryman has the backing of one of the shrewdest managers in the game in his bid for a regular place alongside them.

EVE SETS UT FOR STARDOM

There was an article in the March issue about David Pleat (Player Parade) where you asked if there was another player in the world who could emulate his junior achievements of five appearances for England schoolboys.

Steve Perryman, Spurs 18-years-old midfield starlet, made five appearances for the English schools side — some as skipper — and already has made an England Youth team appearance.

I hope that, unlike Pleat, Steve can break into top stardom.

The way he shaped when Manager Bill Nicholson brought him into the side this

season makes this seem more of a certainty than a possibility.
— Stephen Lovelock, E. Dereham, Norfolk.

STEVE PERRYMAN

Fame at his feet

BRENTFORD reject at 13, first-team player with illustrious Spurs only four years later.

That is the remarkable story of Steven Perryman who is endearing himself to the critical clientele at white Hart Lane.

The irony of that sequence of events must now pain Brentford more than it does Steven who lives in Bancroft Court, Northolt.

Not that Steven ever let that early disappointment sap his confidence or determination.

He says calmly: "I had a trial with them. They didn't ask me back. But it's nothing to be turned down at 13."

His First Division baptism came against Sunderland. Spurs lost 1-0 but Steven's tenacity and intelligent dis-

tribution were widely acclaimed.

"I was very disappointed we lost on my debut. But we were going through a very bad spell after a 5-0 defeat at Derby," he said.

Stevens orders are to patrol the right of the midfield: "I have to blot out the opposition's mid-field men," he says. "Keep them out and once we've got them under the thumb then is the time for me to start to come forward.

"Midfield is an exhausting position in any kind of football at school (Eliots Green Grammar, Northolt) I played inside forward. "I never used to bother about defence. Now I have got to go and win the ball."

His appetite for top-grade football determined Steven to leave school before he had taken any 'O' levels.

"The masters tried to persuade me to stay on. They told me only one in a hundred make it. But I thought I was better qualified at football than anything else."

So with several clubs — including West Ham and Queens Park Rangers — clamouring for his signature he joined Spurs as an apprentice professional.

Eighteen months later — in January — he signed professional forms and since then his career has advanced at breakneck speed.

In the summer after about only 12 reserve team games Steven was selected for Spurs American tour.

His performances in the tour games were so impressive that now it was only a matter of time before Bill Nicholson, Spurs manager, launched him in the First Division.

His only regret after the tour was: "I wish Steven was two years older."

But six months later he gave him his chance in the Sunderland game.

Steven has since displayed a mature blend of combative and creative play. And he appears to be blessed with an even temperament — an invaluable

commodity in the atmosphere of today's First Division games.

With the tendency of managers to nurse their young players gradually into the First Division Bill Nicholson has proved how highly he esteems Steven by keeping him in the first team since his debut.

Steven is not 18 until December. He is a member of the England Youth Squad which has now been whittled down to 30 players.

This season he has played in Spurs youth, reserve and first teams.

It is a record which will take a lot to beat.

In our picture, Steven heads a ball at his home in Northolt.

GAME ON

As a very young kid I played hopscotch a bit. On the journey to school I kicked a stone along the pavement. I ran everywhere, jumped on and off walls, even ran backwards just to do something different. I was a child doing what children did, without any thought whatsoever that it would stand me in good stead later in life. But it built up my fitness and strength from an early age.

That physical fitness was fundamental to my success as a footballer and the longevity of my career. In the 1970–71 season I played the full 42 league games and all but two of 16 cup matches. That was the proper start of a long run of appearances that enabled me to set the record of 866 games for Tottenham Hotspur.

Out of 17 seasons I completed the full 42 league games eight times. I played 40-plus for about 12 of them. I just didn't miss games. That was something to do with my consistency and the trust that Bill Nick and other managers had in me over the course of time.

Not getting injured made me available for consistent selection. There was an element of luck about that. For instance, being injured or carrying a knock when there wasn't a midweek game that I might have missed, and so I had time to recover for Saturday. My height and technique also helped. Because I'm not tall I have a low centre of gravity and so I tackled 'low'. Thus, when challenging for the ball my whole body was behind it. Therefore my knees were not exposed in the way they would have been if I was taller.

But perhaps the main reason why I played game after game was my attitude. I have a high pain threshold, coupled with a very strong desire to play and train – if I missed either, I felt guilty. Added to that I would willingly tell a physio or doctor if I had any physical problems, and take on board their advice. I saw players ignore an injury or keep it quiet, to their and the team's cost, because they broke down in training or a game and were out for longer. My feeling was that if I let the experts know about a niggle or a strain I was sharing the problem, and that made it easier to deal with.

It was also to do with the way I played. From the moment I got in the first team I brought energy and work-rate. I probably had about 18 months where I can't remember doing one thing wrong apart from what was virtually my first touch in the Sunderland game. I got into the team because the rest of them were footballers who could all use the ball but no one could really get hold of it and just give it to someone else to play like I did. Of course the defenders could tackle, Alan Mullery worked very hard and Pat

"I probably had about 18 months where I can't remember doing one thing wrong apart from what was virtually my first touch in the Sunderland game"

Jennings could save it, but in the midfield that simple quality was lacking. I fulfilled a need. It turned into my role; I was doing very well at it and I got better at it.

Bill Nick clearly liked me. I was still only 18 at the start of the 1970–71 season and he must have been feeling protective. I found out from my family some time later that Bill had arranged for Wally Barnes, the ex-Arsenal and Wales player who was at the BBC, to act like an agent for me. Not in the modern sense but more by keeping an eye out for me. Nothing occurred to warrant his guidance – any kind of approaches from people with commercial ideas that were not appropriate for a kid my age, for example. It was probably just an insurance policy from Bill trying to protect me and the club.

That thinking might have stemmed from Bill knowing about the five grand I'd been offered by QPR, and that in the increasingly cut-throat world of professional football, how that might be used against me if it came out. I would have been completely blameless, but it would have created a story and potentially some controversy in the press. I always considered that Bill gave me a little bit more than an even break. I wasn't mollycoddled – far from it – but in his own discreet way he took a bit more care of me. What he really valued was how I played.

I was now firmly part of the first-team set-up. Training was taken by Eddie, who I warmed to more and more. It helped that skills-wise he was as good as anyone. He was a little roly-poly but he could hit the ball beautifully, even at his age. He would run a little routine in the ball court. 'What I want you to do is this: I want the ball moving a little bit. Now, you're going to

A team photo from the August 1970 pre-season game in Spain against FC Cologne, in which I had to face off against the great Wolfgang Overath

TOTTENHAM HOTSPUR

Staand v.l.n.r. Martin Chivers, Roger Morgan, Phil Beal, Pat Jennings, Martin Peters en Mike England. Geknield v.l.n.r. Alan Gilzean, Alan Mullery, Johnny Pearce,

chip it onto that line' – pointing to a line drawn on the wall – 'and it's going to come back and on the second bounce you're going to hit it with a straight half-volley into the circle', indicating one drawn a bit further along the wall.

'Show us then, Ed,' said someone, to a few sniggers. We were all thinking, 'Yeah, Ed, let's see you try.' And guess what: he hit it dead on the line, second bounce, straight into the circle. He turned to us, without a word but with his arms open as if to say, 'See? That's how it's done.' And then he would say, 'How many England caps did I get again?'

He was great. In fact everyone at the club was good as gold. There was nothing flash about any of my teammates. They were proper, proper people, from front to back.

Pat Jennings was by this time looking like the best in the world. Pat unusually missed two games that season so Ken Hancock came in, but Jennings was *the* man. We finished with 33 league goals against us that season, fourth best in the division, and Pat was a major factor why. I always say that Pat could have played outfield. He had an athleticism, and such a leap. We had a physical exercise where you had to jump from a standing start on to the top of gym benches placed on top of each other. Most of us could only manage three benches high but Pat could do four, easy. The span of his legs was unbelievable. When I thought someone was certain to score Pat's legs would just spread out. People talk about his one-handed saves and catches from crosses with those big hands of his but he did save a lot with his legs. Whatever it took to stop the ball going in the net, he could do it.

Pat was a quiet man but had a voice when it was required. When he needed to tell us something at Anfield or Old Trafford, believe you me we heard him; he was the eyes of the back four. He was terrific at letting you know when he was coming for the ball, shouting 'Keeper's!' If a big striker is going to get his head to the ball, it's great to hear your keeper take charge like that. That kind of decisiveness is so important to a team. I talk to young players today and say it's one of the most important calls in the game. Communication was a big part of Pat's game.

He was a really good decision-maker, had excellent distribution and was a very true striker of the ball, but was as good with his arm as any I've ever seen. Pat would usually throw the ball to Cyril Knowles in an arc so that it would come right onto his run.

Pat's value to the team was immense. Brian Clough used to stress the importance of a good keeper, saying of Peter Shilton that he won his Forest team 12 points a season, and Pat was the same. In that era there were a lot of good goalkeepers around – Gordon Banks, and Ray Clemence and Shilton were coming to the fore. But Pat was the best. He was, and still is, unflappable, a brilliant person as well, which makes it even better. In my experience the best players have tended to be the best people. It is a massive attribute to be humble as a famous player, and Pat was certainly one of them, a gentlemen, a proper man. I'm really proud to be the record appéarance holder for Spurs, but if Pat had stayed longer I wouldn't have got anywhere near the tally he would have set.

Cyril Knowles was another Spurs legend and with good reason. What a character he was. Knowlesy had a very northern sense of humour. Me and

PERRYMAN SIZZLER!

STEVE PERRYMAN

The DESMOND HACKETT report

SPURS chief Bill Nicholson and the professor of WEST HAM UNITED, Ron Greenwood, will no doubt be pondering this morning: Why did we fail to win?

The answer, simply, is that neither team were sufficiently fit to carry out their highly paid task of playing for all of 90 minutes.

Both sides thrilled and delighted with soccer that should encourage 53,640 eager paying guests to come again.

But in the last 15 minutes the 22 architects of fine football became panting, heavy-footed, hard labourers, pathetically eager to settle for a draw.

SO GRACEFUL

Manager Nicholson must not have been overjoyed to observe his dearest—at least financially—import Martin Peters reduced to near invisibility for most of the second half.

But in this season of goal-filled promise, let their be rejoicing over the better things.

Eighteen-year-old Steve Perryman looked a five star wonder. He is not only strong and a born game-reader, but possesses the graceful movements that stamps great players. He has, at his age, almost a genius for creating spaces around him.

With Perryman in this form, Alan Mullery less preoccupied wit hshadowing one man—as he did his old mate Jimmy Greaves—and a normal standard Peters, Spurs should have that hard core around which successful teams are built.

The Spurs defence hinges too much on old reliable Mike England. I thought Ray Evans was too impetuous and Cyril Knowles petulant to the point of being fortunate to escape being booked.

And West Ham? It is once again Bobby Moore United. Even with his burden of troubles and his escort of a side-whiskered plain clothes officer, Moore was the greatest.

In two phases in the first half, and then early in the second, West Ham survived largely because of Moore and goalkeeper Peter Grotier.

West Ham were also guilty of over-casual passing. Entertaining yes, but not wholly impressive.

STRUGGLING

Clyde Best, speedy and eager, has not convinced me of his greatness. I was surprised to see Geoff Hurst struggling too often. Jimmy Greaves, bless his dazzling boots, played as he always plays—lurking, lost then lethal.

His goal, a minute after Alan Gilzean had put Spurs ahead, was vintage Greaves.

It was worthy of that 50,000-crowd salute—and quite historic into the bargain.

Because 13 seasons ago he scored in his first League game for Chelsea—into that same Tottenham goal. And that was 348 League goals ago.

Gilzean, with a slick header, and Peter Bennett, with another header, completed the draw.

Grabbing the headlines after the first game of the 1970–71 season against West Ham at White Hart Lane, which ended 2-2

Perryman magic lifts Spurs

SPURS 1, COVENTRY 0
From PETER BLACKMAN

WHITE HART LANE, Saturday.—Spurs, having taken a 12th minute lead through Martin Chivers, failed to punish a slow Coventry defence here today.

Coventry, wearing unfamiliar green and black striped shirts, shook their heads in disbelief when Chivers put Spurs ahead.

It was a glorious 12th minute goal and the biggest cheer from a sun-splashed crowd went to young Steve Perryman, who started it all out of nothing.

Hunt's free kick was edged out to Perryman who suddenly released the break to power the length of the pitch and end with a stunning sideways pass to CHIVERS.

The tall, £125,000 forward did not even look at the target. He thumped away at first time and goalkeeper Bill Glazier hardly moved a muscle as the ball bulged into the back of the net.

Body-swerve

Perryman, grinning hugely, had every right to stick out his chest and seconds later he was swamped by admiring team-mates and deafened by the roar of approval from the crowd

There were other alarms for Coventry and in fact Spurs deserved at least a two-goal half-time lead. They were sharper midfield with the underlating factor being the

standing between Alan Mullery and Perryman.

Half-time: Spurs 1, Coventry 0. Coventry opened the Spurs defence within minutes of the

MAN OF THE MATCH
STEVE PERRYMAN . . . brilliant in defence and attack for Spurs.

restart. O'Rourke and Goodwin linked well on the right, but Martin, going for the final pass, was ruled offside.

Spurs tried a similar raid—Morgan, Mullery and England—but the last pass was too strong for Chivers and Glazier quickly left his line to cut out the danger.

Seconds later came high drama. Chivers forced Glazier to release the ball and it went to Gilzean, who centred across the goal with no Coventry defender guarding the net. Morgan rushed in, challenged

Spurs had a miraculous escape when Knowles tried a back pass to Jennings. The ball ran straight to O'Rourke who ran straight and sent the ball over the bar by Coop, and seemed slow in believing his luck and he fired wide.

It was a ghastly error but

Spurs came back strongly. Kinner and Peters set up a chance for Chivers who steered the ball inches outside a post and then Glazier saved Coventry's bacon with a flying save from Chivers.

Spurs called off Morgan and brought on Pearce, who wasted no time drilling more holes in the Coventry defence. He billowed down the left wing, side-stepped three players and fired in a rising drive which swerved late and went wide.

Attendance: 27,103.

I was not usually Man of the Match. Kindly, people said I often deserved it, but I never really thought that myself

Phil would both have a laugh with him about cricket. We were Middlesex and he was Yorkshire, and would talk up Geoffrey Boycott. But Cyril would also want to discuss things that we wouldn't really want to talk about. He'd be asking me about girlfriends, with a mischievous look. He had no filter – he'd talk about or ask anything.

Cyril always used to call everyone 'Cock'. In a pre-season game once, I went to close an opponent down but he passed it about 10 metres to his team's right-winger, who was up against Knowles playing at left-back for us. So I chased the ball and the opposition winger. Cyril went, 'Go on, Cock, go on!' The winger passed it back to another teammate. I chased the ball and the opponent again. 'Go on, Cock, go on!' said Cyril again. I thought 'No!', and bit back, saying, 'You mean prick, don't you, if I do that'? That caused a laugh, and sort of announced to everyone: 'Stevie's grown up.' I had a voice now.

Knowlesy was a lovely, lovely man, with a big heart. He was big friends with Pat as they had made their debuts on the same day in 1964 and lived in digs together. They had a very strong bond. Cyril could take the piss with the best of them, but he was a superb player with it. He had a fantastic left foot and overlapped very well, which would prove very useful when we played in Europe. Cyril could deliver. He always wanted the ball, in the Spurs tradition of a ball-playing full-back. He was a proper footballer.

Cyril was quite tall and Bill Nick would tear his hair out about him not quite using his height enough to head the ball. When a manager has paid money for a player, the boss wants him to do even better than he is doing. I've been in that situation – you're a bit kinder on a free transfer or home-grown player, but when you spend money on someone it's like a rock around his neck when he's not playing so well because the manager is judged according to the money he has spent.

But Cyril was a great signing with real quality and became an England international. He was confident in his ability. He could take liberties, with the ball and without it. He would do cheeky drag-backs that would leave opponents kicking at thin air and was so cool-headed even on his own goal line. In his younger years he was more physical and he always seemed to have rows with Alan Ball. It all made him very popular. The song *Nice One Cyril* came about after a TV advert for bread which included a character named Cyril. Spurs fans adopted it, and it was turned into a hit record by the Cockerel Chorus. It summed Cyril up and how the fans felt about him.

Tony Want would fill in for Cyril at left-back on occasion, while on the other side Ray Evans stood in for Joe Kinnear. Joe was a good player and got picked for Ireland, although the saying then was if you could keep the ball up six times you would get picked for Ireland. I just felt that if Joe had applied himself a bit more he would have been a better player. But perhaps he couldn't change his natural character – who can, really? He lived the life of a young professional and enjoyed himself. He was very likeable, always well-dressed, jovial and a laugh to be around – a chirpy cockney and a mickey-taker without being an Eddie Baily type.

Phil Beal was, like Joe, another home-grown lad and a piss-taker. I was amazed that he lived in Godstone in Surrey and travelled in all the way from there. He now lives in the West Country and I see as much of him as any of my former teammates. When we were apprentices cleaning the boots, one of the questions we would always ask Cecil Poynton would be who he thought the best player had been in the game the previous Saturday. Cecil almost always said, 'Philip Beal' – not 'Phil', 'Philip' – and I could see why. He was Mr Security, Mr Safe, covering ground and mopping up. He was highly rated and lots of people say he would have played for England more had Bobby Moore not blocked his path. But he didn't quite do enough on the ball to push himself forward. When he scored his one and only Tottenham goal against QPR in January 1969 the most surprised person in the ground was Phil. He loved practical jokes, and I could have a laugh with him. He had a really easy-going manner.

Mike England, the mainstay of our central defence at that time, was a nice bloke as well but had more of a temper. He got really upset with the journalist David Miller one day when he described him as 'Bambi on ice' following a defeat to Man City. The players would say, 'Mike, David Miller's over there in the bar' to wind him up. He'd go steaming in only to find he wasn't there. David came on various European trips with us on charter flights, as spare seats would be sold to the press. Mike took his chance on one such occasion and tore David off a strip.

Mike was an amazing footballer. He was great in the air but he was up there already as he was so tall, but he could also play with the ball at his

A lovely photo of three Spurs captains: Martin Peters, Alan Mullery and me. It was typical of Mullers to have a jacket on. It signified the past, present, and future of Tottenham's on-field leadership

feet. The problem for him was that in his younger days at Blackburn and then when he came to us, he was always needed to play even when carrying a knock. He was often given knee and ankle injections that cost him dear at the end of his career. He had to crawl into a hot bath in the morning when he got up. I think that was all due to cortisone injections and, being such a big man, he had big knees and they suffered.

The midfield at Spurs was where much of the changes were taking place. I was the freshest face, of course, but Martin Peters's arrival from West Ham was big news. He was a World Cup winner, and came with a lot of expectation, even more so because crowd favourite Jimmy Greaves had gone the other way. But Martin had the quality and the intelligence to meet that challenge and succeed.

Martin was a serious talker about football. That stemmed from a good football education at West Ham under Ron Greenwood. Martin knew where the spaces were and could drift effectively, though he suffered a bit from being the type of player who nicked the ball to get possession, rather than someone who tackled. In that era people wanted us to win it. If we did nick it we'd be looked upon by some supporters as maybe not being up for the physical challenge. I disagreed. I saw an elegant player. As they would say now, he could play between the lines, and the obvious modern comparison is with Frank Lampard Jr. Martin didn't appear to be a powerful type but he just got in holes no one else had found. He could find players – Peters would find Gilly all day long. I never saw John White play but from what I heard he was similar to Martin with his ability to ghost into space. It required intelligence and class, and Martin had both.

Martin was very much a thinking player. You could see the wheels turning when he decided to go on a run to get forward and steal into the space unmarked. Peters was big enough to head it, and able and brave enough to put his body in where it hurt. He was a well thought-out footballer. It's why Alf Ramsey said he was 10 years ahead of his time, but it's a debate if that did Martin a good thing or a disservice.

Martin never talked about that label. Instead, as a very sensible guy, he just got on with it. Now sadly he is suffering with Alzheimer's. His

Handing out Gola team kits at a local store as part of a sponsorship deal

contemporaries always speak very fondly of him. When I went to Southend with Exeter, Brian Dear – Martin's former West Ham teammate, who was working at Southend – always wanted to talk admiringly about Martin. I learned a lot from Peters, on and off the field, in how to conduct myself. I was a grammar school boy but I didn't think I was brought up in a 'grammar school household'. It looked like Martin had been brought up in a very classy way. He didn't laugh about stupid things that maybe the rest of us did – he was almost above all that, but a very considered guy and a fantastic footballer. He was an ideal Spurs player.

The dynamic of that Tottenham midfield was given added vigour in the shape of Alan Mullery. Mullers had started playing in the 1950s, and so with the three of us – Mullers, Martin and me – we spanned the decades. Alan could be a raging bull at times, and he's a real character now. I saw him recently after he'd been to Scotland and he said, 'I'm never going to Scotland again – took 12 hours to get home. Twelve hours!'

Mullers had to be enthusiastic, loud and vocal. 'C'mon Steve, let's go, come on, let's do it!' He was a real up-and-at-'em type. He still enjoys talking now, but as a player he was more animated and he verbally attacked everything. He was also a very good player, but I got the feeling that some of the others didn't like him that much, though I could have misjudged that. It was perhaps a generational thing. Clothes became a bit more casual, hair was grown to shoulder length, and players would wear a tracksuit to training. Mullers stayed formal for longer. He was older and he looked it in his dress and style. It was an old school-versus-new school clash, I suppose.

Martin Chivers was a real contrast. He was introverted by comparison, and prone to turning in on himself. He was physically strong, big and powerful, but at times he didn't *look* that way. Maybe that was a mental thing. He had struggled when he first arrived at Spurs and had injury problems. Martin had a bit of arrogance, but underlying it was an element of insecurity. When he was flying, the arrogance would come out and he would take on Eddie verbally. 'Bring a stepladder if you want to talk to me, Eddie,' was his quip. Strikers usually have that bit of edge. They are different, and probably need that individual aspect to their character, to be single-minded.

But, as his goal-scoring record proved, Chivers could deliver. He scored 21 league goals that season, and became even more prolific in subsequent campaigns. He was a force; for two or three years he was the best centre-forward in Europe. Judging that is difficult, but if the ball went up there and Chivers was in on goal I thought, 'He's going to score.' I had full trust, as he did, that he was going to score.

It's a tribute to both players that Martin and Alan Gilzean created such an effective partnership after Greaves's departure. Gilly was just a lovely man. He wasn't as old as he looked, and was fitter than he appeared, but he was a man who loved and enjoyed life. He worked hard and played hard,

I was 'not overawed by stars – they're ordinary blokes'

A wall of Spurs captains – Mullery, Peters and Perryman

and I miss him dearly since he passed away in 2018. I was particularly close to him because I roomed with him, so I knew him inside out. I was going to have a laugh with Gilly for sure.

Gilly was always telling me about Mackay. I would ask him what Mackay would have done in some situation. 'He'd have told him to fuck off,' was the usual response. I could never say that I was in Dave's class as a player or captain but I gained inspiration from him via Gilly's tales. And he provided plenty of material of his own for a few stories. Before one of the early games when I roomed with him, Bill Nick wanted to meet us at 11am for his talk. 'Just before we start,' began Bill, 'the hotel just want to apologise because there was a lot of banging, shouting and even screaming on our floor last night. If it upset any of your sleep, the hotel really apologises. Was anyone's sleep disturbed?'

'Aye,' says Gilly, 'Me and Stevie's. At three in the morning.' Bill looked concerned. 'Aye. It was two dolly birds, bang, bang, bang on our door. To get *out* of the room, that is.'

I'm thinking, 'Oh no, what are you saying Gilly?' And of course, it's not right now to make a joke about that, though it was fair game for humour then. But it indicates the kind of relationship that he had with Bill – they could have a bit of a joke with each other.

Alan told a story once when asked what I was like as a youngster. 'I roomed with Dave Mackay, who was the untidiest, dirtiest son of a bitch,' Gilly explained. 'If we stayed anywhere longer than two days, the maids would go on strike. His underpants would be on top of the wardrobe, his socks beyond the radiator – just a nightmare.

'Dave eventually left and this angel appears in his place rooming with me. Name's Steve Perryman. Cleans my shoes. If I have a bath he not only runs it for me but cleans it out after. Kid's a dream.' He exaggerated, of course, but if we were going to have a cup of tea, I was going make it. If anyone was going to tell the hotel about bringing up newspapers, or to block any calls because we wanted to rest, that would be my job. You really get to know all about someone in that environment. You can't put up any walls.

I judge people a bit by how they write. Gilly would write out a list of people getting tickets for example, and his handwriting was perfect. All in capital letters. Neat, clear, perfect. He took real care, and was obviously educated.

Gilly didn't get the Scotland caps he should have because of the apparent 'Anglos' prejudice that affected Mackay as well: the Scottish FA were said to be resistant to select players who played for English clubs for the national side, preferring those who played for Scottish teams. That was Scotland's loss, because Gilly was a brilliant footballer, just superb, and some athlete. He might have liked a drink but he could still win a 10-lap race. He was a cross-country champion. Terry Naylor was the fittest thing on two legs and one day after Gilly had had a night out someone said, 'Take Terry on for Crissakes – bring him down a peg.' And Gilly did. He beat him.

He was also famously outstanding in the air. Greavesie said Gilly was his best partner and that's enough for me. He knew how to act with people and sign autographs and be a gentlemen. He carried himself so well and he had his own style.

We were thus a team of different characters but a very effective one as well, with a bit of swagger about us. We could play. We had good players. But it was more than that. We had height, we had power, we had overlapping full-backs, we had long throws, near-post corners, the lot. It wasn't direct by any means but it was different to previous Spurs teams.

I used to take near-post corners for Gilly. Some were better than others but Gilly always managed to get his head on them. It was phenomenal how he got to the ball. Sometimes I'd get congratulated for the near-post corner when I'd mis-hit what was supposed to be a deeper corner and it was down to Gilly flicking it on.

That involvement in a set-piece routine illustrated how integral I was becoming to the side, but I was still young and still very much learning, and not just about the game but the club itself. I was sat on the team coach for six months and eventually said to one or the other players, 'Who are those old people down the end of the bus?'

He said, 'They're the directors of the club.'

'What do they do?'

'They fucking direct.' As if to say, 'Don't ask any more stupid questions', because they wouldn't know the answer to that themselves. It was meant to shut me up.

Those directors, led by Sidney Wale, the chairman, were happy to let Bill Nick run the club. Bill would sit upstairs for some games in the directors' box while Eddie was in the dugout. It was an effective way for them to pair up and watch the game, but Bill was certainly not on the board. They wanted to leave it to the man, and they had the right man. Whoever chose Bill Nick did the best job they could ever do for Spurs, because he was precisely the right man. He wasn't up himself, he was

"We were thus a team of different characters but a very effective one as well, with a bit of swagger about us. We could play"

It was an honour to talk football with one of the true greats, Ferenc Puskas, who had brought his side over to train near Northolt. I leapt at the opportunity to meet him

disciplined, he was desperate to improve and he wanted to put the best product he could on that pitch for the club and the fans.

He used to say to us, 'Who are the most important people at this club?' No one would answer because we thought it was a trick question. He'd say: 'It's the supporters. You'll go, I'll go, but they stay till they die. And the people that pay their money up front before we buy a player or get a win at the start of the season, the fans who are the season ticket holders, they are the most important people at this club – not the chairman, not me, not you, not the captain. Don't *ever* think that they're mugs, 'cause I'm telling you, they're not.'

I didn't really have an opinion about the fans then. I was too busy concentrating on my own game and viewed them like any player of any club – they were the supporters who supported their team. But I came to realise that the Tottenham crowd liked my style when I came into the side. There was a feeling that I was 'one of them' because when I did something they liked, such as winning a 50-50, there was a big reaction from the crowd. The roared like it was a goal. You can't not feel that reaction, and I knew they wanted more of it. There is a Japanese phrase, 'The crowd give you power', and I started to feel that power from the fans early on.

During the 1970–71 season those fans were pleased when we got going in the autumn, with each area of the team working well. Part of my job in the midfield was to enable Mullery and Peters to go and do what they wanted to do. Mullery was both attack-minded and defensive; Peters was the most attacking of the three of us, so I had to stay deeper and take care of the opponent when the ball came out, heading towards our goal. I could do that for my life. I could read where it was coming out, just like I could read where the goal kick was going to land when I was a kid playing over at Ealing Park. Nowadays I'd be called the holding midfielder – the percentage player – though it wasn't a term I used myself. I think we had the perfect balance for a three in midfield.

I was very consistent. I can only remember being taken off once against Sheffield United in the League Cup that season, and I missed the later round against Coventry City. Otherwise, I was ever-present. I certainly made my presence felt in a memorable game at Leeds.

It turned out to be an unbelievable 2–1 win, with Chivers scoring twice. Leeds had a reputation for nastiness and would do whatever they could to gain an inch. One aspect of it was that Elland Road was a threatening place.

Early on I turned and Johnny Giles clipped me. Not a problem. We stopped the ball, took the free-kick and carried on. I caught Giles five minutes later. They assumed that I was looking for revenge, but I wasn't. If it was revenge I'd have kicked him a lot harder. All of a sudden there were six of them bending over me after I ended up on the floor. They looked threatening, muttering, 'You little bastard.'

Game on.

Giles said, 'We've got one here.' It was as if they didn't think I was a good enough player to warrant taking me out as a footballer but they wanted to nullify my energy, or perhaps protect Giles. We all judge it differently. If you look at a team and ask what the strengths of that team are, you might target the gifted player. You'd take the goalscorer out if you could, or you'd nullify the midfield delivery. The only way to take the goalkeeper out is to batter him when he goes up for a cross, though they wouldn't try that with Pat. Instead I think they saw me as an energy that needed to be countered. We were a big threat to them and went third in the table that day.

The actual challenges between Giles and I were fairly tame. But it started the aggression against me, as if they were on a mission. It was led by Giles. If you're going to get kicked by Billy Bremner, fine, you know you're going to get kicked, but Giles was a bit more devious. He'd leave his foot in, say, if you were clearing the ball from the box. A lot of players from that era mention Giles when they talk about the physical stuff. Apparently he is disappointed about that and I can see why because he was an excellent player, really top drawer, but I always felt he had a nasty streak. In fact, that applied to many in the Leeds team.

Mick Jones wasn't nasty, Paul Madeley and Paul Reaney were good as gold, and I don't ever remember Terry Cooper kicking me. With Eddie Gray there was not a chance of him being nasty, but Alan Clarke was and so was Peter Lorimer. Big Jack Charlton could dish it out, and Norman Hunter definitely did. His was the more 'honest' approach and he was aptly named. But Bremner and Giles relished the physical stuff, and thereafter I was the target for all sorts of treatment.

Leeds were such a good team, so why did they feel the need to do that bit 'extra'? That must have come from the manager. If Don Revie was behind it, the underlying message was, 'We're not quite good enough,' which I think is awful. If that team just played they could beat everyone.

But at Leeds that day I felt isolated. It was game on for all of us, but I felt I could have been better supported. In truth we all had our contests. Cyril and Lorimer would have been kicking seven bells out of each other for

PERRYMAN'S LOOKING FOR TROUBLE

says JOHNNY GILES of Leeds

STEVE PERRYMAN has been going like a bomb since he got into Tottenham's side. Usually when a youngster gets his big chance he's great for a few games, then, when the first flush wears off, he finds his true level.

But Perryman is all heart. Spurs could be 10 down and he'd still be chasing every ball.

1 COOL HEAD
For a youngster of 19 he's got exceptional temperament. In tight situations he doesn't panic and beat himself, he keeps cool and plays his way out of trouble.

2 FEARLESS TACKLER
He's fearless and very strong in a tackle, going in when it appears he hasn't a chance and winning the ball.

3 BIGGEST FAULT
Now to Perryman's one big fault. To my mind he tries to do too much, possibly because he's inclined to exaggerate DANGER. The moment the opposition begins to build an attack, he sees trouble, he's off back, propping up the right-back, left-back, centre-backs–trying to do it all.

In possession he's not a great dribbler as such but he's quick to see an opening and he's a fine passer of a ball.

4 COUNTER-ATTACK
I was guilty of the same thing when I was a youngster and it hurt my game. Now I only get back when the odds are stacked against my defence. Other than that, I pick up the man nearest me and search out where to hit the opposition when we win back the ball.

Should the attack break down he's stranded, which means more running if he's to link up with his forwards. There's nothing wrong with doing a lot of running provided it's positive, but with Perryman this is not always the case.

PERRYMAN'S RETREAT

GILES POISED TO COUNTER-ATTACK

FIERCE COMPETITOR
Because of his fierce competitive nature, it's said Perryman's a lot like Dave Mackay, Billy Bremner and players like that. This is ridiculous. Like all great players he's got his own individual style. Perryman's like Perryman–nobody else.

TEXT AND DRAWINGS BY TREVILLION

Steve Perryman also earned grudging praise from Leeds after helping Alan Mullery and Martin Peters to dominate in midfield.

Johnny Giles, Leeds schemer, said: "This lad Perryman is certainly a worker and gets stuck in. But I didn't like his attitude at the end. He made a rude gesture as if to show what he thought of me as a player. I thought that was a bit strong."

Johnny Giles's assessment (top) of me came after the famous Leeds game – full credit to him as it was respectful and decent, despite what happened in the match, with Johnny also giving his view of our confrontation (above)

Perryman the magnificent!

LIVERPOOL 0, SPURS 0

From BERNARD JOY

LIVERPOOL, Saturday. — Spurs fought a magnificent rearguard action, with youngsters Perryman and Pratt outstanding, to hold at bay rampant Liverpool in a tense Sixth Round FA Cup-tie at Anfield.

Mullery won the toss, elected to defend the Kop end and promptly subjected his team to a ferocious assault as Liverpool set out to please their most ardent supporters.

Dashing

Spurs were pushed back into desperate defence by the sheer weight of Liverpool's pressure. It may have been mainly one-tracked, with the head of Toshack the main target, but it made up by its persistency.

Collins struggled to match

Toshack, whose chief assistant, the dashing Heighway, called for all Beal's resourcefulness.

At times all 11 Spurs were back in the penalty area when a corner was forced or a free-kick desperately conceded.

The midfield players, especially Pratt, the shock last-minute deputy for Gilzean, and Perryman, performed great things, but were simply overwhelmed by these non-stop Merseyside men.

Yet somehow Spurs held on and, as half-time approached, began to take advantage of the pressure by sharp breakaways.

Hitting the headlines for a performance against Liverpool again

example. I took it personally, but was questioning my teammates. In midfield where were we? I didn't know where my allies were. It was as if to say, 'You're in it, Steve, finish it.' Gilly I think said, 'Stevie, be careful' by way of back-up. But that was as far as it went.

We saw the game out and I had survived unscathed. It was not quite right what I did at the end, but my blood was up and I thought that Giles had wanted to hurt me. But now all of a sudden, in our moment of victory and all our joy – because this was a hell of a scalp – he wants to shake my hand? I told him to fuck off. I shook my hand at him rather than with him. Which is the wrong thing to do at the end of a sporting contest. That was it. I'd lit the firework. Now they all wanted a bit of me in the tunnel. To this day I don't quite know how I got out of it; Pat was there with me, or maybe I put myself alongside him! I heard the sounds of studs coming toward me, and someone from Leeds came from behind, which isn't very brave, and tried to hit me. I saw the blow coming late and just got out of the way of it. I didn't go down from the punch but slipped on the concrete and then there was a big hoo-ha. I was quickly ushered into the dressing room without actually getting hit.

I didn't win the war for Bill Nicholson that day but I won the battle. Bill said as we were coming off, 'Well done, great victory.' Later in the dressing room he said, 'Steve are you all right?' I said I was. 'Bit of trouble at the end?' I told him there was no problem. I didn't want to take it any further: I'd done my bit, we'd won the game and that was the end of it. They were a team of men and it was a dream result. Barry Davis, the BBC commentator, stopped at the table where we were eating after the match and said well done to everyone, and then to me, 'Steve, we're going to highlight the aggression in that game tonight', which didn't do me any harm because I came out of it well: I didn't get booked but had held my own.

Then things took a different turn. The Sunday papers focused on the actual game, but the Monday papers were always about something extra in the game – some different viewpoint, highlighting a player or an incident. Giles was quoted saying something along the lines of, 'He's a good player, Perryman, but he needs to be careful.' Bill Nick picked up on it. He spoke to someone in the press and asked what Giles meant by that and he was told what I had said to Giles.

At the start of training on Monday, Bill told me, 'You wait there' while the others went off running. He said, 'If you ever don't shake someone's hand at the end of the game, you will never wear that white shirt again.'

I can say it was the first and only time Bill Nicholson actually disappointed me. I wasn't expecting him to be all over me with praise, but he saw what I had had to cope with that day and I don't think he paid me any respect whatsoever. I wasn't flash, I wasn't nasty, I wasn't a big head. I thought Bill would have been pleased with me standing up for myself and the team.

My actions at the end were probably not the way to do it. And Bill was right, I should have shaken Giles's hand. But the comment from Bill hurt.

I thought he misread that. I did such a job for him that day and he knew it, and at some risk to myself. I'm still very proud of myself for that day.

That game was an eye-opener into the realities of elite football. It showed this was a tough business. I became battle-hardened, realistic as to what the game was about. This was what I was in. It wasn't always the beautiful game.

Unfortunately, us beating Leeds that day effectively won Arsenal the title. They finished a point above Leeds, while we finished third, a further 12 points behind. We lost four out of six games after the win at Elland Road. That stopped us, as we then lost only one more game all season – but it was to the Arsenal.

I think that after the Leeds win we might have thought we were in with a real chance. But the higher you get the more everyone wants to do you. You have to be better than you were to get to the top if you want to stay there. The run at the end was amazing. A draw used to be a better result: when a win was two points, a draw was half a win, effectively. But we drew too many, 14 in all.

That was typical of my Tottenham career in the league. We never really got close enough. We always underperformed and inconsistency was at the heart of it. We went on a bad run for too long. Unfortunately, George Graham nailed it: if Arsenal played badly they'd get a draw; if we played badly we'd get beaten. It was a different approach; I think there was an element to us that if we went a goal down we'd try to get it back too quickly. There's nothing wrong with that, but you might go a goal down as someone has hit a screamer. When that happens it's nobody's fault that the opposition has had a 'hot' moment, so there's nothing to suggest you should change the way you are playing.

At Spurs, did we panic a bit when we went a goal down? You might get back into it but while panicking the opposition can hit you on the break and

My first major honour: League Cup winners in 1971

you can see the second coming. The crowd wanted us to go forward all the time, and rightly so. It was a cavalier approach but it is what Tottenham have always been about.

The night Arsenal won the title at our place was amazing but for all the wrong reasons. The crowds outside the ground were just enormous, and I had to abandon my car in gridlocked traffic and leave my friends to drive into the car park just so I could get into the ground. I only just made it in time for kick-off.

The game was predictably tasty. I used to play with Charlie George in the England under-23s, and I caught him. He was lying on the floor and looked up at me. 'Is that how it's going to be Steve?' I said it was and he said, 'OK, fine.' Which is lovely. He wouldn't expect anything less. It was a new era. I was the home-grown talent coming through, he was the darling of the North Bank. We were friendly in the under-23s because as far as we were concerned we were from London and the rest of them were mugs. We came from the same place.

I respected that Arsenal team. They were a machine, and we lost at theirs as well. Bastards. Even after all these years I can't help but wonder that a Spurs player could have written himself into the history books if he'd scored in the last second and ruined their league title. I don't think anyone could say that we lay down or that we didn't want to win – we were playing for our club's history. They just found a way. Bill Nick ingrained it in us to hate them and this was the night to hate them. He would have been hurt by the Arsenal defeat, but he knew we'd had a real go. We certainly weren't outplayed, and we'd played worse and won. But good teams find a way, and Arsenal were a good team

The team was distraught after the game but it was the end of a long season and it had actually been a good one. We'd finished third – and won a trophy.

The League Cup was my first taste of silverware, won at Wembley not far from where I grew up. It was the lesser cup competition but gaining in prestige. So it was a major victory, albeit against Third Division Aston Villa. They had beaten Manchester United in the semi-finals but everyone wanted a Tottenham–Man U final, which would have done the competition so much good.

But we couldn't take anything for granted and Villa were a bloody good team. They had some very talented players including Ian 'Chico' Hamilton, Bruce Rioch and Andy Lochhead, who always seemed to cause us problems. They had some experience in there as well. To illustrate the fact that it wasn't going to be easy, I had to kick one off the line at a vital moment in the game. I was always good at anticipating any potential danger. The big stage, with the big crowd and the atmosphere, didn't faze me. In fact I loved it at Wembley. I thrived in that arena. The game was poor but we won it in the end with Chivers scoring twice. He was on fire that day.

Spurs supporters are used to winning things and this was a win. Arsenal won the Double and that overshadowed it, but we had done our job, putting our club back on the main stage. We hadn't been off the stage for that long since the FA Cup win in 1967, but getting a trophy and maintaining high standards at Tottenham was vital.

As a player you have some very low points and some extremely high ones every season, and eventually you might end up with a trophy. Mullers said to me in the bath after the game, 'Enjoy it, because it don't happen very often.' I might have been forgiven in my youthful naivety for thinking, 'Oh, this is handy. My first year and we've won a cup. I could get used to this.' Win whatever you can win, and that happened to be the League Cup.

The important things were that we had won silverware, and it gave us entry into Europe. The next instalment in my young career awaited.

My winners' tankard for the 1971 League Cup victory

At the Spurs Awards night at the end of an eventful and successful season, standing alongside Pat Jennings and Jimmy Hill (left), with Alan Mullery in front. Mullers was Player of the Year, I was Young Player of the Year

**Pictured with
John Pratt, Joe
Kinnear and
Phil Beal on tour
in Japan in the
summer of 1971
(above)**

**The full Spurs
tour party (right)**

Enjoying a meal at a restaurant owned by a Japanese sumo wrestling champion (left). To his right is Chris McDonald, the chap who many years later would present me with a Rolex watch for winning the Japanese Manager of the Year award

Doing my media duties on tour (below). Little did I know that 25 years later Ossie and I would return to the same hotel – the Akasaka Prince in Tokyo – to celebrate winning the Japanese League Cup, and that I would have such an adventure living and working in that amazing country

EUROPEAN ADVENTURES

José Mourinho has said that his priority when he arrives at a new club is to win a trophy. That's why he regarded winning the League Cup, which he did when he first joined Chelsea, as important. It set the tone and provided impetus for further success. Our League Cup win in 1971 was similarly important, as it inspired us to aim for further honours. I wasn't yet a major player in the team. I did my job without being a big influence on the side, but I did have the taste for winning and wanted more of it.

Now we were going to play in Europe. I always thought it was important for Spurs to play in European competition because it was a break from the norm of domestic football and it meant testing yourself against the best from other countries. One of Bill Nick's most repeated quotes is, 'If you're not in Europe, you're nothing' and I know what he meant. There was a freshness of challenge to it all. It was an era of cup replays and 42-game league seasons with small squads, poor pitches and basic treatment for injuries, so we probably didn't need the extra games, but for some reason we thrived on European football. So did the fans, who played a big part in making European nights some of the finest in the club's history.

My first European adventure was in the newly named UEFA Cup. This was the successor to the Fairs Cup and a tougher competition. My later teammate Paul Miller maintains that the UEFA Cup in that era was harder to win than the European Cup, because the best two or three teams from leagues across Europe qualified. You could come across top sides that had won their title recently, and even the European Cup.

Our 1971–72 campaign began in September with a 6–1 win in Iceland against Keflavik. Ralph Coates scored and almost did a lap of honour but with no one chasing him. We said to him, 'What are you doing? You scored a goal – so what?!' Ralph would do more good stuff away from home in Europe than I thought he achieved at home. He had a bit of a name at home and whether people closely marked him more in normal league games I'm not sure, but his running, all-action style worked against foreign teams.

Ralph had joined in the summer as a big-money signing. When Bill met him he was disappointed by his reaction when he asked him how he felt signing for Spurs. It wasn't that Ralph wasn't excited but he didn't show the level of enthusiasm Bill expected. That makes me smile. It was Bill Nick being 100 per cent committed to the club and wanting the same 100 per cent commitment – but a new signing can't be. Ralph had just joined, it was

"I wasn't yet a major player in the team. But I did have the taste for winning and wanted more of it"

The team line-up for 1971–72. Three players pictured here – Jimmy Pearce, Roger Morgan and Pete Collins – sadly picked up serious injuries that finished their careers prematurely

Evening Standard

TOTTENHAM HOTSPUR From the left   Back row: Pat Jennings, Ray Evans, Cyril Knowles, Martin Chivers, Mike England, Peter Collins, Martin Peters, Alan Gilzean, Terry Naylor, Phil. Basi. Front row : Joe Kinnear, Jimmy Neighbour, Ralph Coates, Steve Perryman, Alan Mullery (with the League Cup), John Pratt, Tony Want, Jimmy Pearce, Roger Morgan.

all new to him. Bill Nick was Mr Tottenham and of course entitled to feel the way he did. I was impressed with Bill wanting more enthusiasm from Ralph but his attitude was totally understandable.

That Keflavik match was also notable for Graeme Souness's solitary Spurs appearance, coming on as sub. Phil came on in the home leg and thereafter was picked ahead of Graeme. It spelled the end for Souness at Spurs and he left the following summer. Phil stayed the same, though. 'Chief!' said Bill, 'you can change in the first-team dressing room now.' 'Bill, thanks but I'm OK in here,' Phil said, and stayed with the other reserves and youth players.

We cruised through against Keflavik and were fortunate to defeat Nantes, before two Eastern European trips. Going there at that time, during the Cold War, was a different experience altogether. Rapid Bucharest in December was an afternoon kick-off, dark and dreary in front of a crowd full of soldiers and people in flat caps. Signs of poverty were visible everywhere. Gilly threw a cigarette out of the bus window and all these kids tried to get it. They were clubbed by security forces. It made you grateful for where you were living.

The away leg against Rapid wasn't a good one for me because I hit the hard ground whilst making a tackle and put my collarbone out. I was substituted and Dr Curtin put the bone back in place in the dressing room, which itself felt different – more like an old office. It was good having our doctor with us, as he could put things right there and then; you preferred to put your trust in your own medical people. The game deteriorated into a real kicking match. Jimmy Pearce got sent off with a Romanian player for fighting. After the match there were bodies lying everywhere in the treatment room. I have never seen a dirtier team or a more vicious attack on our players than in that game. It was so bad that Bucharest refused to hand the film of the game over to the BBC to screen the highlights.

We got through, though, thinking that's Romania done and dusted for a season, only to draw another Romanian team, Unizale Textile Arad, in the next round. We won again, in no small part thanks to Eddie Baily's excellent homework on our opponents, which ensured that we were well-briefed and prepared. Eddie could describe a player's game as well as anyone. What also helped was that we were a well-drilled side. We had height, we had class with Peters, Chivers, and Gilzean, and we had the right mentality as well. I think the whole team knew it was game on. I didn't need to change my mentality, because my approach to any game of football was that it was going to be tough.

In Europe, you not only wanted to do it for yourself and your team but also for the crowd. Those nights were like that – it was us against the 'foreigners'. There was an extra edge to it. The war did frame people's thinking in those days, especially when we played a German team. Britain hadn't been at war with all the countries of the teams we faced, but there was a sense of patriotism. It was part of the mindset, and Eddie made sure it was all, 'Fix bayonets, go over the trenches' and all that stuff. We could just keep going in adversity. It *was* a bit warlike. Walking down the street abroad in some place you'd think about the war and what had happened there. In certain cities we played in there would still be bullet holes visible in some of the buildings.

We had nous in abundance as well as talent. There was an urgency about the opponents, coming at you at speed and with purpose. If you didn't start right, with the crowd breathing fire at you – Greece was very hostile, for example – you could wilt under the pressure. European club football was new to me, but my team had experience. Bill had already won in Europe, while Gilly had been to the semi-final of the European Cup with Dundee, which he told me a lot about. Bill continuously communicated the importance of being in Europe. The problem with doing that is if he didn't stress the other games' importance, did it make them seem less vital? Every game to me was important.

We reached the semi-finals of the UEFA Cup in 1972, and our balanced set-up had shown itself well. We were particularly hard to score against in those days with Pat in goal and with England at centre-back. We were a goal-scoring team but we could score from set pieces, long throws, all kinds of ways. Mullery's game was suited to Europe, and we had overlapping full-backs. We were more tactically astute and defensively strong, but with a front end that could do damage.

My role was to be a midfield blanket. Because I was young and naive, I just ran and ran, challenged and tackled, and put pressure on the ball. A team reaped a lot of benefit in Europe by having someone playing that way. I wasn't a dribbler. I played whatever I saw and there was a very effective simplicity about that: I was playing it quick, easy and accurate.

My impact was markedly different in the semi-final, however, when we were drawn against AC Milan. They were one of the biggest names a club could play. This was the glamour tie. They oozed style in their red-and-black shirts and the cut of their shorts. When we got Eddie's pen portraits and photos through, the Italians had a bit more class about them. They were in full colour, not like the black-and-white of the Romanian photos. They had talent in spades. Their skipper Gianni Rivera, for example, you didn't have to be a football nut to have heard about. They had Karl-Heinz Schnellinger,

The first of our two visits to Romania that season, away to Rapid Bucharest in December 1971. I went off injured in this game

who had played in the 1966 World Cup final, and Romeo Benetti, who was nicknamed 'The Englishman' because of the way he played like a bulldog in midfield.

The first leg at White Hart Lane was something of a classic. Years later Irving Scholar got me an hour's recording of the game, not the edited highlights shown on TV, but more extensive coverage. It was a real big-club showdown, with an atmosphere to match. It was cold, unseasonably so, with high winds and a pitch that was bare. We weren't in all-white, as Milan wore white shorts. But the crowd made it one of those special European nights.

Early on I went into a challenge with Benetti and tackled as if I was shooting, putting my laces through the ball. I had always been told not to do that because you risked breaking your leg. There was a split-second to think about what part of my foot to put into the ball and for some reason I went in really hard through the top of my foot. I careered into the air and everyone thought I was injured, but I was OK and it said, 'I'm on it – I'm not frightened.' If I had been more cunning or experienced maybe I wouldn't have gone in so strong, but I thought, 'I've got to put all my force into this.'

I had to deal with Rivera as well. They were basically defensive, looking for Rivera to break from midfield, and they were so classy. I was marking him from a throw-in. He went to the ball and I had to follow, but he checked, took the ball on his chest and glided the other side of me. No one had ever done that to me before. I also saw Rivera do something on John Pratt in the away leg which will stay with me forever. The ball came to Rivera and John went to close him down as he should. Rivera stubbed the ball, so it went forward towards John and then spun back. As Pratty was running back his expression was saying, 'Did I see what I just saw?' And I'm thinking, 'Yeah, you bloody did.' He was something else, Rivera.

At White Hart Lane they scored via Benetti. He was proving he was more than just a hard man, and he could shoot – bang, in the top corner. I was impressed. To beat Pat it had to be some strike. If I didn't know it already, this was top opposition, the genuine quality article. So we were a goal down, and the tone was set: they defended; we attacked. A few minutes later, Knowlesy put one in from an angle with his right foot. Gilly nodded it back, Chivers played it towards Peters, who let it go. I called for it from five yards away. I just said, 'Yes!' I didn't have time to say anything else. In that situation you have to be sure you are going to get it – there's no point calling for the ball if you think you *might* get it – you do so when you are sure. My 'Yes!' was definite. The ball came to me in my stride and bosh – top corner. The goalie got a touch but it was a hell of a strike; through my laces, just like in the tackle I'd made about 15 minutes earlier.

Looking back, the match was a really interesting tactical contest. They were so defensive-oriented. They made contact with us but in a cunning way so as not to give away a penalty, nudging Gilly, Chiv and Peters. They worked out our strengths, were really clever in how they defended and made it difficult for us.

There was a lot of relief when I scored but they still had the advantage due to the away-goal rule, which commentators would always harp on about. So we had a need and a desire to try and win the game. They got a red card when Riccardo Sogliano was sent off in the second half, and Mullers had to almost escort him off the pitch. Alan was having an odd season. He had suffered a long-term injury to his pelvis and then been on loan at Fulham, and it looked like he was on his way out, but Bill Nick brought him back and his experience and will to win was proving vital. Mullers had just returned from Fulham and only got the go-ahead to play at the last minute after the Italians disputed his eligibility.

The crowd had been roaring us on from the start, but they went wild when I equalised. I think sometimes Spurs fans supported according to league position. They could be a bit hard on us when we hadn't won for a few games, but for a European night it was all forgotten. They weren't anything other than for us, willing us to get back. How could they help us get back? The answer was all hands to the pump in the only way they could contribute and that was with their voices.

I think that, generally speaking, in those days the ball would get forward quicker, to encourage a higher tempo. I think that was compounded by the crowd on those nights and they drove us forward. Crowds these days shout 'Shoot!' when a player is around the box. But on European nights even then, Spurs fans let you know they wanted you to shoot, and that led to mysecond goal.

Milan were down to 10 men, which made them not only less able to defend a corner but to then break and score what would have been a killer of a second goal. That gave me a little bit more scope to be less defensive-minded. After a spell of pressure aided by the wind, we were getting corner after corner. Milan were very resolute. We weren't playing Romanians: these were hard-nosed top pros, whose attitude

Mobbed after scoring against AC Milan – my special night under the lights. We wore blue shorts so as not to clash with Milan's white

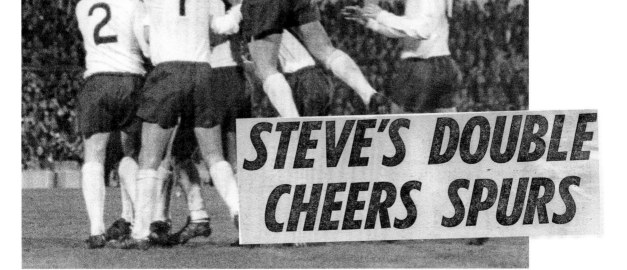

SCORCHER STEVE IS THE SPURS ACE

STEVE'S DOUBLE CHEERS SPURS

TOTTENHAM players arrive in Milan for tomorrow night's second leg of the EUFA Cup semi-final. Pictured are Phil Peal (bottom of steps) who is expected to return to the side after injury, former Northolt schoolboy Steve Perryman, and England striker Martin Chivers.

Spurs confident

TOTTENHAM Hotspur arrived in Italy last night ready for a tough battle against AC Milan in the secon leg of their EUFA Cup semi-final tie, but confident of winning their way into the final.

The 17-man squad, headed by manager Bill Nicholson, travelled to the small town of Appiano Gentile, near Lake Como, to a hotel normally used by the other Milan team,

Internazionale, as their retreat before big maches.

Tottenham won the first leg match by a narrow 2-1 margin in London on April 5.

"We know that it will be a hard, very hard game on Wednesday," Nicholson told reporters at Milan's Malpensa International Airport.

"Milan will have the crowd on their side, while we will have very few supporters. But we will beat them to qualify for the finals. This UEFA Cup is very important to us," he said.

Arriving in Italy before heading to a very warm reception at Inter Milan's training complex – but not such a friendly welcome at the magnificent San Siro

was, 'Score over my dead body.' It was a tough night for Chivers and Gilly, but in focusing on the players who they were expecting to score, Milan weren't thinking about me.

In the 65th minute we had another corner. It was cleared, I brought it down, had a touch forward then – boom! It took a bounce before rattling into the corner of the goal. I was almost embarrassed because me scoring twice, let along from range, didn't happen very often, but it earned us a precious 2–1 win.

AC Milan at home was my game. I'd played really well having not been in a good run of form. I always worked hard but I was better with the ball in some games than others, and this was one of them. It was easy for me to think that work-rate was enough, but the object of the game is to put the ball in the net. I had probably stopped thinking about affecting the other team's goal, focusing instead on protecting ours.

The goals I did score were often about pass and move – that's how I'd been brought up at Spurs. But on that night shooting from distance was what had been required and I had delivered. That game proved to me that even being defensively sound for the team shouldn't detract from anything else in my game. The best place to protect your goal is in their last third, not your last third, after all. There was a positive in me getting forward. It was a very enlightening game for me.

Afterwards I was exhausted, lying flat out in the treatment room. Dr Curtin came in and said something very interesting. 'You know, Bill Nick is a genius, because he was going to leave you out.' 'Hang on,' I thought, 'what was meant by that?' My form hadn't been good, but I don't think I could have given any more. Bill Nick would praise me in the papers, but almost never to my face. He would do so indirectly, saying on a bad day to the rest of the team, 'Why don't you want to run as hard as him?', meaning me. It was a curious thing for Dr Curtin to say, and I wondered if it was at the behest of Bill trying to get a message to me not to get above myself after such a performance.

There was never any danger of that with me, but that didn't mean others thought the same way. For the second leg in Milan we stayed at Inter's training ground. They obviously wanted to see Milan beaten so they helped us. Because the first leg had been on TV, they all saw me as the match-winning star player. I was presented as 'the name'. I wasn't. But when we got into the hotel at the training centre everyone was asking for me. 'Perryman. Where is he?' I was pointed out and they all went 'Ah, Perryman!', because I'd scored two against their big rivals. They must have thought I did that every game!

Bill Nick was clever to get us to stay at Inter Milan's place. It was a stunning set-up – a training ground but like a luxury health complex. It was how I imagined Beverly Hills; it was wonderful. You felt the class and the quality of this Italian set-up. The Italians just oozed sophistication. Having seen it up close, it gave me more respect for people like Liam Brady and Graeme Souness who went to Italy and played there. There was definitely a style about Italy – the clothes, the shoes, the way they carried themselves. I bought some *Capodimonte* porcelain figures in Milan to take a little bit of Italy back home with me.

More importantly, we took an aggregate victory home. We played really well, producing a professional performance and drawing 1–1. I laid a pass on for Mullery in the San Siro to hit and put us a goal up. What a strike it was. It was tense at the end but I don't ever remember thinking that we had got it all to do, and when we went one up it felt like the game was safe. It was played in an intense atmosphere with firecrackers and all sorts of colour and noise. They had stopped our bus in the approach to the ground and supporters were whacking the coach with branches to test our mettle. We passed the test. It was competitive and they put us under pressure but we came through. The freshness of the night in that magnificent stadium – I really wish that it had been the final.

And who did we get in the final? An English side. The news came in that Wolves had beaten Ferencvaros. It was almost a disappointment that we'd reached the pinnacle already in playing Milan. That sounds a bit disrespectful to Wolves, but they were too 'normal'. The final would be played over two legs, home and away. That meant for the away leg there would be no trip abroad and no jet travel, which was disappointing as the players loved going abroad back then. It was a special bonding experience, winning in adversity and being around familiar supporters – people like Morris Keston, his big pal Alan Landsberg and Fred Rhye – as well as the directors and the doctor. If a supporter was taken ill, Dr Curtin would step in and help. Even the air crews would join in the fun, because we used to charter planes, so the crew had to be in the city where we were playing and would often come to the games.

At this time my dad was working for Air France, and all his workmates would come because they got flights for just 10 per cent of the fare. It was a city break for them. There would not be much time for us players to explore the places we played in but we'd go for a walk for a few hours to take in the people, the streets and the architecture. We looked forward to the adventure, but this time the 'adventure' was going to be in the Midlands.

Around that time it seemed like we were always playing Wolves, either in the league or cup, and we had something over them. So it was a bit of an anti-climax. Having beaten AC Milan, we should have been happy because it meant more chance of winning against opposition we knew. And that was how it turned out. Chivers was at his hottest and scored twice in the first leg at Molineux.

He had fully come out of his doldrums period by then. He was so powerful that opponents would bounce off him. Foreign teams must have

The setting for Chiv's 'rocket' night was a familiar one – Molineux

A fitting and triumphant send-off for our skipper and leader, Alan Mullery. He scored with a brave header at White Hart Lane, another goal contributed by our midfielders in a successful UEFA Cup campaign

My UEFA Cup winners' medal and a profile in *Tiger* magazine (right)

been petrified of Chiv. Playing with him in those years, I saw the very best of him. There was a time when there were doubts about Martin, that he wasn't tough enough and picked up too many injuries. Bill Nick even got Mike England to kick Martin to see if he reacted. But by 1972 he'd become a colossus. He had a major effect on results and was a bona fide match-winner.

The final against Wolves might have been an all-English match, but thankfully it still felt like a European tie. We played in the all-white kit, for starters. We got the train home from the away leg and it stopped at a station on the way so we could meet our wives and families – that gave it a feel of 'special arrangements'. The home leg was Mullers's swansong. He scored the opener with a typically brave header that knocked him out cold under a challenge from Wolves keeper Phil Parkes and, although they equalised, we were deserving winners. We didn't know for certain that Mullery was leaving, but the writing had been on the wall since he went on loan to Fulham.

Back then I couldn't see the reasoning behind how the team was picked – why one player was left out and another was in. Bill would always be saying something at half-time like, 'Come on! Lead it!' – not a direct criticism but it was implied that Mullers as captain wasn't doing enough. His reaction was always positive, though. He jumped up and led the team back out. He did against Wolves, and got chaired off at the end. Not a bad way to go out. Bill Nick was very critical afterwards. We had hung on a bit and he let us know it, which actually was not a bad way to start the next season. It stopped us going away for the summer thinking, 'We're great.'

That said, while the phrase 'being winners' wasn't used so much then, that was what we were – and I'm still talking about it 50 years later. It doesn't happen often. Most clubs don't win trophies, and very few win year after year. But I had now won two finals in the less than three years since I had broken into the first team. We also became the first British team to win two European trophies, and that really was something special.

TIGER ▶ REQUEST A STAR

STEVE PERRYMAN WON HIS SECOND FOOTBALL LEAGUE CUP WINNERS' MEDAL WHEN SPURS BEAT NORWICH IN THE FINAL AT WEMBLEY, LAST MONTH, AND STEVE WAS 21 YEARS OLD IN DECEMBER....

IN 1970, STEVE SCORED QUITE A MEMORABLE GOAL FOR TOTTENHAM V. BURNLEY, EXCHANGING PASSES WITH JIMMY PEARCE, THEN ENDING A SPARKLING MOVE WITH A DEADLY SHOT.

PERHAPS YOU REMEMBER SEEING THIS GOAL ON T.V. —OR MAYBE YOU EVEN VOTED FOR IT, AS "GOAL OF THE SEASON"....

PERRYMAN WAS BORN IN EALING, AND WON FIVE CAPS FOR ENGLAND SCHOOLBOYS BEFORE JOINING SPURS AS AN APPRENTICE IN 1967. HE WENT ON TO WIN FOUR MORE YOUTH INTERNATIONAL CAPS WHEN AT WHITE HART LANE, MADE HIS FIRST DIVISION DEBUT IN 1969, AND HAS SINCE PLAYED FOR ENGLAND AT UNDER-23 LEVEL....

STEVE PERRYMAN   TOTTENHAM

FEBRUARY 1971.... AND THE FIRST OF PERRYMAN'S LEAGUE CUP FINALS— AGAINST ASTON VILLA, THEN IN THE THIRD DIVISION... THERE WAS NO SCORE, AND SPURS WERE STRUGGLING. THEN, WITH JENNINGS AND HIS OTHER DEFENDERS BEATEN, A VILLA SHOT ROLLED AGONIZINGLY TOWARDS AN EMPTY NET...

...IT WAS THE COOL STEVE PERRYMAN WHO KEPT HIS HEAD, AND SAVED HIS SIDE. RACING BACK, HE KICKED IT OFF THE LINE IN THE NICK OF TIME!

HERE'S MARTIN CHIVERS (BELOW), SCORING ONE OF HIS TWO LATE GOALS WHICH BEAT HEROIC VILLA THAT DAY. PERRYMAN, AT 19, THE YOUNGEST MAN ON THE FIELD, HEAVED A SIGH OF RELIEF—FOR THE THIRD DIVISION TEAM HAD PROVED A HARD TEAM TO BEAT. AND NOW LITTLE STEVE HAS ADDED ANOTHER CUP WINNERS' MEDAL TO HIS COLLECTION.

PERRYMAN HAS ALSO HELPED SPURS TO WIN THE UEFA CUP — AND HAS HELPED IN THEIR EFFORTS TO DEFEND IT, THIS SEASON. HERE HE ACCLAIMS ONE OF HIS TWO FINE GOALS AGAINST A.C. MILAN, IN THE HOME LEG OF THE SEMI-FINAL, IN 1972.

SPURS BEAT MILAN 3-2 ON AGGREGATE, THEN TOPPLED WOLVES IN THE TWO-LEG FINAL, BY THE SAME SCORE. HERE'S THE SCENE AFTERWARDS...

STEVE PERRYMAN IS ONLY 5 FT. 8 INS., BUT SKILFUL AND TIGERISH IN MIDFIELD, THIS SEASON HE WAS MADE VICE-CAPTAIN OF SPURS, AND A FULL CAP MUST BE HIS—SOON!

NAME ABOVE THE DOOR

I turned up at Cheshunt one day after my brother Bill and I had opened the first Steve Perryman Sports shop. I was driving a brand new all-white Ford Escort estate we'd bought for moving stock. Cyril Knowles drove up next to me. 'New car, Cock?'

I said it was a car for the shop.

'What have you got – a butcher's?'

Knowlesey was taking the piss in his usual gentle, funny way. But having a business and a new car to go with it was a sign of how I was maturing in the early 1970s, not just as a player but as a person.

The story of my sports shops started when I was about 19. My brother Bill was just 21 himself. He'd left school at 17, and was business-minded. He had the idea to open a shop, with my name above the door. If I'd known I was going to be at Spurs for 19 years we would have opened in North London, but we started off closer to home.

The first shop was on Uxbridge Road in Hayes, then we had another on Coldharbour Lane on the road to Heathrow, so the passing business was superb. My involvement was to go to the shop after training, talk to my brother and fill in for him when he took a break. Travelling on the North Circular, I used to break up the by journey sorting out and collecting orders for the shop. I would call into Minerva or Kent Trophies near the police station on Tottenham High Road. Discus Tracksuits were on a trading estate somewhere and Fred Perry had a factory not far from White Hart Lane. My being a Tottenham player didn't seem to do us any harm when dealing with manufacturers.

The sports retail industry was pretty amateur then. We stocked a plain white shirt and had Spurs badges in another drawer for mums to sew on. It was the same for other clubs. That's how it was until Admiral started to make specific team shirts. Kids who wanted to buy the boots players wore, Adidas La Paz for instance, couldn't get them. Shop owners would look at these young customers like they were mad and say, 'Do you know how much they cost?'

I had a presence in the shop without being really prominent. I'd serve customers, but I never felt really comfortable because you have to know about what you're selling. If it was too technical I'd ask Bill. I would do two weeks in the shop every year when he went away. It gave me a sense of how business works – if you're employing someone, they have to generate that money you're paying them plus a little bit more. And actually that's really what a professional footballer is – you're paid to generate money.

"I didn't particularly like 'footballer' pastimes, so the shop was somewhere to go and have a purpose"

The Sunday Times **magazine in September 1972 highlighted the fact that I cost the club nothing**

Lining up for the 1973 League Cup Final (right). Gilly was so laid back he didn't need to talk to anyone. John Pratt and I were more tense!

My winners' tankard from the final

Having a shop wasn't what average young players were doing then. My teammates would go and play snooker or golf in the afternoons. I used to occasionally drop Phil off at the bookies, though he wasn't a big gambler. A sports shop is a gamble. We were gambling thousands of pounds on stock in the belief it would sell.

I didn't particularly like 'footballer pastimes', so the shop was somewhere to go and have a purpose. Clubs wanted you to settle down. They liked you getting married and having children early, getting a mortgage and commitments, the theory being settling down into a 'normal' life would give you stability for your career. That was Bill Nick all over – I can't quite imagine him in the celebrity jungle like Harry Redknapp.

Bill Nick actually helped us with a few items for the shop, including six pairs of shin pads which he gave to me. I said, 'Bill, what do I give you back?' and he said, 'Nothing.' I didn't quite get it; he didn't have to do it. It was probably his way of encouraging me. He was never negative about the shops. I've never phoned anyone for work – if anyone wants me they either know I'm good enough already or not – and the shop was my way of being able to stand on my own feet, which I think Bill Nick admired.

The timing was also good. We opened the shops at the start of a sea change in the sportswear and merchandise industry. Umbro and Minerva had been Bill Nick's trusted brands, provided by Goodmans in Southgate. I played half of my career with no sponsorship on my shirt, around the ground or in the programme. Advertising was almost thought of as dirty money, whereas now it's much-needed revenue. In the early 1970s football was becoming more money-oriented, and that was to have a marked impact on the club.

While we were winning the UEFA Cup in 1972, our league position dipped, beginning a period of decline. The cups were a wonderful compensation at home and in Europe. We won the League Cup again in 1973, beating Norwich City 1–0 thanks to a goal from Ralph Coates. It seems glib to gloss over it now, but it was such a forgettable final, even poorer than the 1971 game, and its importance was in winning another trophy and qualifying for Europe.

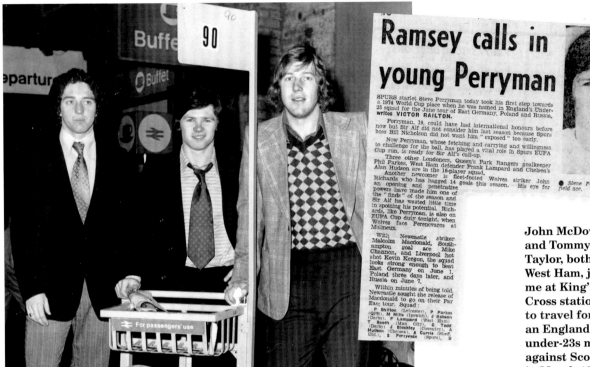

Ramsey calls in young Perryman

SPURS starlet Steve Perryman today took his first step towards a 1974 World Cup place when he was named in England's Under-23 squad for the June tour of East Germany, Poland and Russia, writes VICTOR RAILTON.

Perryman, 19, could have had international honours before now but Sir Alf did not consider him last season because Spurs boss Bill Nicholson did not want him "exposed" too early.

Now Perryman, whose fetching and carrying and willingness to challenge for the ball, has played a vital role in Spurs EUFA Cup run, is ready for Sir Alf's call-up.

Three other Londoners, Queen's Park Rangers goalkeeper Phil Parkes, West Ham defender Frank Lampard and Chelsea's Alan Hudson are in the 16-player squad.

Another newcomer is fleet-footed Wolves striker John Richards who has bagged 14 goals this season. His eye for an opening and penetrative powers have made him one of the "finds" of the season and Sir Alf has wasted little time in spotting his potential. Richards, like Perryman, is also on EUFA Cup duty tonight, when Wolves face Ferencvaros at Molineux.

With Newcastle striker Malcolm Macdonald, Southampton goal ace Mike Channon, and Liverpool hot shot Kevin Keegan, the squad looks strong enough to beat East Germany on June 1, Poland three days later, and Russia on June 7.

Within minutes of being told, Newcastle sought the release of Macdonald to go on their Far East tour. Squad:

P. Shilton (Leicester), P. Parkes (QPR), M. Mills (Ipswich), J. Robson (Derby), F. Lampard (West Ham), T. Booth (Man. City), D. Todd (Derby), J. Bleckley (Coventry), A. Hudson (Chelsea), A. Currie (Sheff. Utd.), S. Perryman (Spurs), D

Steve Perryman . . . midfield ace.

John McDowell and Tommy Taylor, both of West Ham, join me at King's Cross station to travel for an England under-23s match against Scotland in March 1974

On our day we could still beat almost anyone. But it obscured a more general drop in standards and status. We stopped signing 'top liners', the highest quality players. In 1972–73 Mike Dillon and Ray Clarke were home-grown debutants, but there were no 'off-the-peg' additions. It was getting harder to sign the best players, who wanted more money and were being increasingly influenced by agents. Not signing such players led to poorer results, which in turn led to shorter cup runs, falls in attendances and less gate money to play with. It became a vicious circle.

I was still making progress, however, playing game after game and becoming a mainstay of the side. Further recognition came with call-ups to the England under-23s, 17 times in all. Alf Ramsey oversaw the under-23s while in charge of the national side. He was absolutely sure what he wanted and I was to snuff the ball out in midfield or put pressure on.

Nonetheless, Ramsey said to me once, 'What I don't really understand about you, Steve, is why you keep going to the ball. You should let the opposing player come to you more.'

I said that at Tottenham they wanted me to press all the time.

'Well, it's not right *all* the time,' he replied.

I think that underlined a key difference between playing international football and league football – there was an intensity in domestic football that you had to master. At international level there was a bit more time. Bill Nick didn't want me to play too many internationals because I had enough to cope with at Spurs. But I played games for England under-23s and had some interesting trips, including to East Germany, Poland and the USSR in the summer of 1972.

Alan Hudson didn't go on this trip, which left a midfield space open for me to play in. I really enjoyed the experience of being in the England set-up again. In Berlin we had to go through Checkpoint Charlie. We were young

SPURS ACE SENT OFF

England lose two men, but win it in last seconds

Portugal 2, England 3

STEVE PERRYMAN, Spurs' midfield ace and England's captain, was sent off and Everton star Mick Buckley carried off, as the Under-23 international team gained a sensational and dramatic victory here last night.

As a prelude to this evening's clash between the senior sides of the two countries at Wembley it will not easily be forgotten.

Perryman's dismissal came ten minutes into the second half and even on a night of all-syringe decisions, this was just every.

He got the red card of dismissal, apparently for something he said to Spanish referee Urresorran.

Buckley had left this astonishing game after only eleven minutes, following a wild tackle by Portugal's Ferreira.

fine match, crossed from the right and Trevor Whymark headed the ball back from beyond the far post for Ipswich team-mate Johnson to score with a dive header.

STEVE PERRYMAN . . . Shows the red card

From
HARRY MILLER
In Lisbon

THE FOOTBALL ASSOCIATION
LIMITED

Patron: HER MAJESTY THE QUEEN
President: H.R.H. THE DUKE OF KENT
Chairman: SIR ANDREW STEPHEN, M.B., Ch.B.

Telegraphic Address:
FOOTBALL ASSOCIATION, LONDON, W2 3LW

Secretary:
E. A. CROKER

16 LANCASTER GATE, LONDON, W2 3LW

Your Ref: 22nd November, 1974

Our Ref: DR/jc 830

S. Perryman Esq.,
c/o Tottenham Hotspur F.C.,
748 High Road,
Tottenham,
London,
N17 0AP.

Dear Steve,

U.E.F.A. UNDER-23 COMPETITION

PORTUGAL v. ENGLAND - 19TH NOVEMBER, 1974

Just a line to say how delighted I was to hear your result in Lisbon last Tuesday, and to congratulate you and all the boys on getting such a good result over there.

I understand from Gordon Banks and George Eastham that you had considerable problems with the refereeing of the match, and they also both inform me that in their opinion you did nothing whatever to deserve being sent off the field. I can only say to you Steve, try not to worry about this and we shall certainly do everything we can at this end to help your case, although I believe that no provision is made for appealing against a U.E.F.A. suspension.

Anyway, all best wishes, and I hope to see you next month when the under-23 team will be playing Scotland in Aberdeen on 18th December.

Yours sincerely

Don Revie
Don Revie
Team Manager

A report on my sending off for the England under-23s, and a subsequent letter from manager Don Revie assuring me that he understood the decision was unfair and that it wouldn't dent my chances of a future call-up

---

men not really aware of the politics but it was in your face – dogs, armed guards, the lot. It was like something out of a spy thriller.

We went to Kiev, where there was a mix-up over hotel rooms. Ramsey told us, 'Everyone, stay on the bus; this will be sorted.' We were told by one of the management team that he went in and told them we had 20-odd rooms booked. The staff said, 'No, only four.' 'OK,' said Alf, calmly, 'if the other rooms are not available in the next 10 minutes we will go home.' As if by magic, the rooms were made available.

Alf was a very interesting man, a bit aloof and well-to-do, but I liked him. You wouldn't start a conversation with him, but I think I was a bit closer to him than others because of the Tottenham connection. He didn't have favourites by any stretch, but it was obvious how much he appreciated his old Spurs teammate Bill Nick.

Everything was matter of fact with Ramsey – precise and ordered. Jack Charlton tells a story that illustrates how well-spoken and thoughtful Alf was. One game he asked Jack to get tight on a player.

'Do you mean you want me to kick him?' said Jack.

'Oh no.'

'Do you mean nail him?'

'Oh, *no.*'

It was the way Alf said 'no' – posh, stemming from his elocution lessons.

He didn't throw loads of info at you – it was very clear and exact, as if to say, 'This is how it will be, without question.'

My England experience lasted until Don Revie took over. I was in the running to be included in his first senior squad. My battles against his Leeds team, added to under-23 experience, put me in contention. Then in an under-23 game in November 1974, against Portugal, I was sent off. It was assumed I'd been dismissed for dissent, but I hadn't argued; it must have been for what the ref thought was a poor challenge by me. I got a letter from Revie saying that George Eastham and Gordon Banks, who then were in charge of the under-23s team, had told him what had happened, that I wasn't to worry, and it wouldn't affect my chances. But I didn't get the call-up.

In truth, I had more than enough to keep me occupied at Tottenham. Bill Nick continued to sing my praises in the press, if not to me directly, having said I had Danny Blanchflower's anticipation a couple of years before. My work-rate was as intense as ever, getting the ball and serving it to my teammates. I ended up falling out with my brother Ted over it because he said that part of my game had taken over to the detriment of my overall game. In the end he said, 'I'm not watching you play again. You just run about and tackle! Bill Nick is never going to leave you out because you work too hard. But working too hard is not going to help your personal game, so I'm not going to watch it.' I said to Ted, 'Who am I going to please – Bill Nick or you?'

Ted and I still talked and everything else was fine between us. He just stopped coming to watch me. The fact that I didn't progress from the under-23s into the full England team means Ted might have been right. I was seen as a 'job' player who did the best thing for the team.

The Spurs team was now captained by Martin Peters, which was a good education for me. Mullers as a footballer was a serious player and powerful with his body and voice. Martin was more considered, and for me to see the balance of those two was instructive. This education proved important when Martin was injured and couldn't play in the UEFA Cup tie against Lyn Oslo in September 1972.

Bill just said on the night, 'This is the team; Martin's not fit so Steve, you're captain tonight and are also going to be vice-captain from now on, so if Martin is not playing other games you will be captain.'

I was not yet 21 and I was captain of Spurs. Typically, one of my first thoughts was, 'Why me? This is Tottenham Hotspur and I'm leading this team out?' I did think about my family and how proud they were going to be, though there were no mobile phones then to text them, so they heard about it over the loudspeaker at the ground along with everyone else.

I think what earned me that responsibility wasn't just my industry but also my sense of anticipation. That benefited my teammates as I was reading the whole game, not just that affecting my own individual situations. I always gave my opinion, as Ted had told me to do years before, sensing either danger or an opportunity that might affect my teammates and letting them know.

The press reported that my brother Ted was not watching me play anymore, due to how my game had developed

STEVE PERRYMAN

FAMILY TELL SPURS STAR HE RUNS TOO MUCH

Doing the pre-match honours as captain against Olympiakos (left)

"I was not yet 21 and I was captain of Spurs. Typically, one of my first thoughts was 'Why me?'"

Hunter Davies's iconic book, *The Glory Game*. I was surprised Bill Nick allowed Davies the access if I'm honest

My first time in a recording studio – another record, but not one I'm necessarily proud of! The song in question was *Hotspurs Boogie* but it didn't exactly set the charts on fire

Bill Nick told me after the Oslo game that he wanted to see me in his office to talk about captaincy. He gave me a sheet of about 20 things that a captain should do or how he should think. I wish I'd kept it, or at least could remember what was on it! Bill had all the experience; there wasn't a lot that he didn't know. Gilly told me all about Mackay, and I'd seen him with my own eyes as an apprentice, so I knew how a captain should carry himself by seeing him up close. Dave's style was simply to lead by shining example. Mine was more understated by comparison. I can't ever claim I was in Mackay's class.

By now I was also having increased dealings with the press. On the whole I got on OK with journalists. We mixed on European trips and with the under-23s. There is a benefit to a player in talking to journalists: they are people watching games, so surely if you talk to them you can learn something.

I had a personal relationship with most of the top reporters from the papers and it was an era where I don't think they told lies, or got you in trouble just for the sake of it. We were sort of mates – I know that suited them to have that kind of relationship, but there was a trust. You soon knew who to trust to do their job appropriately, guys like Steve Stammers, Michael Hart, Bob Driscoll, Harry Miller, Reg Drury and Norman Giller. It was a an era of good writers.

One of them wrote a broadsheet piece in which they called me 'Death Mask'. They didn't say I couldn't play but that I arrived at grounds, changed, got through the 90 minutes and never smiled, never showed any emotion. I thought that was very unfair. The writer was someone who hadn't spoken to me; if it had been someone who knew me I would have been distraught. I expected, and still do, to be treated fairly, which could be a construed as a bit of a weakness. I might not look like it but behind the 'death mask' you can hurt me with a comment.

The *Daily Mirror*'s Frank McGhee wrote a couple of nasty things about me in that mid-1970s. He wrote that a combination in midfield should be 'bread and jam' but John Pratt and I were 'bread and bread'. In fairness,

he ended up writing some very nice stuff about me towards the end of my career. Maybe I was in a bit of a rut then and John and I weren't the right combination. But it hurt at the time. The *Mirror* was my paper, which made it worse. But in general over the years I've performed better with a bit of needle, so criticism was not always a bad thing.

One of our stranger dealings with the media was with Hunter Davies when he was researching his book *The Glory Game*. It's a classic now, but at the time it was bizarre that the club let Hunter have so much insider access. He wasn't a normal football reporter – his background was in music. I will never understand why Bill allowed Hunter in. It hadn't been done before, and for a club that was so keen on keeping things in-house and discreet it defied belief. The book is a portrait of a time and place when football was moving into a slightly different world. Players' positions in society were changing. Mike England had dinner parties, and Hunter would go to these gatherings. Mike's social circle was an illustration of how the sport was changing: he always seemed a bit more upmarket than the rest of us. I wasn't at Mike's parties but heard, just in passing conversation from players who did go, that there were not just football people there – doctors, solicitors, people from the 'professional classes' apparently attended.

It was a great period for football in terms of the talent that I played with and came up against. There wasn't the wall-to-wall coverage that there is today, so it was hard not to be in awe of many of them. I would look at Bobby Moore like he was unreal, but in a very nice way. He was not a male model but he seemed almost perfect. He spoke correctly and carried himself so well it was almost like it was a statue of him stood in front of you.

The heyday of Best, Charlton and Law was winding down at Manchester United, but they still had it at times. Playing against quality in the 1970s became the norm because so many teams had top players. Manchester City had real talent – Mike Summerbee, who was hard as nails, Francis Lee, who I see now and again in Portugal, Mike Doyle and Colin Bell, who was a thoroughbred. No wonder he was called Nijinsky. Leeds, Liverpool and Derby had quality to burn. Alan Ball went to Arsenal and did well; Joe Royle was up and coming at Ball's old club, Everton; there was Tony Brown at West Brom. I was learning my trade in amongst all that.

For all their talent and star quality, all these players were approachable and normal. I had a funny exchange with Alan Ball in midfield during one game.

'You don't like me, do you?' he said in that squeaky voice of his.

'No Alan; to be honest, I don't,' I said.

'Aye, right. But you would if you played with me.'

And he was dead right.

I met Henry Newton, who played for Nottingham Forest, Everton and Derby, recently. He said, 'Steve, I never kicked anyone before they kicked me.' There was a respect for fellow pros. Players weren't all over each other shaking hands and kissing and cuddling in the tunnel before we went out; there was a robust attitude that we were there to battle. After the match there was always a players' room where we could go and have a friendly chat.

The problem was that by the mid-1970s the game became too much about systems – as if formation and tactics were more important than individual ability. Openness of play was lost. Everything got closed down. I suppose I was part of that as my style was broadly defensive, although I was never

The next step on the international ladder – representing my country for the under-23s against Czechoslovakia in 1974

taught to go out to get a draw, nor waste time to slow the game down. But it did become more and more important not to lose.

Compounding that at Spurs was a gradual reduction in the quality of recruitment. We brought in Neil McNab from Morton for about 40 grand and he became Tottenham's youngest ever player at 16, but he was one for the future. It was as if for more proven players there were better places to go than Tottenham. That could have been the natural cycle of things, as it is incredibly hard for a club to be top all the time – but the talent was not coming through and at the same time we began to lose the quality that we did have. Alan Gilzean left at the end of the 1973–74 season. His final days were on a tour to Mauritius and on his last night out he was heading a lampshade. But laughs then were in decreasing supply.

Jimmy Pearce looked to my inexperienced eye like he was going to be a top player, and Peter Collins seemed as solid as a rock. Along with Roger Morgan, they were all lost to the club through injury, which meant we couldn't raise money via transfer fees when they left. But all told we just didn't have enough about us. It appeared to me that Bill Nick had lost his edge, disaffected by how the game was changing. There were rumours that he needed to watch potential transfer targets too long, and was looking for reasons not to sign players. It was said he didn't like the increasing role of agents, nor how the media was becoming more intrusive or how money was taking over. It wasn't that football was becoming about survival of the fittest but survival of the adaptable, and Bill was struggling to adapt.

In the 1973–74 season we slipped to 11th in the league and swiftly went out of both domestic cups. That happened to other clubs too – Arsenal went from top in 1971 to 10th in 1974. But it was a point where we were relying on Bill Nick's class and experience to keep the wolf from the door.

Europe masked the problems. The year before we beat Red Star Belgrade and Olympiakos in Piraeus, and only went out in the semis on away goals to Liverpool. The next season we were back in the UEFA Cup and knew how to get through the rounds. We beat Cologne in the fourth round. They had Wolfgang Overath in their side. In 1970 we'd played them in the Palma de Mallorca pre-season tournament. They beat us 1–0 and I man-marked Overath. He was so dismissive of me then, looking at me with utter contempt, so it was nice to put one over him when it mattered.

After defeating Lokomotiv Leipzig we reached the final again. That was a fantastic run of success in that competition – two finals and one semi-final in three years. But the 1974 final against Feyenoord was to be one of the darkest, saddest episodes in our history.

It should have been so much better. We were at home in the first leg in front of a big crowd on an early

Phil, Gilly, Cyril Knowles, Mike Dillon and me below the Parthenon in Athens ahead of the game against Olympiakos in November 1972

summer's evening and should have won. But it finished 2–2, after they nicked a second goal five minutes from time through Theo de Jong, who I hadn't tracked back.

The return leg had some light moments. As we came out of the tunnel we saw a fan called Mickey Brown at the side of the pitch. We knew him from our travels away, and he was a bit of a rogue. We said, 'Mickey, what are you doing here?' He had a cameraman's bib and gear and said, 'It was the only way I could get in!' Later, Phil Holder came on for the last few minutes. I think that was Bill Nick wanting 'Chief' to get a share under the bonus scheme for making an appearance in the final. We got a free-kick on the edge of the box and Phil pushed Big Chiv out of the way to take it only to blast the ball just over the bar.

When we swapped shirts at the end of the game, Feyenoord didn't give us the shirts they had worn with badges on them unique to the final, but ones that were ragged and old. In general I felt then that the Dutch were a bit up themselves. They were terrific 'Total Footballers' but clearly thought very highly of themselves.

But we were in no mood to either laugh or complain by then. We had a goal by Chris McGrath disallowed which we were aggrieved about, as Feyenoord ran out 2–0 winners, but that all paled into insignificance because of what happened on the terraces. It was a riot, with running battles between our fans and the Dutch supporters. We were conscious of it on the pitch and worried even if, as professionals, we were trying to retain our focus on the game. I knew that my dad and brothers were in the part of the ground where it was happening. My wife Cherrill was also in the stadium with the other wives.

We were due to stay in Rotterdam for a couple of days, but the one place you didn't want to be as an English person after that game was in Holland. We just wanted to get home. English football fans were looked upon from that moment as out-of-control, ill-disciplined thugs. That might have been true for some, but I maintain it was a small minority. It was a very grim night. The saddest spectacle was Bill Nick having to forget the half-time team talk to go out and appeal for calm over the PA. I felt angry for him that he couldn't be doing his job. This total professional, instead of being with us and plotting our recovery from 1–0 down, was talking to people who probably weren't listening. I'm sure some of it was provoked. If you get a right-hander you're entitled to give one back. But it was as if brains went out of the window and Bill Nick, the man

"We were conscious of it on the pitch and worried even if, as professionals, we were trying to retain our focus on the game. I knew that my dad and brothers were in the part of the ground where it was happening"

Feyenoord changed their shirts at half-time knowing they were due to swap shirts with us at full-time. They wanted to keep the ones with the UEFA Cup Final wording so swapped inferior ones with us. I nearly broke through at one point (right), but we were destined not to score that night in Rotterdam, even having a goal disallowed

these fans supposedly idolised, was not going to have any effect on them.

Bill had enough about him to recognise that what he was witnessing was more important than football; if you knew the man you knew how bad must it have been for him to make that decision to go out onto the pitch. He saw himself as a leader of the 'Spurs Way' and doing things in the right way. He had complete integrity but that night the club's had been crushed. It ripped the heart out of him. He was a proper man, and looking at those scenes devastated him.

It was the beginning of the end. At the start of the next season we lost five out of six, including being beaten by newly promoted Carlisle and getting thrashed 5–2 at Liverpool.

Bill had been getting less patient and more and more critical. Even when we won finals, he was always praising the opponents. Knowlesy seemed to be the butt of everything. And when he started wearing white boots, if ever there was criticism the white boots would be mentioned.

Many years later, I had a discussion with one of Bill Nick's daughters and I felt the same as she did, that she never wanted to let him down. It wasn't out of fear – it was respect and a love for him. No disrespect to my dad, but Bill was my 'work father'. It's why I still feel guilty talking about him in a negative way to this day. But you can get under a cloud as a player with any manager. If you start thinking the manager doesn't rate you it's bloody hard to get out of it. I probably needed Bill Nick to go – and I *really* don't like saying that.

During the crisis time at the club, Bill and Eddie decided I couldn't play any more. At 22 they thought my legs had 'gone' and in a staff meeting they said as much to Charlie Faulkner. Charlie phoned me afterwards and said that he had had a row on my behalf. 'Oh, he's gone has he?' Charlie had said, throwing a cup of tea in anger at Eddie – he wouldn't have thrown it at Bill. 'I'll show you how much he's gone; I'll show you how much I can get for him.'

Charlie told me Bill Nick was going to phone me the next day to ask if I wanted to leave. He said that Spurs had asked Coventry for two players and

Coventry had asked for me in return. Charlie had spoken to Coventry, and they had confirmed it. That could have been seen as almost treasonous by Charlie, but he was protecting me. I didn't think particularly well nor badly of him for it, but it was a risky move.

Bill did call me in the next day, saying he'd never thought of selling me, but that Spurs wanted two players from another club which he didn't name, and that they had asked for me in return.

'What do you think?' he said.

I said, 'I think I'm ready to move. If it's to somewhere like Newcastle, I'm not going; the Midlands, yes.'

Bill said, 'Are you sure about that? Are you really sure what you're saying?'

He probably didn't want me to go but in that case why was he asking me?

'Bill, you're putting it to me,' I replied.

If he really didn't want me to go he wouldn't have mentioned it.

'Well,' he said, sounding a bit bewildered. 'I suggest you go talk to your family and if you feel the same tomorrow, then come see me.'

So I did go to see him the next day and I still said that yes, I wanted to leave. Bill still wasn't telling me where. He just told me to train and he'd tell me later.

I didn't tell anyone I was off. I felt relieved in a way because I just wasn't happy. To say that I'd 'gone' was too strong and I was disappointed in Bill and Eddie's judgement. I might have deserved to be left out for a month or so. I'd been playing football solidly game after game. I had played 53 games the year before, and the year before that 64.

But what I was doing in midfield was clearly not enough. It was as if something had been taken away from me by doing the running in a 'star' team, and now we weren't a star team my running wasn't good enough. Ted's words were coming back to haunt me. I wasn't getting any appreciation, certainly not from Bill, so I felt trapped. Therefore it seemed logical to get out.

Bill had to do something, and this was an option. He could get a couple of players in and while he didn't want to lose me he did want fresh faces. I was married by this point with a baby, Loren. A move would have meant upheaval, but Coventry would have been OK; it would probably have taken me the same time on the M40 to get to there as it did to get round the North Circular.

I was in a bit of a daze. I didn't have an agent. I had little idea about wages or a signing-on fee. On the day it was decided I was leaving, I went home. My wife and I were discussing the move, thinking about the practicalities. And then I got a phone call saying Bill had resigned.

When we went in the next day, Martin Peters asked us, 'Can we say on all of your behalves that we don't want Bill to resign?'

I said, 'Mart, I don't think I can say that.'

I remember him being shocked to hear me say it, though the players' views came to nothing in the end.

There have been rumours since that Bill was sacked and didn't resign. Certainly he was not given a job 'upstairs' as some of the reports said he would be at the time. I don't doubt that he could have been pushed. It was a bad time.

It was also the biggest crisis point in my career, a sliding-doors moment – Bill stays, I'm gone. Nineteen years at Tottenham could have disappeared, just like that. But Bill went, and I was the one who stayed. We would have a

Bill Nick and his wife Darkie returning home from the 1974 UEFA Cup Final. It was very sad because it tipped Bill over the edge and led to him leaving Spurs. He had become disenchanted with the game and less patient. The trouble in Rotterdam was the straw that broke the camel's back

WE WILL RETURN

When the new man was appointed, his name was a surprise. Bill Nick had reportedly been pushing for Danny Blanchflower, Johnny Giles or a combination of the two to take his place. Giles would have been interesting given the flare-up we had had a couple years earlier but by all accounts he did like me as a player. In the event Hull City boss Terry Neill – Arsenal's former player Terry Neill – was appointed.

It was a shock to the supporters, many of whom never took to him, but Terry was given an even break by the majority of players. The senior ones knew that their time was limited. The fact that Pat knew Terry from Northern Ireland international duty and had a decent relationship with him was a positive. If someone was OK by Pat he was usually OK by me.

As invariably happens with a changing of the guard, other faces left. Johnny Wallis stayed but Cecil was close to retiring, while Eddie Baily was sacked, just like that. Terry brought in Wilf Dixon, who had been his right-hand man at Hull.

As for my future, it was settled on day one. Terry walked past me and said simply: 'Steve, you're going nowhere.'

I had come close to leaving – very close – and the change in manager meant a complete switch in fortunes for me. Having Bill Nick as the only boss I'd ever had, of course it was different straight away, but things did feel fresher – not better, necessarily, but different. Every manager has their quirks about what they think should be done within a week or a month of arriving. Terry inevitably drew on his own experiences to do things his way.

A couple of weeks after the start of pre-season I bumped into Bill. I drove past his house coming back from training. He was in his front garden and I pulled over to speak to him. Years later I would knock on his door and go in for a chat. On that day he said, 'I understand you're not doing sit-ups?'

'Not like we did with you Bill.'

'Not right,' said Bill without saying any more than that. He still had his eye on things. There had been no goodbyes from Bill when he left. I phoned him up at some point, and told him, 'I'm sorry, sorry that I didn't do better for you last season. But I want to thank you for all you've done for me.' Bill was fine with it. What a man.

Routines under Terry changed. We trained at Cheshunt more than we did under Bill, though on Fridays we were still back at White Hart Lane. One thing that Terry did introduce was finishing our Tuesday training with

"I had come close to leaving – very close – and the change in manager meant a complete switch in fortunes for me"

Terry Neill stopped my transfer and made certain I would stay at Spurs. The decision made me a 'Spur forever'

a hard sprint running session. I felt that prepared me well for Saturday. Under Bill, we had got into the routine of having 10-lap races round the pitch on a Thursday, which came from what he thought was needed for a player's body to be at its best. I can't say that I was unfit under Bill but Terry's 'sharpener' on a Tuesday with the Wednesday off and then focusing on football on Thursday and Friday suited my body.

Following Bill Nick was not going to be easy and it made sense to ring the changes, so within a year England, Beal and Peters had gone, and Knowles and Chivers would leave soon after. There's a view that Terry allowed Mike to go because he was retiring, only for Mike to go to America to play for Seattle Sounders and there was a bit of a hullabaloo about that.

I think we benefited from a new mental approach. If we messed an exercise up Bill Nick would be upset and let you know it. Terry wouldn't. Bill was a bit of a perfectionist and there's nothing wrong with that because it worked, but with a youngster who is feeling negative or not playing well a manager needs to be careful in how he treats him. I'm not precious by any means, but it doesn't help to be over-criticised.

When Terry joined I was still only 22. From the start he was more appreciative of me. I got more shouts of 'Well done' – whether they were deserved or not – and I felt that Terry and Wilf were on my side. Perhaps it was just hearing a different voice. Jack Charlton said once that five years is long enough to manage one club because after that the players know what you're going to say. I don't think Bill Nick was as readable as that, but things had become predictable.

Naturally there was sadness and disappointment that Bill had left. He had run the whole show, after all, and was so loved by all the staff. As players we didn't really know if Terry was given the same power, right down to how much the tea ladies were paid. But there seemed to be a fairly seamless transition of power. Football clubs move on very quickly.

Another new face appeared when Terry brought in a chap called Keith Burkinshaw. He had previously worked at Newcastle and Terry liked their style of play at that time and saw Keith as well-suited to Spurs. How prophetic that turned out to be, but for the 1974–75 season, there was no real change in tactics. If we played poorly that season it was always put down to Terry's 'Arsenal upbringing', which was unfair. In any system and with any tactic you can play well, badly or indifferently. People forget about individual performances, what the opponents are doing and the overall talent available to managers.

There were new arrivals, in John Duncan, Don McAllister and Bill's last big buy, Alfie Conn. Chris Jones came through the ranks and got a run of games. For me, I was given something of a new lease of life, freeing my head of being so defensive-minded. Terry came up with a plan. 'Steve, when Pat kicks long to hit the front I want you to run on beyond, anticipating that we're going to win it or our striker and their defender both miss it and it runs on. I want you to do that three times a half.'

It was a very simple instruction that was definitely going to reap rewards, because in those days the goalkeeper could pick up the back pass and Pat would have a number of kicks. It's not that we got many goals from it, though I scored six in the league that season. The significance was that I was thinking about getting forward rather than defending. Terry knew that I could recover well. 'You'll get back if we don't win the header; you'll get back as quick as anyone.' For a defensive midfielder, it was a refreshing change of mentality. Terry didn't do me any harm.

He did move Martin Peters on, and Martin did some very good things at his new club, Norwich, playing lots of games. Terry was only 34 when he got the Tottenham job and some of the players he was managing were effectively the same age, and it appeared to be a problem that they weren't quite accepting of him. Martin wasn't being arrogant or flash but was sure of what he needed to do.

Once a manager starts getting 'that feeling' about you and vice versa then both parties are probably better off parting. It was a different for me. I was young, wanting to improve and get my career started again. Martin's departure also opened up the captaincy to me on a permanent basis. The role carried more weight in those days, with more responsibility for skippers to control things on the field. Terry thought my sense of anticipation and having an opinion would be useful in the heat of battle, getting the midfield to drop a bit deeper for example.

Captaincy was not a job with a formal application process. Being judged every day on the way I played and handled myself was my application.

"Naturally there was sadness and disappointment that Bill had left. He had run the whole show, after all, and was so loved by all the staff"

Page 30   DAILY MIRROR, Monday, October 21, 1974

LONDON ON THE BRIGHT SIDE

Fearless Perryman spotlights the path to better fortune

BRAVE MEN OF SPURS..

STEVE PERRYMAN symbolises why Tottenham can go to work with a smile this week while Arsenal will report for training with worry lines showing on almost every face.

By HARRY MILLER

Oh, Daddy, what a funny eye you've got . . . Steve Perryman's young daughter, Loren, examines the damage caused to his left eye during the Spurs–Arsenal derby. Below, he wears a patch to disguise the damage
Picture: ALAN OLLEY

One lovely black eye! Sporting scars after a bruising 2–0 win over Arsenal

My first thought on being made captain was, 'I hope I can handle this'! But there was a degree of naivety involved, and thought I *can* do it. Looking back now I could have been thinking more that I was following in the footsteps of legends – Mackay, Blanchflower, Mullery, Peters, men of real standing. But I adopted my usual attitude towards things: onto the next thing, and captaincy was the next thing.

Wilf Dixon noticed that during one performance I'd gone quiet. He said, 'Steve, you have got to realise that a captain playing poorly can still win the game. You cannot afford to go quiet because you are personally having a bad game.' That's a really good point. If you are going to be captain you have to be captain through thick and thin; you've got to step up even more so when you are not playing well.

That helped make me a good captain. In addition, I knew the culture of the club and how to live up to its values. It had been fed to me right from the off by Johnny Wallis et al. Captaincy carries extra responsibility, as you become the spokesperson for the team and how we act, how we perform and how we are looked upon in the community. I would have to front up in good times and bad, and rightly so: the captain gets to pick the cup up when you win something, and you're in the front line when you've lost the first three games of the season. That's only right.

Not that there was much danger of us lifting a trophy that season. We were poor, losing 21 league games and getting knocked out of the cups straight away. That vicious spiral was continuing. There was the odd highlight – I scored in a 2–0 win over Arsenal in October 1974 – but we had long spells when we couldn't buy a win. There wasn't a single victory in nine games between January and March. We lost five on the spin and got only one draw out of nine at one stage in the spring.

Crowds dropped. We had 12,000 against Carlisle. Life wasn't easy. It was a struggle and that was a new experience for me. For a player who has responsibility so ingrained in him it was tough. We just managed to stay up, winning five games out of the last seven to rescue the situation.

Key in that run was a remarkable home game against Chelsea, another side who had declined severely after having a purple patch. The crowd for that was nearly 51,000. At the coin toss I lined up opposite Ray Wilkins, who was their captain. He was only 18, with so much pressure on his shoulders. I knew Ray because he was brought up in Hayes, and I really liked him and his family. He used to hang about our shop in his school blazer. Brian Moore, the commentator, described that match against Chelsea as the most important game played in the history of both clubs, due to the fear of relegation for both sides. The tension was incredible. Kick-off was delayed because of fighting between fans on the pitch. It was nasty.

I scored the first goal, one of four I got in that seven-game period. I was involved from clearing the ball out from the edge of our box, laying John Duncan in and then joining the attack. Would I have done that in Bill Nick's era? It was almost a tap-in at the end but, maybe because it was against Chelsea, it's one of the goals that I enjoy reminiscing about because it showed my determination and my ability to get from one end to the other. I'd curbed that part of my game for so long.

Alfie Conn missed a great chance that day but he got the second. He'd got a hat-trick away at Newcastle in January, but was always an inconsistent player for us and that frustrated both him and the team.

Chelsea were young and naive – they had a youthful image with the King's Road and all that, and they had a lot of home-grown players in the team. Nothing wrong with that but I wonder if it was all too much for them. We won 2–0, effectively relegating them, and my shop windows paid for it! I can't be certain it was Chelsea fans, but windows were broken five days in succession, and it might have been football related.

The pressure eased against us for a bit but then we lost 1–0 at Arsenal, which meant they stayed up. That was some game: we didn't lie down and it gave us the heart to know that we could go there and play well, albeit lose. Maybe if we'd got a point that day we would have gone into the final game against Leeds with a different mindset, thinking a draw would suit us. There's a dangerous thought. Instead we needed to beat Leeds to stay up, and that probably helped on the night. It is just not in the club's DNA to sit back and contain, but it felt to me over the years that if we needed a win we got it – which is a bit of a damning indictment. A team should need to win every game. It was a mark of those times that there was such inconsistency.

The Leeds match felt very much like a European night – which always felt special – and White Hart Lane was packed. There was a feeling of, 'There's something going down tonight'. We just hoped it wasn't us. As captain I was thinking practically. 'Keep 11 men in this game; focus; concentrate. Don't do stupid things.' We went 1–0 up early through a thunderbolt free-kick from Cyril. 1–0 at home is a very difficult half-time talk because you can concede two just like that. Thankfully Knowlesy scored again and Chivers, recalled after a long spell of being left out, got another in a memorable 4–2 win. Our

Geoff Barnett, in goal for Arsenal, is relieved after Alfie Conn misses a great chance to equalise at Highbury, meaning we needed to win the last game of the 1974–75 season, against Leeds

other scorer was Conn, who during the game did something I thought was practically committing suicide. He got overexcited with how we were playing, and at one point he sat on the ball to mock the Leeds players. It might have been a release of tension for him after a year of frustration. Perhaps some things had been said to him in the game that I wasn't aware of, but from my perspective it was a selfish act for his own glorification or pleasure.

Billy Bremner, a Scotsman, said, 'Steve, tell that Scottish bastard to stop, or we'll start trying.' They obviously had been trying, though there was a lot gossip that they were saving themselves for their European Cup Final a few weeks later.

Alfie deserved any stick. I said to him, 'Do yourself a favour, Alfie,' which I was entitled to say as captain. Stunts like Alfie's I really don't like. Nominating how many nutmegs players are going to do before a game or having a mask ready for when they score a goal, it's totally different to the way I think football should be played. There's a room for nutmegs – if your shot goes through the goalie's legs because you're clever enough to know that in that situation he will spread his legs, that's top-class. But to just pull a trick for its own sake, or say you are going to do something, that's nonsense – it's cheap, unprofessional bullshit.

It could have rebounded badly on Alfie and us. All of a sudden Leeds could have upped their game in anger at being disrespected. Our fans had a laugh but it could have backfired. Still, we won and so stayed up. Just.

Determination and tension written on the faces of the bench as we battle to avoid relegation

There was relief as well as the knowledge that it was not good enough. Why couldn't we play like that more often? The next season saw seven debuts, with six of the players coming through the ranks including Steve Walford, Ian Smith, Micky Stead and Noel Brotherston. Willie Young was the only signing, while Alfie missed a lot of games through injury. Young had critics but he was the man who was going to get his head to things, which at set pieces is always important.

This was now Terry Neill's team. There was a sense of rebuilding as the club as a whole settled down, and it led to a substantial improvement in league position and us reaching the semi-finals of the League Cup. I continued to prosper, scoring six again. I scored in the opening-day win against Middlesbrough, which was very welcome because that fixture had sealed Bill Nick's fate and they were a more than decent side then. I also signed a new contract after negotiating a £10 per week pay rise. Terry eventually said, 'Steve, you've got the £10 because you're my captain.' I made it clear to Terry I wasn't accepting the rise on that basis, as I wasn't *his* captain but captain of the players and the team. I didn't want to be seen as a manager's man.

Another home-grown made his debut that season. We always had one eye on the youngsters, and we had heard about one coming through. You look to see if they are good on the ball and don't panic; someone who seems to have a bit of extra time when you come up against them in training and doesn't allow you to close them as quickly as the other kids. This lad fitted the bill.

Glenn Hoddle was almost untouchable in training. He wasn't a character who would force himself on you with his talk or quips. He was shy, a decent young man trying to make his way in the game. But his talent was unmistakable. We would think, 'Oh, this lad is special.'

I wasn't pushing for him to play in the team. There was a doubt about his strength at that time and growing up he was a bit gangly. I didn't have the clout to tell Terry to pick him, though would certainly air my opinions, but there was something obviously special about Glenn. Someone who could take the ball under pressure like he could was a leader in play. I was a leader in attitude and drive but Glenn – even at that age – was definitely a leader in play.

There were quite a few players coming through the ranks at this point. As someone who had managed to get through all the pitfalls and barbed wire to become captain, my example was a good reason to produce others. It showed it could be done. I had more of an empathy with those players. Once you've had the experience of going through all the stages and milestones of development you can advise on it. It's nice when you've got someone there who can just say a word. 'Relax, you're good enough.' I think I am a major factor in why Tottenham produce their own players, even to this day.

What was obvious about Glenn was that he believed in himself. It wasn't a particularly good team he was coming into, and he was not going to be carried, so he had to do his bit, which was having mastery of that ball. His range of passing, which was already impressive, suited teammates like Chris Jones, who came through the ranks around the same time. Even if Glenn hit someone on the back of the head trying to get it through, you didn't think it was wasted, because he'd seen the opportunity.

Terry did well to ease Glenn in. He came on as sub against Norwich in August and didn't play again until a 2–1 win in February at Stoke in which he scored. Glenn was the future.

You could tell pretty much straight away that Glenn Hoddle was something special

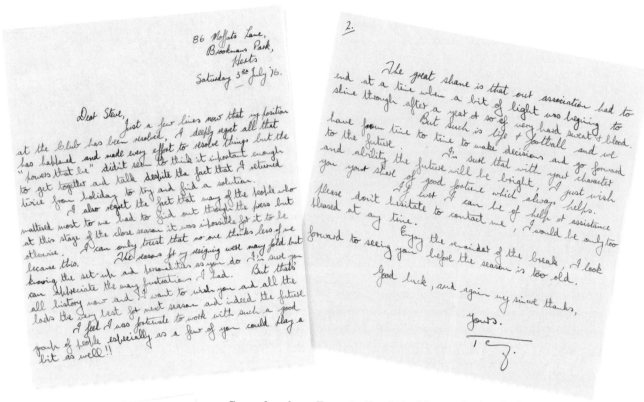

86 Moffats Lane,
Brookmans Park,
Herts

Saturday 3rd July 76.

Dear Steve,

Just a few lines now that my position at the Club has been resolved, I deeply regret all that has happened and made every effort to resolve things but the "powers that be" didn't seem to think it important enough to get together and talk despite the fact that I returned twice from holiday to try and find a solution.

I also regret the fact that many of the people who mattered most to me had to find out through the press but at this stage of the close season it was impossible for it to be otherwise. I can only trust that no one thinks less of me because this. The reason for my resigning will many fold but knowing the set-up and personalities as you do I'm sure you can appreciate the many frustrations I had. But that's all history now and I want to wish you and all the lads the very best for next season and indeed the future.

I feel I was fortunate to work with such a good grouch of people especially as a few of you could play a bit as well!!

The great shame is that our association had to end at a time when a bit of light was beginning to shine through after a year of so of very hard sweat & blood. But such is life & football and we have from time to time to make decisions and go forward to the future. I'm sure that with your character and ability the future will be bright, your your share of good fortune which always helps. I just wish please don't hesitate to contact me, I would be only too pleased at any time.

Enjoy the remainder of the break, I look forward to seeing you before the season is too old.

Good luck, and again my sincere thanks,

Yours,

T.N.

TOTTENHAM HOTSPUR FOOTBALL & ATHLETIC CO. LTD.

748 HIGH ROAD
TOTTENHAM · N17 0AP

5th July 1976.

To Senior Members
of the Coaching and Playing Staff

For your information:

Set out below is the Press Statement issued by the Board on 30th June 1976, concerning the resignation of Mr. Terry Neill as Manager of the Club:-

1. On the 9th June 1976 Mr. Neill wrote a letter to Mr. Sidney Wale, Chairman of Tottenham Hotspur Football Club, in which he tendered his resignation as Manager of the Club "with immediate effect". The Board feels that in all the circumstances it has no alternative but to accept the resignation.

2. In explaining his decision to resign, Mr. Neill spoke of "the attitude of the Board at yesterday's meeting and their complete lack of response to my requests and grievances", which Mr. Neill said "have left me with no alternative but to take this step".

3. The major differences between Mr. Neill and the Board of which the Board is aware related to certain proposals made by Mr. Neill concerning payments which he wished the Club to make to some of its employees. In the opinion of the Board the proposed payments were not such as they could properly authorise.

4. At all times Mr. Neill had full control of team management, and the Board always supported Mr. Neill's requests for transfers of players, and recognises that under his management the team made considerable progress. The Board regrets that Mr. Neill has acted as he has.

Sidney A. Wale
Chairman.

A quick change for Spurs: Terry Neill departs after barely two years. He wrote **some kind words to me, while Sidney Wale made things official (above)**

Spurs fans have Terry to thank for his part in developing that future, but in the here and now of the long, hot summer of 1976 there were only recriminations. Terry walked and went to Arsenal. He'd had less than two seasons, which was not long enough to fulfil his task, but he felt that some players, the supporters and even the board were not with him.

We had gone on an end-of-season tour to Canada and Australasia. We played too many games, nine in total. The mood wasn't great, and there was a suggestion that there had been problems with signing players. At some point Dennis Tueart was mentioned but he didn't come. Terry's standing had got a bit stronger and he perhaps expected more backing. It could have been the call of the club that was close to his heart. But I actually don't think people were too disappointed by it. The cynics would say, 'What would you expect of an Arsenal man?' I first heard he'd gone in the papers. This is a manager I had a good standing with and who kept me at Tottenham. I remember thinking he might try and take one or two with him, but didn't ever consider I could be one. The reaction of my teammates was split.

Keith Burkinshaw was appointed straight away. I didn't really get on with him when he first came. He was northern and blunt and I'd had plenty of that at Tottenham already. But I voted for him when the players had a talk about backing Keith, and I let Sidney Wale know that we wouldn't be too disappointed if it was Keith who got the job.

Unfortunately, the club was on a downer. The decline had deep roots but White Hart Lane was becoming a bit of a depressing place, which will always happen when a club that has done so well, with such tradition and expectancy, goes through bad times. It's a tough crowd at Spurs, and rightly so. The fans had seen a lot better and, as Bill Nick always said, were no mugs.

Chairman Sidney Wale (standing, first from right) tells the squad the club's decision to appoint Keith Burkinshaw (standing, centre) as manager

You could sense the disquiet from the off. There were a number of new signings, including Gerry Armstrong and Peter Taylor, but our form was poor. I started to get hamstring-like niggles that I'd never had before. I'd be fit to play but I think there was a build-up of lactic acid. There could have been a physiological reason for this, and I think stress played a part. I'd finish a game and feel OK, but during Sunday watching TV or being with the family, I'd feel physical discomfort and anxiety. I was taking the job home with me.

The team could still do it on rare occasions. I played one of my best ever games against Liverpool at centre-half. We won 1–0, which was a shock because they were flying. John Toshack and Kevin Keegan taught me a lot about Liverpool's strength at working opponents over. Every time the ball went up to Toshack for him to flick on I was there, anticipating where it would fall and what Keegan would do. All of a sudden from the touchline the message went out to Keegan: 'Drop into midfield.' Ten minutes later they moved him forward again. It was clever, but also respectful of me and seeing how they needed to change things.

Good days like that were rare. When you have positive momentum, you can fly. But when you're losing, you adopt the wrong type of momentum. It's like running through glue. You're not on the front foot, you are expecting the worst. We were too easily beaten and lost 21 games. There was no real backbone, and we lost 8–2 at Derby. That was humiliating. I scored just before half-time to make it 3–2 so in the dressing room we were positive, but we ended up conceding eight goals – with a fella like Pat Jennings in goal. Where do you go after that? We had some woeful games. I wouldn't say we weren't trying, but whatever we were trying wasn't working. We were conceding late goals, letting leads slip.

Despite going down after our last game of the 1976–77 season, the loyal fans stayed and demanded we came back out to the directors' box to wish us well. What magnificent support

In training and the day-to-day it was all too easy to have the needle. I was looking to bring up what I thought the problems were. We went out of the FA Cup against Cardiff and there was a meeting about it. I made the point that I thought Alfie pulled out of about six challenges. His answer wasn't really good enough, something along the lines of, 'Did that cost us the game?' My way of looking at it was what if we all pulled out of six challenges, what chance would we have? People are understandably sensitive to being criticised but I just couldn't understand that thinking. There are team-oriented players and those who are individuals thinking about themselves. A side needs a balance of different types: in the early 1970s Chiv was probably a bit selfish in his attitude but it was productive. In a relegation-threatened team we needed everyone working together.

We retreated in on ourselves. We stopped going into Doll's Caff, as we didn't want to talk to people about the games. A black cloud hung over the place. No one had any respect for you. Walking along Tottenham High Road you felt embarrassed. I got letters. Anything addressed to 'Steve Perryman (captain)' during a run of defeats was likely to be critical, but I read them all and responded. If there was a phone number I'd call but normally I'd write back with something along the lines of, 'You're welcome to your opinion and of course results suggest you're right, although I don't necessarily agree with some of your reasoning.' If there were any accusations of cowardice, I wouldn't have that.

In moments of crisis for me I was always drawn to my parents' home. It was my place of sanctuary. My mum and dad weren't judging me on our last result and I felt out of the heat there. I wondered if that was a weakness in me. But naturally, you're going to find people who love you to help you dodge the bullets.

Right at the end of the season we had a glimpse of hope with a 3–1 home win over Villa, but then we got stuffed 5–0 at Man City, which was the real killer. Maine Road was always a difficult place to play with its big pitch and atmosphere. It was a proper football ground, gritty and northern. At one point when I would normally have passed, I just thought, 'Sod it.' I turned away, got shut down, then turned away again. I wasn't going to give that ball to anyone. I was almost planting a flag saying, 'My team ain't good enough but I am.'

It was me making a stand. The crowd were taking the piss: the Spurs fans were making 'tossers' signs at us. It was no more than we deserved. It was a game where we needed to have the Leeds spirit of two seasons before about us, but we failed miserably.

The last game was against Leicester and we won 2–0. It was a great crowd for those days of 28,000, and there was a banner saying: 'We Will Return.' It felt almost like a celebration game, not the final nail in the coffin, even though other results meant we were down for certain. In a way that Leicester game was the start of the next season. It was a relief in some ways. For weeks it had felt like it was coming. Now it had.

Alfie Conn had been sold back to Scotland by then and wrote a gloating piece in the paper, saying the 'Cockney Mafia' had got rid of him, which I took to mean me, Pratty and Terry Naylor. He also said not only would we not go up the following season but that we'd go down again. I've been accused of not getting on with Scots, usually citing Conn. I knew people like Alan Gilzean and Dave Mackay – I think I know what proud Scotsmen stand for. And if I meet Scots who don't measure up to them, I think what Gill and Mackay would think – 'You don't fancy this, do you?'

I contacted Alfie. I told him he was fine to have his view, but that when we didn't go down and we came back up he was to ring me and apologise. He said he would.

The Tottenham fans were superb that final day. Their support was actually a signpost for better things to come. They showed belief in the club and loyalty. As players we could imagine the stick they were getting at work and at school. So to come and show that spirit on that day was truly humbling. A cynic might take the piss out of it. 'Oh, you got a win, did you? Forgotten how it felt?' But it *was* spirit: it was belief in their club that was going to come right. The attitude of the crowd that day determined everything.

> "The Tottenham fans were superb that final day. Their support was actually a signpost for better things to come. They showed belief in the club and loyalty"

The banner says it all – Spurs would be back

CHAPTER ELEVEN

SCOOPING THE WORLD

There was another banner seen at White Hart Lane around the time of relegation – 'Get The Burk Out'. It was displayed on the Shelf, home to Tottenham's most committed and vocal supporters. But it was an exception. The object of the banner's criticism, Keith Burkinshaw, was not subjected to widespread opposition. It was clear he was determined to restore the club's fortunes, and the fans responded in kind.

Relegation was a humbling experience. For the first time in 27 years, Spurs were not in the top flight, and as captain I was partly culpable for getting us relegated. Part of what a leader does is take responsibility when things go wrong.

I felt a little uneasy with Keith as a coach initially. He was a bit blunt, but that was a strength. He turned out to be good for me because as manager he trusted me, as captain, to have an opinion and voice it. We were a little bit hand in glove. We would speak on the phone for at least an hour every Sunday about how to try and improve things. We'd spend so much time talking about the bloody team when we were getting beaten all the time, we pretty much knew what the other was going to say. But we were always up for it, talking, being honest and facing the challenges head on.

Keith was genuine. He believed in what he said and that's half the battle with managers. If you're a bit grey, players catch you out; you have to believe in everything you're saying. He had shown he was a very capable coach in training. He had a 'working-class' football upbringing as a player with one appearance at Liverpool and then much longer spells at Workington and Scunthorpe. He was schooled in ground-level, old-fashioned football but was willing to try new things. He had belief in his ability and a genuine faith in attacking football.

It was said at the time that Tottenham did not want another manager to get as powerful again as Bill Nick had been. If that's true then it was a misguided idea. You should find the right person and let him be as powerful as he needs to be. Keith always suggested that his authority came from running the whole club. If you are the man you have got to be *the* man.

That said, it was a commendable decision by the board to keep Keith on after relegation. It's unthinkable that it would happen now. There was a risk that it made Keith indebted to the people who kept him in the job, but that was some decision by the board, and no one really got any credit for it. I think they thought Keith had the right ethics and believed in the Spurs Way – he hadn't been great at delivering it so far, but they trusted him to get there in the end.

"Relegation was a humbling experience. As captain I was partly culpable for getting us relegated. Part of what a leader does is take responsibility"

Keith was intent on steering us back to the top flight

One of Keith's strengths was that he provided no surprises. He knew all the young players' names and who their parents were, and always turned up to watch the Sunday games at Cheshunt. That makes a good impression on everyone, inside the club and out. The players also responded well to him. I don't remember anyone being anti-Keith other than Alfie Conn, which is probably because he was soon shown the door.

The fightback began in May 1977. We went to Bergen in Norway, not playing the city's main team but two lower-league sides that we should have beaten and did. The fact that we did so with a togetherness and style meant that everyone left for the summer break feeling good about coming back.

All of us, that is, apart from Pat Jennings. I have never really quite got to the bottom of Pat's departure and move to Arsenal. He was Tottenham through and through and in my opinion wouldn't have wanted to go to Highbury. But what was the alternative – the kids go hungry because dad doesn't want to play for Arsenal?

The popular narrative is that Keith moved him on as a way of showing – to everyone – who was boss. I was with Keith at a fans' event recently and was asked who was the best goalkeeper I played with at Tottenham. I replied that it was a hard choice but opted for Pat. Keith didn't say anything, but gave a little wry look. Another story is that Pat was ignored by the Spurs directors when they walked past him when he and they both knew he was going; none of them said a word and wouldn't look him in the eye. That, sadly, is typical when players leave clubs. It happened to me. But I was really surprised when Pat went. The previous few years had been a struggle, but he could still produce. He got the Players' Player of the Year award in 1976 and joked, 'I want to thank my defence.'

Pat is a man of character and standing, and was a Spurs hero – still is. But it should be noted that Keith had belief in Barry Daines's ability to take over as goalkeeper. That was clearly a factor in his thinking.

During pre-season, Keith opted for the perfect tournament where we would play against a range of clubs, including Leicester, in the north of Sweden. We won that tournament. That's when we started talking about how we were going to play the ball out, how we were going to make better angles – the way we were going to come back.

The change in our approach was instigated by my switch to the centre of defence. Injuries and the personnel available to Keith dictated that to an extent, but I'd played very well in that position the season before against Liverpool as a one-off. In the Second Division it worked a treat. I would play alongside a more orthodox centre-half, either Don McAllister or Keith Osgood.

My personal development and understanding were improving at a time when the club was going backwards. I came to the front in adversity, which I think says something about my character. In the long run it was good for the club. My ability to pick the ball up in defence like a midfield player, to not be rushed and serve passes effectively to our midfield proved highly productive.

Overall we had a small squad of about 18 players. In midfield we had Pratty as a dependable mainstay, a good player in Neil McNab and one who would go on to be great in Glenn. But he was still young and learning. John Duncan would score the goals to get us back up, but the only player to make his debut that season was Colin Lee, who was signed from Torquay. We would have struggled in the top division with that side but in the Second Division we gained confidence as the season progressed. There was a desire to put it right. We had a plan to play positive, attacking football and it gave

the Spurs supporters a reason to turn up and be hopeful. We were winning games again, and the fans responded. Their support was magnificent that season, with large away followings and big attendances at White Hart Lane with a home average bettered by only six First Division clubs. I think the Spurs crowd dictate a lot of what happens at Tottenham, for good and bad. That season they were very much on our side.

The mood at White Hart Lane lifted. We were a club that was being proactive when before we had been reactive. It needed to happen, in a way – the situation was similar to when Manchester United went down a couple of years before us.

We gained breathing space. It was not nailed on that we were going to get back and no one was allowed to be complacent. But my game flourished. Away from the all-action midfield that I'd been used to I was now getting the ball at the back with the game laid out before me. It was like a switch had been flicked. My anticipation and ability to compete physically was ideally suited to my new position. I found openings and angles; I provided for Glenn and the more he had the ball the better team we were.

I think you can relate my situation to any sport. You come to a moment where you think, 'Do you know what this game's about?' There could be many answers to that: being fit, being well-prepared, being imaginative. But reading the game is fundamental. It's about the player thinking about what will or could happen next. That season I always knew what was happening around me. I'm sure it happens to a lot of players; maybe it never happens to some. But for me it was like a flash in my mind.

There was also the undeniable fillip of Liverpool being interested in me. It never came directly – there were rumours that came to me via Andre Ward who worked for the boot manufacturer Gola and also had a

It might not have been a major trophy but lifting the Nolia Cup in Sweden while on tour in May 1977 restored belief within the squad

Colin Lee scores the second of his four goals in the 9–0 thrashing of Bristol Rovers. Look at the packed East Stand: the fans' loyalty was being repaid

link with Liverpool. It was simply, 'Liverpool are seriously looking at you.' It didn't go any further but it's a nice lift when you've been relegated and a club like that is interested. Looking at it dispassionately, it would have been difficult to move. Our family was settled, the kids were at school, and my upbringing meant I didn't want to stray too far from home in the south. Plus, I wanted to stay at Tottenham because I was embarrassed about us going down and I certainly wasn't going anywhere without getting us back to where we were when I joined the club – in the top flight.

Going into the back four and playing games at a slower pace in the Second Division gave me a new lease of life. I occasionally slotted into midfield when there was an injury or a particular need in certain matches, and I found that when I did that I was a much better player having had the experience of playing at the back.

Keith and I discussed a particular idea. I didn't want to do what I often see now, which is defenders passing the ball across the back. Instead I got possession and ran at the space between the two opposition strikers. That forced them into doing something. Usually one or other closed in on me, which created space outside of them for one of our midfielders or full-backs to pull off, and I could then feed them. Glenn was ideal for this tactic and he thrived on the service. McNab was also well-suited to the tactic and it set us in motion and onto the front foot. It was a 'moving set piece'. Why it's not done at the top level now I don't know.

I gained so much confidence playing in the Second Division that the 1977–78 season was the one I enjoyed most in my career. That sounds strange given the level of opposition and that I won trophies in other seasons, but the freedom I had in the second tier was reinvigorating. My centre-half partner would go for the headers, leaving me to play in a slightly 'sweeper-style'. It took nerve to play like that.

We went eight games unbeaten from the start of the season. The only team to cope with our new tactic was Hull, managed by Billy Bremner, who beat us 2–0. It was our first defeat and gave us food for thought. After another win we lost 4–1 to Charlton Athletic. Mike Flanagan, who I used to play with in the Spurs youth team, scored all four, but the scoreline was a travesty. I've never been involved in a game where we lost so heavily having been completely superior. We had total control of the ball and got thrashed.

The Hull match wasn't a freak result because Bremner had worked out how to stop me coming out with the ball. He got one of his players to close me down. So the tactic wasn't unstoppable but we persisted. We had players of quality like Jimmy Holmes at left-back and Terry Naylor, with his athleticism, at right-back. If you set players like that free with the ball, you knew they would hurt other teams.

After the Charlton defeat, we had injuries up front and Keith said to me, 'I'm going to buy a striker.' Colin Lee had been recommended to Keith by Alf D'Arcy, the well-known former amateur player who helped take Spurs on tours around the world and was a real mentor for me. He always had a good opinion on players, saw Colin and thought one of his strengths was that he could jump well. So Keith signed Colin and he met up with us on the Friday before our next league game. 'Hello Colin, nice to meet you and welcome to Spurs,' I said. 'Thanks Steve; I'm injured – I've got a bit of an Achilles,' he said. I obviously looked surprised. 'Don't worry,' Colin said, 'I'll play.'

And so he did – scoring four goals in the famous, record-setting 9–0 win over Bristol Rovers, leaping like a salmon despite his injury. We just clicked that day. That game made us headline news again, and virtually every report made mention of how confident we looked. Confidence is so key: players who had suffered from the tension of last season were now looking completely different. We had a spring in our step and went into matches feeling we could take on anyone.

We had a few tests. It was the year we played Millwall on Boxing Day. 'Harry the Dog' and his Millwall firm promised our lot all sorts in a *Panorama* documentary about football hooliganism. The match was a weird experience because no one wore any colours. There would usually be cheers when your coach arrived and you'd see your fans waving their scarves, but it seemed no one was letting on who they supported out of fear.

We drew 1–1 at Orient in March and I was invited to the *Big Match* studio the day after. Brian Moore told me we were not good enough defensively. I argued politely and logically to the contrary. At the end of filming that sequence, Brian said, 'Ten seconds too long. Sorry Steve, can you do it again?' You can't possibly say the same thing so articulately a second time and I should have said sorry, you'll have to edit it to suit. But instead it was reshot, I suspect to make Brian's point look a bit better. I learned a big lesson that day about television.

We also learned from defeat in the League Cup to Coventry in October, in which I made a mistake when bringing the ball out from defence which led to them scoring one of their goals. We still persisted with the tactic, however. We had belief.

Our big rivals that season were Bolton. They had Peter Reid, who was a hell of a player, along with Sam Allardyce, Frank Worthington and Paul Jones. They were a strong side, and provided major clashes in front of big

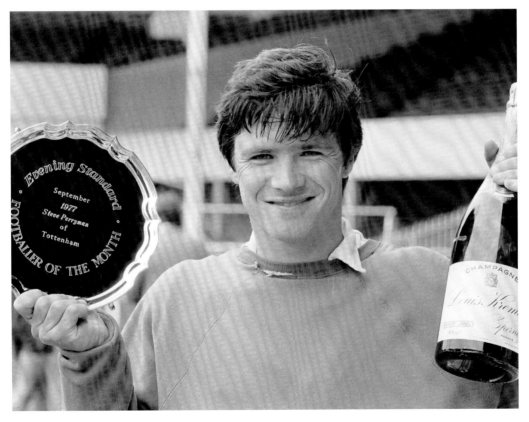

I was the *Evening Standard* Footballer of the Month in October 1977. My move into defence was proving a positive one. Staying at one club so long could make it easy to get into a rut, but a change of manager and position, a change of status from being a young player to an established captain, improved me and freshened up my game

A crucial win over Hull in April 1978, our last home game of the season, in which I scored the only goal

crowds, more than 50,000 when we beat them at White Hart Lane in April thanks to a goal from Don McAllister, who we'd in fact signed from Bolton. We also drew them in the third round of the FA Cup that year, which often happens – intense battles against the same opponents in different competitions. We lost in extra-time in the replay. But perhaps going out early did us a favour.

Bolton went on to finish first, with Southampton, us and Brighton battling for the other two promotion places. We had a wobble at the end, losing three out of the last six, including what could have been a very damaging 3–1 defeat to Brighton. We had a sort-out and I scored the crucial winner in the penultimate game at home to Hull, which meant we needed a point from our final match away at Southampton.

A point was also going to be good enough for them to finish second, which has led to all sorts of rumours about both sides taking it easy for what turned out to be a 0–0 draw. But Alan Ball hit the post, so if they were looking for a draw, he couldn't have been told. One of the things that raised a few eyebrows was Keith and their manager, Lawrie McMenemy, coming out together before the game from the corner at The Dell, walking arm-in-arm.

Those two were obviously more relaxed than we were. It was such an intense game. We had great support that day, especially considering it was difficult to get tickets for the Dell, a small but proper football ground with its own identity, the fans close to the pitch and the changing rooms up the stairs in the corner.

Our celebrations after the draw weren't exactly wild. We had a quick beer but then went straight down to Perranporth in North Cornwall by coach to play a game at Truro City to open their new ground. Keith had accepted Truro's invitation, a typically modest and understated decision by him. We stayed in a hotel in Perranporth with a large group of pensioners who were on a coach trip. Peter Taylor ended up having a dance with some of the old dears. So that was how we celebrated promotion back to Division One.

We went up in third place in the end on goal difference. Our attacking instincts had been vindicated. We conceded 49 compared to Brighton's 38, but we scored 83 to their 63. We had scraped some games – 3–3 against

Mansfield, for example, in the rain and mud – but big victories over the likes of Oldham, Blackburn, Luton and, of course, Bristol Rovers proved invaluable.

Glenn scored a magnificent last-minute free-kick in that Mansfield draw. It was the season when he absolutely came to the fore. He played 41 games, scoring 12 times, in a tough, physical division and on some pretty awful surfaces. He had proved he could cope with the rigours of English football, and how.

I played 42 games, as did Pratty, Dainesy and McNab. Peter Taylor played 41. That says something about a good team: we had a number of players playing every week, providing fantastic consistency.

Peter was a good friend of mine. Spurs had let Jimmy Neighbour go to Norwich and we signed 'Spud' from Crystal Palace as his replacement. He could be the best player ever in some games but couldn't maintain that level game-to-game. Yet he had amazing ability, could kick the ball like a mule and cross it for fun.

It was good quality for the second tier, although at this time the division itself was very strong. We played professional outfits and there were no walkovers. But we played football how it was meant to be played. There was a smile on everyone's face. The last step is the hardest, and when you want something so badly, it's not so easy. But we did it. And no – Alfie Conn never did phone me as he had promised he would when we proved him wrong by getting promoted.

Going up by such a narrow margin, however, also showed our deficiencies. Just because we were promoted it didn't mean we were good enough for the top flight, so Keith started to make plans. The summer of 1978 would prove to be one of the most remarkable in the history of the English game, let alone that of Tottenham Hotspur.

Ding dong at The Dell. Fans swarm onto the pitch as both teams celebrate promotion

SPURS SCOOP THE WORLD

EXPRESS EXCLUSIVE

Ardiles and Villa sign in £750,000 double deal

By Malcolm Folley

TOTTENHAM manager Keith Burkinshaw yesterday signed two of Argentina's all-conquering national side — Osvaldo Ardiles and Ricardo Villa — in a £750,000 deal.

Don't forget the camera... and you won't forget the weekend.

Scotland blacklist Masson, Macari

By John Mann

Burkinshaw buys Argentine stars

OPEN GOLF—TURN TO PAGES 29 AND 31

Read all about it! The signing of Ossie and Ricky was a huge moment for both Spurs and English football

I watched the World Cup in Argentina with much interest. Night games in a football-mad country, the ticker-tape and all that really got my juices flowing, but primarily I was fascinated by the purpose and tempo of the Argentina team. It was the same game of football we played – 11 versus 11 – but it *wasn't* the same game. This was from another planet. It was Kempes, Luque and the nasty but effective Passarella, and they were so impressive to watch.

They also had a little midfielder who stood right out. He had No.2 on his back for starters (even more strangely, in the 1982 World Cup he wore No.1, thanks to the way Argentina numbered their players in the squad by alphabetical order in those days); it was very unusual but then he wasn't ordinary by any means. He was small and thin, a slippery eel who played with amazing speed. He'd get his body in the way to stop a goal going in or drive them on in attack. I was watching and loving it. They were poking me in the eye with their tempo, and this little midfielder was at the heart of it as they went on to win the World Cup in late June.

Unbelievably, a few weeks later I was playing with him and one of his teammates.

The £750,000 double signing of Osvaldo Ardiles and Ricardo Villa was a watershed moment in English football. English clubs just did not sign foreign stars – the Italians and the Spanish did that. But Tottenham, always a pioneering club, tore up the script.

Prior to the 1978 tournament, what we in the UK mainly knew about Argentinian football was the 1966 World Cup meeting at Wembley, Antonio Rattin refusing to walk when sent-off and Alf Ramsey not allowing the England players to swap shirts. Alf had called them 'animals'. Ironically, Keith said that Rattin helped him sign Ossie and Ricky as an intermediary, and that he was the nicest man you could ever meet.

The story of the double transfer unfolded bizarrely, like it was fiction not fact. I was at home in leafy Chalfont St Giles, having recently got married. Season over, promoted, feeling good. I walked down the stairs one morning, picked the paper up and went back upstairs to have a read in bed. Turning to the back page, there was the headline in big capital letters: 'SPURS SCOOP THE WORLD'.

Bloody hell! No sooner had I put down the paper, wondering what the hell was going on, the phone started ringing – and ringing and ringing and ringing. It was mainly press but also friends asking if I had known. I had not heard a whisper.

The story of how the deal was done was remarkable. Keith had been tipped off that Argentina players were looking for moves abroad, and his pal Harry Haslam, manager at Sheffield United and whose coach Oscar Arce was Argentinian, was interested in signing one or two but not those in the higher price bracket like Ossie and Ricky. Harry and Keith talked, Keith flew to Buenos Aires and Sidney Wale gave him the go-ahead to sign Ardiles, and then when Keith was offered Ricky as well, the pair of them.

There were all sorts of rumours flying around, one being that Terry Neill had wanted Ardiles for Arsenal. Ossie told me later he had been thinking he'd be moving to Spain or Italy. England had never come into his mind, but then all of a sudden, there was this guy in a hotel waiting for him. He'd flown all the way from England. How could Ossie not be impressed?

Much later I jokingly said that the secret of Keith and Ossie's relationship was that neither ever understood a word the other said. It was Ossie who during the talks had asked Keith, 'Do you need another one? My friend Ricky could also come.' Ossie also revealed later that at no point did Keith tell him that we'd just got promoted. It would probably have put Ossie off.

But the deal was done and the reaction was incredible. In one fell swoop the club had polished up its act and was shining again in the public light – Spurs were newsworthy, a bit sexy. The positivity surrounding the World Cup-winning Argentina team spread onto us. Everything was heightened – the press interest, exposure, the amazement, not just from our fans but across the football world. We were getting invites to go and play in Saudi Arabia, Dubai, Timbuktu and everywhere in between. The club had woken up from relegation by getting promoted and was now saying – shouting – 'We're here; we're back in the big time.'

But what exactly were we getting? Every time the press asked me this I answered, 'I don't know.' But to the question, 'What do you think about players coming from abroad' I said, 'Why not, if it will improve us?'

'But that means they will be replacing you.'

'I don't know that.'

The press were saying all sorts of things – 'How are they going to be on a wet Tuesday night in February?' and so on. I got some stick in some of the papers, who said, 'Of course Steve Perryman was pleased – they are not going to replace him 'cause he's a defender now.' As if that would enter my head. How could you be that selfish, as a captain, to think that?

Initially there was a little bit of misunderstanding about the type of character and player Ricky was because we'd only seen him come on as sub against Brazil, when he had absolutely splattered someone. We didn't understand that those two countries hated each other. On TV Jimmy Hill and guests were talking about it and saying, 'We don't want that kind of thing here!' But it was very far from the real picture as to what Ricky was really like, as we would soon discover.

I spoke to Keith when he got home. The plan was to reveal them with a press call at White Hart Lane, after Ossie and Ricky were given extra time off after the World Cup. We only met them just beforehand in the dressing room. I always remember thinking, 'What the hell are they gonna think about our training kit?' I just expected they were used to better things.

That first meeting was memorable. They had a little bit of English, Ossie more so, and big smiles. Peter Taylor played a practical joke, wearing a plastic thumb that came off when they shook hands. Childish humour, but they laughed. After that they went back home to Argentina for some more time off then joined us at a sports school in Holland. It was unusual as we roomed in threes. They put Ossie and Ricky in with Peter. He had a nice character about him – they wouldn't have had a clue about his Norman Wisdom impression, but he still did it anyway.

A photo of Ossie which captures his supreme balance perfectly

The *Express* on my growing confidence about our prospects following promotion

Three amigos: the playful side of Ossie's personality shines through

The more we got to know Ossie and Ricky, the more their lovely characters shone through. It was obvious it was going to be all right despite the language barrier, which would mellow over time. Ossie appeared to have the same outlook as me; Ricky was certainly a bit more happy-go-lucky, but both were and are extremely nice people. They'd won the World Cup, which made them a bit special, but I'd played with other World Cup winners in Martin Peters and Jimmy Greaves. Tottenham was a club used to having world-class talent.

Practicalities like accommodation were sorted out by the club. Our task was to help them to settle in quickly. As captain I took on the responsibility of welcoming them. Ossie later said that he did more reading of faces and eyes in that time because of the ribbing and capers the players got up to. Peter taught them all the swear words and tried to trick them into saying them at the wrong times. Or told them that if someone said hello, they should say, 'Half a lager'. Terry Naylor and John Pratt were the biggest piss-takers in the squad and everyone would laugh at their antics, but Ossie and Ricky noticed that my laughter was more restrained. They sensed that I was a bit more serious and wasn't having a cheap laugh at their expense.

Because I'd spent quite a lot of time with Scandinavians, who spoke good English but still needed me to sometimes communicate in ways other than just language, I could do so with Ossie and Ricky. Ricky didn't say much; he just smiled. Ossie soon got the hang of things. One day I walked in and Ossie was very agitated about something he needed at home. He was trying to explain it to the rest but getting nowhere.

'Steebie!' He couldn't quite pronounce the 'v' and has always called me 'Steebie'. 'I need courtoise! Courtoise!'

I thought for a minute, looking at what he was trying to explain with hand signals. 'You mean curtains, Ossie?'

He looked at the others. 'See? Yes! He fucking understand me!'

We'd sit down for dinner, explaining to them about the food. Ossie was always very positive: 'I want this.' His meal would turn up, but then when mine arrived he'd say, 'No, I want yours'. It happened a few times so eventually I said, 'I'll order for you.'

We began to talk a lot about Argentina and their World Cup-winning manager César Luis Menotti. It was fascinating. Menotti had a belief that playing matches was the best form of training. Ossie said, 'If I got caps for every time I actually played a game for Argentina I'd have 200 because we played any team he could find.' Menotti didn't care if they won 1–0 or 12–0, as long his players were doing the right things at the right time. He trusted about five of the group as his lieutenants and asked their opinions. Menotti's reasoning was that in any group there are winners and losers and a middle group that can be swayed. The key is identifying who is going to sway those in the middle. Ossie was a major player for Menotti and brought that winning mentality to Spurs, but also more importantly a style.

Menotti was a very political figure on the left in Argentina and that caused big issues in a country being run by a military dictatorship. Half the crowd loved him and the other half despised him due to the political divide. England was a bit of an escape for Ossie. His wife Silvia's family were close to the government so that when they went out it was under armed guard. England provided a haven and a sense of fair play, even if he wasn't always treated fairly when he played.

And so, after the initial fuss died down, to business. The hard work began in training. Ossie told me later that after a couple of days, he and Ricky said to each other, 'They've only got two players' – meaning me and Glenn! We used to wear cricket-like shirts for training underneath a woollen sweater. Ossie's was about six sizes too big for him. 'What must he be thinking?' I thought. Someone said to him, 'You wait until the winter comes – you'll be glad you're wearing that.'

There were some little issues. At the soccer school camp in Holland, we were doing sit-ups; they were back in again after Terry Neill left. Ossie said, 'No. In Argentina we don't do this.' Naturally, after that the rest of us thought perhaps we shouldn't be doing them. Six months later *The Times* published Menotti's training plan. They did sit-up after sit-up. It might be construed that Ossie was trying to get away with it a bit, though otherwise he did work very hard.

Inevitably, given what dressing rooms are like, the sit-ups thing did make us wonder what else they might be getting away with. 'What are the club giving them?', 'Is that car theirs or is it the club's?' I've never been jealous but that kind of feeling was bubbling in the dressing room a little. Wages are different and players will accept some disparities, but by and large it's got to be all for one and one for all.

Signing Ossie and Ricky was born out of sort of cheapness in a way. Spurs were being asked for so much money for average domestic players, but had landed two World Cup winners for the same money. But it was a great time to be at the club. We all wanted them to succeed, because if they succeeded, we would too.

"Ossie told me later that after a couple of days, he and Ricky said to each other, 'They've only got two players' – meaning me and Glenn!"

Looking ahead to the 1978–79 season

CHAPTER TWELVE

'I'VE GOT A PLAN'

BBC Radio gave a traffic update on 19th August 1978 and reported long delays on the M1 'due to the huge number of Tottenham fans travelling to Nottingham'. At least that's the tale. I do know there were thousands at the City Ground wanting to see our return to the First Division and the competitive debut of our two Argentinian stars. We didn't quite manage a victory but Ricky obliged with a goal in a commendable 1–1 draw.

Four days later we came out to a rousing reception at White Hart Lane for our first home game, against Aston Villa. There were nearly 48,000 supporters in the ground, a deluge of Argentina-style ticker-tape and a fantastic sense of excitement and anticipation. We got stuffed 4–1. Welcome back to the big stage.

This was our rude reawakening to the realities of top-flight football. After a 2–2 draw with Chelsea, a week later came the infamous 7–0 mauling at Anfield. Ossie said he never saw the ball, but there was a hell of a lot of quality about that Liverpool team, which included Graeme Souness. There's a reason why you go down and there's a reason why you get back up – we had been playing lesser opposition. Now we were at the hardest level, and our weaknesses were exposed.

The years 1978 to 1980 were ones of rebuilding and consolidation. Keith rang additional changes by bringing in Ossie and Ricky. He signed John Lacy, Gordon Smith, Mark Kendall and Milija Aleksic. Tony Galvin also joined from non-league football, while Paul Miller and Mark Falco came through the ranks. In all 10 players made their debuts in that 1978–79 campaign. The next season Keith gave another four home-grown players – Chris Hughton, Micky Hazard, Terry Gibson and Peter Southey – their debuts, and brought in Terry Yorath.

The sense of freedom with which we played in the Second Division continued but took a bit longer to bear fruit in the First Division. Spurs hasn't always been a top-flight club throughout its history, but given the club's traditions and trophies some assumed we'd get back to the top level quickly. We were playing open, attacking football and adjusting to Ossie and Ricky, it took a little while before we got it right at the back and the front.

We'd seen a lot of Ossie at the World Cup but it wasn't until we played alongside him that we saw his strength of character and mentality, and his willingness to get the ball in tough situations. He would be clattered, get up, sort of smile and just carry on playing. Opponents promised him all sorts of

"We came out to a rousing reception at White Hart Lane for our first home game, against Aston Villa. We got stuffed 4–1. Welcome back to the big stage"

Crowds flocked to see us back in the top flight, and Ricky rewarded the fans who had travelled to Nottingham to see him with a debut goal

treatment, including Tommy Smith, who had moved to Swansea who beat us in a League Cup replay, but Ossie stood up to it.

He was a bit of everything, not a Luka Modrić as some have compared him to but a livewire over short distances, beautifully balanced and with quick feet. If I was taken on by an opponent Ossie would be biting at his heels, protecting, working and always so dynamic. He said to me one day, 'I run the most in this team.' And he probably did. He had bundles of cheeky humour, but he was a serious footballer. For all his talent he was prepared to run more than anyone.

Ossie and I are the same age and we bonded straight away; we both had that experience of knowing more about how the game is played than most, and there were lots of similarities in our characters. I roomed with him and whenever you room together you always talk more deeply.

He said to me soon after he arrived, 'You remind me of Passarella.'

'Get off,' I said.

'No, really, you do.'

I think Ossie meant it in terms of captaincy and my leadership, but in any case I walked with a bigger spring in my step after he said that; we'd just seen this fella win the World Cup and now I was being compared to him by one of his teammates.

You could almost see the wheels in Ossie's head whirring when he was on the pitch, thinking about angles, position, where to run, where to press, and his mind was just as sharp off it. His humour was wonderful and so clever. He would come out with some pearls. 'Steebie. Some people pass you the ball and it is round; others pass and it is a cube.' Meaning one kind of pass you could use and the other put you in trouble. Another thing he said was, 'I am the most intelligent player in this team. Because Glenn needs to think he's the best player I let him *think* he is the best player – but I know really *I'm* the fucking best player.'

He would talk as he played. When he first arrived and couldn't speak the language, he just said, 'Yes!' to get the ball – and kept on saying it: 'Yes. Yes. Yes!' That got him the ball. If you didn't give it to him he'd give you such a look. As his English improved, he'd have more to say. 'Pass, pass. Pass. Pass! Steebie, why you kick it fucking long? Maxie, why you keep fucking kick it out there? We fucking lose it there!' I had a lot of explaining to do to Ossie about English players and how we did things.

Once, in the middle of December after an away game, a TV programme wanted the players to say something funny for a Christmas show. Ossie told a story about being fouled by a Yugoslavian player who was playing for Middlesbrough. Ossie said, 'I went to the referee and said, "Bloody foreigners!"' The TV crew fell about laughing.

He'd ask me about things such as getting a letter from a school asking him to do a presentation.

'Steebie, I do this?'

'Yeah, you should do it,' I'd say. 'It's not far from your house – just say you can only be there for an hour.'

'OK, you do it with me. You do it Steebie, I do it.'

'No, Ossie, that's not easy for me to get there – it's an hour and a half away.'

'OK. I don't do it.'

'Oh bloody hell. Alright, let's do it then.' He could charm the birds from the trees.

Keith once banned both Ossie and Ricky from taking throw-ins because he thought they were useless at them and threw the ball at people's necks. Ossie was incredulous. 'I'm a World Cup winner!' Another time Keith spent ages telling him, 'Ossie, stay on the right. Stay on the right. Don't go to the left. OK?'

'Yeah, yeah, Keith.'

Within about 30 seconds he was out on the left wing. There wasn't a lot of controlling Ossie. But you could trust him. We wouldn't have done that for any other reason than he thought that was the best place to go.

In training, at first Ricky was the better of the two players – big, tough and hard to knock off the ball – but training is not the same as a match. Your opponent doesn't really want to kick you, and there aren't 26,000 on the Kop calling you all sorts. Ricky was languid, and that trait could be exposed in the white heat of games. He could be inconsistent, though in fairness what he was good at – running with the ball – was difficult on the poor pitches of those days.

There was a contrast in character too. I think Ricky was great for the group because he is such a lovely, friendly guy – not that Ossie isn't but Ricky was gentler in his manner. He would rather smile than scowl. He came into the dressing room once all wrapped up even though it wasn't that cold, which raised a smile even before he said anything. He had a big grin on his face. 'You all right, Ricky?' someone said. He beamed back at us, jumped into the middle of the room and announced, loudly and very deliberately, 'The cat. Sat on. The mat!'

"You could almost see the wheels in Ossie's head whirring when he was on the pitch, thinking about angles, position, where to run, where to press"

Tuning into the FA Cup draw was a new experience for Ossie

His English lessons were obviously coming on a treat, although I wasn't sure how useful that phrase was going to be away at somewhere like Leeds.

Ricky is a heart-on-the-sleeve guy who needed reassurance and understanding. I saw his eyes water on a number of occasions, which is something I never saw with Ossie. An example was in a team meeting, when we were struggling a bit. Ricky said to us, 'I need you give me confidence. Why you no give me confidence?' and his eyes welled up. You felt so sorry for him, but you couldn't feed that feeling and had to say something like, 'Come on, Ricky, for Christ's sake.' Ossie could handle the pressure all day long. He had the tougher mentality. He was very resilient and robust. Ricky knows himself that he was not consistent enough during his career, but by Christ when he performed, he performed.

The combination of Ricky and Ossie makes for such good company. We still spend a week every year together with mutual friends and we just have the best time. I think we were so lucky with the personalities that we signed. We all knew the question marks. Could they play, ride a tackle, stay fit? Could they actually play in Stoke on a cold Wednesday night? But it was also about character in the dressing room, and they were both brilliant. They leant on each other, but Ossie was the main reason that Ricky settled down because he understood him inside out.

The pair of them needed a lot of looking after. I'd see their utility bills on the desk of club secretary Peter Day, and it was obvious that Spurs were paying them. I probably wasn't supposed to see that but it never bothered me; I didn't think, 'Why aren't they paying my bills? When I went to Japan, I certainly needed help with things like that.

One thing that did concern us was when Ossie and Ricky were allowed to come back a week late for their second pre-season. I asked Keith what that was all about and he said it took them three days to get to Argentina and three days to get back. I said, 'Is it our problem that they live in Argentina? I'm the one having to cope with the chaps saying, "Where are they?"'

Keith replied that we would just have to get on with it. When we all got the letter about the formal arrangements for pre-season I phoned Keith, and asked, 'Are we all back on that date?'

'Well, you know Ossie and Ricky won't be back.' I said, 'Phone me when they *are* back.'

We all came back on the same day.

It wasn't a big deal. The bigger picture was that Ossie and Ricky had transformed the dynamic of the club. We were somebodies again. And the biggest plus then was the marriage between Glenn and Ossie. They loved playing with each other – good players appreciate good, special players. They had this bond between them which allowed them to dictate the style of our team. Now we just had to fit the other pieces around them.

We had our struggles in the first season, losing 5–0 at home to Arsenal to add to the 7–0 against Liverpool, and a horrific spell of no wins in 10 in the spring of 1979. We had a good run in the FA Cup, only going out to Manchester United in a quarter-final replay. But something was building. But in the third round we took two games to beat Altrincham, and Wrexham took us to a draw. So the signs were also there that it was *not* right, and we still had work to do to find the right blend.

Terry Yorath, who arrived in 1979, was an important signing. He was a much better player than people give him credit for and he brought experience as well. It freed me up to play in midfield again. I didn't particularly like it but Keith needed me in there. When you've got all these consistent flair players – Glenn was top scorer in 1979–80 – there's a need for a more mundane consistency as well. It was only later in 1980 that I moved to full-back. We ended up with too many midfield players and no obvious right-back. I was always drafted back into midfield when we were struggling with injuries, but my strongest position became right-back.

Key to our progress was the development of Keith as manager and Peter Shreeve as his assistant. Keith was at his best when he was matched up with Peter. Keith wanted improvement every single day while Peter, although being equally ambitious, could temper that with a bit of reality and calm. For instance, if Keith had heard we'd had a night out it was the end of the world. Peter would placate him, tell him to relax and assure him it was OK.

Pat Welton was Keith's assistant at first, and had been elevated to a position that, in truth, seemed to have diverted him away from what he was best at – youth development. There had been talk of Pat getting the manager's job after Terry Neill, but he and Keith were perhaps too similar. Pat had some distractions going on in his private life, whereas Keith was able to devote himself to the team.

From foes to friends: with my old Leeds adversary Terry Yorath

MATCH ACTION

Steve Perryman
Tottenham

Sporting the very classy Admiral away kit that was really popular with the fans

Peter was right on it. He had come through the coaching ranks and brought through a lot of the home-growns. Like Keith, he knew their mums and dads, their weaknesses and strengths – there wasn't a lot that passed Peter by. He was streetwise.

I wasn't close to him before he got the job in 1980. But he would make comments in the dressing room and I'd think, 'He knows what he's doing.' We played Ipswich away one time in four inches of snow. At half-time he spoke first as he often did. He perched on the treatment table, and said: 'Ossie, Ricky – love you. Buenos Aires, 80 degrees – definitely love you. Four inches of snow at Portman Road? I'm afraid you're going to have to come off.'

The delivery was great. He had a cockney wit. He appreciated where the home-grown London players were coming from that Keith sort of understood but not in quite the same way. Bill and Eddie, the bluff Yorkshireman and the chirpy cockney, were mirrored with Keith and Peter. I didn't really know Peter as a player, but he had a very good circle of footballer friends. If we all met up in the Chanticleer, the club's exclusive restaurant and social hangout attached to White Hart Lane, we'd meet Pete's mates, ex-pros like Terry McQuade but also former non-league players like Bobby Cantwell. Pete also knew Alf D'Arcy really well. These people were avid watchers of football. I doubt Peter missed much, but if he did they saw it and gave him their opinion.

Peter took the bulk of training, focusing on things like keep-ball sessions; Keith might take the shooting practice at the end. The routines remained pretty much unchanged from previous eras – at Cheshunt on the grass and some indoor sessions at White Hart Lane depending on the weather conditions. We still played five-a-sides – Friday would be the big kick-up. I don't know how we got away with it but it was proper – no shin pads, hell for leather and you weren't going to lose. Someone had to but it wasn't going to be you.

The ball courts were brilliant for skills and Peter loved it. He used to play with us as much as he could. If it was on a Friday, a slightly more relaxed Peter would say, 'Give me the ball, I've got a plan!' That was his catchphrase, along with 'silky soccer'. If he says either to me today I laugh, having heard them a million times before.

He did a session one day that I'll never forget. It was a keep-ball routine in which you were not supposed to touch the ball until you absolutely had to. If the ball was coming to you and you had someone up your backside of course you had to play it, but in this session it was all about trying to let the ball run to a teammate. It encouraged us to be more aware, think about how the ball was passed and whether or not to take touches. It chimed with me that the best pass is the one you don't have to touch until you're ready. I worry about back passes to goalkeepers in the direction of the goal. It might only happen once in a million times but that ball can bobble over the keeper's foot and into the goal. If you pass the ball directly to the keeper, he has to touch it. But if it's laid at an angle he can choose: one touch and he can wallop it or he can stop it and take two or three touches if he wants to. The point is the pass is not dictating what he does and when; it's offering him the option to do different things. So the best pass is the one that the receiver does not have to touch until he's ready.

Training was competitive, skill-based and interesting. Training with Glenn and Ossie, who had bright minds, meant a coach couldn't do anything mundane with them. Ossie used to detest warm-ups because they were, in his words, 'mind-dulling'. So we had plenty of what we called 'keep-happy days' – all coaches have them whereby they do stuff they know players will enjoy whether it's improving them or not. You can't just be at players all the time to make them learn. There has to be a break to make the game enjoyable, fresh and lively.

Keith effectively ran the whole club, just like Bill. He'd go and see Sylvie Webb, the laundry lady, a lovely, typical North London woman, asking her what she needed. He had the right staff and they would give him the right answers. Having genuine people saves you a lot of time. You don't have to question what they're telling you. That in turn engenders loyalty from the staff to do the best they can – you're not just a number.

The White Hart Lane staff then were still a big team of mostly locals, all pulling together and oozing character and honesty. They were the thread running through the club – people like Sylvie and Bill Fox, the steward in the away dressing room, but also relatively recent additions like John Fennelly in the press office and Gerry Lambert, the unassuming security man to who, when he retired, Daniel Levy gave a season ticket for life. He was such a lovely North London bloke.

One of my favourite ever Spurs photos – the look and demeanour of those ladies says so much about White Hart Lane. As for the fans? All the local barbers must have been going skint!

> "With Keith, anyone with ability thrived under him – Ossie, Ricky, Glenn, Micky Hazard. I think he probably appreciated them because the way they played was opposite to how he was as a character"

It was embodied for me in a wonderful photo from a few years before, of two ladies who must have been members of staff walking around edge of pitch, a packed East Stand in the background, while Roger Morgan is in the foreground. You can imagine their conversation: work finished, heading off and, amid all this frenzy of a football match, one saying to the other, 'Did you lock that door?'

That character, purpose and reliability still ran through the club like a seam of gold. And so too did the ethos of the Spurs Way. Bill Nick was a worker of a player, yet in management and coaching cherished the talent. With Keith, anyone with ability thrived under him – Ossie, Ricky, Glenn, Micky Hazard. I think he probably appreciated them because the way they played was opposite to how he was as a character.

Keith was a straightforward Yorkshireman in the Bill Nick mould, and with a similar football philosophy. He said to me once during this time, 'I'm gonna make a team here, you know.' I couldn't doubt him. He was so determined. One time playing Leeds away we were staying at a hotel. We always went for a walk on the morning of a game but it was freezing cold. We protested. 'We're going to go for a walk because that's what we do,' said Keith, and to prove we should be doing it he strode out, stomping up the hill.

Ossie touched me on the elbow and said, 'Steebie, Steebie, Beatles song.'
'What?'
'Beatles song, Beatles song. *The Fool on the Hill*!'

It was just said in jest. Keith was no fool. His ambition was infectious and it rubbed off. In 1979–80 we drew Manchester United in the FA Cup again, this time in the third round, and in the replay Ossie scored a memorable winner. We were under extreme pressure and Ricky did a long mazy run towards their goal from deep, a sort of a one-man break, which set up the goal. That confidence was obviously a major thing in his game – the ability to run with the ball.

We had started the season with three defeats, and only two wins out of nine. We finished lower in the division than the previous season, 14th as opposed to 11th, but only one point worse off. We were too inconsistent, and lost too many games. It gave Keith a clue as to what needed to be put right.

Celebrating the opening of our second sports shop in Greenford. Bill is on the left, I'm on the right and there's a five-man Spurs wall of Chris Hughton, John Pratt, Paul Miller, Terry Yorath and Peter Taylor in between

Manchester United finished second in the league to Liverpool that season, who had knocked us out of the FA Cup in the quarters with a wonder, if freakish, goal from Terry McDermott. We were just falling short when it mattered – it was sort of obvious that we were playing a type of football that needed a particular type of frontman to bear fruit.

Glenn and I could cross the ball while Ossie and Ricky played great forward passes looking for a one-two. We had genuine, good lads up front but not the type to dominate and tell Ossie and Ricky to put it exactly where they wanted it. I loved Chris Jones's movement but he looked like being a 'nearly player' in that he was not quite getting the goals – it felt like hitting double figures was a stretch too far for him. It was probably a bit about belief. He was brought through with Glenn, could make runs into forward spaces, and trusted Glenn's passing. Who wouldn't? But he just came up short in terms of belief in himself, which meant he lost confidence in how much belief others had in him.

Chris is a smashing bloke and doing really well now with a soccer school in Jersey. But we needed more from our strikers back then. Not scoring enough in turn exposed our weaknesses at the back. We got beaten 4–0 at Forest in March 1980. They were great, Cloughie's mark was all over them. It was like playing against his Derby team again.

Yet there were signs that it was coming together. We beat Liverpool 2–0 in March 1980 and that took some doing. Liverpool were a machine in those days. Relentless. We must have had a bloody good day to beat them. There was a period earlier in the 1979–80 season when we only lost once in 12 games, and in a number of defeats we were not far away, losing by the odd goal.

We had a lot of players making their debuts, particularly home-grown ones, a significant change from when I had come through. There were

Chris Hughton was an outstanding player and is one of the nicest guys in the game to boot

more opportunities, and a greater emphasis on youth. Most good youth programmes are backed up by local school teachers. Get enough teachers 'on the firm' working for the club, people who are seeing kids play either for their own school or others they are playing against, and you are doing the club a favour. Their knowledge began to pay off.

Paul 'Maxie' Miller made his debut away at Arsenal and stood tall. There was a lot of character about him and his generation, including Chris Hughton, who missed only the first three games of the 1979–80 season. Out of that Spurs team, he was probably the one that you least expected to become a manager. Not because he didn't think about the game – he did; he was a considered young man – but because he is one of the nicest men I've ever met. Everyone says it, but it's true. I find myself a bit protective towards him.

People have said to me that he must be a 'yes' man, because he later coached at Tottenham for a long time under a lot of managers. I say to them, 'Do you know him? Have you ever thought it might be because he was good at his job?' To do what he did at Newcastle and Brighton suggests he was a very good reserve-team manager and coach, and he has continued to prove it as a manager himself.

When I came back from Japan many years after we played together Chrissy phoned me. He asked what system the team I had coached had used. An hour and a half later, he was still asking questions, thinking all the time. I was clearing the garage out with the handset wedged to my ear. I couldn't get him off the phone!

Chris was a dream to play with. We used to have a laugh that if ever I had a problem with a winger on my side, I'd say to him, 'Get over to the other wing: you'll have a lovely afternoon with Chrissy, time will fly by and all of a sudden the game will be over. You stay here and it will be different.'

Chrissy did a lift-engineering apprenticeship. He was typical of a home-grown player who was not quite good enough at the usual age for signing as an apprentice, so picked up the safety net of a trade. That showed maturity. On the field he had great balance, covered ground, loved to get forward and would go on to forge a fantastic combination with Tony Galvin.

Chris got his chance because of injuries. Keith asked me on the Friday before a game who we were going to play at left-back. I said, 'Chrissy.' 'But he's a right-back.' I said I'd play left-back and Chrissy could play on the right, but Keith said no, he was not breaking up my service to Glenn.

'So who else can we play?'

'Keith, you haven't got anyone left.'

So Chrissy played left-back and never came out the team. He just took to it, flourished and thrived.

We hadn't really been aware of him coming through. By all accounts he worked hard. If you had a chance to watch the reserves play then you'd notice him. He wasn't blowing anyone away, but he was made of the right stuff: great ethics, honest and very professional.

I did hear that he was political, writing for a left-wing newspaper. Maybe that's why he was so good with another leftie, Tony Galvin, out on the left wing. They probably had meetings over there! But Chris didn't really talk about his politics. He always thought before he spoke. He wouldn't have been a voice in the dressing room when bigger mouths were talking, but he was listening, soaking it up.

What was also obviously different about Chris was his ethnicity. We had black kids starting to come through, but he was the first to really make it, and it was hard for black players. Different times. Chrissy pulled me up one day for what I thought was being respectful in describing someone as 'coloured'. He told me it wasn't. I never had to be told again.

Chris's story shows how it is so vital to take your chance, and how fate plays such a part. It contrasts vividly with that of Peter Southey, bless him, who made his debut against Brighton in September 1979, a month after Chrissy. Peter was going to be a really good footballer but he only got to play that one game.

He wasn't quite ready for the first team but stayed part of the picture. When he came back for the following pre-season, all his running times were down. He was looking tired and a blood test showed he had leukaemia. I think some of the coaching staff felt bad about themselves because he was almost accused of living it up in the summer before the truth came out.

There was nothing malicious in the coaches' treatment of Peter, but there's a lesson there because it's too easy to think the worst about young players. Peter's health gradually declined and he passed away in 1983. We had a players' room at White Hart Lane and we had a picture of him on the wall. When they built the new stand, I said that picture had to stay in the new players' room.

A tragedy like that brought things into sharp focus. There's a lot to worry about when you play at a top club – every defeat hurts. But sometimes something happens to put things in perspective.

For a young group of fit footballers, health should not be a concern. We hear now about depression – I'm sure there was a lot of depression going on back then with injuries, when players got one knock after another. And how must the teammates of John White felt when they lost him?

It definitely makes you take stock of what you're doing. Although you're young, fit and able, you can get knocked down by anything at any age. A real shame. I still think about Peter a lot.

Peter Southey: a sad loss to us all

"Peter was going to be a really good footballer but he only got to play that one game"

CHAPTER THIRTEEN
POSITIVE THINKING

One day, Keith said to our physio Mike Varney, 'I'm stopping all this stretching bollocks.'

Mike had arrived in 1975 and been instrumental in modernising our approach to conditioning, getting us all to stretch better. He asked Keith why he wanted to stop it.

'Ossie never listens to you, and he [pointing at me] can't touch his kneecaps let alone his fucking toes. And yet those two never get injured.'

That was unfair on Mike, who was forward-thinking, and indeed the exchange did not really reflect Keith's attitude to innovation generally – in this case Mike's carefully thought-out stretching exercises designed to improve our conditioning and therefore our performances on the pitch. Keith was always willing to try new ideas to give us a competitive edge. There was a mindset of renewed ambition at the club, and what made us take the next competitive step was the culmination of a long process of positive thinking, rebuilding and improvement from top to bottom.

Some key transfers were also major factors in our progress, and securing the signatures of Steve Archibald and Garth Crooks must rank among the most significant. Their arrival gave us what we had been lacking: the ability to finish off the opportunities created by our highly attack-minded midfield. Archie and Garth would go on to score 36 league goals between them in the 1980–81 season.

I had a role in Garth joining the club. Ray Evans had left us and later went to Stoke. Ray called me to ask if Keith would be interested in Garth, so I passed the message on and he ended up joining us. Garth worked hard and was quick – very quick. He was at his best when he ran in behind rather than when the ball came to his feet when he had his back to goal.

When he first arrived, Garth lacked a little bit in his touch. This was highlighted in small-sided games in the gym, whereas on the pitch there was more space for him to use his running ability. This is where he thrived, using his judgement and intelligence to make well-timed, fast runs. He came to Spurs not quite ready made and quickly improved by playing in a better team – a more glamorous, higher-profile club than Stoke – that suited his manner and character.

It was no surprise that Garth went on to have a media career as it suited him so well – he even co-presented *Top of the Pops* a couple of times. It began while he was actually in the side; he even left the team on a Friday night before a game once to fulfil his commitments to Capital Radio.

"Steve Archibald and Garth Crooks' arrival gave us what we had been lacking: the ability to finish off the opportunities created by our highly attack-minded midfield"

Garth Crooks (second from right) and Steve Archibald (right) were 'the engine of our train'

Garth was showbiz, and a wonderful addition to the dressing-room dynamic. The banter in there revolved around the usual mickey-taking, about how many caps you had, how many medals and so on. Garth could more than hold his own. With my experience and career by then, there wasn't a lot you could have a go at me for, but you could on pace, especially if you were quick yourself, like Garth. My retort would be, 'Garth, there's no man with a starting pistol on the pitch; you have to tell yourself when to go.'

He was so up for fun and laughter and still is. He's a very funny guy. We probably speak two or three times a year, but strangely I feel I am closer to him because of his presence on TV. Sometimes I gently pull him up on something he's said, but Garth knows what his strengths and weaknesses are – he's a clever bloke. And he's always been very respectful to me, which I place great store by.

Chrissy and Garth became great friends. Garth also had a special relationship with Steve Archibald, but Steve was probably the most difficult in the team to read. From the day he arrived from Aberdeen I really rated him as a player. He was top-class, with great speed. I wondered why in training sprints he would start before the instruction to go. Why when someone's so quick would they need to do that? He could have started half a second behind us and still won. It said something about his character and single-mindedness. Steve was a winner.

One thing I couldn't do is read how he was going to be from one day to the next. His face was blank; he never gave any clue as to how he felt. To get a clue I'd say, 'Morning Steve' and he would either mumble something or ignore me.

I suspect he started off being a little negative towards me because of a false reputation I had at the time for not getting on with Scots. He might have been told things by friends, agents or whoever. I can't quite remember how I might have been made aware of that perception, but it sort of hung in the air, possibly something to do with my falling out with Alfie Conn. But I was never the type to go for the easy laugh when England were playing Scotland. When that happened the Scots in your dressing room would be mocked. I was a bit more refined than that.

Steve had worked at Rolls-Royce and had a slightly different background to a lot of the players. He'd also played under Alex Ferguson at Aberdeen, so that no doubt had some influence on his character. It felt like he maybe needed to have the hump a bit to be the player that he was. There was a game in 1983 when we beat Luton 4–2. Richard Cooke made his debut and scored, while 'Archie' scored twice with excellent finishes. John Motson made a comment that Steve had scored 13 goals in 14 games, but that he and Keith were not talking to each other. Their dispute would have been mentioned in the dressing room but not when Archie was there. It was just general dressing-room talk, someone joking saying, 'So what if he's not talking to Keith, he's scoring goals – maybe I shouldn't talk to Keith!'

Goalscorers need to be single-minded. Steve was more than just a goalscorer, but he had his own way of dealing with people. The 1981 team now has a very strong bond, but Steve isn't part of it so much. When we've had anniversary functions he has always been invited and turned up, but my contact with him is generally isolated.

Archie wasn't pally with all the team as he didn't encourage close friendships, although he did have a strong bond with Ossie. But the crowd loved him. With the song that they made up about him – 'We'll take more care of you, Archibald' – it was obvious that they adored him. Even so I think at times he questioned why Glenn was the 'King of White Hart Lane', and not him. There was an arrogance and swagger about him. I confess that I found it difficult to warm to Steve. But in a football squad you're not going to get on with everyone in the same way – that's a fact of life whatever the workplace. We think everyone wants to be liked, yet I don't think Steve was that fussed. The most important thing is that he was a bloody good player. I always talk about the front players being the engine of the train, pulling the rest of the team along, and in combination Archie and Garth became our engine.

The other end of the pitch was another area where we needed to improve, and over the course of the season Keith found the right formula. We had two dependables at full-back in Chrissy and me. And then we had the other two, a pair of Dobermanns in the middle. One was another home-grown player and the other was signed from Weymouth, so there was next to no money spent on what became a highly effective defence.

Graham Roberts and Paul Miller would take on anyone. Chrissy was over on the other side of the pitch from me so I could leave him to it, but I had an effect

Steve Archibald and me putting our heads together for a photo shoot

Paul 'Maxie' Miller talking – just for a change! We had great partnerships up front and in the heart of our defence

on those two. Sometimes I would give them the ammunition – winding them up about an opponent – and they would dish it out physically and verbally.

I always said of 'Maxie' Miller that I didn't know how his parents had a son like him. His late father Dick, a taxi driver, was a lovely man; his mum Joan is a lovely lady. They were publicans in the East End at one stage. It was all said in jest but I'd say to them, 'How did you two, such nice people, bring *that* into the world?'

Keith tried to replace Maxie with other defenders as the side developed, but it wasn't easy because Maxie put so much into his performances. He could kick the ball like a mule, probably went for the ball in the air more than 'Robbo' and cared so much about not allowing the ball to go into his net. And the bigger the game, the bigger his heart.

Maxie, for all his passion, was quite a shrewd player in his decision-making while Robbo was more comfortable on the ground. I think it was Graham's relatively late arrival into the professional game and his lack of experience that led to him becoming a bloody good and effective player. He'd come from non-league after getting rejected as a kid, and broke into professional football late. That gave him hunger and desire. To get turned down by a club was not the end. If you were good enough you just hadn't found the right circumstances yet. Look at Ian Wright – such energy and enthusiasm. To do what he did you have got to have something special about you, and Robbo had that. Graham nearly signed for West Brom but managed to pull out at the last minute and come to us. He got in quickly and ended up playing 21 league games that season.

There was a naivety about his game. Sometimes I'd say to myself, 'He's not gonna take the ball in *there*, is he? Oh blimey, he has. Now pass it,

Robbo! Oh, now he's going to shoot from 40 yards.' And he would and it would hit the bar. He took opponents by surprise, could pass and was very strong in the tackle.

Both he and Maxie could hurt you. They used to pair up taking an opponent on. I'd warn them about Cyrille Regis. 'Don't kick Cyrille; when you do that it only makes him harder.' You could almost see Cyrille's chest swell and the buttons pop on his shirt if it got physical. 'Then he's gonna kick you back – and then kick me.' So I would caution Max and Robbo, 'Just pick him up and say "Sorry Cy."' But they wouldn't listen.

There were some very hard strikers in that era, Peter Withe and Joe Jordan among them, who dished it out. What I liked about our centre-backs was that there was no crying afterwards. They probably told their opponents too much about what they were going to do to them, which the real full-on hard men don't. They just do it. But if Graham and Paul got done themselves they never whined.

Paul and Graham were both strong in the air but neither was the tallest or biggest. I think they were at the perfect stage of their careers to play alongside someone like me and learn from my experience. There were times when Keith said he came into the dressing room and didn't have to do a half-time talk because we were sorting it out amongst ourselves. And as a defence we were really good at organising ourselves to play for offside.

Milija Aleksic and Barry Daines were vying for the goalkeeper spot. Dainesy was the more regular, but by the end of the season Milija became the No.1 choice as Barry's 10-year career at Spurs came to a close. Aleksic had been signed from Luton; he was the son of a Serbian father, and was a good-looking fella, and physically fit. I used to like the way that he wore a white shirt under his green goalkeeper's shirt, with the collar outside.

People talk about my loyalty but Barry Daines was exceptionally loyal. I got into the team at 17, Dainesy had to wait to be a regular until he was 27. He was a very gifted goalie who had the opportunity to move to several other clubs. I knew West Ham were all over him as a schoolboy.

Taking on Hull in the FA Cup – another home tie in front of a big crowd

"Glenn had the skills that I didn't have – the creativity to find the forward ball"

I think he decided not to go there because they had a couple of good young goalkeepers, Steve Death and Peter Grotier. They were understudies to Bobby Ferguson, who the Hammers had signed for a then-world-record fee. Imagine signing for Spurs because you thought you had a better chance of getting games at a club where Pat Jennings was in goal! Dainesy was trustworthy but a quiet personality, which I don't think is the greatest asset for a goalkeeper. The goalkeeper has to have the biggest voice because he can see everything. It's a highly responsible position. Barry's genial character probably worked against him when it came to being dominant in the box.

For much of his career Barry was with the squad on our travels in case the first-choice goalkeeper was taken ill or something. But you can only stand that for so long. There wasn't the loan system that there is now, and there was no substitute goalkeeper. So if you weren't number one you were stuck. These days his agent wouldn't have allowed him to stay so long.

Milija was an excellent all-round sportsman and ended up working at a golf club in South Africa before he died all too young. He was a nice guy who joined in with everything. He was better with his feet than Barry, and made the position his as the season progressed.

Another player who came late into the side and cemented a place was 'TG', Tony Galvin, and like Robbo we saw him as home-grown, although he came from non-league Goole Town. Tony is a bit of an unsung hero. The fans recognised his contribution but he deserves greater acclaim. He was different. I loved his long-striding legs driving down that left wing. 'Just keep going, Tone,' we would think. He could cross it with his left foot, even though his right was stronger. But he was a down-to-earth type of player – northern, able to scrap it out. He had ability but it wasn't eye-catching.

The distances he covered for us were vital, providing width on the left to balance me on the right. I often had to make a decision whether or not to get into the box for Tony's crosses, with an eye on keeping it safe and tight behind me.

Tony was such a willing worker and of great value to the team. It's easy to talk about Glenn and Ossie, but Tony was integral. It had been a long time since we had produced a left-sided player to hold down the position. Tony was probably pound-for-pound the best value player in that team. He cost £30,000, a true bargain.

Facing Tony as a defender, I'd have been hard-pressed to wear him down. He's one of my favourite people – straightforward, no frills, no bullshit. For an international, trophy-winning footballer, he has just slipped back into normal life. No airs or graces. He has been to visit me wherever I have been in my career and has always been supportive.

Tony's hard running was needed in midfield to complement the attacking strengths we had in there. Ossie and Ricky were now settled and delivering. Joining them was Glenn, another home-grown, who had matured into a sensational player and a true superstar.

I devoted a chapter to him in my first book in the 1980s, but I could have written a whole book about him. He was a major talking point in English football, central to the discussion about our game – what it was and where it might be going.

Glenn's elegance is often mentioned. He wasn't very elegant as a kid, and was a bit gangly before he filled out in the early 1980s and truly looked assured. All great players look like they're not rushed, and no one was rushing Glenn. Panic was dispelled from his game because he had unwavering belief in his ability. Even when people targeted him to make a name for themselves, he just threw his shoulder and went the other way. He played the game at his tempo.

Glenn had the skills that I didn't have – the creativity to find the forward ball. It didn't seem to affect him when it didn't work. It was like the goalscorer who says, 'I've missed but there'll be another chance soon.' It said to the players around him, 'Trust me; you make a run and I'll find you.'

Glenn's range of passing was incredible. In one game he ignored playing a simple pass a few yards to me and went for something else a couple of times but neither came off. I said, 'Glenn, give it to me – I'll give it back', meaning, 'I'm here for you.'

'Steve, I didn't see you,' he said apologetically.

The point is that his vision was able to see things that the rest of us couldn't. He didn't need to play the simple ball. In a way it's respectful to say it was natural ability but it's disrespectful to infer he never had to try, because he worked extremely hard. When we finished training at Cheshunt, Glenn would always be doing extra work, hitting balls long distances and landing them on a sixpence

He explained to me once about hitting a forward ball. For the pass to get to say, Archie, before the goalie it's got to be world-class. Glenn said, 'You have to bend it into his run'; it just gives the striker an extra fraction of a second to read it before it gets to the keeper. I'm not sure he was that great at maths and angles at school, but he knew the best way to deliver and give the striker a chance. Glenn could deliver. He could make the ball

I enjoyed making the switch to right-back. The changes in position over the course of my career helped me stay fresh

stop, run through or come back. You can only really do that with practice and more practice.

Glenn had the lot. He was a supreme volleyer, as he showed with his two thumping goals against Manchester United and Forest a couple of seasons before. There was no one else really like him in the English game. If you put Alan Hudson and Tony Currie together, you might have got Glenn.

I remember being nervous of what Glenn would think when my first book came out, because although I oozed praise there was some criticism. I made reference to his deficiencies in covering ground, which many of his critics held against him. In the aftermath of Glenn's recent health problems the views of the media, pundits and others has become kinder. I saw mentions of him being 'the best English player that we've ever seen'. He was, but I stand by what I said about how he could have improved. He was close to being perfect, but he could have been a bit more mobile.

It was an honest appraisal at the time and he was fine with it. He wasn't precious in any way. Glenn always owned up. 'I can't be a John Pratt. That's not my game.' And I think he stayed true to his philosophy. It's like the musician who signs a contract with a record company and they want him to make different music to what is in his heart. Glenn played the way he believed in.

Glenn Hoddle, with Charlie George in the background, during a thrilling 4–4 draw with Southampton in December 1980. Glenn was the conductor of our orchestra

The press clamoured for him to play for England but that was double-edged as it put pressure on managers and their expectations. If Glenn didn't play especially well in an international the backlash would be just as forceful. He was in the right place at the right time at Tottenham. The fact that the opportunity wasn't the same with England was not Glenn's problem. I said in a team meeting once, 'Let's stop talking about what Glenn can't do; let's talk about what he can do because that is so special. We just need to keep him having the ball.'

When he was in poor health he replied to a message I'd sent saying of me, 'As far as I'm concerned there was and is only one Skip.' Glenn was the leader of the orchestra; I was the man who got the orchestra there on time.

People who knew him recognised him for what he was: a straight bat, a proper chap. People who didn't know him could think he was a bit offish, even flash, but there was no way that he was; if anything he was shy.

He wasn't arrogant in any way and did everything that was asked of him – more so because he was home-grown. Tottenham was his club, and he put his heart and soul into Spurs. That in turn led to some negative perceptions, that he was a southern softy – 'Glenda' and all that. An element of distrust developed between football and the media in the 1980s and Glenn probably kept the football writers at arm's length. It was an era when agents handled things more. Dennis Roache was his agent, and tried to control the exposure, but 'media handling' was not kindly thought of by journalists.

None of that should obscure what a genius of a footballer Glenn Hoddle was. His mastery of a ball was absolute. I was interviewed about him for radio during his recent illness and was asked about his 'special left foot'. I said, 'Do you mean you think he was left-footed? He wasn't. He was right-footed, but it's interesting that you couldn't tell the difference.'

Glenn had a big influence on how I continued to develop and improve as a player. It led to another moving set piece, like the one in the Second Division, that was a key part of our armoury. It evolved more than it was devised. When our keeper got the ball in our box, I would move out to the touchline before the left-winger. I would receive the ball and look long, but cut it into Glenn in the middle. I had to deliver it just right because an opponent would be looking to smash him; it had to be measured so that Glenn could let it run across him and then launch it to Tony Galvin on the run. It worked beautifully. Later, when opponents were aware of it, we would sometimes do something to surprise them. Graham Rix, for example, knew that I was going to cut it into Glenn. They were friends, and Rix would have watched us play. But I knew that. So I would feint to give it to Glenn but then run on. 'Fuck! Bastards!' said Graham.

I had to serve Glenn the ball. It wasn't just giving him the ball. It was *serving* him. Glenn told me, 'My dad said, "Glenn, I know you are a good passer, but three of those passes you hit to TG today, my word – where did you get them from?" Glenn said, "Steve P told me to do it, Dad."'

All of this meant that the dynamic at the club was exceptional. We had a Yorkshire manager with a qualified taxi-driver as an assistant. In the team were at least four London home-growns, two non-league players who were virtually home-grown, Latin American superstars and big-money striker signings. Ossie had studied as a lawyer, Tony had a degree in Russian, Archie had worked at Rolls-Royce, Chrissy was a lift engineer, Robbo a pipe fitter's mate and Maxie was brought up in a brothel. Sorry, I mean a pub!

It was a great balance and all of a sudden it came together. Just the right time to bring in a pair of psychologists.

"Glenn was the leader of the orchestra; I was the man who got the orchestra there on time"

The Spurs dugout (from left to right): Ron Henry (then schoolboy coach), Johnny Wallis (trainer), Keith Burkinshaw (manager) and Mike Varney (physio), with Peter Shreeve (assistant manager) standing in the leather coat. Keith and Peter were contrasting in their style and manner but proved a great management pairing. Roy Reyland, who became kit manager, is in the background

Mike Varney is an intelligent chap, despite what Keith thought about stretching. Mike was the first physio to have his name on the back of his tracksuit top, realising the benefit of being on TV since he had his own chain of clinics. The fans even used to sing, 'One Mike Varney' when he ran on to give us some injury treatment.

Mike went on a course to learn about sports psychology and an idea clicked. An injured player having treatment from a physio will be in a situation where they will talk to each other – good things and bad things, the latter especially for injured players at a low emotional point. It was part of the communications system at the club. Mike said to Keith, 'You need to meet these people I've met on this course.'

They were sports psychologists John Syer and his American colleague Christopher Connolly. Keith invited them in. I still speak to Chris; John passed away, sadly. He was the national volleyball coach of Scotland, having played volleyball and hockey, and became very influential, working with a whole range of teams and sportspeople, including the cyclist Chris Boardman.

They didn't know much about football but they knew about communication and how to ask questions. A lot of football chat is piss-taking. John and Chris just made that chat more useful. They gave Keith reports on how he held his meetings, who he encouraged to speak and who was less willing to speak.

They argued that players should be encouraged to express their opinions. For instance, they encouraged the front two to talk together about what they liked about each other or didn't like in terms of football and each other's game. Archie really believed in it. They questioned whether he should try to be nicer off the pitch, but he felt it would dull his edge. So they had him doing a mental visualisation exercise of putting a suit on before he played and then taking it off, to make a distinction between his character on and off the pitch.

It was clever, because it was about improvement. We were given notice in advance of when they were coming in. It was planned right. They used me as the captain – I think I'm a good communicator – as I could get the others to buy in to what they were doing. I walked in one day and said to a couple of lads, 'You look a bit nervous.' They nodded. I said light-heartedly, 'Well, give yourself a bloody good talking too.' It had to be a little relaxed like that.

Players were not forced to speak to them. Micky Hazard didn't want to talk to them, although I think he was one of the ones who would have benefited. But it was probably a step too far at his young age.

What sold it to me is that it confirmed my more practical 'shop-floor football' outlook. I did what they were suggesting. It could be about planning ahead, thinking through a process or a routine.

John and I were going to write a book about football communication combining our two perspectives, but he died before we could do it. We hit it off; we understood each other. It was a really good education for me.

It was very open-minded of Keith and the club to accept them. It's what the old coaching books used to say in that you have got to have an open and enquiring mind. I wonder if there were any restrictions put on the psychologists as to what they could or couldn't say. But they wrote psychology books referring directly to the work they did with us. It was ground-breaking stuff that helped us bond.

Teams are better when you are a band of brothers. That's a throwaway line, but it means it's positive if if you're brotherly enough to be able to say, as you would to a real brother, 'Hold on, that's not right' but always in the context of 'I'm with you: we're together and we'll get through this.' Such togetherness was to prove crucial as we looked to take the next step – winning trophies.

A meeting of minds (left to right): Chris Hughton, John Syer, me, Christopher Connolly, Steve Archibald and Mike Varney. John and Chris were two psychologists who helped create synergy at the club

NAMES IN LIGHTS

B y the time of the FA Cup third round in January 1981, I'd just turned 29 and I was really enjoying my football. I knew what I was doing. It was a lovely feeling hitting that purple patch: I could be a motivator, a captain, a decision-maker, a protector.

During games, people like Garry Brooke and Micky Hazard would say, 'Just keep telling me what to do, Steve.' Brooksie said, 'Steve, I only move to places because you tell me.' I said, 'Well, you're gonna have to learn for yourself. I ain't going to be here forever.' Micky said once, 'I've never had a bad game playing alongside you, Steve,' which is lovely.

My brother Ted started watching me again, having not seen me play for a few years. It all started to come right. I could do a bit of everything, I was on it. Playing football is never easy, but it was getting easier.

The QPR game in the third round was far from easy pickings, however. It could easily have gone the other way, and we only went through after a replay at home. In fact, we played all our games in London right up to the semi-final. We were drawn at home to Hull and then Coventry and saw both of them off quite comfortably.

We drew Exeter for the quarter-final, the weakest team left in the hat. In previous cup runs we'd come up against Manchester United and Liverpool at that stage, so the draw was clearly running for us this time. Unfortunately this season was when there were only three sides of the ground in operation as they were rebuilding the West Stand, so not as many people could get in to see us, but I actually didn't mind the rebuilding going on. Change is good. Change of position, change of manager, different teammates – they all keep you fresh and on your toes. I didn't like seeing the old West Stand go, nor having to park up the road and change in temporary buildings, but it was at least something different.

It seemed like it was all going our way. We could sense it from the crowd. Tottenham fans get very excited: if we win four games on the spin it's 'Here we go!' That was starting to happen in that cup run. John Bond, who had become manager of Manchester City, had tipped us to win the FA Cup that season, which proved to be quite ironic.

We reached the semi-finals. Of the teams left, Wolves would finish fifth from bottom in the league, Ipswich would be runners-up while Manchester City finished 12th. So if we had been able to choose from those three who to play it would have been Wolves. We'd beaten Ipswich 5–3 earlier in the league but that had been a rogue game. A wintry gale had blown in and it

"It all started to come right. I could do a bit of everything, I was on it. Playing football is never easy, but it was getting easier"

With the new West Stand under construction, we played our home cup ties in front of only three stands. We beat Exeter City, but were fortunate to overcome tougher-than-expected opposition on the day

was a little bit of a war. Eric Gates was sent off, and goals were going in all over the place because of the wind. I slid on my arse after a mis-hit shot from Garth that went across the goal and scored.

We drew Wolves and the match was played at Hillsborough. It was my first experience of going to a neutral ground and a big date in the football calendar. In the warm-up, some of our supporters came onto the pitch from where they had been standing on the Leppings Lane terrace. We didn't know what had happened. Archie scored after four minutes and after that more fans were climbing the fences and coming onto the pitch perimeter.

It later transpired that police were letting them climb over and leading them away from the packed terraces. It was a very near miss and tragically the lessons from it were not heeded eight years later. I have to admit that we were not really aware of what was happening. As players, we were so focused on the game and ourselves – the last thing you're thinking about is the crowd. But there was something different about that day. I couldn't put my finger on it but it definitely felt different.

I liked playing at Hillsborough. I didn't play particularly well in that game, and we had to settle for a draw, but Maxie was immense all match. He stepped up that day. I felt responsible for their first goal because I didn't close down the cross. We retook the lead via Glenn but then were robbed in the last minute. The last step to Wembley was taken away from us by a poxy refereeing decision by Clive Thomas who gave Wolves a penalty for a dive by Kenny Hibbitt.

But on the coach going home, we knew we were going to win the replay because we couldn't wait for the game – we wanted it straight away. If it could have been on the Monday we'd have played it, fired up by a sense of injustice. The replay was at Arsenal's ground of all places. There should have been the usual nerves about playing at Highbury, but it didn't occur to us. We were going to win. And then the team sheet came in, and their main striker, Andy Gray, wasn't playing, which was a massive lift. We weren't frightened of him, but that was a lot of their threat taken away.

The match was played on a poor, bumpy pitch. We never really enjoyed playing at Highbury because it seemed smaller than everywhere else, but it didn't seem small that day. It was an unforgettable night. Glenn was doing his stuff, providing for Garth, who scored one of his best ever goals, timing his burst of speed just right and finishing in front of the North Bank, and then Ricky scored a wonderful goal.

The fact that three quarters of the ground was virtually all Spurs made that night special. There are stories that our team vandalised their dressing room or the boardroom, which is insulting nonsense. There was no way we'd do something like that. Nothing could spoil the experience of that game. The ground of your biggest rivals, packed out with your own fans, watching you turn it on. It was one of those evenings, like a European night. We even played in all white because Wolves had dark shorts.

The joy among the players and fans was that we had reached the FA Cup Final. I've heard it said that it was the most important club cup competition in the world back then. It definitely had that reputation and aura. We all grew up believing in the FA Cup. You didn't have to be the best team to win it, but the glory of doing so was huge. It was a massive part of our culture – every FA Cup Final had a story attached.

The beauty was also that it was live on TV; even if you didn't like the two teams that were playing you had to watch the FA Cup Final. There was hardly any live football on television in those days except this game, and now we were going to be playing in it. Our heads were full, thinking about what it meant to our families. If we won the trophy and got our name on it, that was Tottenham back in the big time. Glitz, glamour, wall-to-wall newspaper coverage, cup final songs – this was a different game. Now the spotlight was really on us.

Our league form tailed off, with no wins in the last six games, but not through want of trying. If you go into a game thinking, 'I don't want to be injured', that's the best way to get injured. Taking it easy was never suggested to us or entered our heads. If anything, you try harder because you want to get picked for the final. Some, of course, were more likely to be selected, including me, but this could be a once-in-a-lifetime chance.

I was conscious that I hadn't won anything as skipper. Victory at Wembley would really see my story come full circle, because that's where

Garth Crooks's pace complemented Glenn's passing expertise and resulted in the brilliant second goal in our famous semi-final replay victory over Wolves – at Highbury of all places

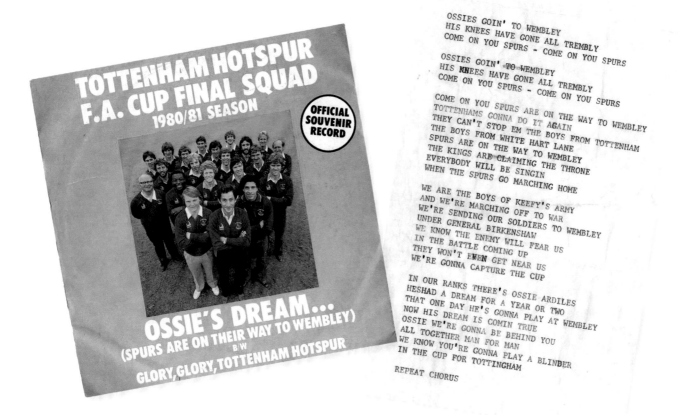

OSSIES GOIN' TO WEMBLEY
HIS KNEES HAVE GONE ALL TREMBLY
COME ON YOU SPURS - COME ON YOU SPURS

OSSIES GOIN' TO WEMBLEY
HIS KNEES HAVE GONE ALL TREMBLY
COME ON YOU SPURS - COME ON YOU SPURS

COME ON YOU SPURS ARE ON THE WAY TO WEMBLEY
TOTTENHAMS GONNA DO IT AGAIN
THEY CAN'T STOP EM THE BOYS FROM TOTTENHAM
THE BOYS FROM WHITE HART LANE
SPURS ARE ON THE WAY TO WEMBLEY
THE KINGS ARE CLAIMING THE THRONE
EVERYBODY WILL BE SINGIN
WHEN THE SPURS GO MARCHING HOME

WE ARE THE BOYS OF KEEFY'S ARMY
AND WE'RE MARCHING OFF TO WAR
WE'RE SENDING OUR SOLDIERS TO WEMBLEY
UNDER GENERAL BIRKENSHAW
WE KNOW THE ENEMY WILL FEAR US
IN THE BATTLE COMING UP
THEY WON'T EVEN GET NEAR US
WE'RE GONNA CAPTURE THE CUP

IN OUR RANKS THERE'S OSSIE ARDILES
HESHAD A DREAM FOR A YEAR OR TWO
THAT ONE DAY HE'S GONNA PLAY AT WEMBLEY
NOW HIS DREAM IS COMIN TRUE
OSSIE WE'RE GONNA BE BEHIND YOU
ALL TOGETHER MAN FOR MAN
WE KNOW YOU'RE GONNA PLAY A BLINDER
IN THE CUP FOR TOTTINGHAM

REPEAT CHORUS

The sleeve for the 1981 FA Cup Final song and the lyric sheet we used in the studio. Ossie was a World Cup-winning footballer, now a pop star – and later a film star thanks to his appearance in *Escape To Victory*

it started – 1967 and signing for the club. We had two players who had won the World Cup and who weren't going to be fazed by it. Glenn was in the England team so was used to playing on the big stage. With my two League Cup Finals I had experience. But there was still nothing quite like an FA Cup Final, and the build-up reflected that.

Tottenham became more open as a club along with the increased commercialism of the game, and famous supporters like Peter Cook were allowed closer to the club. It was known that Chas & Dave were Spurs fans, and their manager, Bob England, was a big fan, so they wrote *Ossie's Dream* for us. It was a bit of fun. It was also a way of them getting something out of their Tottenham link, and why not? It contributed to the players' pool because, whatever anyone says, we were not on great money. An FA Cup Final pool could make a difference.

The pool was a way for teams to collect and share money evenly from commercial activities, media deals, and other sidelines associated with reaching the final. We used Dennis Roach to sort out the pool, with a committee of me plus a couple of others, including Glenn. No one gives you money for nothing – but if it meant a chance to spend a bit more time together then that would be no bad thing. We did 90 per cent of the things that came up and largely shared everything out. If there was fee for an exclusive interview that probably stayed with the player but we had a share of the takings for the post-game banquet, for instance.

I said that Peter Shreeve and Johnny Wallis should be in the pool, and was about to say Keith as well but he said no before I even suggested it; I suppose he thought it might sway his decision-making but fair play to him. That was typically Keith: he played with a straight bat. Everyone who would have made an appearance at some point in the run was entitled to be in the pool.

I was probably earning £25,000 basic a year at this time. We didn't get much over £1,000 each from the pool. The advantage of my era was that no one earned a £100 grand a week more than me. Imagine playing for Real Madrid and you're earning £60 grand a week while someone else is on half a million! I never felt jealousy – it gives you a saner life and the chance to sleep at night rather than worrying about other people and what they are earning.

When we recorded the song, a few drinks helped. It was all pretty strange for the English lads in the squad, so you can imagine how Ossie and Ricky felt, especially about going on *Top of the Pops*. After the show we went to the bar, like everyone does. Paul McCartney walked in and saw Glenn. Glenn saw him and it was like love at first sight!

'It's great to meet you!'

'No, trust me, it's great to meet *you*!'

Shakin' Stevens was on the same programme, as was Eddy Grant, who was a Spurs fan, Kim Wilde, the Nolans and the Undertones. It was such a surreal experience. All of a sudden we were living a different sort of stardom. We were singing about winning and so putting ourselves up for mockery if we failed. Looking back, I can't believe that I did it but you get caught up in the excitement.

In the week before the final we trained at Cheshunt, to keep it as normal as possible. We had a press day on Wednesday. When Ossie heard the match was going to be beamed back live to Argentina he was overcome with emotion. We were aware of the global interest but that really showed how much there was. Then there were tickets to deal with – everyone you knew wanted one or more. You don't want to let people down but you stick to your principles of fair play when it comes to who deserves to go. Family come first, of course.

The suits had been measured and made, and were ready for us where we stayed at the Ponsbourne Hotel near Cheshunt from Thursday to Saturday night. It was a bit of hidden hotel, the kind of place you imagine secret, powerful meetings going on. Ted Croker from the FA came to speak to us about *the* day. He was very personable but left us thinking that we were not the important ones. This was the sport's showpiece. It was about the band, the precise, limited time we were allowed on the pitch and that we had to have a jacket and tie on, even if it was hot. By Friday night the fuss had died down and we could relax. Have dinner, watch telly, don't sit around talking, just relax.

FA Cup Final day arrived. It was muggy, very close and warm. We had a light breakfast, then a team interview. They got Tony Galvin to speak a bit of Russian and then cut to Ossie and Ricky's families all lined up, one big extended family in Argentina. It was a little bit awkward with the satellite delay but touching as well.

The psychologists were with us, having meetings and discussions. The mood was calm, at least on the surface. Everyone had their own thoughts; I went through my usual routines, keeping it as familiar as possible.

We didn't allow cameras on our bus. My view is that, like the dressing room, it's a sacred place. We set off about 12:30pm just to make sure we weren't late. The driver was told not to rush. It's almost as much of a crime in football to be too early as it is to be late, like being on the starting blocks before you are ready. We got a police escort; with 60 million people watching, the last thing anyone wanted was to be held up in traffic.

The journey went through the geographical start of North London and onto the North Circular – Tottenham country. Straight away we picked up

"Looking back, I can't believe that I did Ossie's Dream but you get caught up with the excitement"

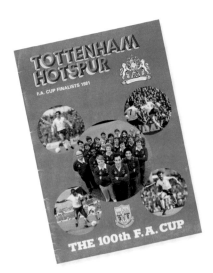

Under strict FA orders, we had to wear suits for the pre-match walk on the pitch

the vibe, with people out waving their colours, hanging out of cars, tooting their horns and cheering us on.

The atmosphere built over a journey that took about an hour. We arrived on time. I was asked to talk to TV the moment we stepped off the coach but the club clamped down on it and said no. Very different to how it would be today. I was trying not to be nervous. It wasn't as if we had mobile phones and texts coming at us and having to send them back. My advice to players now is to let them go – answer three days later. We would get telegrams – from Martin Chivers for example, people wanting you to know that they were thinking about you.

The coach went into the big Wembley tunnel and the gates closed. We went straight into the dressing room, wanting to get on that pitch as quick as we could. When we went for the walk on the pitch we saw the banners, which were great, funny and inspiring, saying things like 'The Year of the Cockerel' relating to the Chinese year, and 'Hod the King of WHL'.

There was a bloke who, with his daughter, used to come to the training ground to say hello and they became quite friendly with us. When I walked out onto the pitch, I looked up and at the very back of the stadium of the old Wembley there was glass between the back wall and the roof. I could see this man and his daughter silhouetted against the glass. The odds must have been thousands to one of seeing them, and we waved to each other.

There was no warm-up on the pitch, so you couldn't check your studs out. In the dressing room we got changed into the very modern Le Coq Sportif kit we'd adopted that season. It felt even better because it was brand new, but something was wrong. Ricky had been given my usual No.6 and I had No.5, and I was not happy. It stemmed from an honest error in the programme, which necessitated the change, but it upset my routine.

Keith and Peter gave us some reminders rather than a long team talk. The Wembley dressing room was not opulent, it was functional, but it reeked of history: you were conscious that Stanley Matthews and Danny Blanchflower had been where you were. Attendants provided a little a bit 'extra', asking if we needed anything. They made the tea, ran the baths, and did the kind of stuff that needed doing when the game was on. Then a bell was rung to let you know it was time to go out into the tunnel. The two teams lined up, not talking to each other. You might smile or nod if one of them caught your attention, like Dennis Tueart, who played in my debut in 1969, or Joe Corrigan, who I was in the England under-23s with. I also knew Gerry Gow from way back in the FA Youth Cup. I knew he was going to be nasty.

The focus then is on you, your team and your thoughts. The tunnel is deep in shadow. You see this little square of light about 75 yards ahead of you. It's pretty quiet apart from a hum. Not noisy, just the hum of so many people outside, gathered in one incredible place. I don't think I could ever accurately describe it – it's a unique noise.

And then you walk forwards, getting closer to that square of light. It's widening and getting bigger as you get closer. The hum grows louder and louder – you want to get to it. That's where it's all going on, out there, and you want be out *there*.

This isn't the walkabout in the suit beforehand. Now you have your kit and boots on, the gear you do your work in. This is it – the ultimate experience you've thought about and dreamed of having, it's happening for real now, and to you. Getting nearer and nearer. This is it; this is the time. It's that moment where you reach the end of the tunnel, go through that square and step out into the daylight. And then it hits you.

There is a burst of noise. Better than anything I'd ever heard from a crowd before. I'd played in front of big crowds at Tottenham and Wembley and experienced amazing receptions. But this is something else. It is two teams coming out together, so no one was booing or jeering. It was 100,000 people roaring at the same time.

A moment of real pride: leading my team out onto the hallowed turf, and hearing that unique Wembley roar

Meeting the Queen Mother before kick-off. We didn't discuss formations in much detail!

It was a release for the fans as well. Much as I didn't like a marching band taking over the pitch, it warmed the crowd up and helped give the final its sense of occasion. But it was crunch time for the supporters as well.

At last, the waiting is over. This is it. The FA Cup Final.

Game on.

We hadn't had a great season and finished mid-table, but we were favourites to win the game. Man City had avoided the threat of relegation, John Bond reshaping the team and doing a fine job alongside John Sainty, City's coach and my first ever coach at Tottenham.

The problem was that we didn't play like favourites. The kick-off was a rehearsed move – knock it back to Maxie, who then sent it out to TG. You wanted your first touch as early as possible. Very early in the game, I nutmegged someone and Jack Charlton, who was doing the expert commentary for ITV, said, 'Oh, he's confident.'

Playing at Wembley, the angles seemed different. At White Hart Lane we had markers – the corner flag or a feature in the stand – to help you get your bearings. At Wembley you can't find the marker. It's almost like it's a new game when you play there. The pitch was heavy and lots of players got cramp.

City took the lead after 30 minutes, a superb header from Tommy Hutchinson. It was the first time we'd been losing in the FA Cup that season and we didn't panic, but we were laboured and made basic mistakes. Ricky especially looked leggy, and was substituted in the second half. He walked off disconsolately to the dressing room rather than sit on the bench. I didn't like that. We found out after it was because he was upset, feeling he'd let people down.

Fortunately we got a free-kick, 10 minutes from time. Glenn was taking it, and told me to just stand a bit closer. I touched it to him, he hit it – goal! There was no real power in it: Glenn went for placement but Hutchinson had come across to try and defend it only to head it past Corrigan and into the net. Tommy should never have been there – he should have trusted his keeper.

We were level and thought we could win it but we had extra-time and by the end I'd never seen two teams so exhausted. We got out of jail.

Barry Daines had rough luck with his testimonial because it was scheduled for after the final but ended up being played between the first game and the replay, and only 7,000 turned up. I think he wanted to put it

Helping Graham Roberts with his cramp. I eventually got cramp in my groin, which had never happened to me before – it had to be due to the tension we were all feeling

off but the club wouldn't allow it. Imagine if we'd won and had been able to parade the trophy at his testimonial!

My son Glenn was only three at the time. He was being babysat by my mum but Ted insisted he'd take him to the match. He asked some supporters to take a picture of him outside the Twin Towers with Glenn on his shoulders, and they happened to be Man City fans. They said, 'You can't have a picture without your colours on.' So they put a Manchester City hat and scarf on my son! When they finished taking the picture Ted said, 'That's the son of the Tottenham captain you've just put your hat and scarf on.'

My daughter Loren went with my wife Cherrill. We had to make arrangements for our children to be taken home after the game because we went to a banquet at the Hilton that was hopefully going to be a celebration for winning. It turned out to be a bit of a damp squib.

Bill Nicholson gave a speech and, typically, told us we didn't play very well. Harsh words but necessary: it gave us added motivation to put it right in the replay. We commanded games at this time without having a ball-winner in midfield because we could dominate with possession. But City had energy and ball-winners and had denied us our usual possession, and on the day that's what it looked like was needed to beat us. And they nearly did.

In the dressing room after the game Keith took me aside and said, 'Would you pick Ricky for the replay?' I said, 'Keith, no, I don't think you can.'

That was more out my frustration with thinking that Ricky had left his team to get on with it. I knew Ricky wasn't like that; I don't even know why I thought it but his body language was giving me the wrong signals. Keith was positive and said straight away in response, 'He's is playing.' And he was right.

I think he asked my opinion so that he could give his to me – almost to make a statement. He told Ricky there and then, 'You're playing.' That was a huge lift for him – it was great psychology and superb timing. Keith was the manager and, boy, did he manage that. It was good for all of us as it got rid of any doubts or distractions.

We had Sunday and Monday at home. Tuesday we did light training, and went back to the Ponsbourne before going to the England–Brazil game at Wembley that evening. It cleared away the hangover from Saturday. The attitude changed. We realised that if we were going to get beaten, then we had better make sure that we at least played football, and if there was any stick to be dished out there were enough of us to do it. We obviously had to step up in terms of our competitiveness.

As it was an evening kick-off, the spotlight was off: there wasn't a whole day of TV devoted to the game. The only thing that was important now was the result. All the ceremony and hullabaloo was done with – this was football for football people.

On the way to the ground it was obvious that there were more Spurs than City fans. Tickets had gone on sale at Wembley on Sunday and most had gone to Spurs fans. It was hard for City supporters to stay down or come back down on a midweek night.

We couldn't wait to get at them. The sun was out but it was a crisper evening. I reverted to my usual No.6. The numbers in the first game had also been a new design – square felt. They had faded when the kit was washed, so for the replay we went back to more traditional stitched-on round numbers.

We came out again. Instantly we saw there were loads more Tottenham supporters there – even in the City end. We did the formal stuff with the dignitaries and then we were off again.

Above: Receiving direction from Keith during the first game of the 1981 FA Cup Final

Below: The picture of Ted with my son, Glenn, outside Wembley before the final, taken by a City fan who insisted on lending Glenn his scarf and hat!

Keith told me a few years later that Glenn was the best player in the replay, that he worked his socks off. I have only ever watched bits of the match but for this book I watched the whole game for the first time and I'll try to describe how the game unfolded as if it was happening now.

We kick off and straight away I see what Keith meant. Glenn is *on* it. Gow leaves one in on Ossie but we're up for this. The pitch still looks heavy, but we're moving the ball over the surface quicker.

Steve MacKenzie has a good shot for them early on but we're OK. Then we break through. Seven minutes are gone when Ossie does his magic out on the left. The ball breaks, good reaction Archie. I'm in the box ready to follow up and there's Ricky – GOAL!

It's a release of energy and a great feeling. See? We are capable. We can play. The crowd are up for it as well. This is our game.

But they hit back quick and in superb style. We clear a cross but it's headed back across our goal for MacKenzie, what a volley, top corner. It's a great goal, and Hutchinson played a lovely header to tee him up.

My thinking is, 'OK, come on. Let's go again. No problem.' However well or bad you're playing it's about the next five minutes, whatever the score is. We get a free-kick on the edge of the area. Glenn hits it – bastard, it's hit the post! This is a better game than the first match already.

I'm reliving the action: 'Well done Tone. Come on Ossie. Well played. C'mon, c'mon Rick.'

I'm putting tackles in, Maxie and Robbo are on it. They are not going to have it their way tonight. We're not going out to hurt anyone, but we will meet fire with fire. Got to be done. In all those youth-team games up against Gow in midfield I was always his sort of governor and he definitely ain't bullying us tonight.

The Spurs supporters were our 12th man on the night. There were many more Spurs fans in the ground for the replay, which was difficult for Manchester City fans to attend due to it being staged in London in midweek

Ricky's first goal – a perfect start after the disappointment he endured during the previous game

'Go on Ossie.' It's flowing more. The slickness, the mojo is back. Short bursts and quick passes.

For such an attacking game there are few actual saves that either keeper has to make. Glenn's winning tackles, he's a different class tonight.

'Pass, pass. Pass! Well done Garth.' He got back well there. Perfect weather now. The sun is down, the lights are on. Game on. Ricky is like a No.10 between the front men and the midfield. Tony and me have to do extra as a result and Glenn is pulled over to the right a bit.

Half an hour gone. We're fine. Ricky has a fierce shot, Corrigan just about keeps it out.

The second half. We come out of the tunnel as if we mean business. We are thinking at this stage it's our game. We're playing football, although I don't think enough.

There's an opening – Garth – ah, nearly in. That was typical of Garth at times in a build-up: do all the good work and then the final bit just isn't quite there.

'Love it, Tone. Ah Chrissy, too readable.' But no, we've got it back. 'Well done.' Closed them down and got it back. These days that would be called the 'high press'. Nothing new.

Five minutes in, we're fine. But Dave Bennett is in, Maxie and Chris come across – it's a pen! I wasn't sure during the game, but I don't think it was looking back decades later. Jack Charlton said Bennett 'went over nothing'. You can see why it was given, but still.

Reeves takes it – ah, Milija, he nearly saved it. OK. Not just a case of keep going. Time to stand up and be counted, Tottenham.

Another one goes in late on Ossie, he's getting angry. 'Press up, press up.' One does it, the others do it to and we're on our way.

'Book him ref!' Right, we've had enough of this. We said after the first game we didn't just accept the physical stuff from City, we took it and didn't do anything. Not this time. We're talking back to them, giving them what for.

They go close again. More passes, we gotta make more passes.

A bit of desire in Tony's run, but then a bit of naivety running into traffic.

'Well played Garth, go on Glenn, magic – oh good save!'

Archie's nearly in. There's a lot of fire from us. That's a bit of a challenge from me. 'Chrissy boy, love it, love it!' But not a good ball forward – I'm disappointed with Chris's lack of quality going forward today.

"It's a release of energy and feeling. See? We are capable. We can play. The crowd are up for it as well. This is our game"

Garth Crooks scores the goal that put his name up in lights. He lit up the scoreboard and our performance that night

Gow in again on Ossie. Ossie bought it a bit. There's a fan coming on the pitch, he's had enough of Gow. The police get him away.

I do a nutmeg – that's two in this final. Not really my style.

City are trying to break our play up, killing time a bit, but nothing like teams do today.

Ossie is on it, really on it. He makes the decision to push up. 'Well played Glenn! Garth, you gotta read that.'

Ooh, there's a tackle from me – that was an important one.

They have had enough chances to win this, having taken the lead twice over the two games. And they've had half-chances in this game.

Glenn is giving all the quality now. That's what good players do when it comes to the crunch.

'Make passes, just make passes.' But we lack targets. That's why we would hit Tony Galvin more.

Milija has barely had a save to make all night. 'That's nice Robbo. Well played Maxie.'

We get a free-kick and, oh dear, I make a bad touch. I don't really like watching myself play. You become self-critical, seeing the errors. I was supposed to make the ball go dead. What an idiot. Still, if that didn't happen who knows, we might have lost!

'Well played Robbo.' He's coming to the front. That's him, a fighter.

'Make passes, just make passes! Play, play, play!' Corner. 'Come on then.' Handball by Caton? It looked like it. OK, go again. 'Great stuff Glenn, what a ball – yes Garth! 2–2!'

What a lovely move that goal was. I'm in there, in case it drops to me or there's a rebound, which is what you have got do when you're chasing the game – take a little gamble. I took a little step back as well so I stayed onside.

The ball from Glenn was lovely, the way he killed it and dropped it in.

Bloody hell, a poxy ball from me.

Milija looks the part, there's no flapping or concern with him.

The crowd are singing 'When Steve goes up to lift that FA Cup...' It's funny how you hear these things later.

'Go on, go on – ooooh Ricky, no! Well done Chrissy boy.'

Now we're moving it well. That's how we've got to play. 'Oh Garth! Aargh, not quite. Archie...' Oh, I'd have waited for it, there could have been a penalty.

There are individual battles all over the pitch. This is the game we want as players and football lovers, the game where our players win their individual battles.

My word, this is a long half – it seems to be taking forever. What's that decision for? Archie did nothing wrong! 'Well done, Garth, get him away from the ref.'

Fifteen minutes to go... 'Great tackle Robbo, well done. And you, Tony. He's given it to Ricky...'

'Go on Ricky. Go on. Go on! Keep going... Ricky – GOAL! GOAL!'

I was coming into the box; you can see me when Ricky hares off on his celebration. It's the greatest goal ever scored in a FA Cup Final, but watching it back now I can't help but find faults. Garth shouldn't be standing still, he should be following Ricky in. He wafts his foot at an imaginary ball as Ricky takes his final touch! Archie is angry, screaming for the ball out by the far post.

I went forward during the move but thought, 'Don't go forward too quick just in case.' And now Tony's steaming down the left – OK, I still gotta be a bit careful. Tony checks back, gives it to Ricky. Ricky is on the slalom. Now I can gamble a bit more going into the box. I'm thinking about Ricky. 'Pass! Pass! Give it!' I might even be on here. 'All right, shoot then. Fucking shoot!' And as you're saying it – he's only gone and done it!

I don't know if it was a joke or not but Ricky once told us about how he used to ride to school on a horse and he didn't play 11 versus 11 for years because of a lack of children until he went to the bigger school when he was about 12. And then when he was playing football the teacher would shout at him, 'Ricky, pass. Pass the ball!' And he was thinking, 'What's this "pass"?' Because the football he had learnt was running with the ball on his farm in and out of the trees. Well, who would have thought that would come in so handy?

As captain my message now is, 'No goals. We do not concede. Nothing stupid. Get back behind the ball, and make it hard for them.'

They bring on Tueart. The crowd are going mad, singing their hearts out. We have to concentrate. A few minutes to go. Just make passes. Ray Ranson and Tony square up, a real northern battle that was.

This game always felt a bit like a World Cup game – at night, it's mild, socks rolled down, an Argentinian has just scored one of the greatest ever goals.

'Play it Ricky. Just make passes, just make passes. Just. Make. Passes.'

I go in on Gow. That'll do.

'Well done Garth.'

Clock is ticking. How long left?

Five minutes to go.

Graham had a poor first half but is storming it in the second. Hoddle's getting stronger. If they did one of those heat maps for him, he'd be everywhere.

There's nearly a hand ball, but it's accidental. Garth is in but it's a poor touch. So close.

A crucial decision by Keith to keep Ricky in the team led to a famous goal and a fabulous celebration

"I've been waiting for this moment, hoping it would come, wondering if it would ever happen. I turn to the fans. I lift the cup. Get in there"

A minute to go. Focus. Concentrate. Pass, pass. Just make passes. It comes back to Tueart. He volleys it, but... it's inches wide.

Time added on, a few more minutes. 'C'mon. Not long now. C'mon. Archie, I love it. Let it run...'

Final whistle. Game over. We've won the FA Cup.

Everyone asks, 'How do you feel?' Relief. Elation. We've done our job. We're back.

There's a kid in a white butcher's coat who gets on the pitch. He's elated because we're back. I felt everything the supporters were thinking and feeling. But how did that kid get on the pitch?

We commiserate with our opponents. You keep it simple – 'Bad luck', something like that. Certainly not anything that can be taken as if you are gloating. It's care for your fellow pros. You have your own thoughts of joy in amongst it but you are also commiserating. You go from a handshake with an opponent to hugging a teammate.

We have to wait. We're hugging, congratulating each other. Such noise and joy, and you're at the pinnacle of it – the fans want to see that trophy picked up because although you've won it you haven't really done it until the captain holds it aloft.

I wasn't explicitly thinking that at the time. When the final whistle goes that is it, I am gone, shattered. At the end of it all it's just release. You've won, you've earned your money. But this time all of a sudden someone taps you on the shoulder. 'Steve. You need to go and pick the cup up.'

I start the walk up the famous 39 steps. Our fans are so close, we're getting mobbed. Its pandemonium and the noise – oh, the noise.

Finally, I get to the Royal Box. It's Princess Michael doing the honours. Shake hands. Take my medal. Receive the cup. Someone told me not to rush if you get to do it. I'm trying to do it right and therefore I put my medal down and take my time.

I've been waiting for this moment, hoping it would come, wondering if it would ever happen. I turn to the fans. I lift the cup. Get in there. A fan comes from nowhere and jumps down in front of me. There's nothing wrong, he hugs me, he's ecstatic, so happy. 'You beauty!' he says.

You beauty, indeed. Get in there.

'When Steve, went up, to lift the FA Cup...' Going to receive the trophy from Princess Michael. From the age of six I had seen somebody else in that situation – now it was my turn

Lifting the FA Cup with Ossie and riding the wave of celebration

Emotionally, we're aglow. We're FA Cup winners. The bad times weighing on your shoulders have been shed. We're back. We'd won the FA Cup when I joined in 1967 – now 14 years later we're back as winners again.

FA Cup history holds its place in the fabric of what we all do as football people. It's Matthews and Nat Lofthouse, the Busby Babes somehow putting a team together after the Munich air disaster, Sunderland, Montgomery's save – as a winner you're part of that history. And Tottenham should always be part of that history. We can't win it every time but we have got to be knocking on the door to win trophies.

Bill Nick said we were nothing without Europe. Well, we are nothing without being at least in contention for trophies. As a winner you are upholding the quality of what the club stands for.

We took team pictures and waited until City were three-quarters of the way round before we started our lap of honour. And then – my word, that was some feeling. Greeting a wall of people. Many of the fans there had been with us through relegation and the Second Division campaign. We owed it to them. You're running towards them on the lap of honour and you think, 'They deserve this.' We were together. Sharing the joy.

Keith and I just shook hands. No nonsense. In the interviews he was very calm and considered. It was his first trophy but he was very respectful. During the game he was in control. He trusted those around him to do the job. He had picked the team and done his bit. We did a few interviews and then it was back to a dressing room of pure elation and unbridled joy. That dressing room was the highlight. There were so many great moments – the goal, lifting the cup, the lap of honour and sharing it with the supporters, but this was more personal. I didn't have any family around but the team was my family in another way.

It was just the players, management team, coaches and physios: nothing different to a normal game in that sacred space, which is how it should be. I looked at people like Johnny Wallis. How was he feeling? How were all the ground staff feeling? They were all there at Wembley and rightly so. The club did it right by the staff in those situations. There had been a club train to take them up to the semi-final in Sheffield. It's an old-fashioned thing to say these days, but it's the people that made me feel at home all those years. I'd done it for myself and my family but I'd also done it for my big family – my club.

That's why it's so disappointing when you lose as I did a few times in my career because you've lost for those people as well. However supposedly low they were down the pecking order made it even more important that they were given credit for their part in any success.

In the dressing room Garth was bouncing, saying, 'My name's in lights!' as he had done on the pitch when he scored and his name appeared on the electronic scoreboard. Ossie was so chirpy, inviting people to have a drink and messing about. That 'English way' of celebrating was new to him, but he was so enthusiastic. We were in the big old bath. He dived in it with the trophy, which might be how the top of the lid got bent over a bit. I stayed in the bath longer than others as usual. We had some lovely photos taken, including one with Johnny Wallis in the bath. We weren't rushing anywhere. We got changed and then got on the bus. And then came that unforgettable moment when we drove out through the tunnel to the street outside.

The trophy had been put right in the front of the bus by the windscreen so it could be seen. That was a bit of a club tradition and we soon saw why. The massive doors opened and we were greeted by a stunning sight. There were hordes there, waiting for us – hundreds, thousands. Tottenham have fans who know how to celebrate. There were people up lampposts, hanging off trees, wherever there was a vantage point they were up there. Wonderful.

If you didn't realise what you've done already, you certainly knew it then. It was like that all the way home to Tottenham. Cars beeping; people

Prized possession: my first FA Cup winners' medal

Keith made sure Johnny Wallis's loyalty was recognised by having him photographed with the trophy

Cockerels crowing: we enjoyed an unforgettable night of celebration in the Chanticleer

in the streets cheering, on top of bus stops – health and safety was out of the window. Along the North Circular past Brent Cross, the traffic was intense; everywhere there were people shouting and cheering, from bridges, the pavements and verges, hanging out of house windows. Amazing.

We'd had a little bit to drink by then – nothing over the top, as we were exhausted and on empty stomachs. By the time we got to Tottenham High Road itself, it was just incredible. It was like a carnival. There were tens of thousands on the streets. The plan was to go to the Chanticleer, the club's own restaurant on Paxton Road. We went first to the boardroom so we could go to the windows that overlooked the High Road. That was our vantage point. Just incredible. People upon people upon people.

I'm sure some of those who had been waiting for us outside the Wembley tunnel had got back to Tottenham somehow. We eventually got through to the Chanticleer. So many people wanted to get in, but it had to be limited. Sorting match tickets had been hard enough – what about tickets for this do?

The celebration was something else. Chas & Dave were singing songs on stage. There must have been some speeches, however incoherent the

The local paper sent a photographer round the day after the match. Here I'm smiling for the camera with my kids Loren (holding the medal) and Glenn

individual was. Keith gave his thanks to everyone; I said some words that I can't remember. But there was a general feeling of, 'We've done it.'

Our families were there with us. That's the main thing: the people really close to us were there to share in the victory. What a night.

My wife and I walked out at about six o'clock in the morning. The fact that it all happened at night made it so special, giving it a bit of a European feel. The morning after some of the squad were going on holidays. They went with a spring in the step, that's for sure. Me? I went home, calling into my mum's first. Special moments. The next day the local paper come round and took a nice picture of my children and me, with my daughter Loren holding my medal. Wonderful times.

A tale of two shirts. Due to a mix-up in the programme I wore No.5 in the first game of the final. The No.5 faded after a wash so we switched to a more traditional numbering style for the replay, when I reverted to my usual No.6

SQUARING THE CIRCLE

I am often asked which my favourite Spurs team was, and I have to say the team of the early 1980s. No disrespect to the 1970s generation but I was just a foot soldier then, whereas I was more of an 'officer' a decade later. I talked to Keith at length about our aims and ambitions before the 1981–82 season began. I wanted to push my teammates. I knew how they all fitted together, what turned them on on the field.

As a team we worked so effectively together, with me central to how we were led. I couldn't really tell Ossie what to do, though. One day he went ape-shit at a referee. Thinking he was going to get sent-off, I said, 'Whoa, Ossie, calm down.' Ossie said to me quietly, 'I'm fucking ice cold, OK?' He was only acting all upset.

I saw him score a goal simply out of anger at Brighton in 1981–82. He got a nasty kick. I went to the referee to speak about it, and Ossie all of a sudden lashed a shot from about 40 yards. I think he meant to kick the ball at the fella who had kicked him but instead it flew into the top corner.

We had a glow about us that season and were on the front foot. We'd become winners, with added belief. Paul Price came in and was a good addition, but I thought he could have had more of a voice given he was Wales captain for a spell. A few new players had made their debuts, including Tony Parks in goal but he wasn't going to get many games after we signed Ray Clemence from Liverpool.

Ray had won championships and was an international, and became fundamental to our professionalism and belief. It could be something he said at half-time, or on the bus driving home after defeat, like, 'We can't do that; that's not what a good team does.' He'd been there and done it.

It was a tricky beginning for him. We drew against Aston Villa in the Charity Shield but Ray didn't have the greatest of games. People were probably wondering had Liverpool let him go because he was past his best? He certainly wasn't. Very soon Ray proved his worth. Keith felt we needed another keeper to improve and Clem improved us. He organised the back line very well, something we had been missing after Pat left.

Spurs suited Ray. We were challenging for honours, and based in London. I think Clem had a long-term goal of being involved in the media and it didn't do him any harm to be in the capital. He said to me one day, 'Do you know what the most important thing in football is these days?' He pointed to the TV camera on the gantry. I think that suggested how much Ray was thinking along those lines. Coming to Spurs was perhaps a career move in the broadest sense for him.

"We had a glow about us that season and were on the front foot. We'd become winners, with added belief"

Peter Shreeve was always up for a laugh and joined us in getting into suitable costume to mark the 100th FA Cup Final

It was still quite a small squad, however. We added consistency and we definitely had a bigger group of young players and potentials. Pat Corbett played one game that year. Gary O'Reilly, Terry Gibson, Ally Dick and Brooksie started to come through, while Micky Hazard played 45 games in total so was becoming fully fledged. Micky was an incredible talent. He could twist and turn with a ball and his working out of angles was outstanding, yet if you asked him how many degrees were in a triangle he couldn't tell you.

Micky was brilliant at playing cards – he could read them. His brain was and is amazing, but he didn't really think about the game when he played, or about his progress. We played Third Division Burnley in 1983 in a League Cup tie when we were on a roll. We went a goal up in five minutes but Burnley won 4–1.

In the bath afterwards Micky said, 'Stevie, I thought we were gonna win by six or seven.'

I said, 'That's exactly why we didn't.'

He didn't speak to the psychologists, as if he might have caught something off them. Micky is very open now; perhaps he is doing the self-analysis he should have done then. I just think he was too passive. He always stepped up when Ossie or Glenn were missing but what about stepping up when they *were* there to make us stronger still?

He would grumble if he wasn't playing. He had the hump with Keith once and in training they arranged an in-house 11-a-side. Micky played with one boot and one slipper and was up against me. I assumed he was downhearted because he knew he wasn't going to be picked for the team.

'Micky' I said, 'go and get your other boot.'

He grumbled and said no.

'Micky, the longer you keep that slipper on the more I'm going to kick you.' Bless him.

The emergence of another home-grown, Mark Falco, as back-up was important. He was very honest, good as gold and good fun, and could handle himself. He came from a solid upbringing without being a goody two-shoes. He was a Spurs fan, but a bit maligned by some fans and journalists; I don't think he got the respect he deserved. He became a scapegoat for some of the fans, but his teammates sure as hell respected him. I don't think a goalscorer ever gets what he deserves: he either gets too much or too little praise rather than what accurately reflects his talent. I don't think God is fair when He gives out goals to strikers. 'Bilko' played 21 league games and scored 11 goals in 1981–82, more than Archie.

I played 42 games again and Chrissy 37, so we had consistency of selection again at full-back. We had all the vital ingredients to be a unit.

We finished fourth in the league, our best position since 1971, and were in serious contention for the title but a number of factors that caught up with us. Our front two of Archie and Garth didn't score 20 between them in the league. There were reasons for that, including injuries and the fact that both wanted the ball to their feet more, which negated their strengths, but that's a big chunk of goals to miss. Opponents were more defensive against us because we made them so. We weren't as effective on the break as we had been. We had to try and open them up more, which is more difficult. The return to European competition was thrilling but added an extra burden on already stretched resources.

Between November and January we only played seven league games due to terrible weather. It meant that in April and May we played a total of 19 games – nearly half a league season in just two months. Our home record wasn't great while the new West Stand was completed, which was not helpful. But the game for the official opening, a 6–1 win over Wolves, was a terrific performance.

The capacity of White Hart Lane had been reduced because the new stand only held 6,500. We got very big crowds at times but this was in an era when attendances generally were declining. Fans had a lot of games to watch and pay for, because we were in so many competitions. The fans were more demanding, which was one of the outcomes of being successful. We were expected to do it again, or better.

We won 3–1 at Arsenal; both derbies that season were very feisty. Chrissy scored and was then sent off in the 2–2 home draw. We were capable of keeping the goals down away from home, until the crunch period towards the end. We drew 2–2 with Liverpool at home in May with over half a team out due to injuries and illness. We went 2–0 up; I played in midfield and scored from 35 yards. They put Graeme Souness on at half-time and could well have beaten us as we ran out of legs.

"The fans were more demanding, which was one of the outcomes of being successful. We were expected to do it again, or better"

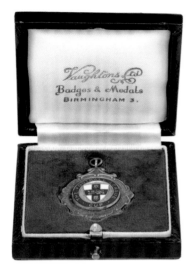

A losers' medal
for my first
Tottenham defeat
in a Wembley
final, but still
a treasured
memory

Wearing
Chelsea's white
shorts in the
process of
beating them at
Stamford Bridge
en route to
another FA Cup
Final

Liverpool back then knew what they had to do to win the league, and in truth we didn't have the same mentality. At one stage I suggested to Keith – and forgive me – 'Let's be a bit more like the Arsenal. On a bad day we could get a draw, rather than a defeat.' Keith said, 'You wouldn't say that if you were sat behind this desk.'

'Forget I said it, Keith.' He had a genuine, committed belief in playing the Spurs Way.

Liverpool also beat us in the League Cup Final in 1982. It was the club's first ever defeat at Wembley. We took the lead early and were so close to winning but Ronnie Whelan equalised three minutes from time and then scored again along with Ian Rush to win 3–1 in extra-time. It was the game where I got the 'Paisley treatment'. Bob Paisley would butter an opposing player up in the press before a game, what would now be called mind games. Did it work? I don't think I played badly. I was battle-hardened and didn't take much notice of it. But it was part of their armoury.

It was also a way of getting a paid-for exclusive, so it fulfilled a few needs: giving a story, getting an exclusive, deflecting attention from your own team – a shot for nothing. Liverpool were very smart. Shankly once got a bit of stick for taking someone off, and when asked why said, 'Aye son, he was playing that good, he was out of sync with the others.' Genius.

They targeted Tony Galvin during that final and Souness laid one on him. That had more of an effect than Paisley's 'treatment'.

We were running on fumes by the season's end. I played all 66 games during that campaign. We were competing on four fronts including Europe, and fell just short in three, but we had more success in the FA Cup again.

It began in the third round against Arsenal. Peter Shreeve did something very clever before the game, putting the FA Cup on the middle of the table in the dressing room. 'Chaps – that's what it's all about.' It made us hungrier. Pat Jennings made an error and let Garth's shot slip under him. It must have been strange for Pat to play against us. In 1983 they beat us in the League Cup at home. There was a big surprise when Eamonn Andrews came on the pitch to say to Pat, 'This is your life.' I was one of the guests and travelled to the studios on the Arsenal team bus. People on the High Road were giving dog's abuse as the coach went past but I saw some going, 'Hang on – that's Steve Perryman on their coach!'

In the FA Cup we beat Arsenal, then Leeds and Aston Villa all at home 1–0. We defended well, played well and scored a goal. It wasn't flash – it was professional, assured and confident. We knew what we were doing.

Chelsea in the quarter-final was the tough one. We hadn't played each other for a long while, there was a lot of trouble and it was reported that 15,000 of our fans went to Stamford Bridge. We had a colour clash with Chelsea's shorts, so we had to borrow their white away shorts to wear with our white shirts. I went to get the ball close to the crowd and got the usual abuse, so I just pointed to the Chelsea badge on the shorts.

We went a goal down in the first half but knew it was coming for us. It was like a knife through butter and we scored three goals, two of which were excellent team moves followed by great finishes from Glenn and Micky. The game ended up being closer than it should have been at 3–2. I made a mistake for their second goal, but confidence was growing again. We beat Leicester City 2–0 in the semi-final at Villa Park without any real problem. More of an issue was something none of could ever have expected – war breaking out between Britain and Argentina.

On the eve of the game I was in my hotel room and kept waking up hearing noise. Ossie and Ricky were in the room below and the noise was them on the phone all night. I didn't find out why until later. They were having frantic discussions with their family about whether they should stay or go home.

Ossie said after the win, 'I'm leaving – I'm not in the final.' He had to go to Argentina to join up with their World Cup squad in any case, but told me, 'There will be things coming out that you will not believe and you'll be right because, trust me, I'm not saying a word – it will be twisted.' Ossie was clever and knew what was going on. I only discovered decades later that Ossie's cousin Jose was in the Argentinian Air Force and was killed in the conflict. Ossie and Ricky were part of us, and we protected them. Success makes you even more solid when things go wrong. Our circle had got stronger, and came to the fore in the build-up to the final. Ricky stayed but didn't play, with Micky taking his place. We shut the Falklands War out of our heads. One of the phrases used by every team is 'no excuses'. We had to cope all the time with injuries, so not having a player like Ricky was normal.

We had no contact with Ossie during the war and very little conversation with Ricky. We stayed away from it because it was a bit too near the bone. We would ask after his family but little more than that. The focus was on the final and wanting to win it again.

Back in the studio: Paul Price and Ray Clemence join a band well-versed in making hit cup-final records!

I was a cover star for the *Radio Times* and got an invite to the magazine's party

A letter from Blue Peter producer Biddy Baxter 'complimenting' us on our singing performance

I was on the cover of the *Radio Times* that month. They used the photo of me lifting the cup in 1981 and then sent the printing plate as a thank you. At the end of the year I was invited to a party where everyone who had been on the cover that year, from all different walks of life, was in attendance. We also recorded another cup final song with Chas & Dave, and got to perform it on *Blue Peter*. Biddy Baxter, the legendary producer of the programme, wasn't happy with our first rehearsal. 'That will not do,' she said. 'If that's the best you've got, gentlemen, then I suggest you go home.'

I suggested to Biddy, 'If you get a couple of cases of lager in, that will help.' It would have been a day when we were OK to have a drink, not too close to a match. So it was done – and it worked. It was a kids' TV programme, so there were no bottles in view of the cameras, naturally.

For the final itself I nearly didn't play. I got injured against Ipswich on the Monday night of FA Cup Final week, and still have a little indentation in a muscle in the top of my thigh resulting from a cortisone injection I had in Harley Street to allow me to play the final. Playing 10 games in 23 days, it was coming. The BBC and Tony Gubba were waiting for me outside the doctors asking if I was going to play. How they knew I was there I don't know, but they were onto the story.

Peter Shreeve had us play a short practice game on the morning of the final to prove me, Tony Galvin and a couple of others were fit. We'd had such a hard season and it showed in the first game. It was very ordinary. Glenn scored in extra-time and then we got caught at the end from a long throw-in, with Terry Fenwick equalising. Their goalkeeper, Peter Hucker, was Man of the Match, so we must have done something right. Terry Venables was managing against his old team and was clever. They had some good players but were lairy. Simon Stainrod and John Gregory said some things, not explicitly against us but it seemed they were over-enjoying the fact they'd got to Wembley – they seemed a bit blasé.

It was still hard work in the replay, but we won 1–0 with a penalty that Robbo earned by going on a surge and being brought down by Tony Currie. I didn't like that we wore all-yellow – both teams had to play in their change kits and I didn't see the reason for that at the time. It was apparently due to QPR winning the toss to decide choice of kit and we assumed they would choose their usual blue and white hoops so we prepared our away strip, only

to discover too late that they had opted for their away colours. There was a slight touch of anti-climax to the game, but you don't win enough to treat anything lightly. We became the first team since the Double side to win the FA Cup in consecutive years, and Keith had achieved something that Bill Nick had done, which isn't too shabby at all. It also meant I joined Newcastle's Joe Harvey and Danny Blanchflower of Tottenham as only the third player in the modern era to captain winning FA Cup Final sides in consecutive years.

It had been a long hard slog. We ran out of steam in the league, a feature that was to persist in the next two seasons, finishing fourth again and then eighth. New players arrived in the shape of Gary Mabbutt and Alan Brazil in 1982–83, and then Danny Thomas and Gary Stevens the year after, as well as a crop of home-growns, though none really made an impact. We lost Ossie for a year in the fallout from the Falklands, and Ricky left for good in 1983.

Playing so many games with relatively small squads was too much to bear. Looking back now in the modern age of squad rotation, what we managed then was remarkable. There were some memorable results and performances, including the famous 5–0 win at home against Arsenal in 1983 (which I missed due to suspension), but the real tangible reward came, as it often has for Tottenham, in Europe.

It was an immense workload. When I think of super-fit modern players who are tracked and monitored to warn when an injury is coming yet play on good pitches but can't play two games in a week, it puts our efforts into perspective. It's too easy an excuse when you play poorly and lose a domestic game after a midweek European match. But I do think travel on top of the game can't be conducive to being fresh.

Another winners' medal: 1982 was not as glamorous a victory as the year before, but still important in the Spurs' annals of success; doing my bit in the extra-time team talk in 1982 (below)

Still, Europe gave us a 'next' to look forward to. The game is about what's next – it's why you can't dwell on results, good or bad. I've always had the mentality of thinking, 'Right, what's next? Once again it was a great adventure. Apart from Clem and Archie, I was the only one in the squad with any experience of playing in Europe. I passed on that experience: how to keep the crowd quiet, keeping possession and taking the sting out of a game.

And what an entry back into it – Ajax, in the European Cup Winners' Cup. They weren't the side of old but were obviously good enough to win something. So to beat them 6–1 on aggregate, with four different scorers, was a hell of a feat.

We had more trouble beating Irish side Dundalk. We played them, Coleraine in Northern Ireland and then Drogheda in successive seasons. Because it was during the Troubles, we had huge security out there, with policemen in the corner flag area with dogs. When you went to take a corner you had to be careful that the dog wasn't on too long a leash. Those games had a bit of eeriness about them. In one game about 10 minutes before half-time there was an announcement.

'Bing bong' came out over the loudspeaker: 'This is an important announcement; this is an important announcement.'

We wondered what was going on, almost to the extent that we stopped concentrating on the game. Has there been a security threat or something?

Handshakes with Barcelona's Antonio Olmo before hostilities commenced in the European Cup Winners' Cup semi-final first leg of 1982

'Important announcement: we've lost the keys to the Bovril hut. So if you're wanting a Bovril at half-time yous are unlucky!' Only in Ireland.

We then saw off Eintracht Frankfurt, playing very well. I played more right-wing than right-back in the home leg, such was our total control. Then came Barcelona. The story is that in the first match, our home leg, they kicked bits out of us. I think we gave it back, but they did start it. The ref, Egbert Mulder, was not doing us any favours, so we had to respond. They certainly weren't the Barcelona we think of these days.

We drew 1–1, Clem making a mistake in letting a long-range effort from Olmo go through his hands. Robbo scored an equaliser five minutes from time via a Glenn free-kick after I'd been hacked down. So that made the second game in Barcelona really tight and tense. The referee, Siegfried Kirschen, and UEFA officials came into the dressing room before the start to say that if there was a repeat of what had happened in the first leg and they thought it was our fault, even if we won we wouldn't win. They would turn the result around.

We were led to believe that it would be a fair match. The game kicked off, the ball came to me and one of their fellas launched himself two-footed at me. Garth and Robbo were also badly fouled. In the Nou Camp tunnel before the game, their players had filed to the right and into a little room on the side. It was a chapel. And then they went out and kicked the shit out of us again. Barcelona was a stitch-up. Paul Miller tells me that years later he chatted with Real Madrid's Uli Stielike. Stielike told Paul, 'In that era we had the referees tied up', which we sort of knew but no one ever confirmed it. I think we're very lucky in England – I don't think I've ever thought of a referee in England as being bent. They might not be great at times, but they are fair.

The squad was really stretched by the Barcelona semi-final. Chris Jones played as a sub in the home leg, having been out of the first-team picture for so long, but the experience from that 1981–82 campaign was invaluable. The next season we went out early to Bayern Munich in the Cup Winners' Cup again but qualified for the UEFA Cup the following season.

The team was changing. 'Mabbsie' had become an integral player having got into the team fairly quickly in 1982 because he could play in various positions. I was impressed by his athleticism and he was great box-to-box, but I always thought he was going to end up as a defender facing the ball rather than a midfielder. He and I were quite similar, though his leap was phenomenal. His father, Ray, had been a pro and gave Gary and his brother Kevin, also a pro, plenty of appropriate exercises as they were growing up.

We were aware of Gary's diabetes, but he managed it very well. He was an unflustered footballer, with a strong purpose of intent about his game. He was genuine, which made it so sad when he had his cheekbone smashed in a challenge by John Fashanu. Gary accepted it with good grace that I don't think I would have mustered.

Gary Stevens was almost Swedish in style, deliberate and measured in his movements, and that's not a weakness. He was positive about his own abilities and accepted his role as either a defensive midfielder or, where he was better in my view, a centre-back, a bit like Mabbutt. I appreciated those players because I was one of them, and that's why I think they benefited from my help on the field.

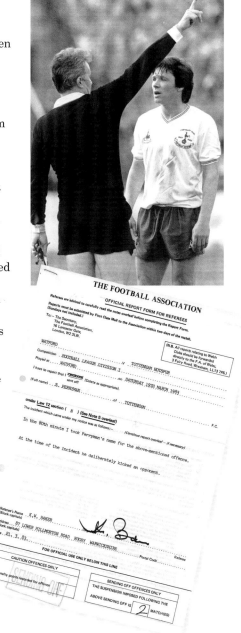

My one and only red card in English league football – and it was deserved. I'd previously got a kick from Watford's Kenny Jackett that was missed by the ref, and clashed with Kenny later. I ended up making Kenny youth team coach when I was manager at Watford and he has become one of my best friends in football

A meeting of the two masters – and Glenn came out on top. Feyenoord's Johan Cruyff went up against Glenn during our UEFA Cup second round first leg match in October 1983. We went 4–0 up after a blistering first half, in which Glenn was described as 'unplayable', and won 4–2

Danny Thomas was a bright, energetic player and a clever guy. He was considered, and ended up being a physio working in the States. He was really good in the dressing room and a lovely fella. He didn't deserve the premature end to his career that stemmed from a tackle by Gavin Maguire in 1987; nor did Gary Stevens, who received similar from Vinnie Jones.

During pre-season of 1983–84, Paul Miller said to me, 'Keith's signed them to replace us,' meaning Gary and Danny. I said, 'Speak for yourself.' But of course that's what a club does – it's an inevitable part of football life. This was a sign of things to come for us, but right then Keith needed all the able bodies he could get.

We beat Drogheda easily, drawing Feyenoord in the next round. Over 35 years later I still think this was the best I've ever seen any of my Spurs teams play. We were on it. I was particularly pleased because Feyenoord in 1974 had been one of the worst nights of my football career.

Johan Cruyff and Ruud Gullit were in the Feyenoord team. It was reported that Cruyff had given Glenn some stick beforehand, claiming he wasn't 'the real deal'. Part of that was playing mind games and there was a suggestion that he hadn't quite said that. But regardless, if he attacked Glenn he was attacking one of us and we made him pay for it.

Archie and Galvin scored two each before half-time at home. Glenn didn't score but he was unplayable. I always said he was the leader of the orchestra. He led the orchestra that night, and we were all in tune. Credit to Cruyff: he admitted he had been wrong about Glenn afterwards.

They pulled it back to 4–2 on the night but we were superbly professional in winning 2–0 in Rotterdam. That performance was what I was trying to describe to Keith about how we should have played after the 1981 FA Cup Final win. Similarly against Bayern Munich, in the next round. We lost 1–0 there but kept it tight and won 2–0 at home in another of the great

European nights. Archie and Falco scored, with Glenn putting it down the inside-left channel for Bilko on his left foot, where he was really strong.

Beating Feyenoord and Bayern Munich was impressive but probably the tougher game was Austria Vienna. We came through that but with a lot of changes for the semi against Hadjuk Split, mainly due to injuries. We went there without Clem, Ossie or Glenn. Thankfully Micky ran the show from start to finish in both games but particularly in the second leg, in which he scored the vital, deciding goal.

Hughton, O'Reilly, Perryman, Falco, Brooke, Hoddle, Hazard, Ian Crook, Parks, Galvin and Roberts, who we regarded as home-grown – that campaign was underpinned by players the club had produced itself and the final was the crux of that. It's why I always make the point that you should never undersell the value of having home-grown players. Home-grown does not mean second-class. Every player, however famous or classy, is home-grown somewhere.

In the first leg of the final against Anderlecht, it was like playing Feyenoord. Anderlecht are Belgian, but the game, setting and players gave it a very Dutch feel. They were very talented – Enzo Scifo was class and Morten Olsen was one of the best I ever played against. They had quality in Frank Arnesen, Alexandre Czerniatynski, Franky Vercauteren and Jacky Munaron, and represented the elite of their league.

We went one-up thanks to Maxie from a corner. There was a bit of a scramble for their goal and Parksy made a slight error. A 1–1 draw was a good result, but I was booked 20 minutes from the end for doing no more than bringing the ball down with my foot to get it under control while contesting possession. Their players ran around like school kids complaining I'd raked my opponent with my studs. In a way it was a compliment to me

My appearance in the 1984 UEFA Cup Final first leg. Morten Olsen was an amazing player who nearly joined Tottenham some time later; he would have been a great acquisition

that they wanted to try something so that I couldn't play in the second leg. I was booked by the referee Bruno Galler and, having been booked earlier in the competition, was duly suspended. He was the ref in 1985 when we lost to Real Madrid and ruled out Mark Falco's goal in the Bernebeu.

My disappointment was nothing beside the heartbreaking story of the young Spurs fan, Brian Flanagan, shot dead by a bar owner in Brussels. I was old enough and professional enough to keep my disappointment in perspective. In any case, the yellow card I'd got in Austria was probably worthy of a red, so perhaps it was karma for me.

Something dragged us up by the bootlaces in that second leg. We found an added dimension; we determined to win. But we came close to not playing it at all.

It stemmed from a dispute over a long-standing bonus scheme for the players in European games. Bill Nick set it up when we won the UEFA Cup in 1972. He knew that we didn't earn enough money from it, so introduced a share scheme whereby round by round we'd get paid a collective percentage, amounting to a third of the profits from the game.

That would vary, depending on the strength of the opposition, gate receipts and so on. The money wasn't much, but the principle was important. You could earn, say, £60 from playing a team like AC Milan. By 1984, the sums could be larger due to the increasing commercialism of the game. If the club are earning more money, it's only right and proper that the players should have their share.

The problem arose when Irving Scholar, who had taken over at Tottenham in 1982 with Paul Bobroff, replacing the old Wale/Richardson ownership, wanted to withhold the TV fee for the Anderlecht home game from the players' bonus scheme. Keith had brought Bill Nick back to the club and Scholar gave Bill a more established role. Bill had devised the share scheme; now Scholar was trying to backtrack on it.

The club had already started to 'knock' us in previous rounds, so we went into the final being owed money and not best pleased. At one point it was even suggested we refuse to play. I said to Scholar directly, 'If the game is televised live that fee surely goes in the pot?' Scholar said, 'No, I'm sure Bill didn't mean that.' I said, 'His office is there – ask him. Knock on his door. If you don't, I will.'

'No, no, no,' said Scholar, worried. He refused to involve Bill Nick and I didn't want to push Bill into taking our side, so the dispute simmered. Eventually Gordon Taylor at the PFA negotiated a deal but it wasn't what we should have got.

As if that wasn't bad enough, Keith was leaving. The received wisdom is he walked, fed up with how the sport was changing. 'There used to be a football club over there,' he is famously supposed to have said the night after the final. The truth is the club had already decided on change. On the day of the quarter-final away leg against Austria Vienna, Scholar and Bobroff knocked on Keith's door at 4pm to say, 'Keith, we've decided we're not going to renew your contract.'

He said, 'You think this is the right time to talk about that?'

They said, 'Well, there's never a right time.' That is never a justification I've bought into.

After the home leg, Scholar brought Vienna's manager up to Keith. He introduced them, as if Keith hadn't already met him across the two games. I think Scholar was showing Keith that he was talking to other managers,

Danny Thomas in his moment of despair, but he was soon lifted by our magnificent supporters

The moment of glory: I saw Tony Parks's famous save from this angle, sitting in the dugout

to send a message, which was 'you're just responsible for the players and the coaching: we run this club now.'

We wanted to win the UEFA Cup for Keith, as he'd played a great part in all of our careers. Most of those players were brought to the club or brought through by him. So it was a case of rewarding him but rewarding ourselves first. We wanted to win it for all the usual reasons.

I didn't play but my routine for the second leg was normal in the dressing-room talks and meetings. I did a couple of TV interviews and then sat on the bench for the actual game. How did I feel about missing out? People make too much of the individual focus on players. John Terry getting a guard of honour in his last game, and the actual game stopped especially for him? Do me a favour. In my era they wouldn't have done that for Pelé. I would have been totally embarrassed.

Sitting in the dugout, I experienced it like a manager would do or an expectant father. It was probably the first time I had sat on the touchline since I was a kid in 1967. Usually, if I was not playing, I'd watch from the stands. I'm not a good watcher, but I shouted and called out as a captain. It was the old story of my brother Ted telling me to have a voice and provide a productive opinion.

We went a goal down, but it felt to me like we couldn't lose – the crowd had come to see us win and the team was going to give it to them. What belief the players had that night. To go forward again and again, for Ossie to hit the bar from a yard out but for Micky to then recover the ball and cross

My teammates made sure I got my hands on the trophy: they were pleased for me as well as for Keith, themselves and the club

it and Robbo to storm his way in and score was special. I really did think it was coming for us. The all-white kit, the floodlights, the atmosphere – it just had to be.

The captain on the night really stepped up. I still say it about Robbo that he did some naive things, but that naivety was his strength. He had that drive and will anyway so imagine how being captain added to it. His performance that night came from pure desire.

It was like we'd got out of jail, and if it has to go to penalties, so be it, and preferable to have them at home. The shootout was the first time I was quite happy I wasn't playing: I'm respectful of anyone who steps up to take a penalty.

When Danny missed – little Danny, a positive character and player – he was obviously bitterly disappointed. But then the reaction of the crowd in singing his name, well, it said it all to me about Tottenham Hotspur supporters. They cared for him within his despair. It makes the hairs stand up even now watching it back. If I'd been Tony Parks hearing that I'd have had an extra spring. And that's what crowds are there for, what they can generate. You can't orchestrate 48,000-odd people to do that. That was done out of pure, instinctive knowledge, support and care. To care for him at that moment was in a different league.

And then the save. *The* save. Parksy set off on a charge and would have got to Seven Sisters if the other players hadn't bundled on top of him. I didn't pile on – I wasn't excitable. I shook Keith's hand, then Olsen's, and applauded our players and the crowd. I got a clue that my suspension had been bent when the Anderlecht players were apologising to me. In their disappointment, having been beaten on penalties, they were apologising to the fella who couldn't play the second leg! Why? It was 100 per cent bent in my mind. It was proved that Anderlecht bribed a referee, for example, to beat Nottingham Forest in their semi-final, and it came back to haunt them.

I got to lift the trophy on the pitch. Robbo had wanted me to go up and get it. It wasn't the time to be thinking like this but as a small protest against Scholar over the bonus row, I wasn't wearing a Le Coq Sportif tracksuit. But I wasn't a sub, after all. I had a personal contract with Adidas at the time, and I wasn't going to wear a suit, so I wore an Adidas tracksuit instead.

Irving came into the dressing room in his wheelchair afterwards. He had snapped his Achilles playing football and wanted to be part of the gang, after all the rows. I think his presence was there to water down Keith's departure. It was as if to say, 'He's gone but I'm here.' Footballers have only got one guvnor at a football club and anyone else should keep out.

I didn't get a medal. I wasn't sat there crying about it, but Ossie came up to me in the dressing room afterwards and said, 'Steebie, this is yours'. He was giving me his medal.

'What do you mean, Os?'

'You deserve it more than me.'

I was bowled over. Officially I wasn't entitled to a medal, so the medal I have is Ossie's. And he's been trying to get it back ever since, but he's not having it back! I jest, what a man to do that. It was a quiet moment in the dressing room, just us, two teammates and great friends. No grand show or gestures. Just proper. For the celebration Clem and I and met some friends of ours in the Centenary Club that was in the stadium then, and we spent a lot of time with the troops in the players' room. It was my sixth and last trophy. It had such a symmetry to it as well. Two League Cups, two FA Cups and two UEFA Cups. It bookended my career very nicely.

There was also a sense of squaring the circle. I'd come into the team as an emblem of Tottenham making their own players and then, towards the end of my career, a home-grown team won a European trophy.

Ossie's winners' medal, which he presented to me – a magnificent gesture. What a man

More celebration pictures from a golden era of success. Wonderful times

CHAPTER SIXTEEN

PARTING OF THE WAYS

By the end of 1984, I was 33 and had seen and done plenty in the game. I'd won six trophies, two in Europe, and had broken Pat Jennings's club record of 590 appearances (the 1981 FA Cup Final replay was my 599th game).

I was also honoured as the Football Writers' Player of the Year for 1981–82. I was not the country's best player – I wasn't the best player at Tottenham. I knew exactly what I was and what I wasn't. My focus, leadership, consistency and loyalty counted. So fair play to the writers. There were many more glamorous players they could have picked ahead of me for plenty of viable reasons. I say as a laugh that I didn't much rate footballer writers' opinions, but that year I think they got it right! Ron Atkinson said I was the wrong choice, that it should have been a player with more flair. Ron had to give an opinion because he was writing a weekly column. Maybe I didn't pull my shorts up high enough for him.

My relationship with the press had evolved as the team's profile increased. I had a row with *Daily Mail* journalist Barry Flatman, who went to my school and stitched me up. Most problems I had were with how something I said was twisted in the headline, and when the journalists insisted they weren't responsible I told them, 'Why don't I speak to the headline writer?' When we started poorly one season, a *Sun* reporter asked Keith, 'Is this a crisis?' Keith said it was. The reporter then phoned me up and, without saying what Keith had said, asked me if it was a crisis. I said 'You're kidding' and explained why there was no need to panic. The next day the angle in the paper was that manager and captain were at loggerheads!

I think everyone at Tottenham was pleased for me winning the award. Chivers sent a telegram, which was lovely. Bill Nick said, 'Well done, Steve – but your passing needs a bit of improving.' It was, in a way, an honour for the club, given that I had received an individual honour when my game was all about improving the team as a whole. I think the people who were most pleased were the supporters.

Further recognition followed in November 1984. We were playing a testimonial for Larry Pritchard at Sutton United, and I arrived a little late. While I was getting changed, Garth had a bit of a chip at me for not being bang on time. I sat down and there were some letters for me that someone at Spurs had brought from the club. I opened one of them and it was an official communication from the Crown saying I'd got an MBE. Garth carried on taking the mick. I said nothing and just showed him the letter. That soon shut him up.

"I knew exactly what I was and what I wasn't. My focus, leadership, consistency and loyalty counted"

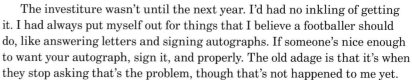

**The letter
explaining
the protocol
for attending
Buckingham
Palace to
collect my MBE
(below) – it was
a wonderful day
out for my family**

The investiture wasn't until the next year. I'd had no inkling of getting it. I had always put myself out for things that I believe a footballer should do, like answering letters and signing autographs. If someone's nice enough to want your autograph, sign it, and properly. The old adage is that it's when they stop asking that's the problem, though that's not happened to me yet.

Even before I got into Tottenham's first team, I was doing presentations for schools, charities, and more. Someone must have nominated me. I have a feeling it was a friend of Phil Holder called Cyril Hardwicke, who was heavily involved with Church Street Traders, a market near Edgware Road. Cyril was active in charity work, organising fun runs around Paddington Rec. I'd go and present the prizes so I think it was probably Cyril who put me forward.

I'd been invited on the Royal Yacht Britannia moored at Tower Bridge a year before with a number of other sportspeople and 11 of the royal family on board. My wife Cherrill wore a stunning red dress. An equerry came over to us and whispered, 'Princess Diana will be coming to you next.' Princess Di duly came over, got introduced and looked amazed by Cherrill's dress! The gathering might have been a test to see how I conducted myself ahead of the MBE being awarded. I'll never forget the tray of drinks: gin and tonic, Scotch and Coke, juice and water. If you wanted a gin and orange you weren't getting one.

According to the official citation, my MBE was for services to football. The ceremony was at Buckingham Palace and the Queen bestowed the honour. Cherrill and I and the kids stayed in a hotel, went out for lunch afterwards and then drove home. It was a bit surreal. It was a great feeling for the family. My family aren't easily impressed but that really meant something to them.

Yet it ranked nowhere compared to what really mattered to me. My biggest honour is the fact that I played the most games for Spurs. I was accepted by the fans and that's the public I was interested in. The awards were bonuses. That's not me devaluing them, but they were a little bit of cream on top.

One honour that had eluded me were senior international caps. I did receive one, but the experience was not positive. Those who say I should have played for England probably saw me a lot and therefore they rated me. Towards the end of my playing career at Spurs, my mum and family were on a game show called *Whose Baby?*, where personalities would be shown photos of someone as a baby and be given clues to help them try to work out who it is. Chas & Dave came on and Dave said something like, 'When Steve is around we have the ball and he can be trusted.' I can imagine Spurs supporters thinking similar – I was consistent and reliable. People who saw me play twice a year were probably looking for a bit more. By the 1980s I think the opinion of me had been formed that I was a job player, and to be an England player you have got to have a bit extra. I came from an era when a lot of good players didn't play for England. As years went on I think lesser players than me *were* getting caps, but that's not a good reason for me to have played more for England.

I did get what was my only cap when Bobby Robson was in charge of what was effectively an England B team that played Iceland in a friendly. It was part of Ron Greenwood's preparation for naming his final 22-man squad for the World Cup in 1982. On the night when I received the Player of the Year award, Greenwood said, 'Steve, if you would do me the favour, I need to select 40 and I'm going to do you the favour of getting you a cap; you're not going to the World Cup so don't see it as a possible step up.'

Ron laid his cards out to me. We went back a long way and there was mutual respect between us. I didn't get that respect from Robson. His opinion of me dated back to the run-ins we'd had with his Ipswich team. He didn't think I was good enough to play for England, and that's fine. But the game I played, brought on as a sub, and the trip as a whole, was poorly handled. He didn't remember my name; I think the only words he said to me were about liking my tie.

I wasn't picked for the England squad for the World Cup in Spain in 1982 – this was the 40-man selection for the warm-up games

My one senior England shirt and cap

I went as an also-ran and was treated accordingly. There was no real communication from the FA: I wasn't told what number shirt I'd be wearing; if there was a team meeting I wasn't invited. There was a mix-up in training – 11 players were named and the rest of us were just sent to one half of a pitch. We weren't even given a ball. When I eventually went on in the actual game, Robson told me to 'man-mark the blond one'. We were playing Iceland. They were all blond.

I felt belittled, used and disrespected. When my first book was serialised in the papers, the headline was unfair to Robson, who was getting hostile press treatment. Everyone was attacking the manager, but I was attacking the man who led us to Iceland, not what he was doing as England manager.

My impression of the England set-up was that it was amateurish. One positive thing that came from it is that it made me realise how professional Tottenham were, which played a big part in me staying at the club so long. An indication of my long service is the fact that as I was still playing for them for seven years after my testimonial in 1979. That testimonial had been a sign of things to come. The game was a 2–2 draw with West Ham, and Jimmy Greaves guested for us. It was the evening that was different. We had a dinner and a lot of celebrities came. The names escape me, but they were the kind of people who were starting to get more involved on the commercial side.

I had seen the game become increasingly money-oriented. Peter Cook, Kenny Lynch and Warren Mitchell were longstanding fans but we started to see their like on the inside more. As players, we were invited to celebrity dinners, boxing nights and Variety Club Great Britain dos. I was on the fringes of it, put off by the black-tie fuss.

Bill Nick wasn't the type to be impressed by it. He wasn't disrespectful but didn't court that world. I went through my career with no name on my shirt and most of it with no sponsor and no adverts in the ground or in the programme other than for the club's own commercial activities. It was almost looked upon as dirty money. Denis Hill-Wood was reported to have said of some fella who was interested in getting involved with Arsenal, 'We don't want his sort here.'

But that world was changing. The commercial manager became busier. We played friendlies and went on tours to places that weren't exactly football hotbeds, like Kuwait. We'd changed from the Umbro kit we'd had for years to Admiral in 1977 with an eye on selling shirts, the start of a number of changes with suppliers. Executive boxes came with the new West Stand in 1982, and Holsten were the club's first shirt sponsor in 1983.

Agents were becoming more prominent. They were and are a necessary evil – how can a young player be expected to negotiate with a seasoned football executive and expect to get fair treatment? Even for a player as experienced as me, they had good uses. Eric Hall, a showbiz and music industry agent, handled anything not to do with football for me. Football contracts and wages were looked after by my trusted solicitor and family friend, Charles Newman.

Eric was a character, not everyone's cup of tea, but I liked his straight talking. I dabbled with a few things like appearing on Radio Luxembourg, for instance, playing my choice of records. I went on *Crackerjack* for a bit of fun, which my kids loved. It's not my world. But you have to try it. I did bits on Breakfast TV and was on *Celebrity Squares*, with Spurs fan Lennie Bennett hosting. Lynda Bellingham, from the Oxo ads, was on it – she was very funny and cracked dirty jokes offstage. I've been told by TV people that if you're

Irving Scholar, the man with high hopes and big dreams who wanted Spurs to be more than a football club

on telly, and you act normal, you come across as so bland. You have to be 'out there'. That wasn't me. I hear commentators and pundits now, trying to scream to make it exciting, people like Robbie Savage. Do me a favour.

The real turning point at Spurs was Scholar and Bobroff taking over in 1982 and making the club a PLC. People say to me that Irving knew his football and loved his Spurs. But what does that matter when actually running a club? He had all sorts of ideas, big and small, some useful, some – well…

One day he said, 'Steve, what do you think about this?' It was a pencil. I said, 'Irving, it's a pencil.'

'Yeah, but what do you *think* about it?'

'Er… it's a red pencil?'

'Yeah, but I can buy them for 3p and we sell them for 30p. Of course not red, and with "Tottenham Hotspur" on them.'

Another day I got a phone call asking me to see Scholar after training. I met him and he said, 'Steve, the new West Stand is nearly finished. You know where the players are parking now?' It was a temporary place down the High Road while the stand, was being built. 'When it's finished you're gonna have to still park there.

'Run that past me again, Irving?'

'We've got 72 private boxes and I want to offer each private box two spaces, so you've all got to stay parking where you are.'

I said, 'Listen, when things are in disarray during the build I understand that. But you're telling me the people who buy a box to watch

Spurs – and football – entering a new commercial era: examples of Scholar taking the club into new ventures

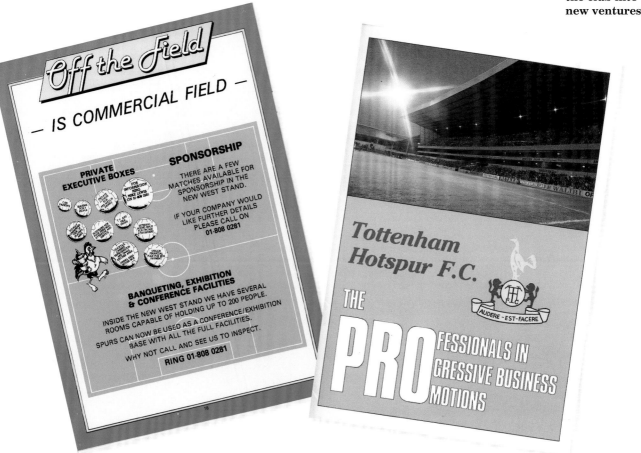

the players play are going to be driving straight in, but we – the players – have got to run the gauntlet from about 200 yards down that road? Have you got a pen and paper?'

Scholar asked why.

'So I can write my resignation letter. If that's the way this club's going, I'm off.'

Scholar didn't follow through with it, I think because I fought it. That's what a captain has to do. But it probably damaged me. The culture of the club was changing. Keith says Scholar rang him 32 times one day, and feels that we allowed the change to happen too easily, but I don't think there was much we could do.

After we had played at Bayern Munich, Bobroff came onto the coach with four of his mates and said, 'Five people get off.' Gilly's old mate, Ricky Prosser, and a couple of Ricky's friends were with us, as would happen to trusted fans sometimes. I sensed they were under pressure to get off so that Bobroff and his friends could have their seats instead, so I jumped up and said, 'C'mon Ricky, I'll get off with you.' Bobroff suddenly said, 'Oh no, not you. We'll get off.' I called their bluff, simply because it was the right thing to do.

A proper club needs leadership in the boardroom, in the manager's office and on the pitch. If you get those three types of leadership on the same page, it functions well. It did not under Scholar because I don't believe he trusted the manager, and by default the captain, because the old model of the manager running the club didn't suit the new model.

Scholar and Bobroff were from a different world of property, young businessmen succeeding in changing times in Britain under Margaret Thatcher, and the two worlds clashed.

Changing faces: new signings John Chiedozie (centre) and Clive Allen (second from right) in our five-man wall against Leicester in August 1984

Victory – at last – at Anfield. It was Peter's first time in charge of Spurs at Liverpool; I'd picked up a slight injury from studs hitting my hand. Spurs managers and assistants were always invited into the Anfield boot room for a chat and commiserations from their Liverpool counterparts in those days, so it must have been an interesting chat that day in 1985!

It wasn't as if I wasn't willing to accept change. We had a marketing campaign that came about initially via a chap I knew, John Jessup, who suggested the club advertise on the radio. The eventual advert had Mike Reid, the actor and comedian, saying, 'So, you get up in the morning, look in the mirror and say, "Come on you Spurs." Then you get to work and you've got 20 mates who support Tottenham and it's 20 voices saying, "Come on you Spurs." Now just imagine how that sounds with 38,000 shouting it. Why don't you go there and sample it?'

It worked well. Scholar blew the agency who did it out and went to Saatchi & Saatchi for a TV campaign. The advert had Ossie leading the team out – suffice to say the club and I were in disagreement over my new contract at the time and I didn't 'play' the role of captain. I haven't got a good record with chairmen. I wanted to do right from a football perspective. I cared little for five-star hotels, first-class travel and all that. I was concerned about what was good for the club. Let's just say Scholar and I had differences of opinion.

It was obvious to me that the new regime wanted Alex Ferguson to take over from Keith but couldn't get him, so promoted Peter Shreeve instead. Peter's assistant was John Pratt, so the managerial voices were new but not *too* new. We all respected Pete. He was very shrewd – not that Keith wasn't, but his manner was more of a good, honest but blunt Yorkshireman – whereas Peter was more subtle in how he communicated.

It was based on down-to-earth, coal-face wisdom. I had similar exposure to it when I talked football chats with Frank McLintock, George Graham, John Docherty and Pat Jennings in the Coolbury Club in Tottenham. With half a million games between us we should have known something about the game.

In 1984 we made good signings in Clive Allen and John Chiedozie, adding to an already strong squad, and had a decent crack at the league. Peter's first game was a 4–1 win at Goodison Park. The 2–1 win at Highbury on New Year's Day put us top. That was in the middle of a 14-game unbeaten run. We lost to Manchester United at home but then memorably beat Liverpool away.

STEVIE BLUNDER

Perryman own goal puts Spurs on ropes

SPURS STAR'S REAL AGONY

Perryman is stunned by the red card ref

It was one of three wins against the best team of the 1980s that season. Crooksie scored both winners in the league, while Clive secured a 1–0 win against them in the League Cup. I'd been to Anfield so many times, so to win there in the league, the first time Spurs had managed it for 73 years, was so welcome. I think we over-celebrated it. It was only a league game, but it was special all the same.

Over the years, I've probably said the phrase 'run to goal' more times than any other . Anything can happen. You've got to go in there optimistic, and run to goal. Garth did it in that game and got his reward for it, following up Micky's shot which had been saved by Bruce Grobbelaar. I think there was an extra fire in our bellies after meeting close-hand the Liverpool team in Swaziland the summer before and not being overimpressed. They were a bit full of themselves, although understandably so having just won the European Cup.

Maxie said afterwards, 'I wouldn't like to be on the *QE2* tonight', in reference to the fact that we hadn't won at Anfield since 1912, the year the *Titanic* went down. Typical Maxie – he could think of something funny at any time. The result put us level with Everton on 57 points. We thrashed Southampton 5–1, before losing to Villa. That set up the key league game of the season, against Everton at home in early April, which was a real classic. They took the lead early when Maxie was caught out from a long goal-kick by Neville Southall and only nodded it into the path of Andy Gray, who hit it first time and scored. Mark Bowen made a mistake and they scored again. Robbo pulled one back from miles out and then Southall produced a stupendous save to stop Falco equalising.

By the end of the season we had finished level on points with Liverpool, with Everton 13 points ahead. They were a good team and were very well led by Peter Reid. It was a familiar story for us: we could be as good as anyone, but also as bad as anyone.

Liverpool won the league yet again the following season. They had something we didn't. In an exhibition game on that tour to Swaziland, I had closed Ronnie Whelan. He moved away under my pressure and should have played it to Phil Neal, but he tried to hit Craig Johnston on the right wing with a 40-yard ball. It missed him by about a yard and went out of play. About six of them – this is a friendly – laid into Whelan. 'Oi! Give it him' – meaning Neal – 'because if you don't, he won't fucking be there next time!' That told me why they were a winning team.

I played all 42 league games again in the 1984–85 season, but the end was coming. The signs had already been there two seasons before. I had been suspended for our 5–0 win over Arsenal in the spring of 1983 and missed the defeat to Brighton before it. At the training ground, when Keith walked up to you clapping his hands, you knew he was thinking about what he was going to say. He did that with me and I wondered what was coming.

'So,' he eventually said, 'you going to get back into this team of ours?'

'What team is that, Keith?'
'The team that beat Arsenal 5–0.'
'Is that the one that lost at Brighton 2–1?'
'Yeah.'
'Yeah, I think so.'

Challenging John Barnes at White Hart Lane at the start of my last season at Spurs. We won 4–0, but it was one of the worst games of my career. I was getting over an injury and had missed a lot of pre-season while doing my coaching badges. Adrenaline got me through the match; playing Barnes while not fully fit was as tough as it got

But I didn't. At least not straight away. For the next game away at Forest I was sub, which was so strange. It was the first and only time in my career. Coming on as sub is like getting on a roundabout while it is already whizzing round. I was 31 then, which is a time when a lot of players would be either leaving, calling it a day or winding down. Your legs can't go on forever.

Later in 1983, Keith and I were talking about a new contract and he said to me, 'What do you need more money for? You've got a shop.'

'OK, Keith, so you're going to allow me to come in and say, "My shops are skint, so pay me more?"' He said no. I replied, 'In that case it's not relevant to what we're talking about.'

My contract was due to expire at the end of the 1982–83 season. We fell out because I swear Keith said he was going to give me a three-year deal but when it came to it offered just a year.

I spoke to Keith and a big row ensued in his office: it's apparently passed into Spurs legend as one of the loudest barneys people ever heard. Someone told Bill Nick about the noise. He pulled me over and said, 'I've heard you've been out of order.' By this time I was a bit braver with Bill and asked him directly how he worked that out. 'I heard you were swearing at the manager.'

'Bill,' I answered, 'I respect you, but if you'd have tried to do to me what Keith tried I'd have had a row with you as well.'

Bill maintained that I had been wrong to shout, but I was incensed and ready to walk away. I think Scholar stepped in as if he was going to be the peacemaker. It was left to my solicitor, Charles, to deal with the club's legal rep, a nice man, Peter Lever. The contract was eventually resolved but it didn't impress me. There were all sorts of tricks going on, as if they were trying to engineer disagreements. I suspect it was also done to try to make Keith look foolish – which in all honesty, I wasn't too much against then because I felt he had tried to turn me over.

Keith almost owned up to me recently when he said, 'You know what my problem was? I tried to keep in the black all the time.' This was to the extent that he was on half the money I was on towards the end of his time as manager. I still believe that Keith genuinely thinks he only ever offered me just a year. I don't think he was being deliberately difficult – things were not written down, which was a big part of the disagreement between us.

In the end I did sign a three-year contract and I lasted almost the whole three seasons in the side. That showed that I deserved three years, and I was very good value for money, given the number of games I played and what we achieved. As that deal was coming to an end of the 1985–86 season, we started negotiations for another new deal. I wanted a two-year contract this time, but was offered only one year. To be honest I was probably asking for too long a deal and the time to conduct negotiations ran out as my existing contract ran down. Tottenham's offer of a one-year deal was withdrawn.

Scholar then offered me the role of assistant to Pete, but only on the existing terms I was on. I declined. The offer wasn't right and I wasn't convinced they wanted to keep Pete in charge in any case, as was shown by the appointment of David Pleat in 1987. I'd crossed swords with the owners and they weren't the types to forget. I don't think Scholar wanted me around as an influence on the players while my contract ran down. I could have stayed right to the end of the 1985–86 season, but there was no point in hanging around.

As I was set to depart, Paul Allen and Chrissy Waddle arrived. Chrissy was a super talent but struggled to settle and play well for quite a while before coming very good. Paul was a little Jack Russell of a player. He had ability, but his energy and drive overpowered it sometimes. It was like he needed to slow down a bit. It came as no surprise that he was very helpful to a lot of players in his time at the PFA because he will help anyone. He was a very good signing for us, and he wasn't a typical Tottenham player. He was more of the type that I had often suggested to Keith that we needed.

That was for another captain to deal with. I scored my last goal for Spurs on Boxing Day 1985 against West Ham; I'd scored my first goal on Boxing Day 1969. My last league game was a 3–1 home defeat to Liverpool on 2nd March 1986. Two days later I played my 866th and final game for Tottenham Hotspur against Everton in a 2–1 home defeat in the FA Cup. I didn't get the chance to say goodbye to the crowd as the decision to leave was made afterwards, which was the biggest shame of all but it was as much to do with me as the club, because I wanted out.

The way it happened was not right. It's very rarely handled right, and not just at Spurs. There was a TV news report of me leaving. I just picked up my stuff in the afternoon, said goodbye to some people like Johnny Wallis, and went. In the days after I had letter after letter from supporters. They let me know how much I meant to them.

Boxing Day 1985 and my last ever goal for Spurs, against West Ham. By strange coincidence I scored my first and last Tottenham goals on Boxing Day in 1969

From Lord Willis

House of Lords

5 Shepherds Green,
Chislehurst,
Kent BR7 6PB.
27th March, 1986.

Steve Perryman, Esq.,
c/o Oxford United Football Club,
The Manor Ground,
OXFORD.

Dear Steve,

I was so sorry to hear that you were leaving Tottenham. I hope that one day circumstances will change and that you will be able to return in a different capacity. We really can't manage without your experience and enthusiasm and deep knowledge of the Club.

In the meantime I wish you every success at Oxford. I know some of the people there and they are a grand crowd and it is a good Club.

All very best wishes.

Yours ever,

Ted

A nice pen portrait by Paul Trevillion and a letter from Lord Ted Willis He'd always had an eye on my career as a devout Spurs fan, as did Paul; I think the description is right – I was a Tottenham club man

MANAGING EXPECTATIONS

I was at a crossroads in my life. Which way now? I didn't have to wait long. I soon heard that Oxford United were interested in me. They were near the bottom of the First Division but I knew their manager, Maurice Evans, a very honest man and a good boss. He brought through some proper players like John Aldridge and Ray Houghton. Trevor Hebberd was a good player; Gary Briggs and skipper Malcolm Shotton were pillars of strength.

Talks were no doubt conducted between Scholar and Oxford's owner Robert Maxwell, who I met in his suite at the top of the *Daily Mirror* offices. The discussion was quick, and I signed there and then. I then drove to Oxford to meet Maurice. His assistant, Ray Graydon, welcomed me but said, 'You realise Maurice had nothing to do with this?'

I was taken aback. 'I assumed if the chairman signed me, it was with the manager's blessing, Are you saying that's not the case?'

Ray was at pains to say it was all OK, and that there was absolutely no issue regarding Maurice and my transfer. 'If that isn't the case,' I continued, 'we need to call a halt now because I'm here to play for the manager, not the chairman.'

I suspected there had been some kind of behind-the-scenes deal between Scholar and Maxwell. I don't know if there was any transfer fee as such, or maybe it had been suggested to Maxwell that, based on all the fan letters I'd received, my signing might put a few more on the Oxford gate. In retrospect I should have joined Oxford on loan, then decided if I wanted to stay there or go back to Spurs.

At Oxford they couldn't believe I'd come to them. My response was that my club didn't want me and their club was the closest to where I lived. Oxford was low-end top-flight football. They were bottom of the league and the Manor Ground in Headington had a capacity of 6,500 and a sloping pitch. And I enjoyed every minute of it.

I was living in Ickenham, which just meant heading the other way up the A40 to what I'd been used to, so it was easy to get there. I had a fight on my hands trying to help keep Oxford up, which was the kind of challenge I always liked. Although they were bottom they weren't a bad team.

They got through to the League Cup Final that season, against QPR, although I wasn't eligible to play. The day before the final, both teams attended the Tottenham–Manchester United game. When it was announced that both sides were in the stands, the crowd chanted my name. That made me feel great. My new teammates were impressed.

"Oxford was low-end top-flight football. They were bottom of the league and the Manor Ground had a capacity of 6,500 and a sloping pitch. And I enjoyed every minute of it"

Even though I was cup-tied for the match, Oxford really made me feel part of their League Cup win, right down to a suit for the final

Cup-tied for the final, I sat on the bench. Oxford won 3–0, with as dominant a performance as I've seen at Wembley. They came alive and passed Rangers to death. Back in the dressing room, the players asked me what they should do with the trophy. I told them to put it in front of the coach, like we had done at Spurs, and that when we drove out of the tunnel there would be hundreds, maybe thousands of people waiting to see the cup that they'd just won. We drove out, and there wasn't a single sod there!

Despite that, the Oxford players asked me for lots of advice. I didn't want to come over as the big 'I am' but I had decades of experience that could be put to good use. They were not mugs by any means, though they did have their own habits which I had to get used to. After my first game at the end of March, a 3–3 draw with QPR, I was told to go to the players' room, which doubled up as the supporters' club. Fine, nothing wrong with mixing with fans. I went in and was asked what I wanted to drink.

'I'll have a small lager, please.'

'We don't serve "small lagers" here, Steve…'

There were other differences. The kit was hung up on a wire hanger. Nothing wrong with that, but it was not Tottenham. The first day at training was different too. We changed at the ground and then got in a minibus. Dave Hogg, an ex-player and coach, was driving. I overheard him talking to someone and it was clear Dave hadn't yet been told where we were training that day. It would be decided each the morning and the location would vary. We would train all over, sometimes the local park, other times lovely university grounds. Oxford was a very different club, but it had such a heart.

A couple of weeks after I'd joined Ossie's testimonial was played against Inter Milan. Oxford had two more games and needed points to stay up, so made it very clear that I would not be allowed to play in Ossie's match. I had to respect that, but wanted to be there for Ossie and went to the game. So did tens of thousands of others, as Diego Maradona was guesting for Spurs. I met him briefly and shook his hand – I'm not sure it was *that* one. I was told that in the dressing room he was unbelievable. While he was signing autographs, he was bouncing the ball on the floor, like a basketball player, but by tapping it up and down with his toe. It was a lovely night for Ossie and thoroughly deserved. I don't think when he arrived anyone would have imagined he'd be at Spurs 10 years later, and they'd be even more surprised that he's still there today doing his bit.

Maurice brought me back into the Oxford team for the next league game, a defeat to Forest, which meant that we needed to win the final game of the season to stay up – against Arsenal. We duly did with a 3–0 win, which was particularly pleasing bearing in mind the abuse I received from the small section of away supporters.

The only tickets that I had been able to get my Spurs-supporting friends were in that away section. I went over there to take a throw-in when we were leading 3–0 and got loads of stick. I had the ball in one hand so I held that up to them, and with the other hand I showed them three fingers – 3–0. Well, you can imagine the abuse.

I got absolutely battered by those Arsenal fans. And I loved it. During the game, I smashed Paul Davis. Graham Rix came up to me afterwards to say, 'That's out of order, Steve.' Apparently I told him 'Eff off, this is serious.' It was a nice little finish to the season.

Back in the dressing room I was shattered as usual when the door blasted open. It was the huge figure of Maxwell. I've never seen such a big suit jacket; it would have made five jackets for somebody else. He had the League Cup trophy in his hand and said, 'OK boys, out. Go. Go to the crowd.' The players looked at each other but in the end had to do it, because he was the guvnor. Shotton took the trophy and led the players out. I just sat there. Maxwell said, 'Perryman. Up. You go. You go.' I said, 'No, I didn't win the cup.'

'Yes, yes, you go. You go.'

He said it in a way that you couldn't argue with. I walked round the pitch about 15 yards behind the group. They took turns to show the trophy to the crowd, asking me if I wanted to parade it. I politely declined – the last thing I'm going to do is show off a cup I had no part in winning.

Until we reached the corner, that is, where the Arsenal fans were still penned in. At this point I thought, 'Actually, I will hold the cup.' I took it, and held it in front of the Arsenal fans. My friends were in the middle of them, and their eyes were saying to me, 'Don't say hello to us; please don't say hello!'

Oxford wanted me to be captain the next season but I said, politely, no chance. Spurs might not have been wrong in moving me on given that in the next pre-season, with none of the bespoke exercises and conditioning that I normally got from Spurs staff, my legs were shot. Even if I could have physically lasted, it wouldn't have been right. Oxford was not my club.

Early in the 1986–87 season, I was playing in midfield and the ball went up to the opposition's centre half, where I knew it was going to drop from experience. But I didn't go. I thought about going but didn't. My legs were telling me they couldn't get there. No one even noticed. But I knew. Maybe Maurice did, too, because shortly afterwards, before another match, he

Challenging Arsenal's Paul Davis at the Manor Ground on the 5th May 1986 on the way to a fine victory – beating the old red neighbours was always fun. However, my Spurs-supporting friends in the away end were not best pleased when I celebrated right in front of them

I went from a player at Oxford to player/assistant manager at Brentford

called me into his little office. He used to drink a small glass of red wine before the game and said, 'Steve, do you want a glass?'

'Does that mean I'm not playing, Maurice?'

'Yes.'

'Go on then.'

It was a very nice way of saying to me, 'This is the end, Steve.' If ever you needed to finish your playing career, you would want Maurice Evans to finish it with.

The next phase in my professional life meant a return close to home, my old childhood stomping ground of Brentford, where Frank McClintock was manager and in need of an assistant. He asked who I could recommend. I said Phil Holder. Frank said, 'Are you telling me that if you become a manager that you would take Phil as your assistant?'

I felt it odd that with all Frank's experience he was asking me about an assistant. My assessment was that in reality he was asking me if *I* wanted to be his assistant. Sure enough, in November 1986, Frank invited me to join him as player/assistant manager at Griffin Park. Frank suggested it would help me get into management. I'd done coaching badges by then so it was a good opportunity and I accepted.

There were problems from the start. My first day was a sign of things to come. I walked into the boot room and there was three inches of water on the floor due to a faulty washing machine that was never repaired. It was amateur. The chairman, Martin Lange, wanted to talk the club up but at ground level it was very poor. We had just five training balls. I went to my shop and took 20 training balls in the next day, at my own expense.

Lange asked me, 'Why don't we produce players?', inviting me to say something critical about Frank. I said, 'Do you know how many balls we had to train with on my first day?' He didn't know, so I told him. 'How are you going to produce footballers with just five balls to work with?' Lange muttered something about that being the manager's fault.

My first job was to drive the minibus, a beaten-up old thing. Again, I wasn't going to be the big 'I am' and refuse. I was backing out of the car park in front of the stand and players were winding me up, banging the side to make it sound like it had hit something. 'Yeah, go on; the school bell is ringing,' I said to them.

Frank signed me and Micky Droy almost in the same week to add playing experience and shore things up in the team for him. It went OK but not well enough for Lange. He sacked Frank on the way home from defeat at Port Vale in January 1987. Frank officially resigned, but he'd been told his contract was not going to be renewed.

Lange phoned to offer me the manager's job – insisted I take it, in fact. I had doubts. I was only 35 by this point. Frank warned me about Lange. He was a self-made property millionaire, and took credit for devising the play-off system. Good for him, but some of his actions were questionable. Frank showed me a letter Lange had written to him – he'd insisted on writing rather than just talking to Frank 'so I can get all my thoughts down without being interrupted'. Even so, Frank advised me to take the job, and after some consideration, I did. And I employed Phil as my assistant.

I soon formed an opinion that Lange was the type who when he put his head on the pillow at night would have all the little worms start turning in his mind, thinking that everyone was cheating him, not doing what they should and wasting his money. I didn't want to waste anyone's money.

There was no money in any case. Walking along the touchline as manager for my first game, someone shouted from the terraces, 'Steve, you must be mad.' I said, 'You might be right.'

I got on with it. I drew on my knowledge of the sports industry and contacts, and all the experience from being at Spurs for so long. The old Third Division was very competitive but my team was never going to lack for competitiveness. We did well, first of all to avoid relegation. I played games when I was needed, in various positions. We gave the fans a bit of hope.

We had three centre-backs who didn't look like particularly good footballers, but I knew I could make them better. We played offside and it worked. I did a lot of ball work and kept training lively and flowing, and we recuperated well. In the Third Division it was fairly rudimentary, a bit of 'position of maximum opportunity' stemming from my FA coaching, but I used Bill Nick and Tottenham's old sayings – 'When not in possession, get into position' and all that.

Over three seasons we built, borrowed and managed a decent squad. We had Terry Evans coming back from injury, Keith Millen and Jamie Bates, and relied heavily on loan players, including Tony Parks. We had the two Joseph brothers, Roger the right-back who went to Wimbledon, and Francis, the lead goalscorer. Robbie Cooke was a goalscorer at the lower levels who Millwall picked up. I brought in Dean Holdsworth from Watford and Gary Blissett from Crewe, so we ended up with a really good strike force. Richard Cadette came in, while Neil Smillie was a machine. Steve Coppell used to watch us when he was at Crystal Palace, and was impressed.

Within the severe limitations Lange put on us, Phil and I wheeled and dealed. We built up the youth system, and got to the semi-final of the FA Youth Cup in 1988–89. Another old Spurs teammate, Colin Lee, came on board as a player and youth coach. I gave him his start in coaching and management, and he did a really good job. We took youngsters released by

Tony Parks was one of the players I brought to Griffin Park, thanks in part to our mutual Spurs links

★ THERE'S a buzz going round that little Brentford are planning to take the sting out of mighty Liverpool in today's FA Cup showdown at Anfield.

★ Bees boss Steve Perryman — and his inflatable mascot — are hoping the boys can swarm into the semi-finals . . . they're not in it for the honey!
Picture: ARNOLD SLATER

STEVE'S STING!

Inflatables were all the rage when I was in charge at Brentford, as this FA Cup preview photoshoot shows. But we were deflated at the quarter-final stage, losing to Liverpool – no shame in that, though...

Andy Sinton, a model young pro who wanted to improve every day and went on to greater things

Spurs, Arsenal and elsewhere and created a team that beat Manchester United in the FA Youth Cup. To complement the great work of our staff, I was drawing on all my experience and contacts, getting every inch out of them. My legs might have run out of steam but my brain hadn't.

The first team had good spells, too, reaching the quarter-finals of the FA Cup in 1989 and losing to Liverpool before getting applauded off by 42,000 people at Anfield. We had bad periods as well including strings of results without a win. We had to sell players – Blissett, Holdsworth, Roger Joseph, Marcus Gayle and Keith Jones, who was like an early N'Golo Kante with legs to burn, all left during my time or just after. It was a survival business at that level.

In the very early days, Lange said to me, 'Get rid of that fat-arsed little waster Andy Sinton.' 'Woah,' I said. 'I understand about the budget, but as you bought him for 25 grand as a youngster from Cambridge United, I suggest you saw something in him.' Lange wanted Sinton to progress quicker because he wanted to turn a profit on him and fast.

That 'fat-arsed little waster' ended up earning Brentford big money. He was a dream to work with. Every day after training he'd say, 'Steve, what can I do better?' He ended up playing for England, Tottenham and Wolves – a more determined character and a nicer young man you couldn't hope to meet. And he wasn't fat – he just had a wide backside!

We also got 90 grand for Roger Stanislaus, a player originally signed for free, after I made a good case at a tribunal in Manchester. On the way back Lange said, 'Who are you going to get to replace Stanislaus? I said I was going to take Gary Elkins from Fulham. From that moment Lange did everything he could to stop the deal.

I told Lange that I knew the full picture – what Elkins was on, what we could get him for and how he suited all the criteria Lange insisted upon, such as being London-based. Everything about the deal was right but Lange was insistent he didn't want Elkins. Exasperated, I asked him why. He said, 'Because Terry Bullivant says that he doesn't like Elkins's eyes. I know this sounds funny Steve – but he stares.' I was almost speechless. Almost.

'Let me just give you a few facts of life, Martin. I don't know Terry Bullivant. I know him as a player; I know he used to play at Brentford. You've mentioned his name three times in front of me in the last couple of years. Your problem is I've got a memory and every time you've mentioned Terry Bullivant it hasn't been positive. Are you now taking his view on Gary Elkins as more important than mine?'

I made the point that Andy Sinton, who we now agreed was the best winger in the Third Division, never had a good game against Elkins. 'It must be because Elkins stares at him, eh, Martin?' I told Lange that if we missed out on Elkins and he went elsewhere, I'd walk. Lange scoffed. Sure enough, top-flight Wimbledon snapped Elkins up. So I walked.

I couldn't reveal the truth of why I had left, so instead all sorts of rumours started to circulate, including a report that I couldn't motivate the players any more, which is the worst thing that can be said about a manager. I took it to court and won £5,000 damages. I'd had grief from Brentford fans when Sinton was sold, it was the era of fanzines and that meant some ill-informed stick, but I knew the truth and I had put my heart and soul into that club. While I was still manager I did a fans' forum in Gunnersbury Park, which is where I spent a lot of my young days, and there was a lot of criticism. I told them how it is: there was a reason why their players were in the Third Division – it's because they were not good enough but that I would make them better.

That's why you're employed – because of your skills in management. I'm terrible at wallpapering. I can't paint. I can't do lots of things. What I can do is know about football. If a chairman doesn't trust that, I'm off. I told the fans, 'The chairman ain't great to work for' and he was sat right there. Those fans weren't used to that honesty.

Lange had all the trappings of wealth but no style in terms of football decisions and actions. In other ways, he was quite innovative. Brentford were one of the first clubs, if not *the* first, to start a 'Football in the Community' scheme, and facilities improved. Overall it was a mixed bag for me, but I was totally happy with what I had done. I had improved players, although Phil joked I'd done it only for someone else to benefit. He knew the score about the club, but I told him to take over as manager regardless. He did, and did a great job, in 1992 taking Brentford up into the Second Division for the first time in 40 years. He was gracious enough to say, 'Steve was a big part of this.'

Jack Petchey at second-tier Watford, my next managerial destination in November 1990, was the complete opposite to what I'd experienced under Lange. Sir Jack is a very astute businessman, and his set-up at Watford was all about structure and communication. You knew exactly where you stood.

The job came about after Colin Lee left Brentford to be Watford youth coach. He eventually got made manager when results were not great. Colin's own results suffered and they were bottom of the league, 11 points from safety. I was out of work and Charles, my solicitor, knew Jack and believed that we could work together. Not everything worked but I saved Watford from relegation with a game to go.

With Elton John – not the owner of Watford by then but definitely happy to avoid relegation

"I found Watford a difficult club, with a fanbase that was hard to please. But we steadied the ship and finished mid-table the next season with an inferior team"

I initially employed Peter Shreeve as my assistant. I wanted his intelligence, shrewdness and innovative thinking. Early on we played an 11-a-side practice match which Peter refereed. He blew his whistle and shouted. 'Stop, everybody. Please stop. I don't know you. Do something that makes me say, "Who the fuck is that?"' Players who witnessed that still mention it to me today!

We had similar challenges as I had faced at Brentford, but in Jack I had a very able chairman. I looked out of my office window one day and saw him drive up in his Rolls-Royce. He got out and spoke to an old fella – the typical type of character you see at any football club. Jack was finding out what he'd seen or heard. Whether Jack acted upon what he learned is another matter but that old boy would go home believing that what he said counted.

We sold one of our best players, Gary Penrice, for £875,000 in March 1991 and I used some of the money to bring in Peter Nicholas, who brought experience and leadership. We had David James established in goal at just 20 and got enough results to keep us up. Peter then left to go back to Tottenham and I replaced him with Peter Taylor, another Spurs connection, though for some reason the Watford crowd didn't take to him – they objected to our set pieces, which Peter devised.

I found Watford a difficult club, with a fanbase that was hard to please. But we steadied the ship and finished mid-table the next season with an inferior team. Jack worked me into his system: monthly meetings, the minutes circulated the next working day which had to be answered 12 working hours before the next meeting. In one of those meetings, Jack pointed to the agreement that I had accepted upon joining, which stated that I could only spend what I had generated. Jack said, 'We ain't got any money. But I want to know, if you had £500k to spend on a No.9, give me a list of who you would sign.'

I was sceptical, but over time compiled a list and gave it to Jack. On it was Paul Furlong. Peter Taylor knew him from when he had managed

Training fun and games at Watford. I was always happy working with and improving players on the training ground, especially younger players

Enfield. Furlong was set to go from Enfield to Coventry for £140,000. I told Jack that was high but Paul was a contender.

Furlong duly went to Coventry, and then later on when we needed a No.9, Jack called a meeting with the directors. I went in and he said, 'Stand here, Steve.'

'So gentlemen, I understand that you all think we need a No.9,' said Jack. They agreed.

'I take it as read that you're not going to put in any money? So let's all rest assured that it's my cash. If we buy a No.9, he [pointing at me] will decide who that player is. Let me just make that clear. Because he is spending my money; he is not spending your money because you've just made it clear that you're not putting any in.'

This was a leader. It was great, no messing about. I reverted back to my list and phoned Coventry's manager Bobby Gould, asking if he wanted to sell Furlong. He didn't but needed to raise funds for other buys and quoted me £200,000 straight, no sell-on fee or any other clauses.

I knew Jack would like the lack of a sell-on because it was on the list of clauses he had given me to ask for if someone bought from us, 'because at the last minute when someone really wants a player they'll give you whatever you ask'. A pre-season fixture was another favourite of his. Jack was very shrewd.

'Go on then,' he said of Furlong for £200k, 'but no more.' Watford ended up selling Furlong for £2.25 million to Chelsea. It was good business and smart management all round.

Watford had a really good set-up for producing home-grown players. David James was one of those and another success for us in the transfer market. Liverpool wanted David and their manager, Graeme Souness, said, 'Steve, you're not getting more than £600,000 for him. If you do, I'll treat you and your little mate Phil Holder to an expensive meal.' We wanted £1 million and we got it, but Graeme didn't treat us to a meal until some time later! That didn't make me clever, it was simply a case of getting the price the player merited. A few months afterwards I sat next to Liverpool's Tom Saunders at a Fulham game where we were both scouting. Over a half-time cup of tea I asked, 'How's David James?'

'How's David James?' he said. 'How *is* David James?' – as if he was about to reveal something shocking. 'I tell you *how* David James is. He only wants a goalkeeping coach!'

I laughed but filled him in on the background. When I took over at Watford we held an introductory player meeting and asked if anyone had any questions. Nobody spoke until 19-year-old David put his hand up. He said, 'Steve, I have Peter Bonetti as my goalkeeping coach twice a week; is it OK if I continue with that?' I said, 'OK, well done for speaking up and good question; let's see how it goes.' So David had previous with a dedicated coach and believed that it worked for him.

Tom said, 'Yes, I know about that. But, as we told him, "Keep the bleedin' ball out of the bleedin' net. Now, do you need any *more* coaching?"' That was the old-school Liverpool way. 'We've paid a million pound for you and you want coaching?!'

Watford was a tough job but made better by working with Jack Petchey. It was a meeting of minds. Jack could have educated a number of owners. He fostered good relationships between the manager, chairman, captain, commercial people and Uncle Tom Cobley and all. Jack was the best chairman I ever worked under by a mile – and I left him. Why? I must have been mad.

All smiles as Watford manager. Still with all black hair, although the grey is definitely in waiting

AN UNHAPPY RETURN

By the 1990s Tottenham had moved on. Few of us from the first half of the previous decade still had any real involvement. There had been new managers in David Pleat and Terry Venables, who later moved upstairs into the boardroom. Ray Clemence had worked under Terry, and with Doug Livermore in tandem effectively managing the first team. Peter Shreeve had come back for a single season as manager. But a new generation of players, including Gary Lineker and Paul Gascoigne, had worn the lilywhite shirt. More significantly, as things turned out, there was a new owner in Alan Sugar. His arrival was to have a big impact on Spurs, and my relationship with the club.

Sugar and Venables had been through a long and bitter dispute over control of the club. I didn't speak to Terry about it at the time but did afterwards, and it seemed it was bruising. There was big unrest with the players, to the extent that their wives and kids protested with placards outside Sugar's house in support of Terry.

It ended up in the High Court and with victory for the Amstrad chairman. One of his first moves after that was to try and placate the crowd because Venables had been so popular. Sugar tried for Glenn Hoddle as manager first, but Glenn declined because he had already agreed to join Chelsea. Again, I didn't speak to Glenn about it. Upheaval like this was part and parcel of how clubs changed direction and managers.

In the summer of 1993 Sugar then turned to Ossie, who was offered the job having done very good things at both Swindon and West Brom. Ossie asked me to come as his assistant, but I said no at first. It took him three weeks to convince me. To be more accurate, I convinced myself that Tottenham was my club and I should go back. I didn't say 'yes' straight away because I would be going from a being a manager at Watford to an assistant manager. I didn't give a lot of thought about what it would be like to work for Alan Sugar. He wasn't stopping me, to put it that way.

The initial issue was leaving Watford. Telling Jack Petchey was going to be hard. He wasn't going to make it easy. In addition I had to think about Charles Newman, my solicitor. Charles had introduced me to Jack and encouraged me to take the Watford job in the first place, so I had to take into account his relationship with Jack. Charles made things a bit easier for me because he said he understood the pull of going back to Tottenham.

I ended up sat in Jack's office. He's Mr Organised and he had three bits of paper in front of him on the table.

> "I convinced myself that Tottenham was my club and I should go back"

'Right' he said. 'We've got to talk about you *possibly* going to Tottenham.'

Jack cut to the chase. 'Sugar is harder to work for than I am.'

I replied that I didn't think Jack was hard to work for. He had been sensible, smart and fair.

'In which case, you agree with me,' he shot back.

'Well, I don't know, Jack…'

'I'm telling you.' Jack knew what he was talking about.

The three sheets of paper were still on the table. We had a little bit of discussion about why he thought I would be wrong to leave, but in the end I said, 'Jack, I'm going.'

The moment I said that, Jack cast aside two of the sheets of paper and focused on one. He'd had the documents prepared for all options. One was 'He's staying', two 'He ain't sure', three 'He's leaving'.

'Right,' said Jack. 'Who is paying for this?'

He went into businessman mode. I said I assumed Spurs would. He said, 'We owe you 10 grand for what you did last year. You're not getting that.'

Peter Taylor had left by then and I had appointed Phil Holder as my assistant. I asked Jack to give that £10,000 to Phil, saying I thought he would then walk away as well, so he wouldn't cost Jack anything more. Phil was on a contract and would have needed to have to been paid off in some way.

'He's not getting that,' Jack said.

I couldn't argue. Jack was playing hardball and rightly so. He hadn't got where he had got by being soft. He had a list of these things he had obviously worked out prior to me walking in. Eventually it was settled. In stark terms: we're done.

Jack ended with one telling comment. 'I'll see how I get on with Sugar', meaning in terms of agreeing compensation for Watford. I should have been thinking about how I would get on with Sugar as well.

The opportunity to work with Ossie was a very interesting prospect. I didn't quite know what I was getting into, but I knew from playing against Ossie's Swindon team with Watford what a good ethic he had in terms of how to play. They had been 2–0 up against us at Vicarage Road in December 1990 and top of the league while we were bottom in a period when I was trying to keep us up. In truth they could have been 8–0 up, not 2–0.

In the second half we got back into it, scored a goal and all of a sudden were pushing and pushing. They were not playing badly, just not as well as in the first half. Late on they hit a ball over the top and their striker, Duncan Shearer, should have gone for goal but instead took it into the corner. We got it back and sent it long, and Gary Penrice equalised with virtually the last kick of the game.

After the final whistle, Ossie kept the Swindon players in the dressing room for an hour. I found out later that he and

Alan Sugar appointed Ossie, who had enjoyed a lot of success elsewhere and was adored by the Spurs fans

Sugar plays Ardiles, his final ace

Alan Sugar: "Surely I have proved this last month that I am a winner. I want Tottenham to be first. Second or third is no good"

**The management
and coaching
team get together
at the start of
the 1993–94
season (from left
to right): Chris
Hughton, Doug
Livermore, Ossie,
Patsy Holland
and me**

Micky Hazard were rucking. Mick was saying Ossie was wrong to say that Shearer should have gone for goal. Ossie said, 'You either score – game over – or it goes a mile over the bar and they end up kicking it long a little later. Be positive: try to win the game.' Micky was sticking up for Shearer, though to be honest Mick and Os could have had a row about what day of the week it was.

I was waiting for Ossie to come into the manager's room and have a drink after the game, half-delighted because we'd got a draw against a very good team. You just knew by looking at Swindon's movement that Ossie was either a very good coach, or he was a good selector of players and system, to be able to get them playing like that. It was like watching chess.

Ossie's mantra was 'Pass, pass, pass.' He would shout from the bench, 'Too many touches! Pass the ball!' When a team passes at tempo it's easy for their players to read where the next ball should go. You don't even have to coach it. That was how Ossie's Swindon team played. It was like poetry.

I knew how Ossie's thought about the game. Lining up against each other in the dugout was a bit odd but we were older and our careers had progressed. Getting back together seemed like the most natural next step in that progression. But in retrospect it was a terrible decision to leave Watford and join Tottenham. Not because it was Tottenham, but because of who I was going to work for. To leave Jack Petchey for Alan Sugar was a disaster, and totally my own fault.

There were some positives. Going back to Spurs in the summer of 1993 meant I was back with people who I knew. I trusted the Spurs public more than I did the Watford fans, which was a big factor.

From my perspective I had returned to Spurs and the club I loved. I went to White Hart Lane to sign my contract. There were some old faces still around, but as it was summer not many. I felt the emotional tug of coming back, but sadly it didn't last long.

The first time I met Sugar was at the training ground offices at Mill Hill. The old training round at Cheshunt had been sold for housing some time before, leaving Spurs to train at a place that was essentially a park and open to the public. Sugar came in to talk to the players on the first morning of pre-season in 1993. It was quite funny because in meetings we had had with the coaching staff – Patsy Holland, Dougie Livermore, Chrissy Hughton and Pat Jennings – Patsy kept asking Ossie, 'What's happening in the first week, Os? What's it look like? Who is training with who? Are the first team in with everyone else? Are we taking defenders and strikers separately, or are we all in together?'

Ossie just said, 'Relax. Leave it to me. No problem.'

Later that first morning at Mill Hill, after meeting the players, Sugar went into a room to speak to Ossie. Sugar had the hump about something. The door was slammed shut. He came out, and stormed off. Ossie emerged, obviously a bit uptight about things as well.

'Steebie,' Ossie said. 'I am a little tense today. You take it. You take training.' So there obviously *was* a problem. I know how to take a session, so it was no hardship, but I'd have liked to have known two weeks before for that session to be planned. It wasn't a big deal. First day of pre-season, you just touch the ball. Nothing too complicated.

But words had clearly been said between Ossie and Sugar. Ossie was a bit shocked about something. It set the tone for the rest of our time there. My feeling was that Sugar sometimes spoke to Ossie in the wrong way. Instead of being encouraging and positive, the tone would often be confrontational. It wouldn't help Ossie to inspire the players straight after he'd been given a dressing-down about something or other.

The tone was set right from the off. Ossie said he needed me to keep the pressure off him. He didn't specify Sugar – Ossie was referring to the overall

The 1993–94 team photo, with Gary Mabbutt as captain

pressure of the job. As former successful players there was expectation around us, but the pressure at a club like Spurs applies to whoever you are. The only thing that dissipates the pressure is results.

Getting those results was going to be difficult. The squad was a bit of a mixture. Mabbsie, Paul Allen and David Howells were there who we knew as players, while Colin Calderwood, David Kerslake and Jason Dozzell were brought in, and Micky Hazard returned. Vinny Samways played a lot of games and Sol Campbell was emerging but Ossie had to use him as a centre-forward because we had injuries. Gordon Durie was there but only briefly. Darren Anderton was a top-class player, as was Teddy Sheringham.

Ossie had to try to mould them into his style of play. I don't think anyone would tell you that they didn't enjoy playing for Ossie. But the enjoyment needed to show itself in results. Teddy was injured and struggled to stay fit. He was done by Bryan Robson in a 2–1 defeat at Man United. It was nasty, and Teddy was out for a long time, which hurt us. We played good football and earned plaudits, but finished eighth from bottom, having needed to beat Oldham towards the end of the season to stay up.

That first season was about getting over the troubles at the club we had inherited. Whoever's decision it had been to go to Mill Hill looked like a poor one. It wasn't home. Selling Cheshunt was a mistake. Historically it had been part of the reason why the club was a step ahead of others. When you control your own training ground you don't have to ask permission to train on a Sunday. Your groundsman lives on site, opens the gate and puts the hot water on for the showers. He might have the hump, but he'll do it.

All of a sudden we were at this place that we couldn't control. You couldn't put a pin in the wall because the building was listed. For a club of Tottenham's stature, at a time when the Premier League TV money was starting to roll in, it was a nonsense. The treatment room was a Portakabin with no running water. People were having to carry buckets of ice – it was ridiculous. The pitches were of a very good quality, until complimentary tickets for the ground staff were cut, that is. Surprise, surprise – the pitches were not so good after that.

Complimentary tickets – 'comps' – were being stopped wholesale. Arsenal were due to play us and George Graham wanted to come and scout with his assistant Stewart Houston. This was normal practice, but George was told, 'Sorry, only one ticket.' So guess what happened when we went to scout Arsenal? We got one ticket, and were seated in the far corner of the stand. Word of this kind of behaviour spread like wildfire in football. 'Tottenham have gone. They are not to be dealt with. Tottenham don't give and take.'

In fairness, there were some good things happening at the club. There was a lot of essential building work and redevelopment required and the Paxton and Park Lane ends had to be upgraded to comply with the Taylor Report. Tottenham came through that time of having to redevelop the ground and get it up to standard, and we did not suffer like other clubs did.

But White Hart Lane was a different place, that was evident. After we beat Derby in the League Cup in October 1993, Sugar phoned Ossie to tell him that he'd appointed a chief executive. Ossie was told that this person would not interfere but that Sugar said he needed someone to be hands on every day. That someone was Claude Littner, who many people will now know from watching *The Apprentice*.

Up until this point, Sugar had been this bold, brash, take-on-all-comers, type. It was as if he was wearing a suit of armour. I am guessing that this

"The tone was set right from the off. Ossie said he needed me to keep the pressure off him"

**Chairman Alan
Sugar holding
court at a Spurs
press conference**

was because it felt like the whole world was attacking him over the Venables split. The players were definitely unhappy about Terry leaving.

It was against this backdrop that the day-to-day side of things at the club wasn't working. There were so many examples that sound petty but to me are very revealing. If the clerk of works wanted to buy four screws, he would have to wait outside Claude's office to get a chit to go and buy four screws. And when he came back to say they only sell them in sixes, the answer would be, 'Well, we don't buy them then.'

It also soon became clear that Sugar was still in negotiation with Jack Petchey and Watford over compensation for me. One day once I was established at Tottenham, I was in my little broom cupboard of an office and got a phone call from Sugar.

'Right,' Sugar said. 'Between you, me and the gatepost, when Ossie got the job here, did you phone him to join him, or did he phone you?'

I said, 'I'm really surprised by that question. I was manager at Watford and very happy. Ossie phoned me.'

'Oh, right.' Brrrr…

Sugar was clearly coming under pressure from Jack and I'm guessing that he wanted me to say that had instigated the move. But it simply wasn't true. Jack ended up getting the deal he needed to get, with part of the agreement being that we would play Watford in a pre-season game before the 1994–95 campaign. And who did we sign that summer? Jürgen Klinsmann. Of course that meant there was huge interest in the game and Jack sold the rights to TV. I don't think Sugar was very happy about that but there was nothing he could do to get out of playing the match. Did Jack do well out of that deal? I don't know, but I would not have blamed him if he did. And it wouldn't have happened if things had been sorted out early between Watford and Tottenham over me leaving.

Tottenham had always had a character of a certain calibre and a way of doing things right. That was changing. The daily milk delivery was questioned and then stopped. They stopped providing bottled water on the team coach. A report was requested to find out how many spoonfuls of coffee there were in a catering-sized tub, so that the club knew how much they were spending every time someone in the White Hart Lane offices had a cup of coffee. Even the system of how match balls were recycled was altered. A used match ball would later be used as a warm-up ball and then as a youth-team ball. Now match balls were used as warm-up balls for longer. When Klinsmann arrived he came into the dressing room after a warm-up before a League Cup tie against Watford. He was holding a tired old ball which had been provided for the warm-up, and he was angry. 'I don't play with this crap. And I don't warm up with it!' he said as he slammed it into the floor.

This was typical of what was happening. Cuts everywhere. Any money that went out of the door was queried. Cutting down on waste is no bad thing. But I think the attitude of the owner was that everyone in football was 'at it'.

Sugar often complained about the business of football and the culture of backhanders and 'bungs', to the extent that he provided evidence to the FA's enquiry at the time. I think that he thought everyone in the game was on the take. I'm not naive enough to think it didn't go on, but I didn't *see* it go on.

I certainly wasn't 'at it'. Neither were the everyday members of staff, but we all came under suspicion and were affected by the determination to root it out, even if 'it' wasn't there.

My brother Ted said Sugar should have had a meeting with all the staff and said, 'I need to make cuts. I might cut too deep. But trust me, I've got to make cuts.' Anyone running an organisation the size of a top-flight football club would be within their rights to say that. He would have been halfway there in explaining and justifying what he was doing. But it wasn't done like that. I felt there was a lack of appreciation of how a football club functions.

For example, there was talk that the club were thinking of changing the way schoolboy players would be treated in the event of being injured whilst playing for Spurs, so that the club would not be liable. The idea was that their parents would be asked to sign a disclaimer agreement to this effect.

When I was told about this I said, "Ah, Ok. Let me tell you something. If you do that, the shares in Arsenal have just gone up double; you're never going to sign another Perryman, Hoddle, Hazard or Barmby from Sunderland, Hull, Harlow or Hayes. You know who you might sign? See those flats over there? Those kids are so indoctrinated by their parents about Tottenham Hotspur that they will sign anything.

'But Tottenham don't just make players from the Tottenham area. They come from all over, including London, but not just Tottenham.'

The idea was shelved, but the message was clear: it was all about saving money. I later said to Ossie that we were mugs – that we should have let them do it. I wasn't concerned about their names being sullied but it would have hurt me if Spurs' good name had been devalued.

I don't know if it was true, but I did know that Ossie and I did not agree with how things were being done because we cared so much about the club.

Ossie looking pensive and in deep thought during a match, while I am a little more demonstrative...

**A stellar
signing – Jürgen
Klinsmann's
arrival at
Spurs provided
everyone at the
club with a lift**

Football is a cut-throat business and from my perspective I don't have a
problem with anyone having a tough-talking style when required. I can deal
with that; at a tender age I dealt with Bill Nick telling me, 'You'll never
wear that white shirt again' for not shaking hands with Johnny Giles. But
at this time I felt there was a lack of respect and trust around the club.

For all the problems, we got through that first season. The club had a big
shock when the FA's bung enquiry found Tottenham guilty of a number of
breaches and handed out a huge punishment of a £600,000 fine and being
barred from the FA Cup for the 1994–95 season. But most damaging was
a 12-point deduction that put us in real threat of going down before a ball
had been kicked. Credit to Sugar for contesting that and being relentless
in eventually getting it all but thrown out. But it was a shock to start the
season with. A more welcome surprise came with the arrival of Klinsmann.

That was some signing. It came out of the blue, with the deal reportedly
agreed on Alan Sugar's yacht moored in Monaco. I didn't know anything
about it in advance; Ossie phoned to tell me we were getting him. I hadn't
really heard of him for two or three years, but Ossie was absolutely
convinced he was what we needed.

When Jürgen came in he was the perfect gentleman. Proper. I can't say
one negative thing about him. Not one. How he spoke to people, how he dealt
with the staff was correct. I loved him for being angry about the warm-up
balls because it showed he was a winner.

The squad was taking on a bit more shape. Teddy was fit, which was
crucial. Teddy and Klinsmann together was an enticing prospect. Nicky
Barmby was coming through; Darren Caskey was quite established and

liked. George Graham once told us that Darren couldn't run, to which I should have said, 'George, you should know that better than anyone.'

Erik Thorstvedt, who I liked very much, had made the goalkeeper position his in seasons past but Ian Walker took over. We also lost Vinny Samways, a good footballer who should have flourished under Ossie, as he loved Vinny's type, but the club decided to sell him to Everton.

We needed fresh blood. I went to scout Ilie Dumitrescu. He was one of only a few players in the Romanian squad that got to the 1994 World Cup quarter-finals who was not playing club football outside Romania. I watched him play in Belfast in March 1994 and it was raining so much it was going sideways.

I phoned Ossie straight after the game from the ground and said, 'I can't say yes to him because I haven't seen enough and the conditions were crap, so I'd like another look if that's possible. But I'd sign Gica Popescu tomorrow. In fact he's walking past me.'

'Go, talk to him,' said Ossie.

I introduced myself to Popescu. 'Perryman, Tottenham. Want to play for us?'

'Hmm. OK. Yeah.'

Popescu signed in September that year, while Dumitrescu signed in time to start the season. He had played in the World Cup and scored goals. Ossie said I'd cost the club another million pounds by not signing him straight away. My reply was that we should wait and see if he could play.

The first game of the 1994–95 season at Sheffield Wednesday was certainly promising, as we earned a famous 4–3 win. Everyone remembers Klinsmann's dive to celebrate his goal, and it was amazing, but we were very fluent going forward. We then beat Everton 2–1 and everything seemed hunky-dory. We lost to Man U, but then won 3–1 at Ipswich. Klinsmann scored twice and crossed for Dumitrescu to score a Cliff Jones-style diving header.

People were starting to tip us for great things. I even heard one comment along the lines of, 'This is the best team since the Double.' The label that was soon attached to our forward line was 'the Famous Five', comprising Barmby, Anderton, Dumitrescu, Klinsmann and Sheringham, but I found

A famous goal celebration at Hillsborough – we didn't know Jürgen and the team were going to do it and it brought a smile to mine and the fans' faces

that difficult to understand because Ossie's typical system was a diamond in midfield.

The accepted wisdom is that it was wonderful to watch going forward but we were wide open at the back, and I wouldn't disagree with that, yet I wouldn't say we lacked defenders. Instead, maybe the reactions were wrong when we lost the ball, because that can make a huge difference.

If you have players that track back, they can go forward as much as you want, as long as they get back into position to defend. Maybe we were too easy to work out in that regard. We had bags of ability, but if opponents coped with that ability and then ran off us, they did well. It's a joke now but Ossie says of that era that he'd say before training started, 'Steebie, I'll take the forwards; you take the defenders. So take them three over there.' The press jumped on the bandwagon of the Famous Five to such an extent that I've since heard that some of the others in the team were introducing themselves as 'one of the Shit Six'.

The good form didn't last. We lost four League games on the spin, and were shipping goals. I always think from a defensive position – safety first. But it's hard as an assistant to know where to pitch yourself. If you're too like the manager, the players suss it. You can't be against the manager: you have to support him. But in private, you need to be saying what needs saying.

However, given what was going on Tottenham the last thing I wanted to do was water Osisie down. There were disappointments every day and your manager did not need to have his focus distracted by all the other stuff that was going on. I had to go with his style, and if I couldn't I should not have been there. In the event neither of us were there much longer. Man City thrashed us 5–2 in late October and in midweek we were beaten 3–0 in the League Cup by Notts County. We then beat West Ham 3–1 but the decision had been made and Ossie was sacked.

I thought they pulled the plug too soon. I'm convinced that Ossie would have got it right if he had had the normal level of support and been trusted to do his job and see it through. It wasn't a case of giving him everything he wanted, but the normal level of support and back-up. He never had it. He had to deal with too much crap. Any togetherness, any morale, was thrown out of the window.

There were seasons when Sir Alex Ferguson would win the title with the best team, make new signings the next season and have poor starts. That's how hard the Premiership is when you are all pulling together, when the man is *the* man, and everyone jumps when he says 'Jump!' Imagine how much harder it is when your club is not all pulling together. Ossie was trying to make things relaxed, but he had to cope with so much anguish behind the scenes.

When he got the sack he called a press conference, which is very unusual; he described the Spurs role as 'the impossible job', which it was. It left me still at the club but not knowing what my

A 'cutting' newspaper cutting: I said to the press, 'You will criticise our lack of imagination and flair the next time England don't qualify for a tournament – but you are part of the problem if you hound a man like Ossie out of his job.' The reporters simply shrugged their shoulders

Facing the press before the Blackburn game as I took the reins for the briefest of times

future was. In truth I was thinking it would not be such a bad thing if we had both been sacked at the same time.

Initially I was announced as caretaker manager. Sugar found me and said, 'So you're going to be caretaker? Because if not, I'll have to give it to Mabbutt or Klinsmann.' I said, 'I work for the club. You're the chairman of club. If you want me to do it, I'll do it.' I knew full well that if I said 'no' and walked there would be no pay-off.

I had one game at Blackburn away, which we lost 2–0. They were champions that year so it wasn't a surprising result. I took Dozzell off after about half an hour because he just kept falling over. I didn't know if he didn't have the right boots on or what, but I had one chance at this and wasn't going to hang about to see if players could stay on their feet.

I had also arranged a friendly at Reading to keep us on our toes – we were out of the League Cup and didn't have a League game for a fortnight – but got told in no uncertain terms by Claude that I would never fix up another game. My arrangements apparently weren't good enough, presumably due to how the gate money was allocated. The terms for what I could do were not made clear. I, of course, knew I had no power, but I wasn't bothered about upsetting Claude.

As for the players' reaction to Ossie's sacking, I would like to think they were very disappointed. But at the club at the time, who knew what was coming next? It was never going to be right the way that the environment was. The team was not going to progress as it could have, given the overall circumstances at the time, which I think was borne out by what happened after. That's not to say our results were better than anyone else's, but Spurs went through a number of managers – too many managers – and it's no surprise because, in my opinion, Sugar and the decision-makers listened to the wrong opinions.

I think he was swayed by reports in the press. I think the journalist Harry Harris was a major influence on whether the manager was doing the right thing or picking the right team, or making the right decisions. It's all

The one and only time I took charge as manager of Tottenham Hotspur – a historic day for me despite the result

right writing about it but get in that dressing room and do it. That's a whole different game. As some of the pundits on TV are finding out, you can be in football all your life and still mess up when you become a manager.

I think Sugar was being advised on things like signing players by people who did not really know enough about the game. That led to disagreements on who we should recruit. The problem was that I knew too much about football for the regime. I knew too much about the history of the club, how it should be run, how it was run and how it was successful. I had an opinion on every move that was made. If people had their opinion, we could have an argument about that, but I think their views were formed by the opinions of other people who were not proper football people.

A club cannot be run like that. Sugar had employed someone who was a world-class player to be his manager. That didn't by default mean that Ossie would be a world-class manager, but I was certain just how good he was. I can't say he was as good as Bill Nick or Keith Burkinshaw because results suggested otherwise. But my feeling was that he knew exactly what he was doing. If it had been backed up properly it could have worked.

Whether the environment was instigated by Sugar, or Claude was just doing it of his own accord, I don't know. In my playing days, Bill Nick made the decisions, but had a board to sanction them, the same as Keith. They had directors who would to listen to a football man doing the football job and making the football decisions. At Spurs at that time I felt that there was there was a general disrespect for our roles. Claude would bring guests into the dressing room to get programmes signed before a match. Fine but do it after the game. Everyone knows the dressing room is a sacred place before a match. One time Ossie was watching a reserve match at the training ground, an important part of his role as manager, and Claude insisted he stop and come inside for a meeting.

It all came to a head in those last few weeks. I had a sick feeling in my stomach every single day. I was getting angry, thinking that the club was being run like just another business, but that Tottenham wasn't just another business. It was my club. And I was spending the whole time worrying about how to shield Ossie from all the stuff that was going on behind the scenes so that he could do his job.

Staff at Spurs had worked long hours for years. At the height of the season 64-hour weeks were common and people would work late into the night. With Terry he would have let them take a day off as a trade-off. If their car broke down the club would repair or replace the car. There was care for the people who worked there. Instead it all went into reverse. Each department had to select staff to be laid off, which in turn meant the ones left had to make up the work.

Little but important things like taking lunch orders and bringing them to people's desks stopped. In my day club staff used to be invited to the Oak Room after games, where the atmosphere was magnificent, especially if we had won. It was like the *Mary Celeste* within a couple of weeks after passes were no longer issued to staff.

There was one incident when Ossie got so pissed off that in the end he said sod it, and we had a drink – not a piss-up – with nice people in the boardroom after a match when everyone else had left. We got a ticking-off the following week for leaving what was claimed to be half-full glasses of Scotch lying around. I think it was the waste of what they thought was expensive Scotch rather than the fact we hadn't cleared away that was the problem. The morale of the place was at the lowest ebb you could possibly imagine. I've been at Exeter, working for nothing, and with no money for the rest of the club, but morale was high. Because we were in it together, all grafting. We weren't all in it together at Spurs.

My time was up when Gerry Francis was appointed as Ossie's replacement. Gerry didn't want to keep me on, which was fine – 'one out, all out' was the usual course of events when a manager goes, and I wasn't expecting anything different. And when it did happen, I was delighted to walk away from that environment, although extremely sad to leave my club.

In 50 years of football, in all those years I have been in the game, the only person ever to have fired me is Alan Sugar. With the later success of *The Apprentice* this has become quite a claim to fame!

Neither was I expecting anything different regarding the rancour over the terms of my departure. I had a few weeks trying to sort a deal out. There is a normal percentage that you get paid up almost without argument. Whatever is left on your deal – a year, two years, etc – you get a percentage of.

Ossie used my solicitor, Charles, but in all fairness didn't really need to, because it was all clearly laid out what would happen in the event of him being dismissed. Then it was my turn. I went into Sugar's office the day I left, and he said, 'It will be all right.' I said, 'Just explain, "It will be all right."' Then he looked at me for the first time.

'What I said, it'll be all right.'

'Well, I'm going to go home and my lady is going to say to me, "Good day?" And I'll say, "Not really, no, I got the sack today." "Who sacked you?"

"In 50 years of football, the only person ever to have fired me is Alan Sugar. With the later success of The Apprentice this has become quite a claim to fame!"

"It got so bad that I didn't want Spurs to win a game while he was in charge. For Steve Perryman to feel that about Tottenham Hotspur... grim times"

"Mr Sugar. His last line was "Pack up your desk, get your stuff and it'll be all right.""

'So, when I tell her you said that, she's going to say, "What the hell does 'It'll be all right' mean?"'

We had a row, him telling me that his people and my people will have to sort it. He swore, shouting that I'd get my money.

'Well,' I said. 'That'll be all right.'

A letter arrived a few days later, offering me much less than what I believed I was entitled to. All the time the deal wasn't agreed, I was supposed to be still getting paid my monthly salary. The first month up, no money arrived. I knew Linda in accounts, so phoned her up to tell her I hadn't been paid. She said she knew.

So I went up there after another couple of weeks, to be told, 'We forgot.' The discussions carried on. A few days later I was with John Newman, who sorts out my pensions, sat in a pub in Brentwood talking about the situation. John said, 'Steve, I'd suggest you have to talk to Mr Sugar. Why don't you go over and see him?'

It was too funny. By complete chance we had decided to meet in Brentwood as it is near John's house and the pub we were in was directly opposite Amstrad's offices. I made the phone call and Sugar said, 'Give me half an hour', presumably so he could check out what was going on with my contract. I went into his office and it was showdown time. We had this almighty row at the top of his building. There was a lot of effing and blinding.

I argued my case and told him I thought he ran the club badly. There was a bit of effing and blinding in the middle of that as well. The office had lots of doors; people were coming along and closing them as our argument raged on. Then a lovely lady came in, saying, 'Steve, would you like a cup of tea?' 'Yes please, one sugar' – no pun intended. The lady went out and shut the door, then it was seconds out, round two. And then the lady came back in with the tea and coffee and we were all nice again. It was comical.

At one point I went to the lift and was pressing G. Sugar came out and pressed the button to keep the door open, insisting we get this sorted. I still went. Eventually, via the lawyers, we came to an agreement and I got what I was entitled to.

In the end I couldn't have been more delighted when I got paid up to go. Sad? I couldn't wait to get out of there, away from the decisions that were affecting everyone's lives. Maybe I wouldn't have felt it so strongly if I didn't love the club and the people, but I did. I went back because I loved it. Yet I could just see the club's reputation sliding out of the door. Any standing Tottenham Hotspur had with anyone was damaged.

It got so bad that I didn't want Spurs to win a game while he was in charge. For Steve Perryman to feel that about Tottenham Hotspur... grim times. The bottom line is because of that experience I fell out of love with football and Tottenham.

In the aftermath, I was out of work for about four months before a Norwegian friend of mine, Lars Ugland, got in touch. Lars was in shipping and had bought a box at Spurs when the new West Stand opened and had it for years but stopped during the Sugar period. Lars was involved with his local team in Norway, but was often in London and was a good contact between Norway and England. He made me aware of this job becoming available on a short-term contract at IK Start.

Their manager, Brede Skistad, had a form of leukaemia that they believed was going to get better, and therefore would I be interested in the short-term just for a change of scenery? I had a very positive view of Norway anyway, and Scandinavia in general due to having sports shops there. So that became the next step in my career.

I left England behind without any fuss or noise. The press were not really interested in what I had to say about what was going on at the club. I suppose from my point of view I thought it would have all sounded like sour grapes if I had dished the dirt. I hadn't signed anything on the pay-off with regard to keeping my mouth shut. But I don't think anyone would really have listened unless they were trying to create trouble for Sugar and Tottenham.

The general line was that Ossie's team couldn't defend and he deserved the sack, and Francis was the obvious candidate to replace him. I was amazed to hear that Gerry had doubts about joining and Sugar apparently said to him, 'Speak to someone like Steve Perryman, he'll tell you about me.'

Francis did well for a while but was one of seven managers during the Sugar years. The last was George Graham. George was no mug but my unspoken advice for him and any of the others was that you can't ask enough questions before you go in there. From a football perspective, he was worth employing, though his Arsenal connections were always going to count against him. But when I heard he got the job my thought was, 'Good luck to you, George. You're going to need it.'

**Time's up,
and time to go**

PERRYMAN-SAN

My stay at FC Start only lasted for six months or so, but it did feature one incident that resonates today. I phoned John Moncur, who was still at Spurs, asking for Stephen Carr and a Scottish international schoolboy, Gary Brady, on loan. John said he'd ask Gerry Francis, who in turn asked If I could be his 'eyes' in Norway on the lookout for talent.

I said, 'Actually I know a player, I've seen him on TV for Molde. This little striker scored one in a 3–1 defeat and two in a 4–2 win. Just the way he puts the ball in the net caught my eye.'

'What's his name?' asked John.

I couldn't pronounce it but said I'd send it over to him. The player in question was Ole Gunnar Solskjaer.

John went to watch him play and faxed me his scouting report. It said: 'I'm physically excited sat in my chair. I want to stand up and say to those around me, "Did you see what he just did?"' In big bold writing underneath the report, John wrote: 'Don't look again at this player – just sign him.'

Francis went to watch Ole play for Norway under-23s (with the manager in Wellington boots, Egil Olsen, in charge). Olsen played Solskjaer on the left of midfield in a 4–5–1 and he didn't get a touch. Gerry wanted a replacement for Nick Barmby but was cautious and offered £300,000, which was rejected. Man United got Solskjaer about a month later for around £1.5 million and the rest is history.

I came back to the UK with my new wife Kim and daughter Ella, who was just over five months old. There had been huge changes in my life. Cherrill and I had divorced, and Kim, Ella and I were in Norway together. Ossie, meanwhile, had been managing Guadalajara in Mexico. He'd asked me to join him out there, and my new family were all set to go but then Ossie got the sack, albeit with his team at the top of the league, after what I understood to be a falling out with the president. So instead he came home to Broxbourne in Hertfordshire, where he'd kept his house. He put Kim, Ella and me up over an enjoyable Christmas and New Year of 1995–96. While we were there the phone rang. It was Alf D'Arcy saying, 'Ossie, there's a job in Japan – fancy it?'

'Steebie. Do we want to go to Japan?'

'Too right we do, Os.'

What was being offered were the manager and assistant manager roles at Shimizu S-Pulse, a club based in the city of Shimizu, between Tokyo

"Japan completely restored my faith in football. It was another world. Pure respect from start to finish"

駐車場出口の為

進入禁止

エスパルスドリームプラザ

TELEPHONE

S-Pulse's official monthly magazine put Ossie and me on the front cover

Our lovely neighbour Mutsumi with our daughters Ella (left) and Jo (right)

and Nagoya. We had a job interview in the West End of London. S-Pulse's executives came well-prepared, gave us the big sell and told us that Shimizu was the best place to live in Japan. They knew our records, and asked me what I thought the reason might be that they had a lot of injuries the previous year. I'd never seen them play, but asked if they had a physical coach. They did and I was told he was Brazilian.

Their manager then was Japanese. I wondered how that worked in terms of training and who dictated it. My instinct was that the Brazilian guy did and therefore suggested to the people interviewing us that the players might be over-trained. It indeed transpired they had lots of stress fractures, caused by being over-trained – jumping on beams and things like that.

I was using my experience and judgement. Ossie talked about how he wanted to play – pass and move – and was very convincing because he absolutely believed in how he wanted his teams to play. We got the jobs and headed out there. Our wives, Ella and my stepchildren Ryan and Hollie joined us a few weeks later – and for the next five years we had the time of our lives.

Japan was an amazing experience, both in terms of work and life in general. It was a total contrast from Tottenham and England. We went from a place of intense pressure and a lack of support to a place where they couldn't do enough for us. It completely restored my love for and faith in football. Japan was another world. Pure respect from start to finish.

Not that it went particularly well at first. Adjusting to a completely new place, life and culture, and getting settled, was difficult. Ella was six months old when we went to Japan; Jo-Jo, our second child, was born there. They grew up effectively as Japanese kids and speaking the language fluently, which was great. But the first six months were horrendous. We thought about going home every single day because we were all packed into a small apartment with boxes that we couldn't unpack until we found a bigger, more permanent place.

Some time later we ended up in a home the size of a three-bedroom detached house but with five bedrooms squeezed in. There was a little park outside the front door. Life started to become normal. On our first day there, there was a knock on the door. A beautiful little seven-year-old girl stood outside. She looked down at a little book.

In slow, very deliberate English, she said quietly, 'You have children?'

'Yes, we do,' I said.

'We play?'

How lovely. Her name was Mutsumi and our girls still speak to her to this day.

Things took some getting used to. If we offered to take Mutsumi out for the day with us, it was not only her parents but her older brother who had to give permission – it is a very male-dominated society. The house has no status in Japan whatsoever. Houses only last 30 years, but we found it ingenious how everything was fitted into ours.

S-Pulse provided us with cars to choose from when we got the jobs. Ossie opted for a Lexus and I chose a Toyota people carrier. It was practical for my family's needs, but caused a bit of a stir with the players. A car is the status symbol in Japan, especially foreign cars. Anyone who owns a Japanese car is considered a bit odd!

S-Pulse was a new club, formed in 1993 when the J-League started, and the least powerful. It was owned by the community.

Most other clubs had been semi-pro, works-based teams – Hitachi and Mitsubishi sides for example. When the game turned professional, clubs weren't allowed to use the company in their name of the club, even if everyone knew it was owned by Kawasaki, Toyota and so on.

Football was already popular in Shimizu because of one man, Mr Hada, and his love for football. He promoted football in schools 10 years before anywhere else. The area in which Shimizu is, the prefecture of Shizuoka, thus became renowned for producing players – a third of the nation's players came from there. The J-League needed one more club to make up the initial 10, and there were no obvious candidates, but out of respect for the area's existing football culture they granted a license to enter a team. Shimizu is a port and does not really have a single big employer. In a way we were a test to see if a club could survive without having a big owner to sign the cheques and keep it solvent.

We had to stand on our own two feet. But nothing was done on the cheap, and we had, like all other J-League clubs (but at the time only three English Premier League clubs), a full-time doctor in Dr Shigeo Fukuoka, who became a good friend of ours. But S-Pulse were not as well-financed as other Japanese clubs and had to be innovative. For their training ground they researched AC Milan's training complex. Injured players riding bikes to regain fitness would be positioned so that they could see the training pitch and watch their teammates as an incentive to get fit – Spurs do something similar today under Pochettino, I hear.

There was a goalkeeper coach, a physical coach, excellent conditioning and an open mind as to how to treat injuries, be it with massage or acupuncture. I found common ground on a number of things. Every Japanese person loves a hot spring to relax. We didn't exactly have a hot spring on Tottenham High Road but I knew that having a good long soak

Signing autographs after training. You would find yourself signing things both on the way in and the way out – the fans were pretty passionate

"I told Ossie, 'We've got a chance here. The other managers are not necessarily picking their best teams – the owners are calling the shots'"

in the bath was beneficial. There was a positive ethical dimension as well. A focus on integrity, hard work and honesty chimed with what I'd been brought up with under Bill Nick at Spurs.

It was brilliant, but not in the beginning in terms of results. The players were very fit when we took over, but technically not quite right. They were enthusiastic, dedicated and intelligent. We couldn't find a problem with any of them in terms of attitude. But improvement was needed. S-Pulse had too many players, something like 50 pros. Ossie had to say to the owners, 'Half of your pros are never going to play in your first team. You're paying them for nothing: they've got to go.' That was unheard of in Japan where it is almost a job-for-life culture. S-Pulse was surely the only club in the country where the management advised them to stop spending money.

After six months we were called into a meeting to discuss what could be done. The club said to us, 'We know it's tough. What do you need?' Ossie was prepared, asking for a whole range of things to do with how we operated. It was all delivered on. We went on a training camp and from the minute we got back we just flew into the second half of the season.

We put certain specifics right. On a matchday there would be two men in suits in the dressing room just before the players went out for the warm-up. We found out they were reps from Puma who were taking orders from the players for Puma gear. That ended, sharpish. Oki-san, a lovely young man, was our 'shadow manager'. He took notes of every session, every meeting, everything we did with the players. It wasn't to spy on us. It was to ensure that everything they could learn from us about football was logged.

We worked the squad hard in training, bringing to bear all our experience and nous. Ossie was relentlessly positive, encouraging his players as ever to 'move the ball, play, play, pass, pass'. In a press conference he said, 'We are the quickest moving, quickest passing team in this country.' I said, to him afterwards, 'Ossie, we aren't.' 'Yeah, but we will be,' he said, 'and the players have got to read that we are.'

Japanese culture is based on hierarchy. They have a special name for the really senior manager in Japan, 'Kantoku'. If you're introduced to the 'Kantoku', you know you're talking to someone very high up. One time Ossie started a session. I was stood on the touchline, watching with Dr Fukuoka. He said, 'We like you two.'

'That's very kind of you,' I said. 'Why's that?'

'Because you pick the best team.'

'What other team is there?'

'Ah, the team that reflects the hierarchy' – meaning the system of social status in Japan, based on things such as age.

That was very revealing. I told Ossie, 'We've got a chance here. The other managers are not necessarily picking their best teams – the owners are calling the shots.'

Ossie did a huge job, improving a number of players so much that they got into the national team. Everyone was pulling in the same direction. *Issho ni* means 'together'. It is another big thing in Japan. Kids at school do an exercise with a large sheet of material. They stand in a circle, lifting the material up to form a dome of air. If everyone's not working together the air escapes, but when they are coordinated it works. That's their mentality: you achieve more by doing things together. But there is also the strict pecking order. Once, the club tried to split the first team and the rest of the squad on a Shinkansen high-speed train into first- and second-class. I insisted we all travelled together.

We saw the value of *issho ni* and brought our own fun element to it. Ossie made the club into a family. The players' wives were isolated and not included beforehand, so we had a karaoke night and barbecues and invited the wives along as well. The players were shocked but loved it. Ossie would have a laugh at the training ground, asking, 'Who is wearing the silliest tie?' The players pointed at Ryuzo Morioka. 'Ok, $10 fine. Now, let's start the team meeting...'

Changes were made to the team. Daniele Massaro, formerly of AC Milan, was in the squad. All the clubs had their big foreign stars – Totò Schillaci, Dunga and Paulo Futre were all there; Luiz Felipe 'Big Phil' Scolari was a manager – all to build the J-League profile. But we let our superstar go. Massaro was getting old and missing games. He said when he left that Ossie had had a Ferrari in the garage but never used it. Ossie replaced him with an Argentinian second-division player, Fernando Oliva, who we came to regard as the best player in Japan.

Toshihide Saito was magnificent for us and in our first year he was voted the best young player in the league. We had a lot of home-grown talent. We never had the money to go for the elite class – Leonardo played for Kashima Antlers in his mid-20s, for example. We could only attract players of a certain level but they were hungry to improve and learn from us.

The combination of a World Cup winner's positivity and my shop-floor approach blended beautifully. It was a fascinating merging of cultures – the

Ossie's first trophy in Japan, the equivalent of the English League Cup. The massive cheques we were presented with were a feature of Japanese competition. We beat Tokyo Verdy in the final, who were managed by Emerson Leão, S-Pulse's former manager

Japanese one of respect, a willingness to learn and the team ethic, Ossie's Latin culture and my Tottenham values and principles. If there was a Spurs influence in Japan it was from me. Unlike Ossie I was brought up from a very young age in the Spurs Way under Bill Nick, which I passed on but with my own stamp on it. I didn't get much praise when I was 17, but was keen to praise the youngsters I was coaching.

Years later I saw a TV programme in which one of the players, Katsumi Oenoki, who is now the general manager of S-Pulse, talked about us. He said, 'We trusted these two.' It was mutual – we passed on our knowledge of how to play better, and we trusted them to heed it and do it. They sucked the knowledge out of us. Again, it was cultural. Japanese people want to improve. In Japan, at 70 years of age it's common for people to learn a new language or take up a new instrument. In England I'll be slowing down at 70. No point in me playing the guitar now.

At Shimizu we had a Brazilian goalkeeping coach, Fuka, an Argentinian manager, an English assistant and a Japanese number three or 'shadow manager', all of us learning from each other's methods and cultures. For example, we learned from the Brazilian the importance of having a dentist: the thinking was that a bad tooth could contribute to causing an injury elsewhere, for example the hamstrings. It is a little difficult to explain but the rationale was that everything was connected, and a problem in one part of the body could have an impact elsewhere. It was League of Nations out there – Africans, South Americans, French, Dutch and Spanish who all brought their own influences. S-Pulse's influence had been Brazilian, as Rivelino was their second manager, following on from Emerson Leão. The South Americans would all hug each other. Ossie would be hugging people and then come away and say all sorts to me about what he really thought of them. Given the investment to grow the game, it was a bit of a gold rush for a lot of people who came over and there was all sorts going on. I spoke to a number two who had left a club and said that the manager who he was assistant to was a right bastard and took 10 per cent of his wages. I told Ossie this and he said, 'See? I was right about him. And how well do I treat you?!'

A night out with staff, players and families, something Ossie encouraged and which represented a big difference to other Japanese teams, who tended to keep families away from that kind of gathering (below); Ossie having fun with my stepson Ryan (below right)

At Tottenham, I wasn't round Ossie's house all the time, though I saw his and Ricky's children grow up. Ossie is godfather to Ella, and we've always been close, but we lived in each other's pockets in Japan. He and Silvia are very generous, amazing people and loyal friends, and we stuck together out there.

Ossie and I did feel like football missionaries. When we first arrived, we went to a meeting of all the J-League managers. I was included, so was there alongside the likes of Arsène Wenger, who became a vast influence on Japanese football. We were all in effect given a mission. Japan was due to co-host the 2002 World Cup with South Korea. At the meeting the organisers said, 'We know that you're going to do well for your club – you have to keep your jobs. But would you also think about improving Japanese players, so that we have some standing and chance in 2002?' Ossie and I treated that very seriously. We started off with no one in the national squad and ended up, when I left five years later, with six or more representing Japan.

When I see Japan play in World Cups and do well, I am so proud. I don't know any of the players because it's too long since I was working there, but I'll bet some of the ideas and methods that Ossie and I introduced are still being used. We signed a kid, Yoshikiyo Kuboyama, from Yokohama Flügels but I had to tell him after three days that he wouldn't make it with us. I'd told him every day about being on his toes but he didn't listen – at least at first. But he knuckled down and came through. He's still there at the club today, teaching the kids, and probably saying the same things to them as I did then. There's a little corner of Japanese football that is Tottenham Hotspur.

The reason why I stayed longer is because I took over from Ossie. We won the J-League Cup in 1996, S-Pulse's first major honour, beating Leão's new team Tokyo Verdy, but after three years Ossie decided to go and manage in Croatia. I think he saw some signs of decline with injuries and players leaving, yet advised me to take over. My contract offer was not great, and I declined. Dr Fukuoka talked me around, emphasising what a good chance this was for me. I was thankful because I enjoyed real success as manager.

Ossie used Spanish in meetings via a translator who knew enough English to be my interpreter by the time I took over. Six of the players had been learning English as well, so there were no real communication issues. My method was to provide continuity from Ossie's time as manager but with my own flavour. I was more regimented about organising the defence at corners, for example. I passed on the things I'd learned in England. Phil Holder told me he'd had a training session with Terry Venables in which Venners said, 'Never run straight on a football pitch with the ball, because you can't turn away. If you run at an angle, you can always turn or have an option. So I told Saito, who joined us from university, 'Don't run straight: you'll get closed down. Go at a 45-degree angle because it gives you more options.'

It just came naturally to think that way. When I was taking my coaching badges with the FA, Robbie Stepney said, 'Steve, you already know it. You don't have to read it in the book: it will come to you. Within training sessions you'll add so much more than what's in the book.'

Getting my message over to the fans via the manager's page in the programme (top) and a fan card used for autographs, supplied by the club for events in the community and other functions (above)

How do you translate 'ooo!'? Eduardo Hanyu (left) held a very important position at S-Pulse as translator. He was the bridge between management and players. He started off as Ossie's Spanish translator but used English when I took over

In Japan I would never allow a midfield player to come back to be goalside of the opponents' strikers if our defenders were already goalside. It would mean we had too many of our players behind the ball. They loved that kind of thinking and explanation in Japan. The lady who translated my programme notes said to me she was told, 'You must be so clever to ask Perryman-san' – 'San' translates as something close to 'Mr' – 'such good questions to get him to write such good notes.' She replied, 'I don't ask questions: he just talks!' I didn't control everything. Players would be signed by the club for the manager. In 1999 Sotaro Yasunaga, a local lad, was brought in to play up front. I relied on the frontmen to be the engine of the train, like Garth and Archie had been at Spurs, but 'Yasu' struggled. I said to him, 'Yasu, this is a difficult question but we're trying to nail down what you think of your game, how you see yourself on the pitch and your role. So to give me a clue: describe your game, your personality, as if it was a car.'

The Japanese are obsessed with cars as status symbols. Yasu said 'Porsche, Perryman-san'. He looked at me as if I was mad but we talked about the kind of qualities his 'car' had. I told him, 'You're not a Porsche; the car

I want you to be is a Volvo Estate – solid, reliable, the driving engine of our team.' Yasu still looked at me as if I was mad, but guess what: he improved.

We went from strength-to-strength, culminating in a remarkable season in 1999. The J-League was organised in two halves, so that in effect there were two championships, with a deciding play-off if there were two individual winners. The rationale was that fans and viewers would switch off if their team was struggling over a single, continuous season, but would maintain interest if at the halfway point the league was reset.

In the 1999 First Stage we finished third, four points behind the winners Jubilo Iwata. These were our big local rivals in Shizuoka. They were effectively owned by Yamaha – their stadium was in the middle of the factory complex.

In the First Stage home game against Jubilo in April, we had felt cheated. They were winning 4–1 with five minutes to go and we pulled one back. It stemmed from my instruction to our strikers to follow a shot or a cross in case of a rebound – just like I'd learned at Spurs, just like Garth Crooks did at Anfield in 1985. Our centre-forward hurried to get the ball back to the centre spot so the game could restart quickly but was pinned in the net by their centre-halves trying to waste time. They manhandled him. Our supporters in a sell-out crowd went mad. The ref eventually sorted the melee out but then sent off our centre-forward and only gave yellows to Jubilo's defenders.

I was fuming, even more so after – via a translator – I heard the Jubilo manager say in his press conference, 'This is a great day for Jubilo; this is a great day for Japanese football because of the quality of our play.' There were no questions, no challenges to what he said. It was explained to me that specialists were not favoured in Japanese society, so the journalists in the press conference could have been covering golf one year, football the next; they rarely asked pressing questions and just wrote up what was said.

My turn in the press conference. I let rip, 'This is a very sad day for Japanese football. I now realise the J-League stands for "Jubilo League". If this is how to win the championship, I don't want it.' I expanded on this, talking about the red card, challenging the journos to explain why our man was sent off. They couldn't answer. I talked about the integrity of the Japanese game being betrayed. It was dynamite stuff.

Eventually I was asked a question. 'You said you don't want the championship if that is how it is won. What if your supporters do want that championship?' 'Great question,' I replied, 'In that case I'm not the man to manage their team.' What a great line for a journalist. In England it would have been headline news, but in the papers the next day – nothing. We had a follow-up press conference the day after the match, and I got someone to clear away all the chairs and tables and just lay out all the newspaper reports of the game on the floor. There was next to no coverage of what I had said the day before. I said to the hacks, 'Just explain to me why what I said was not more reported.' One chap eventually said, 'Jubilo... very powerful.'

That said it all. In the Second Stage we answered in the best possible way by winning it and in style with 12 wins out of 15 games. Yasu scored the goal in the penultimate game that won us the championship against his old team Yokohama F. Marinos. For the last game of the regular season I substituted him and another player with 20 minutes to go. They came off without

> "I told him, 'You're not a Porsche; the car I want you to be is a Volvo Estate – solid, reliable, the driving engine of our team'"

Perryman, our man in Japan

Football
By Ken Dyer

STEVE PERRYMAN'S advice, for all those England fans intent on supporting their team in Japan and South Korea next summer, is to start saving up now. Perryman has been involved in coaching and management in Japan for the past two years, first with Shimizu S-Pulse and now Kashiwa Reysol, the club linked to electronic giants Hitachi and based about a 40-minute fast train ride from Tokyo.

He says: "Tube culture in Japan is based on quality and service but you pay for that.

"My brother is coming over here to see me in a couple of weeks and I want to take him on the train to Hiroshima. It's about a four hour journey and it costs £200 in the Green Car, which is the Japanese equivalent to first class.

"The big difference is that the trains always run on time. They don't even stop for earthquakes unless they have to.

"When I was last back in England I went through Reading station once and there were a group of Japanese tourists taking photos of the information board with all the delays listed on it. They couldn't believe it."

Perryman, the former Brentford and Watford manager, has been in charge of his new club for three months after spending the previous five seasons with S-Pulse, talking them to their first league title in 1999.

"We've started the season okay, winning two, drawing three and losing two.

"With my family back in England, I'm tending to live, breathe and sleep football. If I'm not at the training ground, I'm sitting at home on my own, thinking about the next game."

Perryman watched England's 2-2 draw against Greece on a friend's TV and is as pleased as anyone that the top-point achieved at Old Trafford ensures their presence in the finals next summer.

"I hope England are drawn somewhere in Japan but I keep hearing rumours that they are going to end up in South Korea," he says.

"I've been to Seoul once when I took S-Pulse to play a team called LG Cheetahs and I have to say I was disappointed. The stadium was poor, the pitch terrible and the crowd tiny. I'm sure it has improved since then though."

There have been obvious worries about the debilitating effects of high humidity levels in Japan during the tournament and Perryman would not wish to minimise these concerns.

"It depends to a large extent where you are drawn," he says. "If your base is in the north, on the island of Hokkaido, the England would have little worries. I believe it's on a similar latitude to Great Britain. It snows in the winter and the houses have central heating.

"Go south, however, to Osaka and it's tropical, the kind of climate where you need five showers a day.

"Some of the South American and African countries will be okay but the English players will find it tough if they are down there.

"I'm not all that keen on sunshine anyway and, as a player, I was always useless in August until the temperature dropped and the rain began to fall. You do become desperate to get out of the heat and go somewhere with air-conditioning.

"The problem is the constant change of temperature isn't always good for you either and I know of some American people who went back home because they were constantly catching colds.

"It's obviously important to do your homework thoroughly and Italy may have stolen a march on the rest because I see they're coming over here to play a friendly in Saitamah next month."

The Japanese, according to Perryman, are avid readers and would be aware that England have qualified.

"Ask a Japanese football fan about English football, though, and he will say, 'Manchester United'. If a magazine puts a picture of David Beckham on its front cover, it sells out," he says.

Perryman, however, does see a potential problem with some of the World Cup venues.

"I'm sure the stadia will be top class but some of them are a bit out of the way. There are no World Cup venues, for example, in either Tokyo or Hiroshima," he says.

"It's no good looking for a policeman, either, to ask directions. You hardly ever see one and petty crime is almost non-existent."

Perryman, despite his long and distinguished career, has never been to a World Cup.

"I would love to see some games, if I could," he says. "It's early days yet but the build-up has already started.

"I was walking down a side road here the other day and there, in the window of a little shop, was a colour poster of Michael Owen. I wonder if the kid knows his fame has spread this far."

Steve Perryman celebrates leading Japanese side Shimizu S-Pulse to their first league title

Celebrating S-Pulse's title win. To put our achievement into context, the closest equivalent I can think of is Leicester City winning the Premier League in 2015–16

complaint and smiled at me. I put on a centre-midfielder
and made some other changes and Yasu's look changed
to, 'What the hell is he doing?' The sub then scored from
the edge of the box. Yasu looked at me again as if to say,
'OK, Perryman-san, you might be right.' Jubilo had
fallen away in the Second Stage, and if the points from
the two stages had been added together we would have
been 16 points ahead of them. But in the play-off, Jubilo
won on penalties after we each won our home leg 2–1.
Everything went for them – a dodgy penalty in the
first game, and a sending off for our striker Alesandro
Santos, or 'Alex', after 10 minutes for retaliation.

Dunga was captain of Jubilo and ruled the roost, to
the extent that he effectively controlled the referees. At
the managers' meeting before the start of the next season
it was announced, 'Any dissent – yellow card'. I put my
hand up and said, 'Even for an ex-Brazilian World Cup-winning captain?'

I gave our players instructions on how to handle Dunga. 'Get close. He's
got to hear your breath, hear your feet; you gotta hunt him because he's
Dunga, and eventually he will actually respect you for it.' It was just like
Eddie Baily told me all those years before. I would tell Dunga to 'fuck off'
from the touchline when he was trying to run the show. Dunga came to
Exeter in 2004 to play in a special match commemorating Exeter's visit to
Brazil in 1914 and being the first team to play their national side. I was on
holiday, so sent a note with my kind regards. I was told he read it, raised an
eyebrow and said, 'Ah, Perryman...'

I had managed a team that had won a championship (the Second Stage
title), and was announced as Manager of the Year, receiving a Rolex that
I've never worn. Alex won Player of the Year and got a Saab convertible. Six
of our players were in the Team of the Year – Alex, Sanada, Nobori, Saito,
Morioka and Carlos Santos. We also won the Asian Cup Winners' Cup in
2000 in Thailand; we'd lost the cup final in Japan but qualified for the Asian
Cup as the team we lost to, Flügels, disbanded. The important thing for me
was that I proved I could succeed in management. It was a way of saying,
'Up yours' to any doubters and critics, the people who didn't want either
me or Ossie to work for their club. Wenger did not win what we won in
Japan, despite having the power of Toyota behind him, but then he came to
England and won the Double.

Although he didn't win the championship with us, it was
virtually Ossie's team that won it. He was there on the day
that we won the title and everyone thought it was to support
us. Instead it was to have an interview with Yokohama, who
would be appointing a new manager if they got beaten!

I certainly don't thank Ossie for taking me back to
Tottenham. But if that hadn't happened we wouldn't have
gone to Japan.

Japan was an adventure from start to finish. I couldn't wait
to get my family over, though my mum and dad weren't able to
come. My dad died while I was working out there, and the way
it was all handled was exceptional. On the flight home I was in
business class on JAL and they made sure I was in a quiet place
away from other passengers and left alone. When the tsunami hit

Clippings from coverage of our contentious play-off defeat against Jubilo

My dad, pictured here with my daughter Loren. He sadly never made it out to Japan as he passed away while I was working out there

Life in Japan: With my wife Kim (above); Ella and friends at a game with Oki-san's family (below left); a newspaper interview about our time in Japan (below right). Going there was one of the best decisions I ever made

in 2011 I was naturally very sad for them, but I knew if ever there's a people that can recover from a disaster like that, it's the Japanese.

On reflection I made a big mistake in leaving Japan after five years. I had that team right in my palm. I went back to Kashiwa Reysol for a season in 2001, but as a family we wanted to settle in England, for the girls' long-term education and for a few other things like healthcare, which was good but could be very rigid and prescriptive in Japan.

The school the girls went to in Japan was amazing. We went back for a visit in 2016, and the headmistress was still there. They were very proud of Ella and Jo-Jo, and their photo is still on the wall at the school. The kids had manners lessons, which tells you a lot about that country. If you judge a country by how it treats its old people then Japan must be one of the best places in the world, as the elderly are revered, respected and listened to.

We were not old but we were respected. We went to Kim's favourite department store once in Shimizu, where we were treated so well. An old lady walked towards us and spoke to me – 'Perryman-san...' and the rest I couldn't understand. Ella said, 'Dad, the old lady is saying, "Surely this is our year to win the championship. I support you strongly; I wish you good luck. Please keep fighting for our city and our team, and we believe in you."' Wonderful, and I was so proud that my little daughter of just five years of age could speak Japanese. Kim learned it as well in 18 months. Me? Not so good.

When we came home to live in Gerrards Cross, the first place we headed for was a chippy in Slough that served fish and chips to die for. It must have been happy hour for pensioners as it was packed to the rafters with old people and there was just one table spare for us in the middle.

All the OAPs were looking at the girls, going, 'Ah, how sweet'. Kim put some colouring books on the table and the girls started disagreeing over who had which pencil. All of a sudden, they started raging at each other in Japanese. The whole place stopped silent at the sight of these blue-eyed, rosy-cheeked, blonde-haired girls arguing in the most aggressive-sounding language you've ever heard in your life.

I stood up and said, 'Er, yes, we lived in Japan.'

CUP TRAIL: Perryman, his wife Sue and their daughters enjoy tea-time   Pictures: MATTHEW ASHTON

so big in Japan

Various football shirts and S-Pulse merchandise that I collected during my Japanese adventure: an S-Pulse sweatshirt (right), an S-Pulse jersey signed by the squad (bottom left), a signed Japan national team jersey (centre) and a Reysol jersey (right)

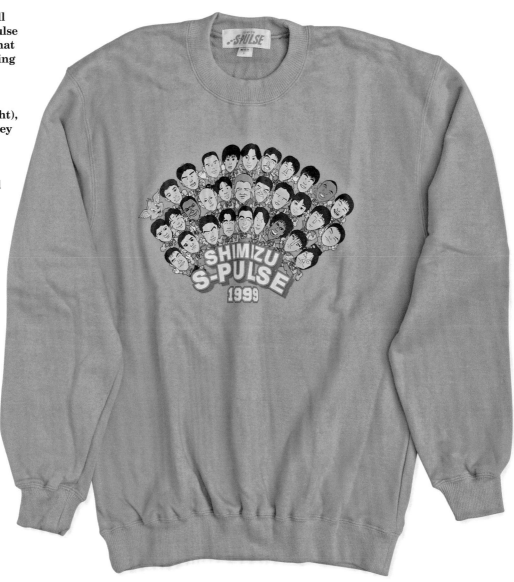

CHAPTER TWENTY

GO WEST

Japan restored me. I'd lost almost everything financially to divorce but went to the Far East, got back onto a sound footing and returned with my confidence high. The next phase of my career was to last 18 years. I'd never have believed you if you told me that was going to happen, but it took my life in a new direction. And once again it was my Spurs upbringing that had a big part in how it played out.

In between seasons in Japan, I did some work at Exeter City. I'd come back in 2001 and I soon got a phone call from Joe Gadston, a nice guy I knew from his time as a youth-team coach at Brentford and who'd played for Exeter in the early 1970s. He asked if I would come down to Devon and help out. Joe had put money into the club, which was floundering on a run of three wins out of 30 and heading for the Conference. I reminded Joe I'd been away for five years and out of the English game, but he was insistent that I provide help to City's player/manager, Noel Blake.

I didn't want to tread on Noel's toes and said I'd only help with his agreement. So I went down and met him. He had made a lot of changes to the team and there was a lack of continuity. I only knew two players – Paul Buckle, who had been a YTS trainee with me at Brentford, and Alex Inglethorpe, who had been my reserve-team centre-forward at Watford and who later did excellent coaching work at Spurs and then Liverpool.

I was clear and honest with Noel. I had learned from a young age at Spurs that Bill Nick's straightforward approach was best. The situation put Noel in a bind. If results improved it would be me who got the credit, even if it wasn't merited. But despite that unfairness he accepted the terms of working together that I proposed. I insisted that all I was offering was an opinion and Noel could take it or leave it.

We looked at the squad together and talked about picking a consistent team and playing a 4–4–2 formation, selecting players Noel trusted. I would come down for a couple of days midweek and go to as many games as I could, giving my advice, and all of it unpaid. Word soon got around. Keith Burkinshaw phoned to say, 'Don't do it – it'll make you look desperate.' I was anything but after the rewarding time I'd had in Japan. I ran into Eddie Baily, who said, 'I hear you're working for nothing – what's that all about?' Kim thought I was mad – we were putting two girls through private education.

I saw their points, but financially I was OK and I knew Exeter didn't have any money in any case. I said to the then-owners, 'You're going to find

> "The next phase of my career was to last 18 years. I'd never have believed you if you told me that was going to happen, but it took my life in a new direction"

Eammon Dolan, the first manager appointed by the Supporters' Trust, the new owners of Exeter City, and a great man. Appointing him was an excellent decision

this very strange, and I can't imagine you're going to argue but I don't want paying. Just cover my expenses.' Unsurprisingly they agreed. A friend of mine reckons my work with Exeter has cost me over £2 million in potential lost earnings. I can live with that, but not having my time wasted.

The first game I went to was a local derby at Torquay. I met Julian Tagg, a Spurs fan who was on the Exeter board and later became chairman and a good friend. Exeter's captain was sent off after 10 minutes; they went a goal down and seemed to spend the rest of the half arguing with the referee. I was asked to speak to the players at half-time so I went down and said, 'Stop fighting with the referee. You're not going to change his decisions: he's only going to get worse if you continue rowing with him. Concentrate on playing football. Hopefully I will be working with you in the future – so show me what you can do.'

It was an echo of Peter Shreeve's request to the Watford players when he was my assistant. 'I don't care if you get beat 5–0,' I continued. 'Just try and play.'

In the second half they were transformed with 10 men, equalised and should have won 4–1, but conceded the latest of late goals. But there had been such an improvement.

Results picked up. After one game Noel asked me to do a radio interview. That went fine so Noel then asked if I'd do another interview, this time for BBC Radio 5 Live, an hour before our home game against Carlisle, who were near the top, kicked off. I had made it clear to the media that I was not Exeter manager and didn't want to be Exeter manager. The first thing the 5 Live interviewer said was, 'So, Steve you're going to be the next Exeter manager…'

Live on national radio I said, 'Right, hold on one fucking minute. I'll tell you about people like you – great at asking questions, useless listening to the answers. So do yourself a favour and listen to this answer; I will never manage Exeter City. I've just been Manager of the Year in Japan. No disrespect to Exeter but why would I want to manage Exeter and take someone's job?' Cue panic on the other end of the line but the interviewer deserved it. I was so distraught at the questions, having done everything entirely the right way in making it clear I wouldn't take the job. I said I wouldn't continue the interview and I didn't.

Exeter rallied and stayed up, and by some margin. As far as I was concerned that was job done, a job well-received by the fans and people at the club. I went back to Japan but in the meantime Noel lost his way and eventually got the sack in September 2001. The club went from bad to worse, suffering relegation to the Conference in 2003 and going into severe debt, with the former directors convicted of fraudulent trading. The supporters formed a trust and rescued the club, putting in a tremendous effort, and appointed the youth coach, Eamonn Dolan, as manager.

Eamonn was a wonderful man whose playing career – and in 2016, his life – was cruelly cut short by cancer. He was at St James Park for 13 years doing everything – player, community coach, youth coach, caretaker manager. During my initial stint in Devon in 2001, I'd be at a loose end in the evening and Eamonn would invite me out for a steak. 'I'm not wasting this opportunity to speak to you, Steve, and pick your brains.'

So we'd go and have a meal and a couple of beers, and talk about football – Japan, my life at Spurs, Bill Nick and all sorts. We built a rapport, so that when Eamonn was offered the manager's job permanently, he said he wouldn't take the job unless I helped him, as I'd helped Noel.

The repercussions of going down hit Exeter hard. They lost their basic Football League share of £400,000 that every club received, and the Centre of Excellence was vulnerable as Exeter were now outside the protection of Football League regulations – any club could now come and take a schoolboy player for nothing.

Exeter's strengths lay in Eamonn and the Supporters' Trust. I bought into it and agreed to help out again, still unpaid, just getting expenses, and my family moved down to Devon. Everyone assumed we did so because of the Exeter job but it was more for the lifestyle in a very beautiful part of the world that we'd grown to love. I picked up the paper soon after to read that I'd been made 'director of football', which was news to me. The club had assumed I wanted the title but I had serious doubts and said no – it suggested all kinds of intrigue and power struggles behind the scenes.

Right from the off I was firefighting. The club had been called before the FA for its disciplinary problems and faced the activation of a suspended fine of £25,000 due to their repeated high numbers of red and yellow cards. If any club did not need that kind of problem, it was Exeter.

I went to the FA hearing with Julian. The board then was formed of seven directors – executives, lawyers and the like – and one trust representative, with a separate trust board. The ratio now is three trust members to five directors, which I think is risky – a club needs expert leadership from outside the fanbase. Julian's background was in teaching sports and he worked at the club's Centre of Excellence. I have seen at close-hand the effort he has put in down the years, even though he hasn't got the praise he deserves from some supporters who seem to be forever suspicious about his motives.

On the train to London for the hearing we were delayed by cows on the line. We finally arrived to meet Barry Bright from the Kent FA – Mr Glum, the type I thought would love to teach us a lesson. We got down to it and, using my experience of standing up to the authorities, said our discipline would improve. When Bright asked how, I cited that under my management, S-Pulse had the best disciplinary record in Japan.

'Oh. So that's gonna work here, is it?' said Bright, dismissively.

I bit back. Julian had the look of someone thinking, 'Oh, no…'

I challenged Bright and pointed out that the suspended fine hadn't worked as punishment. I said to him, 'And you're now questioning whether I'm gonna do something that works? Just let it ride and see if I can do something that does work.'

The hearing decided on fining us a reduced and suspended £12,500. When Eamonn invited me in to meet the players in pre-season I put it straight to them. 'I talked the FA out of us having to pay a fine. If we'd had to, you wouldn't have got paid. So I think there's a lesson here somewhere. The one thing I'm not going to allow this club to do is give money to that poxy FA for red and yellow cards. I'm not going to be embarrassed by your lack of discipline. It is not going to happen. So if I say, "Don't kick the ball away and get booked", don't kick the ball away.'

The following season if we'd been in the league we would have been ranked 19th out of the 92 for discipline based on dismissals and cautions, having been 91st. And Barry Bright never did get back to me to say I was right – my proposal did work.

For another four years I worked at Exeter for nothing. They didn't have any money so it was no good expecting any. Eamonn left to take up the role of academy manager at Reading, with Alex Inglethorpe taking over, before

"For another four years I worked at Exeter for nothing. They didn't have any money so it was no good expecting any"

he in turn went to Spurs and Paul Tisdale replaced him in 2006. 'Tis' has been another of those individuals who has had such a strong influence on me, and I on him. He is a highly innovative manager – intelligent, with terrific ideas and methods. He understands the mentality of players – he'll say to young pros, 'You've got the pretty girlfriend, the tattoos, the nice car. But what haven't you got? A career. Get a career first, then the lifestyle.'

We feed off each other, and the contrasts between us work. Paul says that when he watches football he's focusing on where spaces are. I watch it from a point of view of the individual combat, a legacy of Bill Nick and Eddie's mantra about winning personal battles.

Tis and I worked highly productively together for 12 essentially successful years. We had clear lines of responsibility – him as manager of the team, me overseeing football operations at the club. The team manager is entitled to pick the team to get results and improve; it's the 'DoF''s job to have an opinion about that and be honest. I would advise on whether we should or should not buy a player, providing a view to the board. The DoF is the link between manager and the board who makes sure the football side gets what it needs. I saw my role as very much about football – I hated board meetings if I'm honest.

We restored Exeter's fortunes on and off the pitch. We won promotions and got to League One, and despite reversals and relegations, the club is in a far healthier state from top to bottom. When I first went there, it had little standing and no credibility. I did what I could to help and put the Grecians back on the football map. I helped give them a standing with the rest of football.

An example came when we drew Manchester United at Old Trafford in the third round of the FA Cup in 2005 when we were still in the Conference. We already had a good relationship with United as they were big admirers

Back on the big FA Cup stage, prior to Exeter's plum game against Manchester United. Then manager Alex Inglethorpe, now at Liverpool, is second from right, with managing director Ian Huxham on Alex's left and player/assistant manager Scott Hiley on his right

Exeter's name
up in the Old
Trafford lights

of Eamonn's youth set-up, rating it as the best in the South-West, and their coaches gave demonstrations to our staff and met our players and their parents. Around the cup game, United were first-class from start to finish, liaising with us on everything, making sure the players could exchange shirts, and that all our families were welcomed and treated well.

Everything was totally professional. It had the stamp of Sir Alex Ferguson all over it, just as with Bill Nick at Tottenham – attention to detail and a culture of excellence. I was told that Fergie hand-picked all the staff and it showed. I reciprocated with how I ensured we conducted ourselves. I told our players that regardless of the result not to say one word to anyone about Manchester United unless it was something positive. I made sure we communicated well with United's staff and showed respect at all times.

I sat upstairs in the directors' box for the match, and my wife and kids came too. I'd met Bobby Charlton and his wife at a British Embassy function in Japan once and they took an interest in our girls growing up in Japan. At Old Trafford it felt like Bobby and his wife couldn't wait to see the girls and they treated them so well. We also all saw Sir Alex after the game and had a lovely photo taken with him. My advice to our players was not to end up looking like mugs. United put out a very good second-string that included Wes Brown, Phil Neville and Gerard Pique. With 20 minutes to go and still 0–0 they put on Ronaldo, Scholes and Alan Smith. But they still couldn't break us down. There were 10,000 Exeter fans out of a crowd of 67,000 people, roaring away, and some of them were still in Manchester days later.

Kwame Ampadu, father of Chelsea's Ethan, had been injured and was on the bench. In his place was Danny Clay, home-grown and all heart but liable to give a silly foul away and give the opposition a chance, from the spot or a free-kick. Sure enough he did give a cheap free-kick away but it went over the bar. I switched into manager mode and rang down to Alex Inglethorpe in the dugout, something I hardly ever did, as I wanted to let the manager manage. We agreed to leave the team as it was but then Danny gave away another free kick. I rang again and said, 'Get Danny off and Kwame on quick!'

Alex did so and we saw out a famous 0–0 draw. It was an unbelievable day, and we'd got a replay. In the car park afterwards we were waiting to head off in the coach when a car drove up and stopped. United's Alan Smith got out, jumped on our bus and said, 'Well done chaps, see you next week and have a good journey.' It was so classy.

Alex said that a couple days later at our training ground that there was a United swap shirt left on the table – none of our players had picked it up so Alex in the end took it home. It was Pique's, now one of the most trophied players in the world but back then none of our Conference players fancied having it.

OWN PART OF A CLUB ON THE UP

JOIN THE TRUST TODAY

- FIRST TEAM CHALLENGING FOR PROMOTION TO LEAGUE ONE
- TOP OF THE PREMIER LEAGUE U23s CUP (THE ONLY SIDE BELOW THE CHAMPIONSHIP TO BE TOP)
- U18s SOUTH WEST ALLIANCE LEAGUE CHAMPIONS 2 YEARS RUNNING
- SUCCESFUL LADIES TEAM & GIRLS DEVELOPMENT CENTRE
- CLUB FINANCES SECURE
- TWO NEW STANDS UNDER CONSTRUCTION
- BUILT STATE OF THE ART 3G PITCH
- FURTHER DEVELOPMENT PLANS FOR TRAINING GROUND

THE TRUST

Facing page: Me and Paul Tisdale on a chilly Anfield touchline in January 2016. We'd held them to 2–2 at our place but lost the replay 3–0. But what an amazing experience and a sign of how far Exeter has come as a club

We lost the replay 2–0 live on telly; despite us having a goal given offside. It was so good for Exeter. Our total earnings from the tie were about £1 million, which essentially saved the club. I made sure we welcomed United right, that there were no slip-ups such as letting TV crews to get near the dressing rooms. United were already prepared, bringing security with them: nice fellas albeit proper lumps. But I'm sure United respected us for being professional. Sir Alex said to our Alex afterwards, 'Hey, your team's fit. We have the GPS track opposition sides and your team ran further than any team against us in the last seven years.' A lot of that was chasing the ball but it was an indication that we were a serious, professional club again.

It was all about doing things right and well, lessons I'd learned decades ago at Spurs. Whether it's a five-yard pass, a throw-in or even making a cup of tea, do it right and mean it. Maintain standards. Tottenham gave me integrity and standards which I took with me wherever I went.

After four years, Exeter insisted that my unpaid status couldn't carry on and they were putting me on the payroll as director of football. The club couldn't have done that without the huge amounts of hard work by Tis, by all the managers, Julian, myself, the players, the Supporters' Trust and the board.

I'm one of the very few people who have been involved at all levels of this game. I was involved as vice-president at West London's non-league Yeading with my brothers around the early 2000s and I had some involvement at Yeading from when I was a young player at Spurs. I arranged for Alan Gilzean to present some trophies, and the club were customers of my sports shop. The people who ran Yeading were virtually all Spurs fans. They made me vice-president, and the club put the place on the map.

Some years later I helped Yeading negotiate when they sold Andrew Impey to QPR. It's about financial survival. When Exeter were carrying £4.5 million of debt, Torquay offered to play a pre-season game, with Exeter retaining all the gate receipts. Years later when Torquay were in trouble, Julian wanted to repay the favour. The local paper published a letter from an Exeter fan saying, 'How dare you allow that? We should take a fee. What next – Steve Perryman working for Yeading?' I was incensed. It was at the time I worked for nothing at Exeter. It reflected such small-mindedness about the harsh economic realities of football.

It's a tough game that exacts a physical toll even on those not playing. I had been pretty fortunate with my fitness and health, though I'd had a heart murmur as a kid and I contracted septicaemia in 2010. I'd been to Bergen, tripped over in the hotel room and hurt my hip. Coming back on the plane I felt very ill and was taken to hospital and was diagnosed with a deep vein thrombosis. A day later, just by chance, I took my daughter to hospital for an appointment and a doctor said I wasn't looking well. Septicaemia was diagnosed and I was in hospital for six weeks.

But overall I was in good shape. Dave Mackay was renowned for having a very low heartbeat at rest, a sign of peak fitness. My heart-rate was pretty much the same as Dave's. As a player I was strong in the legs, but also in my heart. Little was I to know then how vital that would be, and means that I'm still here today to tell the story of what happened on 5th May 2012.

It was the last game of the 2011–12 season, home to Sheffield United. We'd already been relegated so I was feeling no stress watching the game. I'd been at home on my own from Friday night, so I'm lucky that what happened did so at the ground, rather than in my house with no one around. During the game

Tis and me at the Charity Shield being presented with the Fair Play award

I had a bad feeling in my chest. I tried to get up to tell one of our staff, Andy Tilson, who was a couple of rows in front of me and I just collapsed.

I was still awake. The pain was intense, so I thought I must be having a heart attack. People rushed to look after me. Andy ran down along the side of the pitch to get the doctor, Peter Riou. He took over and I was put in a wheelchair by St John Ambulance volunteers, taken down the steps and eventually put into an ambulance.

Ella was at the game, about 15 rows in front of me when this all happened. She turned around on hearing the commotion and then saw it was me being wheeled out. She rushed up and I remember kissing her. Ella heard the kit lady, Lou, say, 'I wonder if that's the last time she'll see him?'

I can't remember anything of what happened next. I am told I was rushed to hospital in Exeter, where they did some scans and decided to rush me by air ambulance to Plymouth, where specialists Dr Riou had contacted personally were on standby. I had a seven-hour operation and was in an induced coma for three weeks. The doctors were doubtful that I was going to come out of the coma.

I was lucky to even be in that condition. I had suffered a Type A aortic dissection. The aorta is the biggest artery in the body, supplying blood from the heart to the rest of the body and to the heart itself. And it had split. There is a test to check the health of the aorta at 65, so for anyone reading this, when you get to 65 please have this test done. I don't know the exact technicalities but it's something to do with the gap in the aorta being too wide or too small. It's easy to put right with quite a simple procedure, but if it's left uncorrected and it blows you're in trouble. It's like leaving a hose outside all winter: it perishes and eventually cracks.

The stats for anyone suffering what happened to me are stark: only 40 per cent of people make it alive to hospital. If they survive the surgery, the first 24 hours are absolutely crucial. It was pure luck that due to being at a football match, with Dr Riou, paramedics and an ambulance on the scene, I was looked after straight away.

The doctors weren't sure I was going to come round. The day after I was operated on, they said to Kim, 'He may not ever wake up.' I then caught a dose of pneumonia, which meant the doctors had to put me in a medically induced coma for three weeks.

I had bizarre, vivid dreams. I don't know how long that lasted but Kim was coming every day and they said to her, 'He might stay like this.' She was given two warnings – first that I wouldn't come round from the coma, and second that if I did wake up I might be severely brain damaged.

I was eventually brought round but was kept in hospital for a couple more weeks, still having weird, drug-induced dreams. I was saying all sorts of strange things. I thought I was in a hospital on the Thames at one point. Another time I thought I worked on the haberdashery floor of John Lewis, and I was telling people passing by my bed to buy some material. I claimed that José Mourinho and I were best friends. I kept plotting to escape from the hospital, trying to enlist my visitors to help me. My daughter Ella later told me, 'Before your illness you were starting to talk a bit Devonian, but since you were sort of switched off and on again' – meaning being in a coma – 'you talk like a Londoner again.'

When I was transferred to the Royal Devon & Exeter Hospital, I was moved from one place to another taking all the machines, equipment and drips with me, clunking along the corridors. We stopped once at the lifts,

Kim and me with Ann Ralli (second right) and her daughter (far right) who started Devon Air Ambulance, which played a big part in saving my life

waiting for the doors to open. A fella standing there looked down at me, paused a second and then said, 'Steve, are we going to sign a bleeding centre-forward or not?' The look I must have given him! If it wasn't so serious, it would have been laughable. But the whole experience was just awful. I have flashbacks of the doctors or nurses pulling some tube out of my nose and the pain was excruciating. If ever I know that is going to happen to me again I will refuse, such was the agony.

Kim had been desperate for me to get back to Exeter. When I first went into hospital, all the family came to the house. There were 12 mobile phones going off at the same time, with people calling to try to find out what was happening. My solicitor, Charles, phoned Kim and she explained what I was in hospital for. His wife, Liz, used to be a nurse and he was repeating Kim's words so that she could hear what was happening. When she heard 'aortic dissection' her face apparently said it all. It was a miracle I was alive.

Tis would visit me once or twice a week at Plymouth, which isn't easy for a full-time football manager. He'd phone and say, 'Kim, you said you were going to speak to the surgeon today; have you?' Kim would say 'Yes, he said this, that and the other.' 'Yeah,' said Tis, 'but what was the expression on his face when he said that?' Tis wanted all the exact detail, as per usual.

Of course I was unaware of all this. Kim didn't let me have my phone for six months. When I eventually got it back, I was reading messages sent the minute I was taken ill, the kind people send to someone they care for and love at a moment when they think there is a good chance that person is not going to be around for much longer. Reading that stuff, it was as if I'd died and come back to life to read it.

It was overwhelming. People talk the absolute truth in that situation. They might normally say, 'Steve, you're my mate', the usual football, blokey things. This was heartfelt stuff. Those messages took a bit of doing to look through and reply to. But I had a lot of time because I wasn't going anywhere any time soon.

When I eventually came home after several weeks, nurses visited every so often, and there were follow-up appointments before I basically got back to normal. Never criticise the NHS to me. It not only saved my life but provided so much care afterwards. Some time later I sat next to the South African surgeon who saved my life, Clinton Lloyd, on a flight up to

Sailing to Miami, and cruising to recovery after my aortic dissection

Manchester. It was just a coincidence that I met him in the lounge but then we sat next to each other on the plane. It was a strange feeling to meet the man who saved my life. He and his colleagues were amazing.

I now only have to go back to the clinic once a year for a check-up from Dr Gandhi. As he says, 'Steve, you're going to die of something but you're not going to die of this, we are so on top of it.' How did I survive? I feel it must have been my strong heart. I had no blood going to it for 20 minutes or so but my heart kept going. Perhaps I have all those runs at Cheshunt and Bill Nick's sit-ups to thank. If I have to speculate on what caused my problem, I would say it is because I snore and I hold my breath while snoring – sleep apnoea to give it its proper name. That puts pressure on the cardiac system.

The surgeon actually said to Kim that when they opened me up in the operating theatre, they found the aorta was hanging by a sac of tissue the thickness of cling film. If I had sneezed in that situation I would have been done for.

In the aftermath I found out about all the goodwill people throughout the game had expressed. Players, managers, fans, the media. So many people were thinking of me. I was told later about the Spurs crowd applauding after six minutes of the game against Fulham – six for my shirt number – and giving a big cheer when Paul Coyte, the master of half-time ceremonies, said everyone at the club wishes 'Skip' well. It was immensely touching.

When I was 17 years old I got a ticket for speeding. I was pulled over by the copper, who said to me, 'You know your problem, son? I'm an Arsenal supporter.' He kept calling me 'son' as he was writing out the ticket. As he passed me the ticket, he said, 'And remember, son, your problem is I'm an Arsenal fan.' To which I replied, 'You know, "dad", that's more your problem than mine.'

I tell that story all the time when I meet Spurs supporters. But then I tell the story about the letter from three Arsenal supporters in 2012, saying they hoped I would recover and get back to full fitness. 'Why?' they wrote. 'Because we know a good opponent when we see one.'

I get a bit out of breath now if I walk up a hill. I don't run but I can fast-walk if I need to. I've never had a pain in my chest again. I reflect that I was lucky the air ambulance was available and I've met Ann Ralli, the lady who started the campaign to fund that helicopter for Devon Air Ambulance. She lost her son because one was not available, and has raised lots of money for it.

I've been fine since. Long-distance flights are no problem, and I returned to work as normal. I've not really drunk since but I was never really a drinker in any case. A few months after my illness I had to complete a survey which had questions such as 'Are you depressed?' Out of a score of 100 I had zero. 'Do you ever feel like you're out of breath?' Apart from walking up hills, no. Do you ever feel suicidal?' No. It makes me think, 'Blimey, how well am I?'

I haven't had trauma from it or anxiety. Yet if I wake up in the night with a pain in the hamstring I worry for the rest of the night. It's a hangover from being a player and worrying about being fit. I'd like to say 2012 made me reassess life and all that goes with it. But my life has always been about 'onto the next'. I know that's simplistic but what else can it be? Onto the next chapter.

Clockwise, from top left: Matsuba-san, S-Pulse team secretary, and Ichikawa-san both came to my last game with Exeter at Wembley – that showed huge respect. I picked Ichikawa as a 17-year-old and he got into the national side; Dr Perryman: getting an honorary degree from Exeter University with Floella Benjamin; with my brother Ted at my retirement party; Alex Inglethorpe and I leap for joy as Exeter are drawn against Manchester United in the FA Cup; All smiles at a Spurs reunion

MY CLUB

It's May 2019 and I'm making a trip I've done a thousand times before, coming down from Seven Sisters Tube station in the car. Everything seems the same, but also different. As our party nears our destination I can't quite get my bearings. I'm looking for landmarks that aren't here any more. Warmington House is still there but the Red House, the White Hart pub, the old Dispensary and even Paxton Road itself are gone. But there's the age-old feel of a big football match: hordes of fans making their way to the game, an expectant buzz in the air.

My first sight of it is from the High Road. It's a real 'wow' moment. I've seen the photos, but to see it for myself is some experience. There it is – this incredible, gleaming new stadium right in the middle of Tottenham. I just love the shape of it. There are no straight lines; I love the curves. I'm so pleased to go to the new stadium because it feels a little bit like the old place. It's not White Hart Lane, but it's in virtually the same location on the High Road. It feels comfortable. It's home.

We head down Worcester Avenue into the underground car park – an underground car park! It seems to go on forever. We get a lift up to the directors' lounge. So my first sight of the stadium from inside is coming up through the stairs into the director's box. Wow. Just wow.

We have arrived early, so go up one more floor, where Ossie is going to be in something called 'The H Club'. I look out of the windows there. It's all just stunning. I love the floodlights. I think it's very special. It was worth waiting for. I don't envy anyone else having to build a new stadium, because they have got it all to do. Go on, have a try. See if you can do better than Tottenham Hotspur FC. My club.

It's not good. It's spectacular. It's not about how much money you spend, it's about how you get the best out of that money. The club is in good hands. I was invited to the Training Centre recently and it felt like a happy place. Of course the buildings and the pitches were as if from another planet, but the positive feeling that everyone was pulling together for Spurs was similar to what I remember at Cheshunt – and very different from the club I left after my short spell as Ossie's assistant.

That was the lowest point in my life, when I fell out of love not just with Spurs but football itself. Japan restored my love for the game, and now I have reconnected with my club. Daniel Levy and the board have made a real effort to bring me back into the fold and I thank them for that. As I approach retirement I sincerely hope that I will be spending even more time at the new stadium.

> "Japan restored my love for the game, and now I have reconnected with my club. Daniel Levy and the current board have made a real effort to bring me back on board and I thank them for that"

Bill Nick. You just didn't want to let him down

Back to the game and we're playing Everton after we've reached the Champions League final, so understandably the mood is great. Everyone has a big smile on their face. I meet up with a lot of old pals and players – Ossie, Ricky, Mabbs, Ledley King, Chiv, Robbo, Maxie, Micky. It's clear they are all really pleased to be here. They're proud. That's not me putting words in their mouths: you can see they think this is something special.

We are surrounded by people who want to say hello and wish us all well. Us players have had a part to play in this stadium being built. The success we earned has helped sustain the club down the years, as of course have the supporters. The fans are the lifeblood of the club. The plan is for this to be a sporting arena, and host concerts and other events. But at its heart it's a football stadium. This place is about football.

I sit down to dinner with Cliff Jones and Bill Nick's daughter, Jean, there with her husband Steve, at a table hosted by Daniel Levy's wife, Tracy. Cliff and I are talking about Bill and his discipline and yet how he never fined anyone. He used to change with us in the dressing room. If you were late, you had to walk in in front of him; you just felt his eyes burn in the back of your head. You didn't need to be fined; that look was enough.

Jean says: 'I went on a school trip to Wimbledon tennis once, and we were told to be back for the minibus at a certain time. But Angela Mortimer was playing on an outside court so we couldn't get through this crowd of people. So me and my two mates were late and the bus went without us. We had just enough money to scramble together to get the train home.

'When I got home my mum went potty about the school leaving us to make our own way back. My dad was sat at the table listening to all this, my mum saying it was all the school's fault and eventually he said, "You're talking nonsense. You shouldn't be late." It was typical of my dad.'

It was lovely hearing that; talking to Bill's daughter, with Cliff, one of the heroes of the Double, in the new ground.

There are so many people to see. Dave Clark from the Dave Clark Five is sitting close to us – talk about being glad all over! I'm thinking about how new and dazzling this all is, but also about the old days, mostly golden ones. I think about a lot of people, the staff and characters at White Hart Lane back in the 1960s and 1970s – Mrs Wallace, Mrs Bick, Johnny Wallis, Charlie Faulkner, Dickie Walker and Dodger Joyce amongst others. I think about dear, young Peter Southey. All the people down the years. It was wonderful to be there.

I've been in the game for more than 50 years now. 2019 marks a full half-century since my first-team debut, and the club kindly invited me back to the Premier League game against Southampton on the date of the anniversary.

My return to Spurs came in 2002, not long after Daniel Levy and Enic had taken over. I initially had contact from acting chairman David Buchler, who told me, 'This club has had too much of the F-word,' to me implying there had been too much aggravation before. Daniel later phoned to tell me they'd had a vote about renaming a lounge after a player and I had got half the votes, so would I consider allowing my name to be used for the lounge? I said I was happy to do so and was invited to be a guest at the game against Blackburn. Tottenham had been through plenty of changes by then. Glenn was manager and striving to get Spurs back among the elite.

I later played a significant part in Spurs signing Kazuyuki Toda. He'd played for us at S-Pulse and was one of the best Japanese players. Alf D'Arcy and his son were acting to get him a move and got him a trial at Sunderland. He travelled at his own expense, which was a bit odd. I was asked to look after him so he spent the night with us and then I drove him to Heathrow to get a flight up north. When I got home the phone rang. It was Daniel saying he and Glenn wanted to sign Toda. He hadn't had the greatest time at Sunderland and had been pretty much left to his own devices, and didn't know what to do. I got him back to ours, Glenn came over and had a chat with him and Toda said he wanted to join Tottenham. I advised him honestly what his prospects would be at a club like Spurs and how difficult it might be to get games, which proved to be the case once he did sign.

I can't say I was thrilled to be acting as an intermediary. Football today is full of them – too many. I am so pleased to be out of that aspect of the game. I don't want to deal with another agent as long as I live. I've heard stories of agents getting money from a house sale. A player comes to London, wants to live in a nice area, buys a £3 million house and the player's agent gets his cut out of the sale from the estate agent. There can be a lot of malpractice when there's that kind of money floating around. Money attracts the best and the worst. A bit like the Wild West. There are no checks on anyone. Sharp operators, sharp practices.

My core beliefs and values, nurtured and sustained by my time at Tottenham, have not altered in those 50 years. Since leaving Exeter, I have been associate director at MK Dons – helping Paul Tisdale, who became manager there in 2018. I say to players now, 'If you just turn up and your attitude is, "I'm here, give me my kit, tell me what to do, pay me and then I go home", that ain't enough. Everything you do – do it right, with purpose and intent. If it's a ten-yard side-foot pass in training, mean it. Put effort into it.'

Take handwriting. Why doesn't it improve as we get older? It gets worse if anything, because we just scribble something out quickly. Unless you write with the active thought of improving your handwriting, it won't improve. It's the same with football, and the earlier good, regular practice

"I've been in the game for more than 50 years now. 2019 marks a full half-century since my first-team debut"

**Harry Kane
presents
me with a
commemorative
cap to mark
the 35th
anniversary
of our famous
UEFA Cup win**

is introduced, the better. You can't wait until players are 21 and in a team because then there is the pressure of getting results; it has to be done with kids under 10, when they are not under pressure.

It's a bit like the Dutch philosophy, of playing non-competitive games, which is kind of how I learned to play. I didn't really play competitive football until quite late. I don't think coaches should worry about teaching youngsters how to play offside. Focus on the ball and using it. Touch is key. Pace is important but it doesn't make you a footballer – just look at Usain Bolt.

I tell the coaches who I give sessions to, 'You may use just one of these 20 exercises I've shown you and you might want to adapt it: that's what coaching is.' It's what management is, really. Thinking, planning, being adaptable. There are thousands of decisions to make every day. And there's a mistake round every corner. In a game of fine margins, put in the planning and practice to try and mitigate any errors.

Practice might not make perfect but it will make a player improve. I was doing that as a six-year-old, knocking a tennis ball against the wall but with imagination and purpose. Think about one of the greatest goals ever – Brazil 1970. The ball comes to Pelé, he knocks it off to Carlos Alberto so precisely, so purposefully, a pass honed by years of repeated practice, that Carlos Alberto didn't have to do anything except hit it – bosh. Vincent Kompany today is a prime example. He's not the world's best but what he does, he means.

I think Mauricio Pochettino works to that ethos. I've been told that when Spurs finish practice with potential new youth players, the kids are then told to sprint back 60 yards to the halfway line. Anyone who doesn't sprint back doesn't get invited back. His mantra of telling new players that they have signed to train not play – i.e. don't assume you'll just get in the team – is very clever, and has strong echoes of Bill Nick.

I'm a huge admirer of Pochettino and his coaching team's work. He's done a remarkable job assembling a wonderful side and putting Spurs back on the big stage. I would just love to see them win a trophy. They came so close to winning the biggie, the Champions League, and the run to the final was so thrilling, but the chances of landing the big prizes are slim without building up to them.

The modern team have been a joy. Dele is a thoroughbred, and I love the flow in Christian Eriksen's movement. I prefer Eric Dier at centre-half. I like Jan Vertonghen, who got back to his best in the 2018–19 season, having refound his emergency gear, to speed up when required. I think Spurs are still a bit too deliberate and lacking in purpose and pace, but have a real superstar in Harry Kane. He has become such a tremendous player. He played a pass the other day I didn't know he was capable of – I think he might even have looked the other way as he played it.

Sometimes players have ability but then stop improving, like Joe Hart, whose career stalled. Harry's ability has prompted him to look like he's always searching for the next thing to do, be it a goal-scoring record or whatever. You might not hear him say he's after the next record but there's something driving this Spurs man on. My thought when I first saw him was that he was another Mark Falco. No disrespect to Mark, but Harry has come on so well.

I'm not one of those bitter old pros who constantly say it was better in my day and moan about the money players are on now. Good luck to them. I do think the body of a player in my era might not have been as fit as today's players, but that it was more robust. Today's players are sharper and quicker. They are also subject to so much more scrutiny and how they cope with it is admirable. It's so dissected – how Harry deals with it is exceptional. Every near-miss is picked apart in minute detail and the criticism is just ridiculous. 'Harry never scores in August.' We didn't know when Jimmy Greaves scored and didn't score. We just knew he scored more than enough.

Cliff Jones made a brilliant point to me. He said, 'Steve, have you ever been asked if you could play in this modern team?'

'Yeah, it's difficult to answer.'

He said, 'Turn it around. Ask if these players could have played in our time? Terrible pitches, heavy balls and boots. Injuries, the treatment of injuries. Conditioning and diet then. That's the best answer you can give.'

It's all got to be kept in perspective. Imagine Jimmy Greaves being subject to such intense exposure like players are today? Jimmy would be put on a pedestal so high you couldn't reach him. I found my way into a team of British internationals at 17. Maybe I would do the same today. I would probably have been training from eight years of age, instead of having my first professional coaching session at 15. When it was noticed that I lacked half a yard of pace that would have been worked on. So it's all relative.

I feel there is too much focus on tactics in the modern game. They are of course vital and, believe me, managers agonise over every detail to do with systems and formations. But football is a game of so many variables, and mentality is fundamental. Alex Inglethorpe, my former manager at Exeter and now academy director at Liverpool, said to me that both Liverpool and Tottenham's wins in the semi-finals of the Champions League in 2019 were about mentality. They had nothing to do with tactics.

I am all for innovation. Jürgen Klopp brought in a throw-in coach at Liverpool and was mocked, but why? He's trying to improve his team. Not everything that's new is bad. Video analysis is wonderful. But it comes back to what Graeme Souness said recently about the need to win the ball before deploying tactics. The fundamental question is, 'Can you get to the ball first?' If you don't have the ball you can't play. That's a bit old-fashioned, but it's an essential truth. People can apply whatever spin they like, talk about 'transitions' and use modern terminology – it's not that what is said is wrong, but that it is not new. 'Playing between the lines' was finding space. The 'high press' was closing down.

The basic characteristics remain the same. Play on the left or right; quick or slow; heroes and villains. It's all the same – the same dimensions, the same pitch. Everything going on outside might be different but essentially the game is the same. Football is still a great game. It still turns people on. There cannot have been a better week of football than in May 2019, with Man City beating Leicester, then the two Champions League semi-final second legs – Tottenham's incredible comeback at Ajax and Liverpool beating Barcelona. It was magnificent.

What I certainly don't like is that dreaded phrase 'game management'. I grew up with integrity at Tottenham and I find it very hard to witness some of the goings-on. Time-wasting is a particular bugbear. Why do refs wait until the 87th minute, for example, to book a goalkeeper for time-wasting? That's not what the fans pay to watch. In my era, playing away we would make the home crowd quiet by keeping possession, not by running the ball into the corner or taking a minute to take a throw-in.

Critics lambast VAR for how long it takes. But what about players wasting 30 seconds at a throw-in? Do five of them and that's over two

> "The fundamental question is, 'Can you get to the ball first?' If you don't have the ball you can't play"

minutes wasted. I appreciate the financial gulf between clubs means some teams cannot afford to play open. But to have a chance of winning you have got to have a go. A good rule change was to award three points for a win in the 1980s. I think the next change might need to be no points for a 0–0. But I actually don't want to change things too much because all players, from whatever era, should be judged equally against each other. Jimmy Greaves's goal-scoring record should be challenged on the basis that anyone trying to beat it is playing essentially the same game to the same laws, rules and regulations. They just need to be better applied.

Watching that game against Everton in 2019 in the new stadium I reflect on what's changed and what's stayed the same. I was thinking about how captaincy has altered. I can't name a lot of skippers in the Premier League, which is probably an illustration of how the role has changed. Tony Adams and John Terry were very good captains – both home-grown. You need that bit of extra knowledge of the club that you play for to fulfil the role.

I look around and see my old teammates in the stands enjoying the spectacle like me – the 'limping legends' as some might call them! Ex-players have been brought into the fold more and I think Tottenham handle that as well as anyone, giving them hospitality roles. It's not for me, in all honesty. I've been too busy with Exeter and MK Dons to go to many games. I missed the last game at White Hart Lane. I would have loved to have been there, but Exeter had a play-off semi-final that I obviously could not miss.

The fans know what the club means to me in any case. I went back to White Hart Lane for a match against Everton in November 2014, taking Paul Tisdale's son with me to stand in the tunnel, before I was introduced to the crowd at half-time. I wanted to hear it one more time – 'when Steve went up to lift the FA Cup...' It was marvellous. I meet lots of fans at events. It maintains a link between the supporters and players and I hope that continues.

I think about how White Hart Lane used to dominate the area and how the new stadium does even more so. I do wonder what Tottenham would be like without Spurs. I'm always surprised but really pleased when someone from there succeeds – Adele, for example. It's long seemed to me that you

With Cliff Jones, journalist Patrick Barclay, Pat Jennings, John Pratt and Phil Beal after Alan Gilzean's funeral

start life a bit further down the social scale if you come from Tottenham, so anyone who is successful really deserves it.

Alan Gilzean got a fantastic reception the first time he came back to Spurs after many years. I'm glad he got to see what he meant to the supporters before he passed away in 2016. I had the honour of meeting his ex-wife, Irene, for the very first time at his funeral and seeing his two boys, Kevin and Ian, again. In such sad circumstances it was a delight. Everyone was telling stories about how great Gilly was. I said to her, 'I know this is difficult, but are you OK?' And she said, 'Yeah, it's really nice to meet you. I've heard your name and so much about you.' All the people there were great. If someone can be judged by the quality of people at their funeral, my word, that showed what a man Gilly was.

Gilly wasn't a recluse, as some say; he just didn't crave any attention. I helped bring him back into the Tottenham fold. I got a phone call from BBC Scotland in 2009 requesting an interview as Gilly was going to get inducted into the Scottish Football Hall of Fame. I met him in Bristol for the interview and encouraged him to come to the Lane again. Gilly said, 'Stevie, you are like your dad!' He still had his old swagger. I can just see him walking on the pitch the same way.

I miss Gilly. I miss too many of my old colleagues and friends who we've lost: young Peter Southey; Eamonn Dolan and Adam Stansfield at Exeter; Sanada-san, our goalkeeper at S-Pulse; Eddie Baily; Johnny Wallis; dear Bill Nick and his wife Darkie; Justin Edinburgh; Cyril Knowles; Jimmy Neighbour; Milija Aleksic; and Ralph Coates.

I think also of all the old characters around the Lane and other places. Coming to the new ground, it was shock that the White Hart pub is no longer there. The guvnor was a very nice bloke called Joe Louis and many players, legends of old, used to drink there. It was also a rogue's den full of old London characters like One-Armed Lou (we never did find out how he lost it), Johnny 'the Stick' Goldstein and Stan Flashman. I was asked to sign some photos one day by one of these types. It was for the Kray brothers, who, the chap claimed, were Spurs fans. I wasn't going to argue.

I think of the old fans as well, like Morris Keston (RIP), Alan Landsberg the jeweller, Peter King who worked the market at Covent Garden, Gilly's mate Ricky Prosser and Fred Rhye the old boxer, who travelled on the coach with us sometimes. These people would give players something at Christmas – a box of nuts or oranges, clothes, a bottle of wine, whatever their trade was. Such colourful, larger-than-life personalities who helped give Spurs its unique character and style.

I love the crowd today. The passion that they put into their team is inspirational, and it's not just in London and England. I've been privileged recently to visit Iceland and New Zealand and feel the passion of Tottenham supporters around the globe. It helps to prove what a big club we are, that even without periods of success, the support remains so staunch, passed from generation to generation. A club like ours, with the tradition of support we have at Tottenham, means we were lucky to play for it. The club deserves success now but the supporters deserve it as much if not more, because they are the ones that underpin it. Just like Bill Nick said.

I enjoy meeting fans. Everyone's got a story to tell – about how they saw me play my first game, or how they have been a supporter for years. Why should I not listen to their story? Fans should be treated with respect and courtesy.

BILL NICHOLSON OBE MEMORIAL SERVICE

WHITE HART LANE SUNDAY, NOVEMBER 7, 2004

I look back on my role in the story of Spurs, and can reflect that I did my bit. Sound judges have often praised me during my career. John McDermott, head of the academy at Spurs, told me I should write a PhD on football, on how it works from the inside. Keith Burkinshaw has said that I was the best reader of the ball off the turf that he ever worked with. Keith was highly rated and respected himself; there's a story from when David Pleat took over in 1986. A local scout – more of a contact than a proper scout – said to Pleat, 'David, this is the greatest day in Tottenham's history. I told those mugs before you to sign so-and-so; they just ignored me but now we've got a brain in charge of us.' David asked who this chap was and he was told it was a scout. David said, 'Get rid of him. Anyone who thinks Keith and Shreevsie are mugs knows nothing.'

Phil Holder and I talk about the people and the past every day. One of my regrets is that Phil and I didn't play more in the Spurs first team together because me holding down a place inhibited his progress in a way. He was man enough that it didn't affect our friendship. I dropped Phil off at home once on a Friday. I wasn't going to play the next day due to injury, with Phil taking my place. His dad said, 'I hope he keeps you out.' And I think he was right to feel that way.

You have to be competitive to make it in this game. I have no competitiveness left for anything else. If I play table tennis, I'm happy to just keep the ball going backwards and forwards – winning doesn't bother me. But put a football in front of me, well...

Phil was in the QPR dressing room once when his good mate Harry Redknapp was managing. Harry was asking after me, and Rangers' goalkeeping coach, Kevin Hitchcock, formerly of Chelsea, joined in to tell a story. 'My mate Glyn Hodges was at Wimbledon,' said Kevin. 'Growing up, Glyn was a mad Spurs fan and his favourite player was Steve Perryman. One midweek game he was picked to play left-wing against Steve. Glyn says, "We line up. I'm playing on the pitch of my dreams – White Hart Lane. I'm facing Steve Perryman. The game starts, the ball goes out, now Steve's alongside me. I say, 'Hello Steve.' And he says, 'Hello? Who the fuck are you talking to?' Steve was the most horrible bastard I'd ever met, and tackled hard."'

And where did I learn to tackle? In Bill Nick's office of all places. He called me in once. 'Steve, open that cupboard!' In it were orange Minerva footballs. They hadn't been used and had lost a bit of air, but Bill got me to block tackle him in his little office with an orange ball.

I think back to all those places and people at White Hart Lane. Helping out in the office, saying hello to Julie Bick and Barbara Wallace, though we never called them by their first names. Their part of the offices was probably the only part of the whole stadium where we get a more motherly approach. They always called me 'Stephen' like my mum would. Lovely ladies, but smart, acting as Bill Nick's eyes and ears, finding out those little personal details that might be important. They weren't spying, they were caring.

They found out about a girl who worked in the club's pools office, which developed into the commercial department. She had taken a shine to me and started to follow me around a bit. I mentioned it in passing to Mrs Wallace and suddenly the girl left. The club clearly didn't want her distracting me. Was she sacked? I don't know, but I still feel bad about it and I do wonder what happened to her.

"I look back on my role in the story of Spurs, and can reflect that I did my bit"

Left: Chris Hughton's 60th birthday with Ossie, Chris, Garth Crooks, Paul Miller and Tony Galvin

Following pages: A moment of reflection in the tunnel at Tottenham Hotspur's new stadium. I was kindly invited to the match against Southampton in September 2019 to mark the 50th anniversary of my Spurs debut

I have happier memories of meeting up with old pals and teammates. A few of the 1980s team met up for Chrissy's 60th, prior to his very unfair sacking at Brighton. Garth was good fun as ever. He looks well – and well fed! We had a reunion not so long ago for the 1970 FA Youth Cup squad, which was wonderful. Graeme Souness came along. A few years ago Harry Redknapp hosted a party at the Redknapps' favourite Italian restaurant in Bournemouth. Phil attended. He told me it was a lovely evening and all of a sudden Harry looked across and said, 'There's Graeme Souness coming in the door.' Harry asked him over to sit down and join the party.

Graeme said, 'Harry, how nasty was I as a player?'

'Ooh, nasty,' said Harry.

'Yeah? Well, see him,' said Graeme, pointing to Phil, 'And his mate' – meaning me – 'I was scared shitless of them two. I never walked around the corner before looking around it first just to see if either of them two were coming.'

It was said in jest but it reflected a nice, long-lasting respect. It was about standing our ground and fighting our corner, which Graeme was still admiring decades later. That means a lot to me. I was with a friend at a cup final a few years back. We were in a lounge and Denis Law walked in, surrounded by people, but then he saw me and almost pushed people aside to come and say hello. That makes me feel good, because it indicated a lasting mutual respect. Liam Brady said I was one of the fairest defenders he ever played against. Coming from an Arsenal man I'll take that. I've often heard people with Arsenal connections talking about who they would least want to see in the Tottenham dressing room before a North London derby today, inspiring the current team, and they usually say, 'Steve Perryman.' Because I get what this club is about.

My mind has been drifting on this sunny day in in May 2019. My attention turns back to the game. Oliver Skipp comes on as a sub. He reminds me of myself 50 years ago, a bit older but a home-grown lad trying to make his way in the game and play for Tottenham Hotspur. Eddie Baily used to say of me, 'His heart is bigger than his head.' I hope Oliver uses his head and plays with his heart. For my club. Best of luck, young man.

A SPUR FOREVER!

I would like to express my thanks to all the managers and coaches I played for, all my teammates who won and lost alongside me, and all my colleagues who have shared the dugout with me in my coaching career. It has been quite a journey.

Thanks also to my two brothers, Ted and Bill, and Phil Holder, John Newman, Charles Newman and Alf D'Arcy, for always looking out for me and helping me in my goal of becoming the best player and person that I could.

I would also like to thank the following who have helped me put together this book. My co-writer, Adam Powley, who has done a tremendous job, designer Doug Cheeseman, and Jim Drewett, Toby Trotman and Ed Davis at Vision Sports Publishing, as well as Nick Maroudias for the fantastic portrait photography.

And finally, to the Spurs supporters – my second family that is extended all over the world. I may not have been the most gifted player you ever saw, but there was no one who ever pulled on the lilywhite shirt who cared more about our club than me.

TOTTENHAM SIGN UP PERRYMAN

STEPHEN PERRYMAN, the 15-year-old, and much sought-after inside-forward, has finally signed for Tottenham Hotspur.

Stephen, an England Schoolboy international who comes from Northolt and went to Eliots Green Grammar School, has signed on as an apprentice professional, having trained at White Hart Lane last winter.

This brings an end to a chase for his signature which has involved Manchester United and several London clubs, including Queen's Park Rangers who were just beaten by Spurs.

TOTTENHAM HOTSPUR FOOTBALL CLUB

Tour to UNITED STATES OF AMERICA AND CANADA

14th May to 4th June, 1969

DEBUT for Spurs boy

TOTTENHAM HOTSPUR FOOTBALL & A

MEMBERS OF THE FOOTBALL ASSOCIATION AND THE FOOTBALL

LEAGUE CHAMPIONS 1961

SECRETARY: R. S. JARVIS

748 HIGH ROAD
TOTTENHAM. N.17

CHAIRMAN: FRED. WALE

26. 6. 67.

R. Perryman Esq.,
39 Bancroft Court,
Lime Trees Estate,
Northolt.

Dear Mr. Perryman,

to say that you have
rue that they do not
egards to your decis
to leave school th
of our local head
hool can take no a
eems that everyth:
gistered by a Pro
Natu
to be ours and I
ever have been
Club. Charlie
on wednesday
shall be more than pleased, and any
he family too.

I am very pleased to hear of
of the F/L which seems to have been a
sal of the attitude they were taking in
You must also be happy and relieved
it was worth all the worry.

Closing in haste with best

Yours sincerely,

H Nicholson,

Manager.

AUDERE · EST · FACERE

Nicholson: This proves we can find our

Boy Perryman Spurs stars

By JEFF POWELL

STEVE Perryman, 17, stands this morning on the threshold of the First Division in defiance of those who doubt Tottenham's capacity to produce players of their own.

Whether or not he plays against Sunderland, he is destined to become one of the youngest ever to appear in Spurs' first team.

Skipper Mullery with Perryman yesterday
Picture PATRICK LARKIN

STARMAN STEVE

Young Steve Perryman turned in star-man performances against both West Ham and Coventry.

FOOTBALL LEAGUE—DIVISION ONE

TOTTENHAM HOTSPUR
v.
SUNDERLAND

Official Programme

Price SIXPENCE

Saturday, 27th Sept., 1969
KICK-OFF 3 p.m.

SEASON 1969-70   Vol. 62   No. 11

The Spurs boy wh